Directory of

Professional Preparation Programs in TESOL in the UNITED STATES and CANADA

1999–2001

Ellen Garshick, Editor

T E S O L Teachers of English to Speakers of Other Languages, Inc.

Founded 1966

Typeset in Slimbach
by Capitol Communication Systems, Inc., Crofton, Maryland USA
and printed by
Pantagraph Printing, Bloomington, Illinois USA

Additional copies of this directory may be obtained from:

Teachers of English to Speakers of Other Languages, Inc. (TESOL)
1600 Cameron Street, Suite 300
Alexandria, VA 22314 USA
Tel. 703-836-0774 • Fax 703-836-7864 • e-mail: publ@tesol.edu •
http://www.tesol.edu

Director of Communications and Marketing: Helen Kornblum
Marketing Manager: Ann Perrelli
Cover Design: Ann Kammerer

ISBN 0-939791-75-7

Contents

Preface

This 11th, revised edition of the *Directory of Professional Preparation Programs in TESOL in the United States and Canada, 1999–2001*, provides basic information about college and university programs in the United States and Canada leading to a degree, certificate, or diploma in the teaching of English to speakers of other languages (TESOL).

The *Directory* lists 194 U.S. institutions offering more than 300 programs in TESOL: 29 doctoral programs, 194 master's programs, 46 graduate certificate programs, and 81 undergraduate programs. Among these are 107 programs leading to a state teaching credential in TESOL. It lists 19 Canadian institutions offering 33 programs in TESOL: 3 doctoral programs, 9 master's programs, 13 certificate or diploma programs, and 8 undergraduate programs, including 13 programs leading to a provincial credential in TESOL. It includes brief descriptions of the programs offering degrees and certificates in the field of TESOL as well as state and provincial certification requirements for TESOL. Also included is a geographical index of institutions.

As in previous editions, information was compiled from questionnaires sent to the institutions. Each institution is thus responsible for the accuracy of the information contained in its entry. The entries are not detailed, and we suggest that the reader obtain further information from the individual institution as desired.

For persons interested in teacher education institutions in Australia, the English Language Intensive Courses for Overseas Students (ELICOS) Association of Australia has published *Teacher Training in TESOL: A Directory of Courses in Australia and New Zealand*. Readers may write to the ELICOS Association, Level 3, 162 Goulburn Street, Sydney, NSW, Australia 2000 to obtain a copy. The ELICOS World Wide Web site is at http://www.elicos.edu.au/. Available from the *EL Gazette* is *The ELT Guide*, which lists courses in Great Britain and abroad for practicing and prospective teachers. Inquiries should be sent to ELT Guide, 5th Floor, Dilke House, 1 Malet Street, London WC1E 7JA, United Kingdom.

Special thanks, as always, to the program administrators who responded to the questionnaires. English language educators will be pleased to see from the scope of this volume that their programs are many and varied to match the needs of both prospective and practicing TESOL professionals.

June 1998

Helen Kornblum
Director of Communications and Marketing, TESOL
Alexandria, VA USA

PART 1

THE UNITED STATES

◆ ADELPHI UNIVERSITY, School of Education

Degree Offered: MA in TESOL.

Length of Program: 3–4 semesters. Students may be full-time or part-time and may begin their study at the beginning of any semester. Rolling admissions are in effect.

Program Requirements: In-service teachers, 33–36 credits; precertification students, 45–48 credits. Six credits in a language other than English is required for New York State TESOL certification. Practice teaching is required. Neither a thesis nor a comprehensive examination is required.

Courses Offered: (*required) *TESOL I: Developing Language Arts Skills; *TESOL II: ESL in the Content Areas; *Foundations of Bilingual Education; *Evaluation and Testing in ESL and Bilingual Education; *Structural Linguistics; *History of the English Language; *Language and Culture; *TESOL Student Teaching or Practicum; *Educational Research; *Historical, Social, and Moral Foundations of Education.

Full-Time Staff: Alan Sadovnik, Eva M. Roca (director), Judith Johnston.

Requirements for Admission: The university's requirements for admission are a baccalaureate degree with a concentration in one of the liberal arts and sciences, a GPA of 2.75 or higher, three letters of reference, and an essay.

Tuition, Fees, and Aid: $470 per credit hour. Fees are $150.

General: The program leads to New York State certification (provisional or permanent).
One hundred fifty-three students completed the program in 1996–1997.
The university has an intensive English language program for nonnative speakers of English.

Summer Session: Yes

Further Information: Prof. Eva M. Roca, Director
TESOL/Bilingual Education Programs
School of Education
Harvey Hall Room 126 B
Adelphi University
South Avenue
Garden City, NY 11530

Telephone: (516) 877-4072
Fax: (516) 877-4097

◆ ALABAMA, UNIVERSITY OF, Department of English

Degree Offered: MA-TESOL.

Length of Program: 4 semesters. Students must be full-time and must begin their study at the beginning of the fall semester. The application deadline is January 10.

Program Requirements: 30 semester hours. Competence in a language other than English is required for native speakers of English. Practice teaching is required. A thesis is optional. A comprehensive examination is not required.

Courses Offered: (*required) *TESOL Methods; *Second Language Development; *Teaching Academic Writing to ESL Students; *Teaching Academic Writing Through Literature; *Special Topics; Multicultural Literacies; Dialectology; Testing and Evaluation.

Full-Time Staff: Catherine Davies (director), Vai Ramanathan.

Requirements for Admission: The university's requirements for admission are an undergraduate degree in the humanities, strong writing samples and references, and a GPA of 3.5 or higher.

Tuition, Fees, and Aid: Teaching assistantships and fellowships are available.

General: The program offers a strong combination of theory and practice. The teaching experience that graduate students get includes teaching in the program's ESL composition classes, in the English Language Institute, and in the community's schools.

Students may go overseas (e.g., to Guatemala or Korea) to teach in the summer while earning units toward their degree.

Ten students completed the program in 1996–1997.

The university has an intensive English language program for nonnative speakers of English.

Summer Session: Yes

Further Information: Vai Ramanathan or Catherine Davies
Department of English, MA-TESOL
Box 870244
University of Alabama
Tuscaloosa, AL 35487

Telephone: (205) 348-5065
Fax: (205) 348-1388
E-mail: cdavies@english.as.ua.edu;
vramanat@english.as.ua.edu

◆ ALABAMA, THE UNIVERSITY OF, IN HUNTSVILLE, Department of English

Degree Offered: TESOL certificate (graduate).

Length of Program: 3 semesters. Students may be full-time or part-time and may begin their study at the beginning of the fall or spring semester. There are no application deadlines.

Program Requirements: 18 semester hours. Competence in a language other than English is required; English meets the requirement for nonnative speakers of English. A practicum and (as of 1999) a comprehensive examination are required. A thesis is not required.

Courses Offered: (*required) *Graduate Survey of General Linguistics; *Advanced English Grammar Studies; *History of the English Language; *Second Language Acquisition (Special Topics); *Strategies for Methods and Research in TESOL; *TESOL Practicum.

Full-Time Staff: John Mebane (chair), Madeleine Youmans, Cynthia Walker.

Requirements for Admission: The university's requirements for admission are a minimum average of B (3.0) on the undergraduate record and a score of 1500 on the GRE General Test. Nonnative speakers of English must have a minimum TOEFL score of 500. The program requires a score of 50 on the Miller Analogies Test and requires nonnative speakers to take the English department's English Language Placement Test.

Tuition, Fees, and Aid: For in-state students, $1,674 per semester; for out-of-state students, $3,332 per semester. After completing 9 units in the program, students are eligible for part-time ESL teaching positions. Tuition scholarships are also available.

General: The student body is diverse and nontraditional, leading to stimulating interaction in class. Students are offered a forum to discuss their personal experiences with and ideas about TESOL. The program's relatively small size allows for extensive one-on-one contact with professors and individual attention. The program will lead to an Alabama credential in TESOL as of 1999.

Six students completed the program in 1996–1997.

The university has an intensive English program for nonnative speakers of English.

Summer Session: No

Further Information: Dr. Madeleine Youmans
Department of English
Morton Hall 222
The University of Alabama in Huntsville
Huntsville, AL 35899

Telephone: (205) 895-6320
Fax: (205) 890-6949
E-mail: youmansm@email.uah.edu

◆ AMERICAN UNIVERSITY, Department of Language and Foreign Studies

Degree Offered: TESOL certificate.

Length of Program: 2 semesters. Students may be full-time or part-time and may begin their study at the beginning of any semester. Application deadlines are fall semester, February 1; spring semester, October 1; summer term, March 1.

Program Requirements: 15 semester hours. Competence in a language other than English is optional for native speakers of English; English meets the language requirement for nonnative speakers of English. Neither practice teaching, nor a thesis, nor a comprehensive examination is required.

Courses Offered: (*required) *Principles of Linguistics; *Theory and Practice of English Language Teaching I and II; Structure of English; Language Analysis; Second Language Acquisition; Cultural Issues in the ESL/EFL Classroom; Teaching English for Specific Purposes; Bilingual Education; Language Teaching and Testing; Computer Applications for Language Teachers.

Full-Time Staff: Naomi Baron (chair), Theresa A. Waldspurger, Brock Brady (coordinator).

Requirements for Admission: The university's requirement for admission is a minimum of a high school diploma or the equivalent. Graduate-level students must have a baccalaureate degree from an accredited institution. Nonnative speakers of English must have a TOEFL score of 600 or higher. A cumulative GPA of at least 3.0 is expected.

Tuition, Fees, and Aid: $655 per semester hour. No financial aid is available.

General: The TESOL certificate enables people from any educational background to gain an essential theoretical foundation plus hands-on teaching experience in order to pursue teaching opportunities either in the United States or abroad. Through the annual American University Summer TESOL Institute, students may complete the program in a single summer.

Twenty-three students completed the program in 1996–1997.

The university has an intensive English language program for nonnative speakers of English.

Summer Session: Yes

Further Information: Brock Brady, TESOL Coordinator
Department of Language and Foreign Studies
Asbury 322
American University
4400 Massachusetts Avenue, NW
Washington, DC 20016-8045

Telephone: (202) 885-1446
Fax: (202) 885-1076
E-mail: bbrady@american.edu

◆ AMERICAN UNIVERSITY, Department of Language and Foreign Studies

Degree Offered: MA in TESOL.

Length of Program: 4 semesters. Students may be full-time or part-time and may begin their study at the beginning of any semester. Application deadlines are fall semester, February 1; spring semester, October 1; summer term, March 1.

Program Requirements: 33 semester hours. Competence in a language other than English is encouraged but not required for native speakers of English; English meets the language requirement for nonnative speakers of English. Practice teaching, an oral comprehensive examination, and a portfolio based on work and research completed during the program are required. A thesis is not required.

Courses Offered: (*required) *Principles of Linguistics; *Theory and Practice of English Language Teaching I and II; *Structure of English; *Language Analysis; *Language Acquisition *or* Second Language Acquisition; *Cultural Issues in the ESL/EFL Classroom, *or* Topics and Language and Culture, *or* Topics in Applied Anthropology: Anthropology of Education; *Practicum in ESL; Reading and Writing in the ESL/EFL Classroom; Teaching English for Specific Purposes; Bilingual Education; Language Teaching and Testing; Computer Applications for Language Teachers; Global and Multicultural Education; Selected Topics; thesis option.

Full-Time Staff: See TESOL certificate program description.

Requirements for Admission: The university's requirement for admission is a baccalaureate degree from an accredited institution with an average cumulative GPA of at least 3.0. Nonnative speakers of English must have a TOEFL score of 600 or higher.

Tuition, Fees, and Aid: $655 per semester hour. Some financial aid, including merit-based awards such as graduate assistantships, is available.

General: The MA in TESOL is distinctive in its focus on experiential learning. Students plan lessons, observe classes, and design tests for English language classes. Faculty draw on their extensive teaching experience, research, and interaction with other cultures to provide pragmatic lessons and advice. Courses are also offered during the Summer TESOL Institute.

Individual international internships may be arranged.

Eighteen students completed the program in 1996–1997.

The university has an intensive English language program for nonnative speakers of English.

Summer Session: Yes

Further Information: Brock Brady, TESOL Coordinator
Department of Language and Foreign Studies
Asbury 322
American University
4400 Massachusetts Avenue, NW
Washington, DC 20016-8045

Telephone: (202) 885-1446
Fax: (202) 885-1076
E-mail: bbrady@american.edu

◆ AMERICAN UNIVERSITY, Department of Language and Foreign Studies/School of Education

Degree Offered: MAT: ESOL.

Length of Program: 4 semesters. Students may be full-time or part-time and may begin their study at the beginning of any semester. Application deadlines are fall semester, February 1; spring semester, October 1; summer term, March 1.

Program Requirements: 39 semester hours. Competence in a language other than English is strongly recommended but not required for native speakers of English; English meets the language requirement for nonnative speakers of English. Practice teaching and a comprehensive examination are required. A thesis is not required.

Courses Offered: (*required) *Principles of Linguistics; *Theory and Practice of English Language Teaching I and II; *Structure of English; *Second Language Acquisition; *Cultural Issues in the ESL/EFL Classroom; *Reading and Writing in the ESL/EFL Classroom; *Language Teaching and Testing; *Foundations of Education; *Foundations of Education; *Foundations of Education for Exceptional Children *or* Overview of All Exceptionalities: The Arts in Special Education; *Theories of Educational Psychology and Human Development; *Student Teaching with required seminar.

Full-Time Staff: Naomi Baron, Theresa A. Waldspurger, Brock Brady (coordinator). School of Education: C. A. Tesconi, Jr., M. Wineburg, F. Jacobs, D. Sadker, S. L. Smith, F. E. Huber, S. Irvine, D. Thompson, C. E. Messersmith, D. D. Miller, R. Ralph, L. Fox, A. Prejean.

Requirements for Admission: The university's requirement for admission is a baccalaureate degree from an accredited institution with an average cumulative GPA of at least 3.0. The program requires a satisfactory score on the Miller Analogies Test or the GRE. Nonnative speakers of English must have a TOEFL score of 600 or higher and demonstrate the oral skills necessary to teach in a U.S. public school.

Tuition, Fees, and Aid: $655 per semester hour. Federal government loans and merit-based awards, such as graduate assistantships, are available.

General: The MAT: ESOL is designed for students with no previous background or preparation in education who wish to acquire ESOL teaching certification for Grades K–12. The degree prepares graduates to work effectively with diverse populations. The program, which began in 1997, is offered in conjunction with the university's School of Education and leads to a state credential in TESOL.

The university has an intensive English language program for nonnative speakers of English.

Summer Session: Yes

Further Information: Brock Brady, TESOL Coordinator
Department of Language and Foreign Studies
Asbury 322
American University
4400 Massachusetts Avenue, NW
Washington, DC 20016-8045

Telephone: (202) 885-1446
Fax: (202) 885-1076
E-mail: bbrady@american.edu

◆ THE AMERICAN UNIVERSITY IN CAIRO, English Language Institute

Degree Offered: Graduate diploma in TEFL.

Length of Program: 2 semesters. Students may be full-time or part-time and must begin their study at the beginning of the fall or spring semester; fall semester is preferred. Application deadlines are fall semester, January 29; spring semester, October 29.

Program Requirements: 18 semester hours. Competence in a language other than English is not required. Practice teaching is required. Neither a thesis nor a comprehensive examination is required.

Courses Offered: (*required) *English Grammar; *Introduction to Linguistics; *Methods of Teaching a Foreign Language (2 semesters); *Second Language Acquisition; one elective.

Full-Time Staff: Amira Agameya, Yehia El Ezabi, Fred Perry, Jayne Sowers, Paul Stevens (chair).

Requirements for Admission: The university's requirement for admission is a BA or BS with an overall GPA of 2.75 and of 3.0 in the major. Nonnative speakers of English must have a TOEFL score of 580.

Tuition, Fees, and Aid: For in-country students, $1,470 per semester; for out-of-country students, $4,900 per semester.

General: The program offers a U.S.-style education in a multicultural, multilanguage setting and combines rigorous academic standards with a balance between theory and practice.

The university has an intensive English language program for nonnative speakers of English.

Summer Session: Yes

Further Information: Ms. Mary Davidson, Student Coordinator
TEFL Program, English Language Institute
American University in Cairo
420 Fifth Avenue, 3rd Floor
New York, NY 10018-2724

Telephone: (212) 730-8800
Fax: (212) 730-1600
E-mail: davidson@aucnyo.edu

◆ THE AMERICAN UNIVERSITY IN CAIRO,
English Language Institute

Degree Offered: MA in TEFL.

Length of Program: 5 semesters. Students may be full-time or part-time and must begin their study at the beginning of the fall or spring semester; fall semester is preferred. Application deadlines are fall semester, January 29; spring semester, October 29.

Program Requirements: 30 semester hours (thesis track); 36 semester hours (comprehensive examination track). Competence in a language other than English is not required. Practice teaching and either a thesis or a comprehensive examination are required.

Courses Offered: *English Grammar; *Introduction to Linguistics; *Methods of Teaching a Foreign Language (2 semesters); *Research Methods and Experimental Design; *Second Language Acquisition; *Advanced Research Methodology (thesis track only); Testing and Evaluation; History of English; Computer-Assisted Language Learning; English Syntax; Contrastive Analysis and Error Analysis; Pragmatics; Sociolinguistics; Language and Society in the Middle East; Teaching and Assessing EFL/ESL Writing; Teaching Children ESL/EFL; Role of Grammar in TEFL.

Full-Time Staff: See program description for graduate diploma in TEFL.

Requirements for Admission: The university's requirement for admission is a BA or BS with an overall GPA of 2.75 and 3.0 in the major, or, for nonnative speakers of English, a TOEFL score of 580 with a TWE score.

Tuition, Fees, and Aid: For in-country students, $1,470 per academic year; for out-of-country students, $4,900 per academic year. Fellowships are available.

General: The program offers a U.S.-style education in a multicultural, multilanguage setting and combines rigorous academic standards with a balance between theory and practice.

Nine students completed the program in 1996–1997.

The university has an intensive English language program for nonnative speakers of English.

Summer Session: Yes

Further Information: Ms. Mary Davidson, Student Coordinator
TEFL Program, English Language Institute
American University in Cairo
420 Fifth Avenue, 3rd Floor
New York, NY 10018-2724

Telephone: (212) 730-8800
Fax: (212) 730-1600
E-mail: davidson@aucnyo.edu

◆ THE AMERICAN UNIVERSITY OF PARIS,
Department of Continuing Education

Degree Offered: Certificate in TESOL.

Length of Program: 1 semester. Students must be full-time. The program is offered each fall. Rolling admissions are in effect.

Program Requirements: 3 credits. Competence in a language other than English is not required. Practice teaching is required. Neither a thesis nor a comprehensive examination is required.

Courses Offered: *TESOL Methodologies; *Pedagogical Grammar; *Techniques in Language Teaching; *40-hour practicum.

Full-Time Staff: Danielle Savage (coordinator), Roberta Vellvé, Erin Link.

Requirements for Admission: The university's requirement for admission is a BA or the equivalent.

Tuition, Fees, and Aid: 21,350 French francs plus a 300-franc application fee. Stafford loans are available.

General: Located in Paris, the program offers the opportunity to work in an EFL setting. Job placement is available for those able to work in France.

Twenty-one students completed the program in 1996–1997.

The university has an intensive English language program for nonnative speakers of English.

Summer Session: No

Further Information: Danielle Savage, Coordinator
TEFL Program, English Language Institute
Department of Continuing Education
The American University of Paris
102, rue St. Dominique
75007 Paris
France

Telephone: (33-1) 40 62 05 72
Fax: (33-1) 40 62 07 17
E-mail: ce@aup.fr

◆ AMÉRICAS—PUEBLA, UNIVERSIDAD DE LAS, Language Department

Degree Offered: MA in applied linguistics.

Length of Program: 3 semesters. Students may be full-time or part-time and must begin their study at the beginning of the fall semester. The application deadline is July 11.

Program Requirements: 40 credits. Competence in Spanish and English is required. Practice teaching, a thesis, and professional development points are required. A comprehensive examination is not required.

Courses Offered: (*required) *Methodology in Second Language Teaching; *Introduction to Linguistics; *Bilingual Education; *Language Acquisition; *Introduction to Syntax; *Testing and Evaluating in Second Language Teaching; *Statistics and Research Design; *Practicum; *Development of Educational Organization I; *Selected Topics in Applied Linguistics; *Thesis Proposal; *Thesis; 13 electives.

Full-Time Staff: Peter Ecke, Lydia Giles, Christopher Hall (chair), Connie Johnson, José Antonio López y Maldonado, Guillermo Rivero.

Requirements for Admission: The university's requirements for admission are a minimum GPA of B or 3.0, a notarized copy of the applicant's birth certificate with apostille, and a notarized copy of the applicant's diploma with apostille. The program requires three academic letters of recommendation, an updated curriculum vitae, an example of academic prose writing in the applicant's native language, and interviews with faculty.

Tuition, Fees, and Aid: $2,500 per semester. Teaching assistantships and U.S. college–funded loans are available.

General: All courses may be taught in Spanish or English, as all permanent members of the faculty are bilingual speakers. This program is the only master's in applied linguistics program in Mexico that is accredited by the Southern Association of College and Schools. Students must complete their professional development points by attending conferences or publishing in journals. All students may teach at the undergraduate level once they have met departmental and university requirements. The university participates in several exchange programs with U.S. universities.

Six students completed the program in 1996–1997.

Summer Session: Yes

Further Information: Dr. Lydia Giles, Program Coordinator
Edificio 31
Universidad de las Américas Puebla
72820 Sta. Catarina Martir
Puebla, México

Telephone: (22) 29-31-19
Fax: (22) 29-31-01
E-mail: lgiles@mail.pue.udlap.mx

◆ ARIZONA, THE UNIVERSITY OF, English Department

Degree Offered: MA in ESL.

Length of Program: 4 semesters. Students may be full-time (preferred) or part-time and must begin their study at the beginning of the fall semester. The application deadline is February 1.

Program Requirements: 32 credits plus 8 credits of prerequisite course work. Four semesters of work in a language other than English or equivalent proficiency is required; English meets the requirement for nonnative speakers of English. A comprehensive examination and practice teaching are required. A thesis is not required.

Courses Offered: (*required) Prerequisites: Introduction to TESL: An Overview, Introduction to Linguistics, Modern English Grammar; *Teaching of Composition; *Grammatical Analysis; *Second Language Pedagogy: Observation and Analysis; *Second Language Pedagogy: Testing; *Cultural Dimensions of Second Language Acquisition; *Second Language Acquisition Theory; *Second Language Acquisition in Formal Contexts; *Seminar: Second Language Acquisition Research; *Internship: Applied ESL; *a reading course; 6 units of electives in such areas as testing, computer-assisted language learning, language for specific purposes, ESOL/literature, program administration, discourse analysis, and code switching.

Full-Time Staff: Douglas Adamson, Roseann D. Gonzalez, Donna M. Johnson, Frank Pialorsi, Muriel Saville-Troike (director), Rudolph C. Troike.

Requirements for Admission: The graduate college's requirement for admission is a baccalaureate degree with a minimum 3.0 GPA. In addition, the program requires a two- to three-page statement of purpose, three letters of recommendation (preferably from academic sources), GRE scores, and, for nonnative speakers of English, a TOEFL score of 550 (preferably over 600) plus a TWE score or a writing sample.

Tuition, Fees, and Aid: For in-state students, $1,029 for 7 or more units per semester; for out-of-state students, $255 per unit through 6 units, $3,326 maximum. Fees are $72 per year. Teaching assistantships through the English Department and other language departments, fellowships, tuition scholarships, registration scholarships, and minority fellowships are available.

General: This program emphasizes advanced training and leadership development for TESOL professionals. The Center for ESL serves as a laboratory for the study of teaching, program administration, and language acquisition. Electives can be chosen from a wide variety of courses. Tucson, a multicultural, multilingual city, provides a rich environment for research in second language acquisition and sociolinguistics.

Ten students completed the program in 1996–1997.

The university has an intensive English language program for nonnative speakers of English.

Summer Session: Yes

Further Information: Director, English Language/Linguistics Program
Department of English
Modern Languages 456
The University of Arizona
PO Box 210067
Tucson, AZ 85721-0067

Telephone: (520) 621-7216
Fax: (520) 621-7397
E-mail: maesl@u.arizona.edu
http://www.coh.arizona.edu

◆ ARIZONA STATE UNIVERSITY, Department of English

Degrees Offered: Master of TESL; MA in English with a concentration in applied linguistics.

Length of Program: 4 semesters. Students may be full-time or part-time and may begin their study at the beginning of any semester. Application deadlines are fall semester, September 15; spring semester, February 15 (if applying for financial aid) or April 15 (if not applying for financial aid).

Program Requirements: 30 semester hours. Competence in a language other than English is required; English meets the requirement for nonnative speakers of English. Neither practice teaching, nor a thesis, nor a comprehensive examination is required. An applied project is required.

Courses Offered: (*required for the master of TESL) *Research Methods; *English Linguistics; *Theories Underlying the Acquisition of ESL; *Methods of Teaching ESL; *Applied Project; Advanced Studies in ESL; Sociolinguistic Aspects of Second Language Acquisition; Grammar for TESL; Special Topics; Seminar; American English; History of the English Language; Phonetics and Phonology; Semantics; Syntax; Pragmatics and Discourse.

Full-Time Staff: Karen L. Adams, Dawn Bates, Marysia M. Johnson, Roy C. Major (program director), James W. Ney, Don L. Nilsen, Elly Van Gelderen.

Requirements for Admission: The university's requirement for admission is a BA from an accredited institution with a minimum GPA of 3.0 for the junior and senior years. Nonnative speakers of English must submit a TOEFL score of 580 or higher and a TSE score of 50 or higher.

Tuition, Fees, and Aid: For in-state students, $99 per semester hour up to 6 semester hours; $942 for 7 or more semester hours. For out-of-state students, $330 per semester hour. Teaching assistantships and in- and out-of-state tuition waivers are available.

General: Because of its location in greater Phoenix, where a multitude of languages are spoken, the program offers a wide variety of teaching opportunities through internships and employment.

Twenty-five students completed the program in 1996–1997.

The university has an intensive English language program for nonnative speakers of English.

Summer Session: No

Further Information: Roy C. Major
Director, Programs in Linguistics and TESL
Arizona State University
Tempe, AZ 85287-0302

Telephone: (602) 965-3188
Fax: (602) 965-3451
E-mail: Roy.Major@asu.edu

◆ AZUSA PACIFIC UNIVERSITY, Department of Global Studies and Sociology

Degree Offered: MA/TESOL.

Length of Program: 6 terms. Students may be full-time or part-time and may begin their study at the beginning of the Fall 1 or Spring 1 term. Application deadlines are Fall 1, July 15; Fall 2, September 15; Spring 1, November 15; Spring 2, February 10.

Program Requirements: 36 semester units. Six semester units in a language other than English are required; English fulfills the requirement for nonnative speakers of English. Practice teaching, membership in TESOL or California TESOL, and either a thesis or a comprehensive examination are required.

Courses Offered: (*required) *Second Language Acquisition; *Teaching English Grammar; *Teaching English Pronunciation; *Language and Culture; *Second Language Pedagogy I and II; *Observational Practicum; *Sociolinguistics and Language Teaching; *Teaching Practicum; *Language Program Design; Approaches to Grammar; Research Methods in TESOL; Thesis Preparation; Principles of Language; Special Topics in Language Development; Special Topics in Educational Technology.

Full-Time Staff: Donald Dorr, Richard Robison, Richard Slimbach (chair).

Requirements for Admission: The university's requirement for admission is a bachelor's degree from an accredited college or university with a minimum GPA of 3.0. Candidates with a GPA of 2.50–2.99 may be considered for provisional admission; those with a GPA below 2.5 may petition for consideration. Nonnative speakers of English must have a TOEFL score of 550 or higher.

Tuition, Fees, and Aid: $335 per unit. Federal Stafford loans are available. California Graduate Fellowships are available for U.S. applicants who are prospective college teachers.

General: The program is exclusively geared to training teachers of adult populations. Practical training is emphasized in two methods courses and two practica. Situated in greater Los Angeles, the program offers teaching opportunities with more than 150 cultural groups; approximately half of the students in the program are internationals. The program offers the option of an international teaching practicum on an independent study basis. Opportunities are also available to teach abroad with a team of classmates and faculty.

The university offers a cooperative program with the English Language Institute/China.

Fifteen students completed the program in 1996–1997.

The university has an intensive English language program for nonnative speakers of English.

Summer Session: No

Further Information: Director, Graduate TESOL Program
Department of Global Studies and Sociology
Azusa Pacific University
901 East Alosta Avenue
Azusa, CA 91702-7000

Telephone: (626) 812-3055
Fax: (626) 815-3801
E-mail: iss@apu.edu

◆ AZUSA PACIFIC UNIVERSITY, School of Education and Behavioral Studies

Degree Offered: MA in language development.

Length of Program: 6 terms. Students may be full-time or part-time and may begin their study at the beginning of the Fall 1 or Spring 1 term. Application deadlines are Fall 1, September 1; Fall 2, November 10; Spring 1, February 1; Spring 2, April 15.

Program Requirements: 36 semester units. Competence in a language other than English is required; English fulfills the requirement for nonnative speakers of English. Practice teaching and a three-part final growth assessment are required. Neither a thesis nor a comprehensive examination is required.

Courses Offered: (*required) *Language Acquisition and Development; *Methods of Bilingual English Language Teaching; *School Practicum in English Language Development; *Teaching and Cultural Diversity; *Literacy Development; *Curriculum Planning; *Family, Community, and School Connections; *Assessment and Evaluation; *Special Topics; *Research for Educators.

Full-Time Staff: Dan Doorn (director), Maria Pacino.

Requirements for Admission: The university's requirement for admission is a bachelor's degree. The program requires a teaching credential for public schools, K–12, or significant teaching experience. Applicants must either meet the foreign language requirements for the California CLAD certificate or fulfill them during the program.

Tuition, Fees, and Aid: $325 per unit. Loans and grants are available.

General: Students earn the California CLAD certificate for K–12 teaching of ESL students. Courses are offered in 9-week terms in evening classes at four sites in the Los Angeles area. Students conduct their own action research study and develop curriculum units across courses.

Thirty-five students completed the program in 1996–1997.

The university has an intensive English language program for nonnative speakers of English.

Summer Session: Yes

Further Information: Director, Language Development Program
School of Education and Behavioral Studies
Azusa Pacific University
901 East Alosta Avenue
Azusa, CA 91702-7000

Telephone: (626) 812-5371
Fax: (626) 815-5416
E-mail: ddoorn@apu.edu

◆ BALL STATE UNIVERSITY, Department of English

Degree Offered: MA in TESOL.

Length of Program: 3 semesters. Students may be full-time or part-time and may begin their study at the beginning of any semester, although fall semester is preferred. There are no application deadlines.

Program Requirements: 32 credit hours. Competence in a language other than English is required; English meets the requirement for nonnative speakers of English. A creative project is required. Neither practice teaching, nor a thesis, nor a comprehensive examination is required.

Courses Offered: (*required) *Introduction to Linguistic Science; *Theory and Research in TESOL; *Methods and Materials in TESOL I (Grammar and Speaking); *Methods and Materials in TESOL II (Reading and Writing); *Approaches to Modern English Grammar; *Second Language Acquisition; *Linguistic Phonetics; *Contrastive Analysis; Language and Culture; Language and Gender; Methods and Materials in TESOL(Pronunciation); Proseminar in Computer-Assisted Language Learning.

Full-Time Staff: Christopher M. Ely, Carolyn MacKay, Elizabeth Riddle, Herbert Stahlke, Frank Trechsel.

Requirements for Admission: The university's requirement for admission is an undergraduate GPA of 3.0. The program requires the equivalent of 2 years of college-level study in a foreign language, a two-page autobiography including a statement of academic purpose, a sample of scholarly writing, three letters of recommendation, a GRE score for native speakers of English, and, for nonnative speakers of English, a TOEFL score.

Tuition, Fees, and Aid: For in-state students, $1,658 per semester; for out-of-state students, $4,436 per semester. University fellowships and departmental assistantships are available.

General: The program emphasizes reflective teaching, including knowledge and skill related to communicative, linguistically effective ESL/EFL instruction. Students receive a solid, practical grounding in TESOL methods and second language acquisition as well as in cross-cultural pragmatics, sociolinguistics, and in-depth linguistic analysis of ESL materials. Special facilities include a state-of-the-art computer-assisted language learning lab. An ESL endorsement of a state teaching license is available.

Exchange programs exist with universities in Great Britain, South Korea, Taiwan, and Indonesia. Opportunities exist for teaching in France, Brazil, South Korea, Japan, and the People's Republic of China.

Fifteen students completed the program in 1996–1997.

The university has an intensive English language program for nonnative speakers of English.

Summer Session: Yes

Further Information: Director of Graduate Programs
Department of English
Robert Bell Building, Room 295
2000 West University
Ball State University
Muncie, IN 47306

Telephone: (765) 285-8415
Fax: (765) 285-3765
E-mail: 00blyates@bsu.edu

◆ BALL STATE UNIVERSITY, Department of English

Degree Offered: MA in TESOL and linguistics.

Length of Program: 4 semesters. Students may be full-time or part-time and may begin their study at the beginning of any semester, although fall semester is preferred. There are no application deadlines.

Program Requirements: 42–45 credit hours. Competence in a language other than English is required; English meets the requirement for nonnative speakers of English. A creative project or a research paper is required. Neither practice teaching, nor a thesis, nor a comprehensive examination is required.

Courses Offered: (*required) *Introduction to Linguistic Science; *Theory and Research in TESOL; *Methods and Materials in TESOL I (Grammar and Speaking); *Methods and Materials in TESOL·II (Reading and Writing); *Approaches to Modern English Grammar; *Second Language Acquisition; *Phonological Analysis; *Grammatical Analysis; *Language and Culture; *Linguistic Phonetics; *Introduction to Historical Linguistics; *Contrastive Analysis; Language and Gender; Methods and Materials in TESOL (Pronunciation); Proseminar in Computer-Assisted Language Learning.

Full-Time Staff: See program description for MA in TESOL.

Requirements for Admission: See program description for MA in TESOL.

Tuition, Fees, and Aid: See program description for MA in TESOL.

General: The program is designed to provide teachers with a strong foundation in ESOL instruction (see program description for MA in TESOL) as well as the ability to bring to their instruction informed, sophisticated linguistic knowledge. An ESL endorsement of a state teaching license and a separate MA in linguistics are available.

Exchange programs exist with universities in Great Britain, South Korea, Taiwan, and Indonesia. Opportunities exist for teaching in France, Brazil, South Korea, Japan, and the People's Republic of China.

Five students completed the program in 1996–1997.

The university has an intensive English language program for nonnative speakers of English.

Summer Session: Yes

Further Information: Director of Graduate Programs
Department of English
Robert Bell Building, Room 295
2000 West University
Ball State University
Muncie, IN 47306

◆ BALL STATE UNIVERSITY, Department of English

Degree Offered: PhD in applied linguistics.

Length of Program: Variable. Students may be full-time or part-time and may begin their study at the beginning of any semester, although fall semester is preferred. There are no application deadlines.

Program Requirements: 90 credit hours. Competence in two languages other than English is required; for nonnative speakers of English, English meets the requirement for one language. A thesis and a comprehensive examination are required. Practice teaching is not required.

Courses Offered: (*required) *Advanced Composition; *Introduction to Linguistic Science; *Approaches to Modern English Grammar; *History of the English Language; *Applied Linguistics; *Phonological Analysis; *Grammatical Analysis; *Sociolinguistics; *Language and Culture; *Proseminar in Linguistics; *Linguistic Phonetics; *Introduction to Historical Linguistics; *Research Methods; *Topics in English Grammar; *Topics in Phonology; *Topics in Grammatical Analysis; *two literature courses; *one (24-credit) or two (15-credit) cognates.

Full-Time Staff: See program description for MA in TESOL.

Requirements for Admission: The university's requirement for admission is an undergraduate GPA of 3.0. The program requires a a two-page autobiography, a statement of academic purpose, samples of scholarly or critical writing, five letters of recommendation, a graduate GPA of at least 3.3 (3.5 preferred), a combined GRE score of at least 1500 for native speakers of English, and, for nonnative speakers of English, a TOEFL score of at least 575.

Tuition, Fees, and Aid: See program description for MA in TESOL.

General: This program, which combines work in applied linguistics and linguistics, is designed to prepare its graduates to teach and carry out research in a wide range of areas. Available cognates include TESOL, composition/rhetoric, computer science, anthropology, and sociology.

Five students completed the program in 1996–1997.

The university has an intensive English language program for nonnative speakers of English.

Summer Session: Yes

Further Information: Director of Graduate Programs
Department of English
Robert Bell Building, Room 295
2000 West University
Ball State University
Muncie, IN 47306

Telephone: (765) 285-8415
Fax: (765) 285-3765
E-mail: 00blyates@bsu.edu

◆ BELOIT COLLEGE, Department of Education

Degree Offered: Certificate in TESL.

Length of Program: Students may be full-time or part-time and may begin their study at the beginning of any semester. Application deadlines are fall semester, August 1; spring semester, December 15; summer session, May 1.

Program Requirements: 14 semester hours. Competence in a language other than English is recommended. Thirty hours of field experience are required. Neither practice teaching, nor a comprehensive examination, nor a thesis is required.

Courses Offered: (*required) *Introduction to Teaching ESL/EFL; *Introduction to Language *or* Linguistic Analysis; *Second and Foreign Language Acquisition; *Grammar, Curriculum, and Materials in ESL.

Full-Time Staff: Jan Bigalke, Melanie Schneider (director).

Requirements for Admission: The college's requirement for admission is completion of a college preparatory program. A minimum TOEFL score of 550 is required for nonnative speakers of English. The program requires applicants to be current undergraduate students or to have an undergraduate degree from an accredited institution.

Tuition, Fees, and Aid: Variable based on part-time, full-time, degree, and nondegree status. Ful-time students are eligible for work study, scholarships, and loans. Part-and full-time students who are at least 25 years old or who have an undergraduate degree may apply for regular financial aid or receive reductions in tuition. Limited scholarships are available for summer study.

General: The TESL certificate is designed for individuals interested in teaching English abroad or in non–public school settings in the United States. Students may earn the certificate in one summer if they have already completed a linguistics course. Course work for the TESL certificate may be applied toward K–12 certification through Beloit College.

Some opportunities for international and urban field experience exist in programs associated with the college.

Ten students completed the program in 1996–1997.

The college has an intensive English language program for nonnative speakers of English.

Summer Session: Yes

Further Information: TESL Program Director
Department of Education
Beloit College
700 College Street
Beloit, WI 53511-5595

Telephone: (608) 363-2325
Fax: (608) 363-2718
E-mail: klinek@beloit.edu

◆ BELOIT COLLEGE, Department of Education

Degree Offered: K–12 certification in ESL.

Length of Program: Students may be full-time or part-time and may begin their study at the beginning of any semester. Application deadlines are fall semester, August 1; spring semester, December 15; summer session, May 1.

Program Requirements: 52 semester hours (for initial certification). Competence in a language other than English (6–9 semester hours or the equivalent) is required. Practice teaching and 100 hours of field experience (for initial certification) are required. Neither a comprehensive examination nor a thesis is required.

Courses Offered: (*required) *Introduction to Teaching ESL/EFL; *Introduction to Language *or* an introductory linguistics course; *Second and Foreign Language Acquisition; *Teaching ESL in the Schools: K–12; Grammar, Curriculum, and Materials in ESL; *six professional education courses (for initial certification); *one course each on culture and language.

Full-Time Staff: Jan Bigalke, Melanie Schneider (director), Sonja Darlington, Kathleen Greene, William New, Thomas Warren (chair).

Requirements for Admission: The college's requirement for admission is completion of a college preparatory program. A minimum TOEFL score of 550 is required for nonnative speakers of English. The program requires applicants to be current undergraduate students with a GPA of 2.5 or higher or to have an undergraduate degree from an accredited institution.

Tuition, Fees, and Aid: See program description for certificate in TESL.

General: Certification in ESL (K–12) may be either the primary certification or a secondary (add-on) certification (requiring fewer courses). Course work may be completed during the academic year or the summer.

Some opportunities for international and urban field experience exist in programs associated with the college.

Six students completed the program in 1996–1997.

The college has an intensive English language program for nonnative speakers of English.

Summer Session: Yes

Further Information: TESL Program Director
Department of Education
Beloit College
700 College Street
Beloit, WI 53511-5595

Telephone: (608) 363-2325
Fax: (608) 363-2718
E-mail: klinek@beloit.edu

◆ BIOLA UNIVERSITY, Department of TESOL and Applied Linguistics

Degree Offered: Undergraduate minor/certificate in TESOL.

Length of Program: 2 semesters, upper division. Students may be full-time or part-time and may begin their study at the beginning of any semester. Application deadlines are fall semester, August 1; spring semester, January 1.

Program Requirements: 19 semester units. Competence in a language other than English is not required. Practice teaching is required. Neither a comprehensive examination nor a thesis is required.

Courses Offered: (*required) *Introduction to Language and Linguistics; *English Pronunciation and Grammar; *Introduction to TESOL; *Intercultural Communication; *Materials Evaluation and Preparation; *Communicating Values Through TESOL; *Practicum in TESOL.

Full-Time Staff: Marguerite G. Kraft, Katherine B. Purgason, Herbert C. Purnell (chair), Peter J. Silzer, Peggy A. Velis.

Requirements for Admission: Applicants should consult the university's catalog. A minimum TOEFL score of 600 is required for nonnative speakers of English. In addition, the program requires upper-division standing in any undergraduate major with a minimum GPA of 2.5. Although unaffiliated with any church or denomination, the university accepts students only from the Christian evangelical community, its primary constituency.

Tuition, Fees, and Aid: $7,143 per semester.

General: The Department of TESOL and Applied Linguistics is part of the School of Intercultural Studies at Biola and thus has a strong cross-cultural emphasis. Department faculty average over 14 years living or working abroad or in minority communities. Up to 6 units of the undergraduate minor in TESOL may be applied toward the graduate programs.

Ten students completed the program in 1996–1997.

The university has an intensive English language program for nonnative speakers of English.

Summer Session: No

Further Information: Chair
Department of TESOL and Applied Linguistics
Marshburn Hall
Biola University
13800 Biola Avenue
La Mirada, CA 90639-0001

Telephone: (562) 903-4844

◆ BIOLA UNIVERSITY, Department of TESOL and Applied Linguistics

Degree Offered: Certificate in TESOL (graduate level).

Length of Program: 2 semesters plus 1 interterm. Students may be full-time or part-time. Fall entry is preferred. Application deadlines are fall semester, August 1; spring semester, January 1.

Program Requirements: 9 prerequisite units plus 16 program units. Competence in a language other than English is not required. Practice teaching is required. Neither a thesis nor a comprehensive examination is required. Transfer of prerequisite units is possible.

Courses Offered: (*required) Prerequisites: Introduction to Linguistics, Intercultural Communication, Bible/Theology; *Structure of English; *Introduction to TESOL; *Materials Evaluation and Preparation; *Communicating Values Through TESOL; *Second Language Acquisition; *Practicum in TESOL.

Full-Time Staff: See program description for undergraduate minor.

Requirements for Admission: The university's requirements for admission are a bachelor's degree with a minimum GPA of 3.0, transcripts, letters of recommendation, and completion of the regular application packet. A minimum TOEFL score of 600 and a TWE score of 5 are required for nonnative speakers of English. Although unaffiliated with any church or denomination, the university accepts students only from the evangelical Christian community, its primary constituency.

Tuition, Fees, and Aid: $307 per semester unit. Limited aid is available.

General: See program description for undergraduate minor.
   Six students completed the program in 1996–1997.

Summer Session: No

Further Information: Chair
   Department of TESOL and Applied Linguistics
   Marshburn Hall
   Biola University
   13800 Biola Avenue
   La Mirada, CA 90639-0001

   Telephone: (562) 903-4844

◆ BIOLA UNIVERSITY, Department of TESOL and Applied Linguistics

Degree Offered: MA in TESOL.

Length of Program: 4 semesters plus interterm. Students may be full-time or part-time. Fall entry is preferred. Application deadlines are fall semester, August 1; spring semester, January 1.

Program Requirements: 9 prerequisite units plus 32 program units. Competence in a language other than English is recommended. Practice teaching and either a thesis or a comprehensive examination are required. Program prerequisites and 8 additional graduate units may be transferred in.

Courses Offered: (*required) *All courses in the certificate in TESOL program; *Advanced Methods and Techniques in TESOL; *Language Testing and Assessment; *Comprehensive Exam; *Bible/Theology; electives (8 units), including English: Past, Present, and Future; Applied Linguistics; Sociolinguistics; Phonetics; Discourse Analysis; Course Design in TESOL; English for Specific Purposes; Topics in TESOL; Readings in Language Learner Strategies; Reading in the ESOL Curriculum.

Full-Time Staff: See program description for undergraduate minor.

Requirements for Admission: The university's requirements for admission are a bachelor's degree with a minimum GPA of 3.0, transcripts, letters of recommendation, and completion of the regular application packet. A minimum TOEFL score of 600 and a TWE score of 5 are required for nonnative speakers of English. Although unaffiliated with any church or denomination, the university accepts students only from the evangelical Christian community, its primary constituency.

Tuition, Fees, and Aid: $307 per semester unit. Limited aid is available as teaching assistantships or grants.

General: See program description for certificate in TESOL. Degree students may begin their program off-campus with distance education courses. They may also complete their program off-campus, taking two electives and the comprehensive exam at a distance.
   Ten students completed the program in 1996–1997.
   The university has an intensive English language program for nonnative speakers of English.

Summer Session: No

Further Information: Chair
Department of TESOL and Applied Linguistics
Marshburn Hall
Biola University
13800 Biola Avenue
La Mirada, CA 90639-0001

Telephone: (562) 903-4844

◆ BIOLA UNIVERSITY, Department of TESOL and Applied Linguistics

Degree Offered: MA in applied linguistics.

Length of Program: 4 semesters plus interterm. Students may be full-time or part-time. Fall entry is preferred. Application deadlines are fall semester, August 1; spring semester, January 1.

Program Requirements: 12 prerequisite units plus 33 program units. Intermediate-level competence in a language other than English is required; English meets the requirement for nonnative speakers of English. Either a thesis or a comprehensive examination is required. Practice teaching is not required. Program prerequisites and 9 additional graduate units may be transferred in.

Courses Offered: (*required) Prerequisites: Introduction to Linguistics, Phonetics or Phonology, Syntax; *Applied Linguistics; *Seminar in Applied Linguistics; *Planning, Evaluation, and Research in Applied Linguistics; *Intercultural Communication; *Comprehensive Exam *or* Thesis; *Bible/Theology; 18 units of electives, taken generally or in one of the following concentrations: language surveys, linguistics, literacy, TESOL, or translation.

Full-Time Staff: Stephen Barber, Marguerite C. Kraft, Katherine B. Purgason, Herbert C. Purnell (chair), Peter J. Silzer, Peggy A. Velis.

Requirements for Admission: The university's requirements for admission are a bachelor's degree with a minimum GPA of 3.0, transcripts, letters of recommendation, and completion of the regular application packet. A minimum TOEFL score of 600 and a TWE score of 5 are required for nonnative speakers of English. Although unaffiliated with any church or denomination, the university accepts students only from the evangelical Christian community, its primary constituency.

Tuition, Fees, and Aid: $307 per semester unit.

General: See program description for certificate in TESOL.
One student completed the program in 1996–1997.
The university has an intensive English language program for nonnative speakers of English.

Summer Session: No

Further Information: Chair
Department of TESOL and Applied Linguistics
Marshburn Hall
Biola University
13800 Biola Avenue
La Mirada, CA 90639-0001

Telephone: (562) 903-4844

◆ BOSTON UNIVERSITY, Department of Developmental Studies and Counseling

Degree Offered: MEd in TESOL (certification program).

Length of Program: 3 semesters. Students must be full-time for at least 1 semester and may begin their study at the beginning of any semester. Application deadlines are fall semester, July 1; spring semester, December 1; summer semester, May 1.

Program Requirements: 48 credits for pre-K–9 certification; 52 credits for 5–12 certification. Competence in a language other than English is required; English meets the requirement for nonnative speakers of English. Full-time practice teaching (300 clock-hours) is required. A major project on the development of teaching materials is required. Neither a thesis nor a comprehensive examination is required.

Courses Offered: (*required) For pre-K–9 or 5–12 certification: *Linguistic Problems in TESOL; *Introduction to Language; *Educational Issues in Bilingualism; *Intercultural Education; *Foundations of Educational Practice; *Literacy Development: Instruction and Assessment; *Student Teaching Practicum; *Student Teaching Seminar. For pre-K–9 certification: *Bilingualism and Biliteracy; *Special Education: Curriculum and Instruction; *Methods in Bilingual Education and TESOL. For 5–12 certification: *Second Language Acquisition; *Introduction to Adolescent Development; *Methods of Teaching ESL 5–12.

Full-Time Staff: Steven J. Molinsky (chair), Maria Brisk, Robert Saitz, Marnie Reed, Mary Catherine O'Connor, Bruce Fraser, Yuan Feng, Phil Tate, Thomas Cottle.

Requirements for Admission: The university's requirement for admission is an accepted degree from an accredited college or university. The program requires a minimum GPA of 3.0 in the last 2 years of work in the undergraduate major and a minimum score of 50 on the Miller Analogies Test. Students have the option of taking the GRE. A minimum TOEFL score of 600 is required for nonnative speakers of English. Candidates must show evidence of the ability to communicate in a language other than English at the intermediate college level. If the undergraduate transcript does not show course work in mathematics, science, social studies, and language arts, the deficiency must be made up as part of the graduate program to fulfill certification requirements.

Tuition, Fees, and Aid: $10,985 per semester or $344 per credit. Full-time students pay a $69 union fee; part-time students pay a $40 registration fee. Some financial aid, scholarships, teaching assistantships, and research assistantships are available.

General: The program is interdisciplinary with an emphasis on training teachers to be creative and innovative. Programs are offered at the pre-K–9 and 5–12 grade levels to comply with Massachusetts state ESL certification requirements.

Thirty students completed the program in 1996–1997.

The university has an intensive English language program for nonnative speakers of English.

Summer Session: Yes

Further Information: Marnie Reed
Graduate TESOL Program, Department of Developmental Studies and Counseling
School of Education
Boston University
605 Commonwealth Avenue
Boston, MA 02215

Telephone: (617) 353-3233
Fax: (617) 353-3924
E-mail: tesol@bu.edu

◆ BOSTON UNIVERSITY, Department of Developmental Studies, School of Education

Degree Offered: MEd in TESOL (noncertification program).

Length of Program: 2 semesters plus one course. Students may be full-time or part-time and may begin their study at the beginning of any semester. Application deadlines are fall semester, July 1; spring semester, December 1; summer semester, May 1.

Program Requirements: 38 credits. Competence in a language other than English is desirable; English meets the requirement for nonnative speakers of English. Practice teaching is required. A major project on the development of teaching materials is required. Neither a thesis nor a comprehensive examination is required.

Courses Offered: (*required) *Introduction to Linguistics; *Linguistic Problems in TESOL; *Second Language Acquisition; *Methods of TESOL; *Student Teaching: College and Adult; *Seminar in TESOL; *Intercultural Education; *Perspectives on Inquiry; one elective in a TESOL-related area.

Full-Time Staff: Steven J. Molinsky (chair), Robert Saitz, Mary Catherine O'Connor, Bruce Fraser, Marnie Reed, Yuan Feng, Paula Menyuk.

Requirements for Admission: The university's requirement for admission is an accepted degree from an accredited college or university. The program requires a minimum GPA of 3.0 in the last 2 years of work in the undergraduate major and a minimum score of 50 on the Miller Analogies Test. Students have the option of taking the GRE. A minimum TOEFL score of 600 is required for nonnative speakers of English.

Tuition, Fees, and Aid: See MEd in TESOL (certification program) description.

General: The program is interdisciplinary with an emphasis on training teachers to be creative and innovative. A project on the development of teaching materials is required of all students. A number of students' projects have been published. This program is intended for those wishing to teach ESL/EFL in college and adult programs as well as internationally.

Thirty students completed the program in 1996–1997.

The university has an intensive English language program for nonnative speakers of English.

Summer Session: Yes

Further Information: Steven J. Molinsky, Director
Graduate TESOL Program, Department of Developmental Studies and Counseling
School of Education
Boston University
605 Commonwealth Avenue
Boston, MA 02215

Telephone: (617) 353-3233
Fax: (617) 353-3924
E-mail: tesol@bu.edu

◆ BOSTON UNIVERSITY, Department of Developmental Studies, School of Education

Degree Offered: MEd in TESOL: specialization in EFL/ESL for children.

Length of Program: 2 semesters. Students may be full-time or part-time and may begin their study at the beginning of any semester. Application deadlines are fall semester, July 1; spring semester, December 1; summer semester, May 1.

Program Requirements: 36 credits. Competence in a language other than English is desirable. Practice teaching is not required. Neither a thesis nor a comprehensive examination is required.

Courses Offered: (*required) *Methods of TESOL; *Seminar in TESOL: Issues in EFL/ESL for Children; *Introduction to Language; *Linguistic Problems in TESOL; *Bilingualism and Biliteracy; *Intercultural Education: Theories and Methods; *Perspectives on Inquiry; two electives.

Full-Time Staff: Maria Estela Brisk (director), Steven J. Molinsky, Mary Catherine O'Connor, Robert Saitz, Marnie Reed, Judith Schickedanz, Bruce Fraser.

Requirements for Admission: See MEd in TESOL (noncertification program) description.

Tuition, Fees, and Aid: See MEd in TESOL (noncertification program) description.

General: This specialization is a response to the growing trend abroad to begin English language instruction in the elementary grades. The program was begun in the 1997–1998 academic year.

The university has an intensive English language program for nonnative speakers of English.

Summer Session: Yes

Further Information: Maria Estela Brisk, Director
Bilingual Program, Department of Developmental Studies
and Counseling
School of Education
Boston University
605 Commonwealth Avenue
Boston, MA 02215

Telephone: (617) 353-3260
Fax: (617) 353-3924
E-mail: tesol@bu.edu

◆ BOWLING GREEN STATE UNIVERSITY, Department of English

Degree Offered: MA in English with a concentration in TESL.

Length of Program: 4 semesters. Students may be full-time or part-time and may begin their study at the beginning of any semester. Application deadlines are fall semester, March 1 (funded students), May 1 (fee-paying students); spring semester, October 1 (fee-paying students).

Program Requirements: 33 semester hours. Competence in a language other than English is not required but is helpful. Practice teaching, a comprehensive examination, and participation in testing and placement are required. A thesis is not required.

Courses Offered: Teaching of Writing; Modern English Linguistics; Language Variation; Theories in TESL; Resources and Research in TESL; Applied Syntax; Applied Phonology; Methods in TESL; Practicum in TESL; *Supervised Internship.

Full-Time Staff: Virginia S. Martin, Shirley E. Ostler (coordinator), Harender N. Vasudeva.

Requirements for Admission: The university's requirements for admission are a BA or BS from an accredited institution and submission of a GRE score. For nonnative speakers of English, the program requires a minimum TOEFL score of 600.

Tuition, Fees, and Aid: For in-state students, $7,824 per year (3 semesters); for out-of-state students, $14,208 per year. Four teaching assistantships are awarded each year. Recipients must demonstrate the ability to teach freshman composition.

General: The program is small and has an excellent job placement record. Students acquire experience in ESL testing and placement. Funded students usually teach 3 semesters of freshman composition. Optional internships are available in ESL administration and international student advising. Double degrees with German or Romance languages are possible. Students are encouraged to become professionally involved through attending and presenting papers at conferences and by developing research for publication, both independently and with faculty.

The internship may be taken in Mexico or Korea.

Five students completed the program in 1996–1997.

The university has an intensive English language program for nonnative speakers of English.

Summer Session: Yes

Further Information: Dr. Shirley E. Ostler, Coordinator
MATESL Program
Department of English
Bowling Green State University
Bowling Green, OH 43402

Telephone: (419) 372-6864
Fax: (419) 372-0333
Email: sostler@bgnet.bgsu.edu

◆ BRIGHAM YOUNG UNIVERSITY, Department of Linguistics

Degree Offered: TESOL certificate.

Length of Program: 2 semesters. Students may be full-time or part-time and may begin their study at the beginning of any semester. The application deadline is February 1.

Program Requirements: 21 credits (24 for nonnative speakers of English). Competence in a language other than English is not required. Practice teaching is required. Neither a thesis nor a comprehensive examination is required.

Courses Offered: (*required) *Introduction to ESL Methodology; *Student Teaching; *Language, Mind, and World (prerequisite); *ESL Advanced Composition (for nonnative English speakers); Teaching Culture; Language Acquisition; Advanced Methodology; TESL Supervision-Administration; ESL in Elementary School; Reading and Writing; Grammar and Usage; Phonology of Modern English; Materials Development; Language Testing; Bibliography and Research; Humanities Computing Project; Interlanguage Analysis.

Full-Time Staff: Neil J. Anderson; Robert W. Blair; Rey L. Baird, Lynn E. Henrichsen, Melvin J. Luthy, Glen W. Probst, John S. Robertson (chair), Diane Strong-Krause, Mark W. Tanner.

Requirements for Admission: The university's requirements for admission are a baccalaureate degree from a recognized university, a completed application, three letters of recommendation, a GPA of approximately 3.6 for the last 60 hours of study, an honor code commitment, and a letter of intent. A minimum TOEFL score of 580 is required for nonnative speakers of English. The program requires a GRE score.

Tuition, Fees, and Aid: Latter Day Saints, $1,550 per semester; others, $2,325 per semester. Partial tuition scholarships, a limited number of teaching and research assistantships, and part-time teaching in the English Language Center are available.

General: This program's course offerings combine practical and theoretical insights from current research. Students have access to an array of technological resources. The TESOL certificate is a graduate program. It is also the first year of the TESOL MA. A student may stop after earning the certificate or, if qualified, continue in the MA program. With some modification, the program can lead to a state endorsement in TESOL.

Thirty-two students completed the program in 1996–1997.

The university has an intensive English language program for nonnative speakers of English.

Summer Session: Yes

Further Information: John S. Robertson, Chair
Department of Linguistics
2129 JKHB
Brigham Young University
Provo, UT 84602-6278

Telephone: (801) 378-2937
Fax: (801) 378-8295
E-mail: Lingsec@JKHBRC.BYU.EDU

◆ BRIGHAM YOUNG UNIVERSITY, Department of Linguistics

Degree Offered: TESOL MA.

Length of Program: 2 semesters beyond the TESL certificate. Students may be full-time or part-time and may begin their study on completion of the TESOL certificate and satisfactory completion of Bibliography and Research.

Program Requirements: 38 semester credit hours. Competence in a language other than English is required; English meets the requirement for nonnative speakers of English. Practice teaching and a thesis are required. A comprehensive examination is not required.

Courses Offered: (*required) *18 credit hours from the certificate program; *Master's Thesis; *TESOL Seminar; *Research Design and Bibliography; *Language Acquisition; 12 additional credits.

Full-Time Staff: Neil J. Anderson, Robert W. Blair, Rey L. Baird, Lynn E. Henrichsen, Melvin J. Luthy, Glen W. Probst, John S. Robertson (chair), Diane Strong-Krause, Mark W. Tanner, C. Ray Graham.

Requirements for Admission: The university's requirements for admission are an application, ecclesiastical endorsement, and adherence to the Honor Code. The program requires a GPA of at least 3.0 in 19 hours beyond the TESOL certificate.

Tuition, Fees, and Aid: See TESOL certificate program description. Some computer lab part-time positions are also available.

General: The MA program provides opportunities for development of research and critical writing skills. Students have access to an array of technological resources. Faculty have university support for overseas research. With some modification, the program can lead to a state endorsement in TESOL.

Fifteen students completed the program in 1996–1997.

The university has an intensive English language program for nonnative speakers of English.

Summer Session: Yes

Further Information: John S. Robertson, Chair
Department of Linguistics
2129 JKHB
Brigham Young University
Provo, UT 84602-6278

Telephone: (801) 378-2937
Fax: (801) 378-8295
E-mail: Lingsec@JKHBRC.BYU.EDU

◆ BRIGHAM YOUNG UNIVERSITY–HAWAII, Languages and Linguistics Division

Degree Offered: BA in TESOL.

Length of Program: 4–5 semesters. Students may be full-time or part-time and may begin their study at the beginning of the fall or winter semester. There are no application deadlines.

Program Requirements: 45 semester hours. Competence in a language other than English is required (4 semesters); English meets the requirement for 2 of these semesters for nonnative speakers of English. Practice teaching, a comprehensive examination, a senior paper, and maintenance of a GPA of 2.5 in the major are required.

Courses Offered: *Critical Introduction to Literature; *History of English; *one of the following: Semantics, Ethnic Literature, Genre Literature, American Literature to the Mid-19th Century, American Literature (Mid-19th Century to World War I), American Literature Since World War I, Victorian Literature, Modern British Literature, Shakespeare, Adolescent Literature; *Intercultural Communication; *Introduction to Linguistics; *Phonology; *English Grammars; *Sociolinguistics; *Language Acquisition; *Introduction to TESOL; *TESOL Methods and Materials; *TESOL Testing and Research; *TESOL Listening and Speaking; *TESOL Reading and Writing; *TESOL Practicum; *Senior Seminar; *4 semesters in foreign language.

Full-Time Staff: Margaret P. Baker, Brent Green, Lynne Hansen, Mark O. James (chair), Fawn Whittaker, Earl D. Wyman.

Requirements for Admission: The university's requirements for admission are high school transcripts, ACT or SAT scores, and a GPA of 2.7 or higher from high school or previous university experience. International students must have taken the TOEFL or MELAB. The program also requires completion with a C+ or better of Introduction to Linguistics and Introduction to TESOL.

Tuition, Fees, and Aid: For Latter Day Saints, $1,066 per semester ($553 per term); for others, $1,596 per semester ($798 per term). Pell grants, Stafford loans, BYU-Hawaii short-term loans, division scholarships and loans, internships, and research associateships are available.

General: The characteristic that sets BYU-Hawaii apart from other universities is its multicultural setting: About 40% of the student body is international. This fact plus living and going to school in Hawaii yields numerous opportunities to gain a sensitivity to multicultural issues. Students can work as tutors or interns and gain much experience and insight.

Fifteen students completed the program in 1996–1997.

The university has an intensive English language program for nonnative speakers of English.

Summer Session: No

Further Information: TESOL Program Division Chair
Languages and Linguistics Division
Brigham Young University–Hawaii
55-220 Kulanui Street
Laie, HI 96762

Telephone: (808) 293-3602
Fax: (808) 293-3448

◆ CALIFORNIA, UNIVERSITY OF, BERKELEY EXTENSION, Education Extension

Degrees Offered: TESL certificate; TEFL certificate.

Length of Program: 1½ years. Students may be full-time or part-time and may begin their studies at the beginning of any semester. No application is needed.

Program Requirements: 17 semester units. Competence in a language other than English is not required. Practice teaching and an English language proficiency test are required. Neither a thesis nor a comprehensive examination is required.

Courses Offered: (*required) *Fundamentals of Linguistics for ESL Teachers; *Methods and Materials for TESL; *Second Language Acquisition; *Cross-Cultural Communication; *Practicum in TESL; Language Acquisition Through Art, Music, Poetry, and Play; TESL in Japan; Sheltered Instruction: Language Development in the Content Areas; Introduction to TESL in the Workplace; Methods of Teaching Specially Designed Academic Instruction in English; Fundamentals of Grammar for the ESL Teacher; Teaching English Overseas; Testing and Evaluation in the ESL Classroom; Reading Instruction in the ESL Classroom; Fundamentals of Classroom Management; Teaching Writing in the ESL Classroom; Teaching for Literacy in the ESL Classroom; Developing the Reading and Writing Connection in ESL; Methods of Teaching Bilingual and English Language Development; Introduction to TESL; Teaching Pronunciation as a Communicative Skill; Developing Multisensory Language Teaching Activities for ESL/EFL Classrooms; Cooperative Learning in Language Classrooms; Developing Oral Fluency Through Cooperative Group Work; The Role of Literature in the ESL/EFL Classroom; Language Acquisition and Classroom Interaction.

Full-Time Staff: Margaret R. Wilcox, Barbara B. Patterson.

Tuition, Fees, and Aid: TESL program: approximately $3,000; 3-month intensive TEFL program: approximately $4,000. Some loans are available.

General: The program provides comprehensive training that includes both a theoretical foundation and practical application and experience. Organized practice teaching is provided. Courses within the TESL program can be used for a California specialized authorization in CLAD.

Sixty-five students completed the program in 1996–1997.

The university has an intensive English language program for nonnative speakers of English.

Summer Session: Yes

Further Information: Director, TESL/TEFL Programs
Education Department
University of California, Berkeley Extension
1995 University Avenue
Berkeley, CA 94720-7009

Telephone: (510) 642-1173
Fax: (510) 643-8683
E-mail: TESL@unx.berkeley.edu

◆ CALIFORNIA, UNIVERSITY OF, DAVIS, Department of Linguistics

Degree Offered: MA with a concentration in applied linguistics.

Length of Programs: 6 quarters. Students may be full-time or part-time and must begin their study at the beginning of the fall quarter. The application deadline is April 1 (March 1 for overseas applicants).

Program Requirements: 38 quarter units for general track; 42 units for applied track. Competence in a language other than English is required. Practice teaching plus either a comprehensive examination or a thesis is required.

Courses Offered: (*required) *Methods of TESOL; *Materials of TESOL; *Recent Research and Special Projects in TESOL; *Theory of ESL; *Research on Second Language Acquisition; *Individual and Social Aspects of Bilingualism; Linguistic Theory (Phonology, Morphology, Syntax, Semantics); Historical Linguistics; Sociolinguistics; Romance Linguistics.

Full-Time Staff: W. A. Benware, Patrick Farrell, Steven LaPointe, M. Manoliu, Barbara Merino, Almerindo Ojeda, Mary Schleppegrell, Maximo Torreblanca.

Requirements for Admission: The university's requirement for admission is a baccalaureate degree from an accredited institution. The program requires three letters of recommendation and submission of a GRE score. International students are required to take the TOEFL.

Tuition, Fees, and Aid: $1,490 per quarter. Out-of-state students pay a fee of $2,995 per quarter. Teaching assistantships are available for second-year MA students. Fellowships are also available.

General: The program is strong in the practicum; students teach 3 hours a week each quarter in the UCD ESL clinic during their first year. They are fully responsible for planning course syllabi and lessons. Over the year trainees may teach all areas of English with advanced and high-intermediate students. As teaching assistants in the second year, students teach sections of academic credit courses offered to undergraduate and graduate students at the university.

Three students completed the program in 1996–1997.

The university has an intensive English language program for nonnative speakers of English.

Summer Session: No

Further Information: Program Director
Department of Linguistics
110 Sproul Hall
University of California, Davis
One Shields Avenue
Davis, CA 95616

Telephone: (530) 752-3464
Fax: (530) 752-3156
E-mail: embrown@ucdavis.edu

◆ CALIFORNIA, UNIVERSITY OF, IRVINE EXTENSION, Department of Education and Social Sciences

Degree Offered: Certificate in TESL.

Length of Program: 3 quarters. Students may be full-time or part-time and may begin their study at the beginning of any quarter. There are no application deadlines.

Program Requirements: 26 quarter units. Competence in a language other than English is not required. Neither practice teaching, nor a thesis, nor a comprehensive examination is required.

Courses Offered: (*required) *Methods of TESOL; *Culture and Cultural Diversity; *Language Structure and Use; *Language Assessment; *Second Language Acquisition; *The Grammar of English; 8 units of electives.

Full-Time Staff: Jia Frydenberg (director), Laura Franklin, Haley Dawson, Kathleen Phelan.

Requirements for Admission: Extension courses have no formal admission requirements. Nonnative speakers of English must show a TOEFL score of 530 or the equivalent.

Tuition, Fees, and Aid: $60–$90 per quarter unit. Student loans are available.

General: The program is a practical, hands-on course that is continually updated and refined. Specializations in adult education and teaching internationally are offered. A full-time academic adviser is on staff. As of fall 1998, a 4-month intensive TEFL certificate program will be offered twice each year.

Ninety-six students completed the program in 1996–1997.

The university has an intensive English program for nonnative speakers of English.

Summer Session: Yes

Further Information: Haley Dawson, Academic Advisor
Department of Education and Social Sciences
Extension Building D-100
University of California, Irvine Extension
PO Box 6050
Irvine, CA 92616-6050

Telephone: (714) 824-7579
Fax: (714) 824-3651
E-mail: hmdawson@uci.edu

◆ CALIFORNIA, UNIVERSITY OF, LOS ANGELES, Department of TESL and Applied Linguistics

Degree Offered: MA in applied linguistics and TESL.

Length of Program: 6 quarters (2 years). Students must be full-time and must begin their study at the beginning of the fall quarter. The application deadline is December 15.

Program Requirements: 40 quarter credits. Competence in a language other than English not required. A thesis is required. Practice teaching is optional. A comprehensive examination is not required.

Courses Offered: (*required) *Research in Applied Linguistics; *Functional Foundations of Language; *Foundations of Language Acquisition; *Foundations of Language Assessment; *Social Foundations of Language; *MA Thesis Research and Preparation; Language Acquisition; Experiential Seminar: Second Language Learning; Discourse-Centered Language Learning; Topics in Psycholinguistics; Language Socialization; Current Issues in Language Acquisition; Advanced Seminar: Interlanguage Analysis; Cross-Linguistic Topics in Language Acquisition; Design and Development of Language Assessment Procedures; Analysis and Use of Language Assessment Data; Experimental Design and Statistics for Applied Linguistics; Current Issues in Language Assessment; Assessment Laboratory; Discourse Analysis; Cross-Linguistic Topics in Functional Grammar; Topics in Semantics and Pragmatics; Ethnographic Research Methods; Advanced Seminar: Cohesion Analysis of English Structure; Advanced Seminar: Contextual Analysis of English Structure; Discourse Laboratory; Theories of Language Education and Learning; Writing for Second/Foreign Language Teaching; Materials Development for Second/Foreign Language Teaching; Structure of Present-Day English; Second/Foreign Language Teaching Practicum; Current Issues in Second/Foreign Language Teaching; courses in anthropology, education, linguistics, neurobiology, psychology, sociology, and several foreign language departments.

Full-Time Staff: Asif Agha, Roger W. Andersen, Lyle Bachman, Donna Brinton, Marianne Celce-Murcia, Charles Goodwin, Janet Goodwin, Christine Holten, Linda Jensen, Elinor Ochs, John F. Povey, John H. Schumann (chair), Evelyn R. Hatch, Russell Campbell, Earl Rand.

Requirements for Admission: The university requires a B (3.0) average and a GRE General Test score. Nonnative speakers of English must have a TOEFL score of 625 (recommended). The requirement is waived for applicants who have completed a minimum of 2 years' full-time study at an English-medium university. The program requires a statement of purpose, three letters of recommendation, an academic research/writing sample, and transcripts from all colleges and universities attended.

Tuition, Fees, and Aid: For out-of-state students, $9,000 per year. Fees are $4,800 per academic year for all students. Merit-based aid; teaching assistantships in ESL, freshman composition, foreign languages, psychology, education, and linguistics; and fellowships are available.

General: Understanding the theory and research in the fields of language acquisition, language assessment, discourse analysis, functional grammar, and cross-linguistic research are the primary foci of this program. Intended primarily for individuals who wish to pursue a career in applied linguistics, the program is designed to provide both breadth of knowledge in several areas of applied linguistics and the specialized knowledge and skills needed to plan and conduct research in one. Although some students also take an elective course of study that includes a language education and practical element (observing classes, preparing lesson plans, and classroom teaching), these activities are viewed in light of their theoretical underpinnings and the research opportunities they offer. The program leads to a California credential in TESOL.

Through a liaison with the Language Resource Program, students can participate in programs in Armenia, China, Korea, and Mexico as well as nationwide projects in language teaching.

Eight students completed the program in 1996–1997.

The university has an English language program for nonnative speakers of English.

Summer Session: No

Further Information: Lyn Repath-Martos, Student Affairs Officer
Department of TESL and Applied Linguistics
University of California, Los Angeles
Rolfe Hall 3300
405 Hilgard Avenue, PO Box 95131
Los Angeles, CA 90024-1531

Telephone: (310) 825-4631
Fax: (310) 206-4118
E-mail: lyn@humnet.ucla.edu

◆ CALIFORNIA, UNIVERSITY OF, LOS ANGELES, Department of TESL and Applied Linguistics

Degree Offered: PhD in applied linguistics.

Length of Program: 12–15 quarters. Students must be full-time and must begin their study at the beginning of the fall quarter. The application deadline is December 15.

Program Requirements: 52 quarter credits. Competence in a language other than English is required; English meets the requirement for nonnative speakers of English. A dissertation and two qualifying papers are required. Practice teaching is not required.

Courses Offered: (*required) *Language Acquisition; *Phonology I; *Syntax I; *two courses in syntax/semantics or phonetics/phonology or discourse analysis/functional grammar; specialized courses on current issues, including Neurobiology of Applied Linguistics, Critical Period, Learning and Memory, Metaphor and Literal Speech, Ethnographic Research Methods for Discourse Analysis, Moral Discourse, Narrative, Problem-Solving Discourse, Cross-Linguistic Topics: Mood, Tense, Aspect, Topics in Semantics and Pragmatics, Language Socialization, Research Design and Statistical Analysis, Design and Development of Language Assessment Procedures, Analysis and Use of Language Assessment Data, Discourse Laboratory, Assessment Laboratory, Cross-Linguistic Laboratory; courses in applied linguistics, neurobiology, anthropology, education, linguistics, neurobiology, psychology, sociology, and several foreign language departments.

Full-Time Staff: Asif Agha, Roger W. Andersen, Raimo Antilla, Lyle Bachman, Donna Brinton, Marianne Celce-Murcia, Steven Clayman, Susan Curtiss, Alessandro Duranti, Charles Goodwin, Janet Goodwin, Marjorie Goodwin, Bruce Hayes, John Heritage, Thomas Hinnebusch, Christine Holten, Nina Hyams, Linda Jensen, Sun-Ah Jun, Patricia Keating, Edward Keenan, Hilda Koopman, Paul Kroskrity, Ian Maddieson, Anoop Mahajan, Pamela Munro, Elinor Ochs, Russell Schuh, John H. Schumann (chair), Carson Schutze, Emanuel Schegloff, Dominique Sportiche, Edward Stabler, Donca Steriade, Robert Stockwell, Timothy Stowell, Anna Szabolcsi, George Bedell, William Bright, Russell N. Campbell, Victoria Fromkin, Evelyn R. Hatch, Peter Ladefoged, Earl J. Rand.

Requirements for Admission: The university requires a B (3.0) average and a GRE General Test score. Nonnative speakers of English must have a TOEFL score of 625 (recommended); the requirement is waived for applicants who have completed a minimum of 2 years' full-time study at an English-medium university. The program requires a statement of purpose, three letters of recommendation, a master's thesis or other academic sample, and transcripts from all colleges and universities attended.

Tuition, Fees, and Aid: See program description for MA in applied linguistics and TESL.

General: Through the interdepartmental structure of this program, students may focus on and specialize in unique aspects of language acquisition, language assessment, and discourse analysis/functional grammar. Participants are encouraged to explore relevant topics through a variety of academic perspectives and fields.

Nine students completed the program in 1996–1997.

The university has an intensive English language program for nonnative speakers of English.

Summer Session: No

Further Information: Lyn Repath-Martos, Student Affairs Officer
Department of TESL and Applied Linguistics
University of California, Los Angeles
Rolfe Hall 3300
405 Hilgard Avenue, PO Box 95131
Los Angeles, CA 90024-1531

Telephone: (310) 825-4631
Fax: (310) 206-4118
E-mail: lyn@humnet.ucla.edu

◆ CALIFORNIA, UNIVERSITY OF, RIVERSIDE, University Extension, International Education Program

Degree Offered: TESOL certificate.

Length of Program: 4 quarters. Students may be full-time or part-time and may begin their study at the beginning of any quarter.

Program Requirements: 25 quarter units. Competence in a language other than English is not required. Practice teaching and a comprehensive examination are required. A thesis is not required.

Courses Offered: (*required) Prerequisites (may be exempted by examination): Standard English, Fundamentals of Writing; *History and Survey of ESL Methodologies; *Introduction to Linguistics; *Language Development and Acquisition; *Lesson Planning for the ESL Classroom; *Grammar Methodologies A; *Grammar Methodologies B; *Student Teaching; *four of the following: TESOL Listening Methodologies, TESOL Reading Methodologies, TESOL Conversation Methodologies, TESOL Vocabulary Methodologies, TESOL Pronunciation Methodologies, TESOL Writing Methodologies, Teaching American Idioms.

Full-Time Staff: Linda Adler, Peggy Cleve, Wendy Crockett, Sheila Dwight (director), Carol W. Kisch, Jeanette LaPorte, Hank Mantell, Gregory McCoy, Dave Myers, Debbie Peterson, Greg Richey, Fredith Laub.

Requirements for Admission: The requirement for admission is a high school diploma. In addition, students must pass examinations in writing and English usage.

Nonnative speakers of English must have a TOEFL score of 500 and a TSE score of 200.

Tuition, Fees, and Aid: $2,500 for the program. The application fee is $50.

General: The program emphasizes practical classroom applications of teaching methodologies. In the final course of the program, Student Teaching, students are assigned a mentor teacher and teach an ESL course for students from the community.

The program has sister school relationships with Hokuriku, Josai, Fukuyama, and Gifu universities in Japan and sends teachers to these schools and to Korea.

Twenty-five students completed the program in 1996–1997.

The university has an intensive English language program for nonnative speakers of English.

Summer Session: Yes

Further Information: Dr. Sheila Dwight
International Education Programs
University of California, Riverside, Extension
1200 University Avenue
Riverside, CA 92507

Telephone: (909) 787-4346
Fax: (909) 787-5796
E-mail: ucriep@ucx.ucr.edu
http://unex.ucr.edu/iehomepage.html

◆ CALIFORNIA, UNIVERSITY OF, SANTA BARBARA, University Extension, International Programs

Degree Offered: TESL/TEFL certificate.

Length of Program: Approximately 1 year. Students may be full-time or part-time and may begin their study at the beginning of any quarter. The application deadline is 1 week before a course begins.

Program Requirements: 24 quarter units. Competence in a language other than English is not required. Practice teaching is required. Neither a thesis nor a comprehensive examination is required.

Courses Offered: (*required) *Language Structure and Usage; *Language Development and Acquisition; *ESL Methods and Materials; *Art and Craft of ESL Teaching; *Cross-Cultural Communication; *Practicum in ESL Teaching; 7 elective units in skills development (reading, writing, speaking, listening, grammar, pronunciation), methods and materials (student-centered approach, cooperative learning, English through drama and music, use of videos and computers, textbook evaluation and materials writing, lesson planning, testing and assessment, error correction), and English for specific student populations (English abroad, English in the workplace, adult learners, the multilevel classroom, business English).

Full-Time Staff: Nancy Overholt (director), Peggy White.

Requirements for Admission: The program requires 2 years of college course work, an associate's degree, or the equivalent. A BA is required for the issue of the certificate. Admission into the program is not necessary for those taking course work for professional growth only. Nonnative speakers of English must have a TOEFL score of 530 to enroll and a score of 550 to do the practicum and receive the certificate.

Tuition, Fees, and Aid: $150–$250 per course. Limited discounts are available on a needs basis.

General: Visiting students and teachers from abroad enhance the cultural depth and understanding of second language acquisition processes and foster international networking. Courses are offered in four counties (Ventura, Santa Barbara, San Luis Obispo, and Kern) and on weekends to accommodate working adults. Up to 6 units of transfer can be requested for comparable course work.

Sixty students completed the program in 1996–1997.

The university has an intensive English language program for nonnative speakers of English.

Summer Session: Yes

Further Information: Brice Taylor, Certificate Adviser
UCSB Extension
6550 Hollister Avenue
Goleta, CA 93117

Telephone: (805) 893-3816
Fax: (805) 893-4943
E-mail: btaylor@xlrn.ucsb.edu

◆ CALIFORNIA POLYTECHNIC STATE UNIVERSITY, Department of English

Degree Offered: TESL certificate.

Length of Program: 3 quarters. Students may be full-time or part-time and may begin their study at the beginning of any quarter. Application deadlines are fall quarter, November 30; summer quarter, February 28; winter quarter, June 30.

Program Requirements: 29 quarter units. Competence in a language other than English is required for native speakers of English. Practice teaching is required. A comprehensive examination is required only if the certificate program is taken with the MA in English. A thesis is not required.

Courses Offered: (*required) *Introduction to Linguistics; *Modern English Grammar *or* Seminar in English Linguistics; *Topics in Applied Linguistics *or* Seminar in Applied Linguistics; *Intercultural Communication; *Language and Culture; *Practicum in TESL; Theories of Language Learning and Teaching; Approaches to TESL.

Full-Time Staff: John Battenburg (coordinator), Barbara E. Cook, Steven T. McDermott, Johanna Rubba, Habib Sheik.

Requirements for Admission: The university requires students pursuing the certificate to be matriculating students.

Tuition, Fees, and Aid: For in-state students, $743 for more than 6 units; for out-of-state students, $164 per quarter unit in addition. Teaching assistantships are available for students who are also enrolled in the MA in English program.

General: The program offers courses from the departments of English, social sciences, and speech communication. A practicum is required for practical ESL classroom experience.

Fifteen students completed the program in 1996–1997.

Summer Session: No

Further Information: Dr. John Battenburg, Coordinator
TESL Program, English Department
California Polytechnic State University
San Luis Obispo, CA 93407

Telephone: (805) 756-2945
Fax: (805) 756-5748
E-mail: jbatten@calpoly.edu

◆ CALIFORNIA STATE UNIVERSITY, DOMINGUEZ HILLS, Department of English

Degree Offered: Certificate in TESL.

Length of Program: 2–3 semesters. Students may be full-time or part-time and may begin their study at the beginning of any semester. There are no application deadlines.

Program Requirements: 24 semester units. Competence in a language other than English is not required. A practicum and a thesis are required. A comprehensive examination is not required.

Courses Offered: (*required) *Phonology; *Morphology; *Syntax; *Linguistic Analysis; *Seminar in Linguistics; *Psycholinguistics; *Second Language Acquisition; *ESL Teaching Methods.

Full-Time Staff: Burckhard Mohr, Vanessa Wenzell, Ed Zoerner.

Requirements for Admission: The university's requirement for admission is a baccalaureate degree from an accredited institution. Nonnative speakers of English must have a TOEFL score of at least 550.

Tuition, Fees, and Aid: For in-state students, $459 per 6 units; for out-of-state students, $246 per unit in addition. Fees are $119. No financial aid is available.

General: The postbaccalaureate TESL certificate is offered to teachers and prospective teachers seeking competence in TESL. The program combines upper-division and graduate courses in the areas of English, linguistics, and education. Courses completed or required as part of other programs of study may be applicable toward the certificate.

Five students completed the program in 1996–1997.

The university has an intensive English language program for nonnative speakers of English.

Summer Session: No

Further Information: Vanessa Wenzell, TESL Coordinator
English Department
California State University, Dominguez Hills
1000 East Victoria Street
Carson, CA 90747

Telephone: (310) 516-3322

◆ CALIFORNIA STATE UNIVERSITY, DOMINGUEZ HILLS, Department of English

Degree Offered: MA in English with a TESL option.

Length of Program: 2–4 semesters. Students may be full-time or part-time and may begin their study at the beginning of any semester. There are no application deadlines.

Program Requirements: 30 semester units. Competence in a language other than English is not required. A diagnostic exam after the first semester of study and a final project are required. Neither practice teaching nor a comprehensive examination is required.

Courses Offered: (*required) *Second Language Acquisition; *ESL Teaching Methods; *Pedagogical Grammar for TESOL; *Linguistic Analysis; *Psycholinguistics or Sociolinguistics; *Current Issues in TESL/Applied Linguistics; *Topics in Linguistics; *Research Methods in Applied Linguistics; *Seminar in English Literature; History of the English Language; History of American English.

Full-Time Staff: See program description for certificate in TESL.

Requirements for Admission: The university's requirement for admission is a baccalaureate degree from an accredited institution with a GPA of at least 2.5. Nonnative speakers of English must have a TOEFL score of at least 550. Three prerequisite courses (phonology, morphology, and syntax) must be taken before the program or during the first semester.

Tuition, Fees, and Aid: See program description for certificate in TESL.

General: The program is designed for graduate students planning careers in TESL/TEFL at the college or university level in the U.S. or internationally. This program combines upper-division and graduate-level courses in English, linguistics, and education with practical experience and a final project.

Ten students completed the program in 1996–1997.

The university has an intensive English language program for nonnative speakers of English.

Summer Session: No

Further Information: Vanessa Wenzell, TESL Coordinator
English Department
California State University, Dominguez Hills
1000 East Victoria Street
Carson, CA 90747

Telephone: (310) 516-3322

◆ CALIFORNIA STATE UNIVERSITY, FRESNO, Department of Linguistics

Degree Offered: MA in linguistics with an ESL emphasis.

Length of Program: 4 semesters. Students may be full-time or part-time and may begin their study at the beginning of any semester. Application deadlines are fall semester, August 1; spring semester, October 1.

Program Requirements: Competence in a language other than English is optional. Practice teaching and a comprehensive examination are required. A thesis is optional.

Courses Offered: (*required) *General Linguistics; *Phonology; *Syntax; *Teaching Basic Written English; *Seminar in TESOL; *Testing and Evaluation in TESOL; *Phonology Seminar; *Syntax Seminar; *Historical Linguistics; Sociolinguistics; Methods of TESOL; Practicum in TESOL; Practical English Grammar.

Full-Time Staff: Armando Baltra, Barbara Birch, Ritva Laury, Ellen Lipp, Gerald McMenamin, Karen Mistry, P. J. Mistry, Joel Nevis, Shigeko Okamoto, G. W. Raney (chair), Vida Samiian, Graham Thurgood, Raymond Weitzman, Jack Zeldis.

Requirements for Admission: The requirements for admission are a BA in an appropriate field with a GPA of 3.0 or higher, and GRE scores of 450 (verbal) and 430 (quantitative). International students must score 550 or better on the TOEFL. Students who do not have a BA or minor in linguistics must complete a minimum of 9 units of upper-division courses in linguistics with a GPA of 3.0 or better.

Tuition, Fees, and Aid: For in-state students, $901 per semester; for out-of-state students, $246 per unit. Limited fellowships are available for out-of-state students and foreign nationals. Graduate students are expected to teach in the American English Institute. Limited teaching assistantships are available in the department.

General: The program provides a linguistics core in the ESL MA option. Faculty members work closely with students.

About 20 students completed the program in 1996–1997.

The university has an English language program for nonnative speakers of English.

Summer Session: Yes

Further Information: G. W. Raney, Chair
Department of Linguistics
California State University, Fresno
Leon S. Peters Building, Room 383
5245 North Backer Avenue
Fresno, CA 93740-0092

Telephone: (209) 278-7525
Fax: (209) 278-7299
e-mail: geor@CSUfresno.edu

◆ CALIFORNIA STATE UNIVERSITY, FULLERTON, Department of Foreign Languages and Literature

Degree Offered: Certificate in TESOL.

Length of Program: 3 semesters. Students may be full-time or part-time and must begin their study at the beginning of the fall semester. Admission begins November 1 and continues until slots are filled.

Program Requirements: 24 semester hours. Competence in a language other than English is required; English meets the requirement for nonnative speakers of English. Practice teaching is required. A thesis and a comprehensive examination are optional.

Courses Offered: (*required) *Principles of TESOL (oral-aural emphasis); *Principles of TESOL (reading-writing emphasis); *TESOL Practicum; *Spanish-English Contrastive Analysis, Japanese Contrastive Analysis, *or* Language Transfer and TESOL; electives chosen from English, foreign languages, linguistics, or another appropriate field.

Full-Time Staff: Nancy T. Baden, Jan Eyring (coordinator), Ronald M. Harmon, Marjorie Tussing.

Requirements for Admission: The university's requirement for admission is a baccalaureate degree from an accredited institution with a minimum GPA of 2.5 in the last 60 semester hours attempted and a minimum GPA of 3.0 in the major. In addition, the program requires 2 years of one foreign language or 1 year each of two foreign languages with a minimum GPA of 3.0, Advanced College Writing and Structure of Modern English with a minimum grade of B, and oral and written proficiency in English to be determined at the time of the application. Applicants without a baccalaureate degree from a postsecondary institution where the principal language is English must have a minimum TOEFL score of 575 and a minimum TSE score of 55–60.

Tuition, Fees, and Aid: For in-state students, $640.50 for 0–6 units, $973.50 for 7 or more units; for out-of-state students, $246 per unit in addition.

General: The program prepares teachers to enhance their employability by demonstrating additional competencies in TESOL. It also serves prospective teachers or students who wish to teach English in the U.S. or abroad. Located in the heart of southern California's most diverse nonnative English-speaking communities, the program offers many opportunities for students to gain knowledge of TEFL/TESL theory and practice. A variety of university-approved teaching and tutoring opportunities are available, including the Business Resource Center, the Writing Assistance Center, the Distance Learning Program, and the American Language Program.

Six students completed the program in 1996–1997.

The university has an intensive English language program for nonnative speakers of English.

Summer Session: Yes

Further Information: TESOL Coordinator
Department of Foreign Languages and Literature
Humanities Building, Room 835C
California State University, Fullerton
800 North State College Boulevard
Fullerton, CA 92834-6846

Telephone: (714) 278-3534
Fax: (714) 278-5944

◆ CALIFORNIA STATE UNIVERSITY, FULLERTON, Department of Foreign Languages and Literature

Degree Offered: MS in education with a concentration in TESOL.

Length of Program: 30 semester units. Students may be full-time or part-time and must begin the program at the beginning of the fall semester. Admission begins November 1 and continues until slots are filled.

Program Requirements: 30 semester units. Competence in a language other than English is required; English meets the requirement for nonnative speakers of English. Practice teaching and a comprehensive examination are required. A thesis is not required.

Courses Offered: (*required) *Principles of TESOL I (emphasis on aural/oral communication); *Principles of TESOL II (emphasis on reading and writing); *Theory of Bilingual Language Acquisition; *Curriculum and Program Design for TESOL; *Second Language Assessment; *Practicum; electives from culture, linguistics, English and speech communication, and professional education.

Full-Time Staff: Nancy Baden, Janet Eyring (coordinator), Juan Carlos Gallego, Ronald Harmon, Marjorie Tussing.

Requirements for Admission: See program description for certificate in TESOL. In addition, this program requires a survey course of English or American literature and a course in descriptive linguistics, both with a minimum grade of B. Applicants without a baccalaureate degree from a postsecondary institution where the principal language is English must have a minimum TOEFL score of 575 and a minimum TSE score of 55–60.

Tuition, Fees, and Aid: See program description for certificate in TESOL.

General: The program is well integrated and dedicated to creating TESOL professionals with a strong knowledge of theory and practice. The culminating experiences of the program are the practicum and the master's exam. The program serves teachers at all educational levels, including K–12, intensive, adult, community college, and university in the U.S. and abroad, and meets individual needs by offering late afternoon and evening courses and seminars. Proximally located to some of southern California's most diverse nonnative English-speaking communities, the program offers many opportunities for students to gain ESL practice teaching experience. A variety of university-approved teaching and tutoring opportunities are available, including the Business Resource Center, the Writing Assistance Center, the Distance Learning Program, and the American Language Program. Fourteen students completed the program in 1996–1997.

Summer Session: Yes

Further Information: TESOL Coordinator
Department of Foreign Languages and Literature
Humanities Building, Room 835C
California State University, Fullerton
800 North State College Boulevard
Fullerton, CA 92834-6846

Telephone: (714) 278-3534
Fax: (714) 278-5944

◆ CALIFORNIA STATE UNIVERSITY, HAYWARD, Department of English

Degree Offered: MA in English—TESOL option.

Length of Program: 6 quarters. Students may be full-time or part-time and may begin their study at the beginning of any quarter. Applications are accepted until capacity is reached.

Program Requirements: 45 units. Competence in a language other than English is not required. Practice teaching and a portfolio are required. A comprehensive examination is not required.

Courses Offered: (*required) *Theory and Practice of Teaching ESL I and II; *Second Language Acquisition; *Morphology and Lexical Semantics; *Sociolinguistics; *Testing and Evaluation for TESL; *Computer-Assisted Language Learning and Teaching; *Theory and Practice of Composition; *Supervised Tutoring and Teaching; *Departmental Thesis Project.

Full-Time Staff: Keoko Tanaka (coordinator), Charles DeBose, Marilyn Silva, Alison Warriner.

Requirements for Admission: The university's requirement for admission is a relevant baccalaureate degree with a GPA of 3.0 overall. Those without a relevant baccalaureate degree may be accepted into the program by taking prerequisite courses.

Tuition, Fees, and Aid: For in-state students, $590 per quarter; for out-of-state students, $164 per unit in addition. Grants and fellowships are available.

General: Students have an opportunity to teach courses in the ESL Program as a part of the practicum. Students also work closely with faculty to gain practical experience in conducting research, administering learning centers, and making professional presentations.

Opportunities to teach overseas are available.

Twenty-three students completed the program in 1996–1997.

The university has an intensive English language program for nonnative speakers of English.

Summer Session: Yes

Further Information: Keiko Tanaka
Department of English
Warren Hall UM71
California State University, Hayward
25800 Carlos Bee Boulevard
Hayward, CA 94542

Telephone: (510) 885-3521
Fax: (510) 885-4797
E-mail: ktanaka@csuhayward.edu

◆ CALIFORNIA STATE UNIVERSITY, LOS ANGELES, TESOL Program

Degree Offered: Certificate in ESL/EFL.

Length of Program: Students may be full-time or part-time and may begin their study at the beginning of the summer or fall quarter. Application deadlines for U.S. students are summer quarter, April 1; fall quarter, June 5; winter quarter, October 1; spring quarter, February 1. Application deadlines for international students are fall quarter, March 1; winter quarter, September 1; spring quarter, October 1.

Program Requirements: 32 quarter units. Competence in a language other than English is required for native speakers of English. Practice teaching is required. Neither a thesis nor a comprehensive exam is required.

Courses Offered: (*required) *Theories of Teaching/Learning Second Languages; *Pedagogical Grammar for ESL Teaching *or* Modern English Grammar; *Methods for Teaching Second Languages; *Teaching ESL for Academic Purposes; *Language Testing; *Practicum in ESL; *Educational Sociolinguistics *or* Language and Culture; *ESL/EFL Course, Curriculum, and Materials Design; Using Computers in the Language Classroom; English Phonetics for Second Language Teachers; Current Issues in Language Testing; Language Planning and Language Policy; Evaluation of Educational Research; Statistics in Education; Issues in Classroom Second Language Acquisition; Current Issues in Second Language Research; Educational Psycholinguistics; electives from other departments.

Full-Time Staff: Janet Fisher-Hoult, José L. Galvan (chair), Lia D. Kamhi-Stein, Patricia A. Richard-Amato, Marguerite Ann Snow.

Requirements for Admission: The university's requirement for admission is a GPA of 2.75 in the last 90 units attempted. The program requires 1 year of college-level foreign language study or the equivalent; nonnative speakers must have a minimum TOEFL score of 600 (or a score of 550 plus a TWE score of 5).

Tuition, Fees, and Aid: For in-state students, $1,754 per year; for out-of-state students, $5,900 per year. University scholarships, graduate assistantships, teaching assistantships, fee waivers for international students, and School of Education scholarships are available.

General: The program prepares students for a wide variety of instructional settings from kindergarten through adult levels, both in the United States and abroad.

Four students completed the program in 1996–1997.

The university has an intensive English language program for nonnative speakers of English.

Summer Session: Yes

Further Information: Coordinator, TESOL Program
Charter School of Education
King Hall C-2098
California State University, Los Angeles
Los Angeles, CA 90032-8413

Telephone: (323) 343-4330
Fax: (323) 343-5336
E-mail: blee@calstatela.edu

◆ CALIFORNIA STATE UNIVERSITY, LOS ANGELES, TESOL Program

Degree Offered: MA in TESOL.

Length of Program: Students may be full-time or part-time and may begin their study at the beginning of the summer or fall quarter. Application deadlines for U.S. students are summer quarter, April 1; fall quarter, June 5; winter quarter, October 1; spring quarter, February 1. Application deadlines for international students are fall quarter, March 1; winter quarter, September 1; spring quarter, October 1.

Program Requirements: 45 quarter units. Competence in a language other than English is required for native speakers of English. Practice teaching is required. A thesis or a comprehensive exam is required.

Courses Offered: (*required) *Theories of Teaching/Learning Second Languages; *Pedagogical Grammar for ESL Teaching *or* Modern English Grammar; *Methods for Teaching Second Languages; *Teaching ESL for Academic Purposes; *Language Testing; *Practicum in ESL; *Educational Sociolinguistics *or* Language and Culture; *Evaluation of Educational Research; *Comprehensive Examination *or* Thesis/Project; *(for thesis students) Statistics in Education; Using Computers in the Language Classroom; English Phonetics for Second Language Teachers; Current Issues in Language Testing; Language Planning and Language Policy; Discourse Analysis in the Language Classroom; ESL/EFL Course, Curriculum, and Materials Design; Issues in Classroom Second Language Acquisition; Current Issues in Second Language Research; Educational Psycholinguistics; electives from other departments.

Full-Time Staff: Janet Fisher-Hoult, José L. Galvan (chair), Lia D. Kamhi-Stein, Antony J. Kunnan, Patricia A. Richard-Amato, Marguerite Ann Snow.

Requirements for Admission: The university's requirement for admission is a GPA of 2.75 in the last 90 units attempted. The program requires completion of Introduction to Linguistics with a grade of B or better and 1 year of college-level foreign language study or the equivalent. Nonnative speakers of English must have a minimum TOEFL score of 600 (or a score of 550 plus a TWE score of 5).

Tuition, Fees, and Aid: See program description for certificate in ESL/EFL.

General: The program is mainly a teacher-training program, though it also provides a research knowledge base that aids teachers in becoming effective consumers of research and prepares them for advanced training in applied linguistics.

The program is offered in Buenos Aires, Argentina, taught by California State, Los Angeles, faculty. The university participates in U.S. Agency for International Development–funded training of EFL teachers in Egypt.

Fifty students completed the program in 1996–1997.

The university has an intensive English language program for nonnative speakers of English.

Summer Session: Yes

Further Information: Coordinator, TESOL Program
Charter School of Education
King Hall C-2098
California State University, Los Angeles
Los Angeles, CA 90032-8413

Telephone: (323) 343-4330
Fax: (323) 343-5336
E-mail: blee@calstatela.edu

◆ **CALIFORNIA STATE UNIVERSITY, NORTHRIDGE,**
   Linguistics Program

Degree Offered: BA in linguistics.

Length of Programs: 8 semesters. Students may be full-time or part-time and may begin their study at the beginning of any semester. Application deadlines are fall semester, July 1; spring semester, November 1.

Program Requirements: 124 semester units. Competence in a language other than English is not required. Neither practice teaching, nor a thesis, nor a comprehensive examination is required.

Courses Offered: (*required) *one of the following: Anthropological Linguistics, Language and Linguistics, Language and Symbolic Processes; *Phonetics and Phonology; *Syntax; *Child Language Acquisition *or* Second Language Acquisition; *Semantics and Pragmatics; *Languages in Contact; *15 units in linguistics *or* a minor (18–24 units) in an approved discipline.

Full-Time Staff: Sharon Klein (coordinator), Daniele Dibie, Alan Harris, Barbara Hawkins, Barbara Kroll, Rebecca Litke, Evelyn McClave, Rei R. Noguchi, Sabrina Peck, Wendy Snyder, Christine Strike-Roussos, Elizabeth Weber.

Requirements for Admission: Students should consult the Office of Admissions.

Tuition, Fees, and Aid: For in-state students, $990 per semester; for out-of-state students, $246 per semester unit in addition.

General: The program provides students with a solid foundation of linguistic theory complemented by a range of course work in second language acquisition and methodology. In cooperation with the College of Extending Learning's ESL program, students will do a practicum in a conversation course. The program attracts a large number of international students, whose own languages and English learning experience enrich the overall program.

Fourteen students completed the program in 1996–1997.

The university has an intensive English language program for nonnative speakers of English.

Summer Session: Yes

Further Information: Dr. Sharon Klein, Coordinator
Linguistics Program
Sierra Hall 103
California State University, Northridge
18111 Nordhoff Street
Northridge, CA 91330-8251

Telephone: (818) 677-3453
Fax: (818) 677-7094
E-mail: hflin001@csun.edu; sharon.klein@csun.edu
http://www.csun.edu/ ~ hflin001/csunling.html

◆ CALIFORNIA STATE UNIVERSITY, NORTHRIDGE, Linguistics Program

Degree Offered: MA in linguistics with a concentration in TESOL or general linguistics.

Length of Program: 4 semesters. Students may be full-time or part-time and may begin their study at the beginning of any semester. Application deadlines are fall semester, July 1; spring semester, November 1.

Program Requirements: 30 units. Competence in a language other than English is required; English meets the requirement for nonnative speakers of English. A thesis or a comprehensive examination is required. Practice teaching is optional.

Courses Offered: (*required) *Seminar in Phonology; *Seminar in Transformational Generative Grammar; *Seminar in Cognitive Linguistics; *Seminar in Historical-Comparative Linguistics; *18 units in TESL track *or* general linguistics.

Full-Time Staff: See program description for BA in linguistics.

Requirements for Admission: The university's requirement for admission is an undergraduate GPA of 3.0 or a score at or above the 50th percentile on one portion of the GRE. A minimum TOEFL score of 550 is required for nonnative speakers of English. Students must complete the equivalent of the undergraduate minor in linguistics (about 18 units).

Tuition, Fees, and Aid: See program description for BA in linguistics.

General: See program description for BA in linguistics.
Twelve students completed the program in 1996–1997.

Summer Session: Yes

Further Information: Dr. Sharon Klein, Coordinator
Linguistics Program
Sierra Hall 103
California State University, Northridge
18111 Nordhoff Street
Northridge, CA 91330-8251

Telephone: (818) 677-3453
Fax: (818) 677-7094
E-mail: hflin001@csun.edu; sharon.klein@csun.edu
http://www.csun.edu/ ~ hflin001/csunling.html

◆ CALIFORNIA STATE UNIVERSITY, SACRAMENTO, Department of English

Degree Offered: MA in TESOL.

Length of Program: 3 semesters. Students may be full-time or part-time and may begin their study at the beginning of any semester. Application deadlines are fall semester, April 24; spring semester, November 21.

Program Requirements: 27 semester hours. Competence in a language other than English is required; English meets the requirement for nonnative speakers of English. Practice teaching is required. A comprehensive examination or a thesis is required.

Courses Offered: (*required) *Research and Testing in TESOL; *Sociolinguistics; *Second Language Acquisition; *ESL Reading Pedagogy; *ESL Writing Pedagogy; *Pedagogy of Grammar in ESL; *Pedagogy of Spoken English; *Practicum; *thesis or comprehensive examination; two electives.

Full-Time Staff: Linda Callis Buckley (chair), Dana Ferris, Marie Helt, Fred Marshall.

Requirements for Admission: The university's requirements for admission are a baccalaureate degree with a GPA of 3.0 and undergraduate transcripts. The program requires completion of Introduction to Linguistics, Introduction to ESL Methodology, Grammar for ESL Teachers, and Advanced Composition.

Tuition, Fees, and Aid: Teaching assistantships and graduate assistantships are available for second-year students; some university scholarships are available.

General: The program is committed to offering a strong pedagogical background to all graduate students. Currently a pedagogical class is required in each skill area. A joint program is offered with the Peace Corps, and most faculty are involved in research projects with students.
  Nineteen students completed the program in 1996–1997.

Summer Session: Yes

Further Information: Dr. Linda Callis Buckley, Coordinator
Department of English
138 Calaveras Hall
California State University, Sacramento
6000 J Street
Sacramento, CA 95819-6075

Telephone: (916) 278-5725
Fax: (916) 278-7609
E-mail: buckleyl@csus.edu

◆ CARDINAL STRITCH UNIVERSITY, Department of Education

Degree Offered: Add-on certification in ESL, 1–9 and K–12.

Length of Program: 2 semesters. Students may be full-time or part-time and may begin their study at the beginning of any semester. Application deadlines are fall semester, August 20; spring semester, January 15; summer semester, variable.

Program Requirements: 24 credits. Competence in a language other than English is required; English meets the requirement for nonnative speakers of English. Neither practice teaching, nor a comprehensive examination, nor a thesis is required.

Courses Offered: (*required) *Applied Linguistics for Second Language Acquisition; *Advanced Writing; *Intercultural Communication; *Minority Groups in American Society; *Intercultural History; *Methods of TESL.

Full-Time Staff: Joanne Anderson, Judith DuMez, Mary M. Kasum, Gabrielle Kowalski, Marcia Lunz (coordinator).

Requirements for Admission: The university's requirements for admission are a high school diploma or the equivalent, a rank in the upper 50% of the graduating class; a GPA of C or higher; an ACT score of 20 or higher or an SAT cumulative score of 840 or higher; and courses to fulfill the high school English, mathematics, social studies, and science requirements. The program requires completion of Introduction to Education, Initial General Clinical Experience, and Portfolio Presentation plus an overall GPA of 2.75.

Tuition, Fees, and Aid: $250 per credit. Fees are application and matriculation, $40; technology, $25. Federal and state grants, federal loan programs, college scholarships, and student employment are available.

General: The add-on certification in ESL enhances the student's basic preparation for teaching. This new program qualifies the student to apply for ESL positions in the United States or abroad.

Opportunities for international fieldwork are available on a volunteer basis.

Summer Session: Yes

Further Information: Chair
Department of Foreign Languages and ESL
Bonaventure Hall Room 17
Cardinal Stritch University
6801 North Yates Road
Milwaukee, WI 53217

Telephone: (414) 352-5400

◆ CARDINAL STRITCH UNIVERSITY,
Department of Education

Degree Offered: MEd in professional development with a concentration in ESL.

Length of Program: 2 semesters. Students may be full-time or part-time and may begin their study at the beginning of any semester. Application deadlines are fall semester, August 20; spring semester, January 15; summer semester, variable.

Program Requirements: 31 credits. Competence in a language other than English is not required. Practice teaching and a comprehensive examination are required. A thesis is not required.

Courses Offered: (*required) *Applied Linguistics for Second Language Acquisition; *Intercultural Communication; *Reading/Language Arts for ESL Learners; *Language, Cognition, and Literacy; *Methods of TESL; *Practicum in TESL; *Professional Development Seminar; *Research and Statistics; *Multiculturalism in Today's Schools; *Renewing the Professional Knowledge Base; *Interpretation of Research Literature; an elective from ESL courses.

Full-Time Staff: Nancy Blair, Mary M. Kasum, Gabrielle Kowalski, Marcia Lunz (coordinator), Robert Pavlik.

Requirements for Admission: The university's requirements for admission are an application form, transcripts of all previous undergraduate and graduate work, and a minimum GPA of 2.75.

Tuition, Fees, and Aid: $260 per credit. The application and matriculation fee is $40. Federal loan assistance is available.

General: This new program prepares the student for teaching ESL to adults of college age and older. A solid core of education courses is paired with a core of courses concentrating on the skills and background necessary for successful ESL teaching in the U.S. or abroad.

Opportunities for international fieldwork are available on a volunteer basis.

Summer Session: Yes

Further Information: Chair
Department of Foreign Languages and ESL
Bonaventure Hall Room 17
Cardinal Stritch University
6801 North Yates Road
Milwaukee, WI 53217

Telephone: (414) 352-5400

◆ CARROLL COLLEGE, Department of Education

Degree Offered: BA TESOL.

Length of Program: 8 semesters. Students may be full-time or part-time and may begin their study at the beginning of any semester. Application deadlines are fall semester, July 31; spring semester, December 18.

Program Requirements: 40 credits for the major. Competence in a language other than English is required for native speakers of English and optional for nonnative speakers of English. Practice teaching is required. A thesis is optional. A comprehensive examination is not required.

Courses Offered: (*required) *Intercultural Communication; *Introduction to Instructional Computing *or* A Survey of Computer Science; *Educational Psychology; *Teaching in the Secondary School; *Tests and Measurements; *Introduction to Language; *English Grammar; *TESOL Methods and Applications: Reading and Writing; *TESOL Methods and Applications: Listening and Speaking; *TESOL Practicum; *an advanced English writing course; the equivalent of 2 years of study of a modern foreign language; 6 credits in cross-cultural classes such as history or geography.

Full-Time Staff: Lynette Zuroff (chair), Ron Stottlemeyer, Ron Thronson.

Requirements for Admission: The college's requirements for admission are graduation from high school with a GPA of 2.5. The program requires faculty recommendations, a writing assessment, and an interview.

Tuition, Fees, and Aid: $5,745 per semester. Scholarships and other forms of financial aid are available.

General: TESOL students at Carroll will find excellent opportunities to apply classroom theory to practical situations during their practicum. The Carroll Intensive Language Institute provides a setting for practice teaching. The program leads to a Montana credential in TESOL.

Ten students completed the program in 1996–1997.

The college has an intensive English language program for nonnative speakers of English.

Summer Session: Yes

Further Information: Linda Lang, Director
International Programs
O'Connell Hall 113
Carroll College
161 North Benton Avenue
Helena, MT 59625

Telephone: (406) 447-4469
Fax: (406) 447-5461
E-mail: llang@carroll.edu

◆ CARSON-NEWMAN COLLEGE, Department of Graduate Studies

Degree Offered: MAT in ESL.

Length of Program: 3 semesters. Students may be full-time or part-time and may begin their study at the beginning of any semester. Application deadlines are spring semester, December 1; fall semester, August 1; summer semester, May 1; May term, April 1.

Program Requirements: 36 credits. Competence in a language other than English is optional. A practicum is required. A comprehensive examination and a thesis are optional.

Courses Offered: (*required) *History of the English Language; *Language and Culture; *English Phonology; *English Syntax; *Language Acquisition; *ESL Curriculum; ESL Materials and Methods I: Speaking and Listening; *ESL Materials and Methods II: Reading and Writing; *Evaluation in ESL; *Practicum in ESL; Topics in ESL; Advanced Writing and Research Skills; Advanced Speaking Skills (international students only).

Full-Time Staff: Mark Brock (coordinator), Li Jun, Donald Midkiff, Brenda Young-Ferrell.

Requirements for Admission: The college's requirements for admission are a baccalaureate degree with a 2.5 GPA overall, two official transcripts, three letters of recommendation, and scores on the GRE General Test, the NTE Core Battery tests in General Knowledge and Knowledge of Communication Skills, or the Praxis Series. Nonnative English-speaking students must submit satisfactory TOEFL scores (550 minimum) or complete basic and advanced English language study.

Tuition, Fees, and Aid: $180 per credit hour. Graduate and teaching assistantships are available.

General: The program offers small, seminar-style classes, a blend of theory and practice, and opportunities to apply knowledge in local ESL classrooms. Faculty and students work closely together, striving for academic and teaching excellence in a Christian environment. The college has been recognized by several national publications for the quality of the education experiences it provides to its students. The program leads to a Tennessee credential in TESOL.

Students have completed field work and practicum requirements at sister universities in China.

Thirteen students completed the program in 1996–1997.

The college has an intensive English language program for nonnative speakers of English.

Summer Session: Yes

Further Information: Dr. Mark Brock
Graduate TESL Program
Carson-Newman College
Box 7000215
Jefferson City, TN 37760

Telephone: (423) 471-4793
Fax: (423) 471-4748
E-mail: Brock@CNCACC.CN.EDU

◆ CENTRAL CONNECTICUT STATE UNIVERSITY, Department of English

Degree Offered: Undergraduate concentration in TESOL.

Length of Program: Students may be full-time or part-time and may begin their study at the beginning of any semester. Application deadlines are fall semester, May 1 (April 1 for international students); spring semester, November 1.

Program Requirements: 21 semester hours. Six semester hours in a language other than English are required; English meets the requirement for nonnative speakers of English. Practice teaching is required in the major area and encouraged in the TESOL minor. Neither a thesis nor a comprehensive examination is required.

Courses Offered: (*required) *TESOL Methods; *Second Language Acquisition; *The Study of Language; *Introduction to Linguistics *or* Analytical Skills in Language *or* electives in modern languages; Introduction to Ethnology; Intercultural Communication; Studies in Linguistics and the English Language; Culture and Civilization of Other Lands; Minorities and Social Inequality; Practicum; History of the English Language; The Study of Culture.

Full-Time Staff: Andrea G. Osburne (coordinator), Gerald Tullai, Leyla Zidani-Eroglu.

Requirements for Admission: The university's requirements for admission are graduation from an accredited secondary school or equivalency program and SAT scores. Admission is based on record, rank, and SAT scores. Transfer students must have a GPA of 2.0 or higher. Nonnative English-speaking international students must have a TOEFL score of 500 or higher.

Tuition, Fees, and Aid: For in-state students, $1,031 per semester (fees, $776); for out-of-state students, $3,337 per semester (fees, $1,209). The health care fee is $244. Financial aid includes scholarships, loans, and work-study programs.

General: Methods training emphasizes the successful diffusion of educational innovation. Opportunities for overseas practice teaching are available through several university exchange programs.

Three students completed the program in 1996–1997.

The university has an intensive English language program for nonnative speakers of English.

Summer Session: Yes

Further Information: Dr. Andrea G. Osburne
Department of English
318-1 Willard Hall
Central Connecticut State University
1615 Stanley Street
New Britain, CT 06050

Telephone: (860) 832-2748
Fax: (860) 832-2784
E-mail: osburnea@ccsua.ctstateu.edu

◆ CENTRAL CONNECTICUT STATE UNIVERSITY, Department of English

Degree Offered: Certification in TESOL (graduate level).

Length of Program: Variable. Students may be full-time or part-time and may begin their study at the beginning of any semester. Application deadlines are fall semester, August 1; spring semester, December 1.

Program Requirements: Variable. Students who did not satisfy the state requirement of 39 semester hours of general education in English, natural sciences, mathematics, social studies, foreign language, and fine arts as undergraduates must do so. Competence in a language other than English is optional. Practice teaching is required. Neither a thesis nor a comprehensive examination is required.

Courses Offered: (*required) *Analytical Skills in Language; *Second Language Acquisition; *Second Language Testing; *Philosophy of Education or Foundations of Education; *Learning Theories in Secondary Education; *Principles and Evaluation in Education (K–12); *TESOL Methods; *Second Language Composition; *Student Teaching, TESOL K–12; *Instructional Computing; *Introduction to Education Learners With Exceptionalities; *Child and Adolescent Development or Lifespan Development; three electives in English language, linguistics, and literature; three electives in foreign language or bilingualism; at least two electives in culture and intergroup relations.

Full-Time Staff: See program description for undergraduate concentration in TESOL.

Requirements for Admission: The university's requirement for admission is a baccalaureate degree from an accredited institution with a minimum GPA of 2.7 (3.0 in any postbaccalaureate course work). A GRE score may be required in individual cases. A TOEFL score of 550 is required of nonnative speakers of English.

Tuition, Fees, and Aid: For in-state students, $1,252 per semester (fees, $746); for out-of-state students, $3,490 per semester (fees, $1,164). Financial aid includes loans and scholarships for U.S. students. Some assistantships are available in the English, modern languages, and education departments. International students may not hold assistantships during their first semester of study.

General: Most required courses are offered in the evening. Methods training emphasizes successful diffusion of educational innovation. The program, which began in 1997, leads to a Connecticut credential in teaching Grades pre-K–12.

Opportunities for overseas practice teaching are available through several university exchange programs.

Summer Session: Yes

Further Information: Dr. Andrea G. Osburne
Department of English
318-1 Willard Hall
Central Connecticut State University
1615 Stanley Street
New Britain, CT 06050

Telephone: (860) 832-2748
Fax: (860) 832-2784
E-mail: osburnea@ccsua.ctstateu.edu

◆ CENTRAL CONNECTICUT STATE UNIVERSITY, Department of English

Degree Offered: MS with a concentration in TESOL.

Length of Program: 3–4 semesters. Students may be full-time or part-time and may begin their study at the beginning of any semester. Application deadlines are fall semester, August 1; spring semester, December 1.

Program Requirements: 36 semester hours. Competence in a language other than English is optional. Practice teaching is strongly encouraged. Either a thesis or a comprehensive examination is required.

Courses Offered: (*required) *Analytical Skills in Language; *Contemporary Educational Problems; *education elective; *Modern Phonology; *Modern Syntax; *Research in TESOL; *Second Language Acquisition; *Introduction to Sociolinguistics; *TESOL Methods; *one of the following: Practicum, Second Language Composition, Second Language Testing, History of the English Language; Bilingual-Bicultural Education; Multicultural Education; Comparative Education; other electives in modern languages, history, education, and anthropology.

Full-Time Staff: See program description for certification in TESOL.

Requirements for Admission: The university's requirement for admission is a baccalaureate degree from an accredited institution with a minimum GPA of 2.7 (3.0 in any postbaccalaureate course work). A GRE score may be required in individual cases. A TOEFL score of 550 is required of nonnative speakers of English. Native speakers of English must have had 3 semester hours of a language other than English. The requirement may be waived for admission but must be completed by graduation.

Tuition, Fees, and Aid: See program description for certification in TESOL.

General: See program description for certification in TESOL.
Twelve students completed the program in 1996–1997.

Summer Session: Yes

Further Information: Dr. Andrea G. Osburne
Department of English
318-1 Willard Hall
Central Connecticut State University
1615 Stanley Street
New Britain, CT 06050

Telephone: (860) 832-2748
Fax: (860) 832-2784
E-mail: osburnea@ccsua.ctstateu.edu

◆ CENTRAL MICHIGAN UNIVERSITY, Department of English Language and Literature

Degree Offered: MA in TESOL.

Length of Program: 2 semesters. Students may be full-time or part-time and may begin their study at the beginning of any semester. U.S. students should apply at least 6 weeks before delayed registration for the semester begins; international students should begin the admissions process 6–12 months before they plan to begin their studies.

Program Requirements: 30 semester hours. Competence in a language other than English is required. Practice teaching and a comprehensive examination are required. A thesis is not required.

Courses Offered: (*required) *TESOL; *TESOL Materials, Assessment, Curriculum; *English Phonology for Language Teachers; *English Grammar for Language Teachers; *Introduction to Second Language Acquisition; *Applied Linguistics in Written Communication; *Seminar in English Linguistics; *Practicum in TESOL; Reading and the English Classroom; Linguistics and Reading; Applied Sociolinguistics; Fundamental Issues in Language; Problems in Teaching English; Foundations of Bilingual Bicultural Education; Methods and Materials for Bilingual Bicultural Education; Statistics in Education.

Full-Time Staff: Peter H. Fries, Leslie T. Grant, William C. Spruiell.

Requirements for Admission: The university's requirement for admission is a baccalaureate degree from a college or university of recognized standing with an overall undergraduate GPA of 2.5 or of 2.7 in the last 60 hours of graded course work toward the degree. The department requires an undergraduate major or minor in English, linguistics, language arts, reading, or a foreign language with a GPA of at least 2.7 in the major and 2 years of college foreign language study (or its equivalent). Nonnative speakers of English must have a TOEFL score of at least 550 and a TWE score of at least 5, or a MELAB score of 85. Students with TOEFL scores below 550 may need to enroll in English Language Institute courses.

Tuition, Fees, and Aid: For in-state students, $35.40 per credit hour; for out-of-state students, $268.80 per hour. Fees are $480 per year. A limited number of teaching assistantships and fellowships for U.S. and non-U.S. students, federal financial support for U.S. students, and teaching positions in the composition program and the English Language Institute are available.

General: Course work involves theory, application, and practice. The practicum is waived for experienced teachers. The program cooperates closely with the university's English Language Institute.

Three students completed the program in 1996–1997.

The university has an intensive English language program for nonnative speakers of English.

Summer Session: Yes

Further Information: Dr. Clara Lee Moodie
Chair, Graduate Studies in English
Department of English Language and Literature
Anspach Hall 215
Central Michigan University
Mount Pleasant, MI 48859

Telephone: (517) 774-3574
Fax: (517) 774-1271
E-mail: Clara-Lee.Moodie@cmich.edu

◆ CENTRAL MISSOURI STATE UNIVERSITY, Department of English and Philosophy

Degrees Offered: Certificate in TESL; MA in TESL.

Length of Program: 3 semesters for the MA. Students may be full-time or part-time and may begin their study at the beginning of any semester. Suggested application deadlines for U.S. students are fall semester, July 5; spring semester, November 15;

summer session, May 5. Suggested application deadlines for international students are fall semester, May 15; spring semester, October 10; summer session, March 15.

Program Requirements: Certificate, 21 semester hours; MA, 32 semester hours. Two semesters of a language other than English (or the equivalent) are required for native speakers of English; English meets the requirement for nonnative speakers. Practice teaching is required. A thesis is optional. A comprehensive exam is not required.

Courses Offered: (*required for MA) *Introduction to Graduate Study in TESL; *Linguistics; *Introduction to Second Language Teaching; *Language and Culture; *Teaching ESL: The Oral Language; *Teaching ESL: The Written Language; *Advanced Grammar for TESL; *Advanced Applied Linguistics; *Practicum in TESL; *6 semester hours from such courses as Computers and Language Learning, Comparative Cultures, Second Language Testing/Assessment, Comparative Education, Cognitive Psychology, Language Development, and Statistics in the Behavioral Sciences.

Full-Time Staff: Cheryl Eason (coordinator), Ronald W. Long, Robert A. Yates.

Requirements for Admission: The university's requirement for admission is a baccalaureate degree from an accredited institution. The program requires an undergraduate GPA of 2.5 for students who earned undergraduate degrees in the United States and a minimum TOEFL score of 565 for nonnative speakers of English.

Tuition, Fees, and Aid: For in-state students, $132 per semester hour; for out-of-state students, $264 per semester hour; for residents of the Midwest Student Exchange States (Kansas, Minnesota, Michigan, and Nebraska), $198 per semester hour. A limited number of teaching assistantships in freshman composition, ESL, and the Educational Development Center are available. Graduate assistantships, tuition scholarships, and work study are also available.

General: Students receive an introduction to linguistics and a strong foundation in applied linguistics as well as training in ESL/EFL pedagogy. Practicum opportunities are available in the public schools, intensive language programs associated with junior colleges and universities, support courses for new international students, and adult ESL programs for immigrants and refugees. The program leads to a Missouri credential in TESOL.

Night courses are offered on campus for in-service teachers, and distance learning opportunities are being explored. Summer course are rotated so that teachers and other part-time students can complete the MA program in about 3 years by attending classes at night and in the summer.

Twenty-two students completed the program in 1996–1997.

The university has an intensive English language program for nonnative speakers of English.

Summer Session: Yes

Further Information: Graduate Coordinator, MA-TESL Program
Department of English and Philosophy
Martin 336
Central Missouri State University
Warrensburg, MO 64093-5046

Telephone: (660) 543-8507, 4425
Fax: (660) 543-8544
E-mail: eason@cmsuvmb.cmsu.edu

◆ CENTRAL WASHINGTON UNIVERSITY, Teacher Education Programs Department

Degree Offered: BEd TESL.

Length of Program: 4–5 quarters. Students may be full-time or part-time and may begin their study at the beginning of any quarter. The application deadline is the beginning of each academic quarter, provided students have been accepted to the teacher education program.

Program Requirements: 24–27 quarter hours. Competence in a language other than English is required if students are also in the bilingual program; TESOL-only minors must have completed 2 years of a foreign language. Practice teaching is required. Neither a thesis nor a comprehensive examination is required.

Courses Offered: (*required) *Methods in Teaching ESL; *Testing ESL; *Reading ESL; *Education Linguistics; *Culture and Curriculum; *Language in Culture; *Practicum; *Language Acquisition.

Full-Time Staff: Minerva Caples, Dale Otto, Carol Butterfield, Linda Klug.

Requirements for Admission: The teacher education program requires a GPA of 3.0, California Achievement Test scores, three letters of recommendation, and the completion of legal requirements pertaining to background.

Tuition, Fees, and Aid: For in-state students, $168.40 per credit hour; for out-of-state students, $597.40 per credit hour. No financial aid is available for students pursing endorsement in ESL, but university financial aid is available.

General: The program addresses the preparation needs of teachers of Grades K–12. It leads to a state endorsement in ESL.

Thirty students completed the program in 1996–1997.

The university has an intensive English language program for nonnative speakers of English.

Summer Session: No

Further Information: Minerva L. Caples, Director
Teacher Education Programs Department
Black Hall
Central Washington University
Eighth Street and Chestnut
Ellensburg, WA 98926

Telephone: (509) 963-1951
Fax: (509) 963-1162
E-mail: caplesm@cwu.edu

◆ CENTRAL WASHINGTON UNIVERSITY, Department of English

Degree Offered: MA in English: TESL/TEFL.

Length of Program: 5 quarters. Students may be full-time or part-time and may begin their study at the beginning of any quarter. Application deadlines are fall quarter, April 1; winter quarter, October 1; spring quarter, January 1; summer quarter, April 1. Teaching assistant applications are due February 15.

Program Requirements: 55 quarter credits. Competence in a language other than English is required; English meets the requirement for nonnative speakers of English. Practice teaching and either a portfolio or a thesis are required. A comprehensive examination is not required.

Courses Offered: (*required) *Methods and Materials in TESL/TEFL; *Second Language Acquisition; *Phonetics and Phonology; *Advanced Grammar; *Language in Society; *TESL/TEFL Seminar; four electives in language, literature, culture, or pedagogy.

Full-Time Staff: Patricia Callaghan (chair), Loretta Grey, Linda Klug, Xingzhong Li, Carl Rosser.

Requirements for Admission: The university's requirements for admission are a GPA of 3.0 in the last 90 hours of graded work and a GRE score. A background in language study is desirable.

Tuition, Fees, and Aid: For in-state students, $1,400 per quarter for 10–18 credits; for out-of-state students, $4,260 per quarter for 10–18 credits. Teaching assistant-ships are available.

General: Theory and practice are integrated in most of the classes. Pedagogical courses focus on adult ESL/EFL education. With an additional sequence of education courses, students may earn a Washington State credential in ESL. Graduate students have the opportunity to do their practicum in intensive English program.

International fieldwork in practice teaching may be arranged.

Seven students completed the program in 1996–1997.

The university has an intensive English language program for nonnative speakers of English.

Summer Session: Yes

Further Information: Graduate Student Coordinator
Department of English
Central Washington University
400 East 8th Avenue
Ellensburg, WA 98926-7558

Telephone: (509) 963-1546
Fax: (509) 963-1561
E-mail: olsons@cwu.edu

◆ CINCINNATI, UNIVERSITY OF, Division of Teacher Education

Degrees Offered: EdD and MEd in literacy education with a concentration in TESL; K–12 validation in TESL; certificate in TESL.

Length of Program: 7 quarters. Students may be full-time or part-time and may begin their study at the beginning of any quarter. Application deadlines are summer/autumn quarter, January 2; winter/spring quarter, June 1.

Program Requirements: EdD, 135 credits; MEd, 54 credits; validation, 30 credits; certificate, 22 credits. Competence in a language other than English is required. Practice teaching is required. A thesis, a project, or a comprehensive examination is required for the MEd.

Courses Offered: (*required) *Phonetics for TESL; *Analysis of Language; *Theories of Second Language Acquisition; *Methods of TESL I and II; *TESL Practicum; *Sociolinguistics; *Assessment and Evaluation in TESL; *courses in social/cultural issues, human learning, research, technology, and computer literacy; electives in literacy, language, and literature.

Full-Time Staff: Ruth Benander, Mary Benedetti, Susan Jenkins (chair), Holli Schauber.

Requirements for Admission: The university's requirement for admission is a bachelor's degree from an accredited institution. The program requires a GPA of 3.0 in relevant course work, a GRE score, and 1 year of foreign language at the college level (may be taken as pre- or corequisite). Nonnative speakers of English must have a TOEFL score of 620 or higher, a TWE score of 5, and a TSE score of 50.

Tuition, Fees, and Aid: For in-state students, $1,856 per quarter; for out-of-state students, $3,502 per quarter. The general fee is $160 per quarter. University graduate scholarships and assistantships are available.

General: Graduate assistants have the opportunity to participate in teaching, research, and administrative aspects of the ESL program. A variety of practicum sites are available. The K–12 validation in TESL program leads to an Ohio credential in TESOL.

Ten students completed the program in 1996–1997.

Summer Session: Yes

Further Information: Program Chair
Department of Teacher Education
Room 505, Teacher College
University of Cincinnati
PO Box 210002
Cincinnati, OH 45221-0002

Telephone: (513) 556-3590
Fax: (513) 556-2483
E-mail: SusanJenkins@uc.edu

◆ CLARK UNIVERSITY, American Language and Culture Institute

Degree Offered: Certificate in teaching ESL to adults.

Length of Program: This is a continuing education program. Students must be part-time and may begin their study at the beginning of any semester. There are no application deadlines.

Program Requirements: 7 units. Competence in a language other than English (beginning college-level course) is optional. Practice teaching is required for students without prior on-site teaching experience. Neither a thesis nor a comprehensive examination is required.

Courses Offered: (*required) *Methods and Materials for Teaching Diverse Second Language Students; *Introduction to Linguistics; *First and Second Language Acquisition; *Modern English Grammar; Instructional Technology and Second Language Education; Practicum; Capstone Project.

Full-Time Staff: James T. Raby (director), David P. Williams.

Requirements for Admission: The requirement for admission is a bachelor's or master's degree.

Tuition, Fees, and Aid: $900 per course. College of Professional and Continuing Education scholarships and tutorial positions are available.

General: The university has an intensive English language program for nonnative speakers of English.

Summer Session: Yes

Further Information: Director
ALCI
Clark University
950 Main Street
Worcester, MA 01610

Telephone: (508) 793-7794
Fax: (508) 793-8887
E-mail: alci@clarku.edu

◆ CLARK UNIVERSITY, American Language and Culture Institute

Degree Offered: Graduate certificate in teaching ESL in Grades 5–12.

Length of Program: This is a continuing education program. Students must be part-time and may begin their study at the beginning of any semester. There are no application deadlines.

Program Requirements: 12 units. Competence in a language other than English (intermediate college-level course) is optional. Practice teaching is required. Neither a thesis nor a comprehensive examination is required.

Courses Offered: (*required) *Foundations of TESL; *Methods and Materials for Teaching Diverse Second Language Students; *Introduction to Linguistics; *First and Second Language Acquisition; *Curriculum Content and Its Adaptation for Second Language Learners; *Procedures for Evaluation and Assessment in the Bilingual/ESL Classroom; *Experience of Adolescence; *Focusing on a Discipline: High School; *Practicum.

Full-Time Staff: James T. Raby (director), David P. Williams.

Requirements for Admission: The requirement for admission is a bachelor's degree in the arts and sciences. Nonnative speakers of English must have a TOEFL score of 600 or higher.

Tuition, Fees, and Aid: See program description for certificate in teaching ESL to adults.

General: See program description for certificate in teaching ESL to adults. The program leads to a Massachusetts credential in TESOL.

Summer Session: Yes

Further Information: Director
ALCI
Clark University
950 Main Street
Worcester, MA 01610

Telephone: (508) 793-7794
Fax: (508) 793-8887
E-mail: alci@clarku.edu

◆ COLORADO, UNIVERSITY OF, AT BOULDER, Department of Linguistics

Degree Offered: MA in linguistics.

Length of Program: 4 semesters. Students may be full-time or part-time and are advised to begin their study at the beginning of the fall semester. Application deadlines are fall semester, January 15; spring semester, October 1.

Program Requirements: 30 semester hours (24 if a thesis is written). Competence in a language other than English is required; English meets the requirement for nonnative speakers of English. A comprehensive examination is required. Practice teaching is not required. A thesis is optional.

Courses Offered: (*required) *Phonetics; *Morphology/Syntax; *Phonology; *Grammatical Analysis; *Semantics/Pragmatics; *Diachronic Linguistics; Structure of English for TESOL; Techniques in Teaching TESOL; 9 hours of electives in second language teaching, second language acquisition, anthropology, and intercultural education.

Full-Time Staff: Alan Bell, Barbara Fox, Zygmunt Frajzyngier, Lise Menn (chair), David Rood.

Requirements for Admission: The university's requirements for program admission are a recognized baccalaureate degree with a GPA of 2.75, a GRE score, and considerable knowledge of a foreign language.

Tuition, Fees, and Aid: For in-state students, $930 per semester; for out-of-state students, $3,768 per semester. Required fees are about $200. Almost no financial aid is available. Experienced teachers may qualify for teaching assistantships.

General: The program is primarily an MA in linguistics with some TESL course options. The program cooperates with University of Colorado at Denver in course offerings.

Six students completed the program in 1996–1997.

The university has an intensive English language program for nonnative speakers of English.

Summer Session: No

Further Information: Chair
Linguistics Department
Campus Box 295/Woodbury 308
University of Colorado
Boulder, CO 80309-0295

Telephone: (303) 492-8041

◆ COLORADO, UNIVERSITY OF, AT DENVER, Department of English

Degree Offered: MA in English, applied linguistics (ESL).

Length of Program: Students may be full-time or part-time and may begin their study at the beginning of any semester. Application deadlines are spring semester, October 25; summer semester, March 2; fall semester, May 25.

Program Requirements: 30 credits. Competence in a language other than English is required; English meets the requirement for nonnative speakers of English. Practice teaching is required. A project, a comprehensive examination, or a thesis is required.

Courses Offered: (*required) *Language Theory; *Principles and Practices of Adult Second Language Acquisition; *Teaching Second Language and Second Dialect Writers; *Teaching Second Language and Second Dialect Speakers; *Critical Inquiry and Classroom Research; *Rhetoric and the Teaching of Writing; *one of the following: History of the English Language, Rhetorical Theory: Teaching Writing, Special Topics in Rhetoric; one elective.

Full-Time Staff: Joanna Addison, Richard Van De Weghe, Ian H. G. Ying, Rex Burns.

Requirements for Admission: The requirements for admission are a minimum undergraduate GPA of 3.0, GRE General Test verbal and analytical scores of 600, four letters of recommendation, and successful completion of the department's writing exam. For nonnative speakers of English, a TOEFL score of 580 or higher and a TWE score of 4 or higher are required.

Tuition, Fees, and Aid: For in-state students, $1,284 per semester; for out-of-state students, $4,182 per semester. Teaching assistantships are available.

General: This new program provides students with a comprehensive background in the theoretical and practical issues of teaching ESL to adult learners both overseas and in the United States.

Fieldwork or practice teaching is possible at the program's Beijing and Moscow campuses.

The university has an intensive English language program for nonnative speakers of English.

Summer Session: Yes

Further Information: Joanne Addison or Ian H. G. Ying
Department of English
Campus Box 175, PO Box 173364
University of Colorado at Denver
1051 Ninth Street Park
Denver, CO 80217-3364

Telephone: (303) 556-8304
Fax: (303) 556-2959
E-mail: jaddison@carbon.cudenver.edu;
hying@carbon.cudenver.edu

◆ COLORADO STATE UNIVERSITY, Department of English

Degree Offered: MA in TESL.

Length of Program: 4 semesters. Students may be full-time or part-time and may begin their study at the beginning of any semester. Application deadlines are 6 months before the semester of enrollment (exceptions allowed).

Program Requirements: 35 semester hours. Competence in a language other than English is required for native speakers of English. Practice teaching, a thesis, and a comprehensive examination are required.

Courses Offered: (*required) *Teaching English as a Foreign/Second Language; *Theories of Foreign/Second Language Learning; *Descriptive Linguistics; *Phonetics and Phonology; *Syntactic Analysis; *Semantics, Pragmatics, and Discourse Analysis; *Workshop in TESOL; *Research in TESOL; *Supervised Teaching; electives in applied linguistics and education.

Full-Time Staff: Gerald P. Delahunty, Douglas E. Flahive, James J. Garvey, Karl J. Krahnke.

Requirements for Admission: The university's requirements for admission are a baccalaureate degree with a minimum GPA of 3.0 and a GRE score. The program requires three letters of reference.

Tuition, Fees, and Aid: For in-state students, $1,300 per semester; for out-of-state students, $4,945 per semester. Fees are $338 per semester. Teaching assistantships are available.

General: The program balances work in linguistics and language study, research and applied linguistics, and pedagogical applications. It is currently under revision and will likely offer more electives.

Ten students completed the program in 1996–1997.

The university has an intensive English language program for nonnative speakers of English.

Summer Session: No

Further Information: Karl Krahnke, Coordinator
Graduate Program in TESL
Department of English
Colorado State University
Fort Collins, CO 80523

Telephone: (970) 491-6428
Fax: (970) 491-5601
E-mail: krahnke@lamar.colostate.edu

◆ COLUMBIA INTERNATIONAL UNIVERSITY, TEFL Program

Degree Offered: MA in TEFL/intercultural studies.

Length of Program: 1 or 2 years. Students may be full-time or part-time and must begin their study at the beginning of the fall semester. The application deadline is July 15.

Program Requirements: 68 semester hours for Program I; 37 semester hours for Program II. Competence in a language other than English is not required. Practice teaching and a comprehensive examination are required. A thesis is optional.

Courses Offered: (*required) *Introduction to World Religions *or* Folk Religions; *Cultural Anthropology *or* Cross-Cultural Communication; *Introduction to TEFL; *Linguistics 1; *Techniques of TEFL: Listening, Speaking, and Reading; *Linguistic Ministry; *Biblical Theology of Missions; *Linguistics 2; *Techniques of TEFL: Structure and Writing; *Language Program Design, Administration, and Supervision; electives.

Full-Time Staff: Nancy S. Cheek (director), Kay Herbert, Lindsay Hislop, Maura Mask.

Requirements for Admission: The university's requirements for admission are an approved Christian character, evidence of conversion and development in Christian character, evidence of the ability to pursue an academic program successfully (including a minimum GPA of 2.7 in undergraduate study or a score above the 50th percentile on the GRE), evidence of effective use of English, and a baccalaureate degree from an accredited institution. Nonnative speakers of English must have a TOEFL score of 600 or higher.

Tuition, Fees, and Aid: $285 per semester hour. Limited financial aid is available.

General: Students have the opportunity to do a summer internship overseas.

Twenty-three students completed the program in 1996–1997.

Summer Session: No

Further Information: Brian O'Donnell, Admissions Director
Admissions Department
Columbia International University
PO Box 3122
Columbia, SC 29230-3122

Telephone: (800) 777-2227
Fax: (803) 786-4209

◆ COLUMBIA UNIVERSITY IN THE CITY OF NEW YORK, American Language Program

Degree Offered: Certificate of professional achievement in TESOL.

Length of Program: 1 semester. Students may be full-time or part-time and may begin their study at the beginning of any semester. Application deadlines are fall semester, August 27; spring semester, January 8; summer semester, June 25.

Program Requirements: 18 credits. Competence in a language other than English is not required. Practice teaching is required. Neither a thesis nor a comprehensive examination is required.

Courses Offered: (*required) *Methods in Language Teaching; *Applied Phonetics and Phonology; *Curriculum Design and Materials Development; *Teaching English Grammar; *Classroom Applications of Second Language Acquisition Research; *Practicum in TESL.

Full-Time Staff: Patrick Aquilina, Frances Boyd, Karen Brockmann, Robert Cohen (chair), Mary Jerome, Linda Lane, Carol Numrich.

Requirements for Admission: The university's requirements for admission are a bachelor's degree or the equivalent. Nonnative speakers of English must have a TOEFL score of 600; students scoring 550 may be admitted to enroll in a combination of certificate courses and advanced ESL courses.

Tuition, Fees, and Aid: $368 per credit. No financial aid is available.

General: This program begins in spring 1999. The faculty are senior lecturers and lecturers in the internationally recognized American Language Program at Columbia University and well-known professionals in the field of ESL. Students have the opportunity to practice their teaching skills under the guidance of highly experienced ESL faculty members and can earn the certificate in one 8-week summer term.

The university has an intensive English program for nonnative speakers of English.

Summer Session: Yes

Further Information: Coordinator of Student Services
Department of Continuing Education and Special
Programs
Lewisohn Hall, Room 203
Columbia University
2970 Broadway, Mail Code 4119
New York, NY 10027-6902

Telephone: (212) 854-2820
Fax: (212 854-7400
E-mail: sp-info@columbia.edu

◆ DELAWARE, UNIVERSITY OF, School of Education

Degree Offered: MA in ESL.

Length of Program: 3–4 semesters. Students may be full-time or part-time and may begin their study at the beginning of any semester. Application deadlines are fall semester, May 30; spring semester, November 30.

Program Requirements: 33 credits. Competence in a language other than English (intermediate level) is required for native speakers of English. Practice teaching is required for state certification. Neither a thesis nor a comprehensive examination is required.

Courses Offered: (*required) *Second Language Acquisition; *TESL; *Second Language Testing; *The Structure of English; *Language Syllabus Design; *Educational Research Procedures; *Psychology of Teaching *or* Models of Instruction; *Advanced Educational Psychology *or* Cognition and Instruction; *Ethnic Studies and Multicultural Education, Philosophy of Education, Social Philosophy of Education, *or* Politics of Educational Policy.

Full-Time Staff: Gabriella Hermon (coordinator), Louis Arena, Anna Bergstrom, Cynthia Brown, Ludwig Mosberg, James Raths, Nancy Schweda-Nicholson, William Stanley.

Requirements for Admission: The university's requirements for admission are an undergraduate cumulative index of 3.0, a GRE score, and three letters of recommendation. Nonnative speakers of English must present a TOEFL score.

Tuition, Fees, and Aid: For in-state students, $2,060 per semester; for out-of-state students, $5,085 per semester. A limited number of teaching assistantships are available.

General: The program is a joint program in linguistics and education. There is an emphasis on multicultural education; student teaching placements are provided in both ESL and bilingual classrooms in Delaware. The program is approved by the state.

The program has an option of placing students in Panama for student teaching.

Eight students completed the program in 1996–1997.

The university has an intensive English program for nonnative speakers of English.

Summer Session: Yes

Further Information: ESL Coordinator
Department of Educational Studies
201 Willard Hall
Main Street
University of Delaware
Newark, DE 19716

Telephone: (302) 831-2324
Fax: (302) 831-4445

◆ DELAWARE, UNIVERSITY OF, Department of Linguistics

Degree Offered: MA in linguistics.

Length of Program: 4 semesters. Students may be full-time or part-time and may begin their study at the beginning of any semester. Application deadlines are fall semester, July 1; spring semester, December 1.

Program Requirements: 30 credits plus a qualifying examination, or 36 credits. Competence in a language other than English is not required. A comprehensive examination is optional. Nether practice teaching nor a thesis is required.

Courses Offered: Historical Linguistics; Phonology I and II; Syntax I and II; Introduction to Morphology; Language Planning; Methods of Teaching Foreign Languages; Language Syllabus Design; Second Language Testing; Theory and Techniques of Interpretation; Introduction to Acoustic Phonetics; Language Acquisition; Second Language Acquisition and Bilingualism; The Structure of English; Introduction to Sociolinguistics; Semantics I, II, and III; Sociolinguistics of English in the Inner City; TESL; Issues in Teaching Limited English Proficient Students; Old English; Middle English; Linguistic Principles of Translation; Lexicography and Lexicology; Advanced Studies in ESL Methodology; Seminar in Second Language Testing; Topics in Syntax; Seminar in Language Development; Linguistics and Writing; Linguistic Field Methods; Topics in the Structure of Chinese; Topics in the Structure of French; Topics in the Structure of German; Topics in the Structure of Italian; Topics in the Structure of Japanese; Topics in Phonology; Acquisition of Phonology; Projects in Acoustic Phonetics; Second Language Acquisition; Soviet Psycholinguistics I and II; Studies in Linguistics.

Full-Time Staff: Mark E. Amsler, Louis Arena, Sandra Carberry, John Case, Peter Cole, William Frawley, Roberta Golinkoff, James Hiebert, James Hoffman, Helene Intraub, Seymour Levine, Frederick Masterson, Frank Murray, Evelyn Satinoff, Nancy Schweda Nicholson, Thomas Scott, Richard Venezky, Alfred Wedel.

Requirements for Admission: The program's requirements for admission are combined verbal and quantitative GRE scores of 1050 or higher and a writing sample. Foreign applicants must have a TOEFL score of 550 or higher.

Tuition, Fees, and Aid: For in-state students, $1,832 per semester; for out-of-state students, $5,224 per semester. Fees are $185 per semester. No financial aid is available.

General: Four students completed the program in 1996–1997.

The university has an intensive English language program for nonnative speakers of English.

Summer Session: No

Further Information: Director of Graduate Studies
Department of Linguistics
University of Delaware
46 East Delaware Avenue
Newark, DE 19716-2551

Telephone: (302) 831-6806
Fax: (302) 831-6896
E-mail: creswell@udel.edu

◆ DELAWARE, UNIVERSITY OF, Department of Linguistics

Degree Offered: PhD in linguistics.

Length of Program: 8 semesters. Students must register for 1 year of full-time study and may begin their study at the beginning of any semester. Application deadlines are fall semester, July 1; spring semester, December 1.

Program Requirements: 69 credits. Competence in a language other than English is required; English meets the requirement for nonnative speakers of English. A thesis and comprehensive examinations are required. Practice teaching is not required.

Courses Offered: (*required) *Phonology I and II; *Syntax I and II; *Psycholinguistics *or* Sociolinguistics; *at least three 800-level seminars. For other courses, see program description for MA in linguistics.

Full-Time Staff: See program description for MA in linguistics.

Requirements for Admission: See program description for MA in linguistics.

Tuition, Fees, and Aid: See program description for MA in linguistics. Teaching, assistantships, fellowships, and research assistantships are available.

General: Three students completed the program in 1996–1997.
The university has an intensive English language program for nonnative speakers of English.

Summer Session: No

Further Information: Director of Graduate Studies
Department of Linguistics
University of Delaware
46 East Delaware Avenue
Newark, DE 19716-2551

Telephone: (302) 831-6806
Fax: (302) 831-6896
E-mail: creswell@udel.edu

◆ EAST CAROLINA UNIVERSITY, Department of English

Degree Offered: MAEd in English with a concentration in TESL.

Length of Program: 3 semesters. Students may be full-time or part-time and may begin their study at the beginning of any semester. Application deadlines are fall semester, June 1; spring semester, October 15; first summer session, March 15; second summer session, May 1.

Program Requirements: 33 semester hours. Recent experience with a language other than English is required for native speakers of English. Practice teaching and a comprehensive examination are required. A thesis is optional.

Courses Offered: (*required) *The Structure of English: Phonology and Morphology; *The Structure of English: Syntax and Semantics; *TESL: Theories and Principles; *Applied Linguistics for Language Teachers; *Linguistics, Education, and ESL; *Descriptive Linguistics; *Introduction to Research; Internship in TESL; electives.

Full-Time Staff: Debra O'Neal, Terese Thonus, James Wright, Bruce Southard (acting chair).

Requirements for Admission: The university's requirements for admission are a bachelor's degree from an accredited institution with a GPA of 2.5 or higher overall or of 3.0 in the major, and a satisfactory GRE score.

Tuition, Fees, and Aid: For in-state students, $450 per semester; for out-of-state students, $4,014 per semester. Fees are $466 per semester. Teaching assistantships, out-of-state tuition waivers, and supplemental graduate scholarships are available.

General: After completion of the program, teachers holding a North Carolina teaching license may add on ESL certification. Elective courses are available from a number of disciplines (e.g., English, communication sciences and disorders, reading anthropology, and educational leadership) chosen to reflect students' interests and career plans.

The program has an exchange internship program with the University of Belize. Three students completed the program in 1996–1997.

Summer Session: No

Further Information: TESL Coordinator
English Department
GCB 2201
East Carolina University
Greenville, NC 27858

Telephone: (919) 328-6041
Fax: (919) 328-4889
E-mail: southardo@mail.ecu.edu

◆ **EASTERN COLLEGE, Department of Education**

Degree Offered: Master's in multicultural education.

Length of Program: 2 years. Students may be full-time or part-time and may begin their study at the beginning of any semester.

Program Requirements: 30 credits.

Courses Offered: (*required) *A Christian Perspective on Social and Philosophical Foundations of Education *or* Sociology of Education; *Issues in Special Education; *Seminar in Developmental Psychology; *Learning and Cognition; *TESL; *Multicultural Education; *Urban Education; *Statistics; Developmental Reading; Research Design.

Full-Time Staff: Bernice Baxter, Helen Craymer, David Greenhalgh, Marie Koals, Helen W. Loeb (chair).

Requirements for Admission: The requirements for admission are NTE scores if the student's GPA is below 2.5, a personal statement, official transcripts from all colleges and universities attended, and two letters of recommendation.

Tuition, Fees, and Aid: $352 per credit. Fees are $150 for full-time students. Grants and assistantships are available to full-time students.

General: The college offers unique graduate programs that have a strong spiritual emphasis.

Summer Session: Yes

Further Information: Megan Miscioscia
Graduate Admissions
Andrews Hall, 2nd Floor
Eastern College
1400 Eagle Road
St. Davids, PA 19087-3696

Telephone: (610) 341-5972
Fax: (610) 341-1466
E-mail: gradad@eastern.edu

◆ EASTERN KENTUCKY UNIVERSITY, Department of English

Degree Offered: BA in English/teaching with TESL endorsement.

Length of Program: 8 semesters. Students may be full-time or part-time and may begin their study at the beginning of any semester. Rolling admissions are in effect.

Program Requirements: 128 semester hours. Competence in a language other than English is required. Practice teaching is required. A thesis and a comprehensive examination are optional.

Courses Offered: (*required for the endorsement) *Introduction to Linguistics; *ESL; *History of the English Language; *Methods and Materials of TESL.

Full-Time Staff: Joy Allameh, Helen Bennett, Ordelle Hill, Alan Hunt, James Kenkel, Marshall Myers.

Requirements for Admission: The university has open admissions. The program requires a 2.5 GPA on the last 60 semester hours, a writing proficiency exam, and computer literacy.

Tuition, Fees, and Aid: For in-state students, $1,970 per year; for out-of-state students, $5,450 per year. Academic scholarships are available.

General: The program has an exchange arrangement with Yamanashi University in Japan.

Eight students completed the program in 1996–1997.

The university has an intensive English language program for nonnative speakers of English.

Summer Session: No

Further Information: Dominick J. Hart
Department of English
Case Annex 467
Eastern Kentucky University
Richmond, KY 40475

Telephone: (606) 622-5861
Fax: (606) 622-1604
E-mail: enghart@acs.eku.edu

◆ EASTERN KENTUCKY UNIVERSITY, Department of English

Degree Offered: MA in English with an emphasis in ESL.

Length of Program: 2–3 semesters. Students may be full-time or part-time and may begin their study at the beginning of any semester. Rolling admissions are in effect.

Program Requirements: 30 semester hours. Competence in a language other than English is required. Practice teaching is not required. A thesis or a comprehensive examination is required.

Courses Offered: (*required) *ESL; *two to four of the following: Introduction to Linguistic Theory, History of the English Language, Advanced Study of Language: Theory and Application, Seminar in Linguistics, Old English, Seminar in Scholarship and Writing, Methods and Materials of TESL.

Full-Time Staff: Joy Allameh, Helen Bennett, David Elias, Ordelle Hill, Alan Hunt, James Kenkel, Marshall Myers.

Requirements for Admission: The university's requirements for admission are an undergraduate degree and a combined GRE score of at least 1000. The program requires a combined GRE score of 1150 and an undergraduate GPA of 3.0 or higher.

Tuition, Fees, and Aid: For in-state students, $2,150 per year; for out-of-state students, $5,990 per year. Graduate assistantships are available.

General: Five students completed the program in 1996–1997.

The university has an intensive English language program for nonnative speakers of English.

Summer Session: No

Further Information: Dominick J. Hart
Department of English
Case Annex 467
Eastern Kentucky University
Richmond, KY 40475

Telephone: (606) 622-5861
Fax: (606) 622-1604
E-mail: enghart@acs.eku.edu

◆ EASTERN MENNONITE UNIVERSITY, Department of Language and Literature

Degrees Offered: Minor in TESL; MA in education with a concentration in TESL.

Length of Program: 1 year for the minor. Students may be full-time or part-time and may begin their study at the beginning of any semester. There are no application deadlines.

Program Requirements: 18 semester hours for the minor. Competence in a language other than English is required for native speakers of English. Practice teaching is required. Neither a thesis nor a comprehensive examination is required.

Courses Offered: (*required for the minor) *The English Language; *The Grammars of English; *Psycholinguistics; *Methods of TESL; *TESL Practicum; *a foreign language through the intermediate level.

Full-Time Staff: Carroll D. Yoder (chair), Ervie L. Glick, Karin de Jonge-Kannan, Cynthia Yoder.

Requirements for Admission: The university's requirements for admission are a GPA of 2.0, SAT scores or 880 or ACT scores of 19, and one reference attesting to academic ability and promise.

Tuition, Fees, and Aid: $12,600 per semester. Academic scholarships and need-based aid are available.

General: The program is designed to meet the needs of public school teachers as well as those planning to teach abroad or in community-based programs. It leads to a Virginia credential in TESOL.

Twenty students completed the program in 1996–1997.

The university has an intensive English language program for nonnative speakers of English.

Summer Session: Yes

Further Information: Dr. Ervie L. Glick, Director, TESL
Department of Language and Literature
CC-347
Eastern Mennonite University
1200 Park Road
Harrisonburg, VA 22802

Telephone: (540) 432-4161
Fax: (540) 432-4444
E-mail: glicke@emu.edu

◆ EASTERN MICHIGAN UNIVERSITY, Department of Foreign Languages and Bilingual Studies

Degree Offered: MA in TESOL.

Length of Program: 4 semesters if started in September; longer otherwise. Students may be full-time or part-time and may begin their study at the beginning of the fall or winter semester. Application deadlines are fall semester, March 15; winter semester, July 15.

Program Requirements: 32 credit hours. Competence in a language other than English is not required. Practice teaching is required. A thesis is optional. A comprehensive examination is not required.

Courses Offered: (*required) *Observation and Analysis of ESL Programs; *Theoretical Foundations of Second Language Pedagogy; *A Pedagogical Grammar and Phonology of English; *Methods of TESOL: Reading, Writing, Grammar; *Methods of TESOL: Listening, Speaking, Pronunciation; *Foreign Language Testing and Evaluation; *ESOL Materials: Review, Adaptation, and Development; *TESOL Practicum; *TESOL Seminar; *two courses in linguistics.

Full-Time Staff: JoAnn Aebersold, Thom Cullen, Cathy Day, Glenn Deckert, Betsy Morgan.

Requirements for Admission: The university's requirements for are official transcripts from all colleges and universities attended and a GPA of at least 2.5. The program requires 1 year of college foreign language study and two letters of recommendation. Nonnative speakers of English must submit a TOEFL score of 550 (520 for conditional admission) or a MELAB score of 6 (4 for conditional admission).

Tuition, Fees, and Aid: For in-state students, $145 per credit hour; for out-of-state students, $339 per credit hour. Fees are $15 per credit hour. Graduate fellowships and graduate assistantships are available.

General: The focus and greatest strength of the program is the consistent application of theory to classroom practice. Graduate teaching candidates are systematically exposed to students in the undergraduate ESL program, culminating in an intensive practicum. Graduates believe that the hands-on approach has been the most important preparation for working as professional ESL teachers.

Twenty-two students completed the program in 1996–1997.

The university has an intensive English language program for nonnative speakers of English.

Summer Session: Yes

Further Information: TESOL Advisor
Department of Foreign Languages and Bilingual Studies
219 Alexander Building
Eastern Michigan University
Ypsilanti, MI 48197

Telephone: (734) 487-0130
Fax: (734) 487-0338
E-mail: aebersold@online.emich.edu

◆ EASTERN WASHINGTON UNIVERSITY, Department of Modern Languages and Literatures

Degree Offered: Certificate in TESOL.

Length of Program: 3 quarters. Students may be full-time or part-time and may begin their study at the beginning of any quarter. Application deadlines are fall quarter, August 15; winter quarter, December 12; spring and summer quarters, March 5.

Program Requirements: 26–27 quarter credits. Competence in a language other than English is optional. Practice teaching is required. A thesis and a comprehensive examination are optional.

Courses Offered: (*required) *Methodology in TESL/TEFL; *Second Language Materials Development and Adaptation; *Assessment in ESL/EFL; *Second Language Acquisition and Teaching; *Reading Instruction in ESL; *(for endorsement) Language Arts and ESL Instruction *and* Anthropological Linguistics; Grammar for Teachers; Modern Grammar; Phonetics; Sociolinguistics.

Full-Time Staff: Janine Alden, Mary Brooks, Cynthia Hallanger, Mark Landa (director), Evelyn Renshaw, Robert Werckle.

Requirements for Admission: The university's requirements for admission are completion of 15 high school units as follows: English 4, mathematics 3, social science 3, sciences 2, foreign language 2 (in one language), and fine arts 1 (or an additional unit in another named area); transcripts; and ACT or SAT scores. Nonnative speakers of English must provide evidence of proficiency in English. The program requires junior standing (senior standing preferred) and recommended prerequisite courses.

Tuition, Fees, and Aid: For in-state students, $2,430 per year; for out-of-state students, $8,616 per year. Grants, loans, work study, and scholarships are available to U.S. students.

General: Students have opportunities for practical training and observation in the university. In addition, students may observe in other intensive language programs and in the public schools. The program cooperates closely with the Education Department. The program leads to a teaching endorsement from the College of Letters and Social Sciences that is recognized by the state of Washington.

There are opportunities to teach abroad.

Twenty students completed the program in 1996–1997.

Summer Session: Yes

Further Information: Mark Brooks, Minor Program Director
ESLG Department of Modern Languages
Patterson Hall 358F, Mail Stop 34
Eastern Washington University
Cheney, WA 99004-2431

Telephone: (509) 359-6939
Fax: (509) 359-7855
E-mail: mland@ewu.edu

◆ FAIRFIELD UNIVERSITY, Graduate School of Education and Allied Professions, Department of TESOL, Foreign Language, and Bilingual/Multicultural Education

Degree Offered: MA in TESOL.

Length of Program: 4 semesters. Students may be full-time or part-time and may begin their study at the beginning of any semester. Rolling admissions are in effect.

Program Requirements: 33 credits. Competence in a language other than English is not required. Practice teaching is required only for initial certification. Either a thesis or a comprehensive examination is required.

Courses Offered: (*required) *Philosophical Foundations of Education; *Introduction to Educational Research; *Introduction to Educational Technology; *Contemporary Issues in Education; *Principles of Bilingualism; *Methods and Materials for Second Language Teaching; *Teaching and Learning Within Multicultural Contexts of Education; *Culture and Second Language Acquisition; *Testing and Assessment in Foreign Language, ESL, and Bilingual Programs; Special Learners in the Bilingual/ESL Classroom; Teaching Grammar in Second Language Settings; Methods and Materials in Bilingual Programs; Thesis Seminar; The English Language Learner in the Regular Classroom; Historical and Sociopolitical Issues in Bilingual/Multicultural Education; Directed Observation and Supervised Student Teaching; *Certificate of Advanced Study Practicum in Teaching.

Full-Time Staff: Sr. M. Julianna Poole (chair).

Requirements for Admission: The university's requirement for admission is an undergraduate cumulative quality point average of 2.67. The Praxis I is required in the teacher preparation program. The program requires proficiency in English. Credits obtained from foreign universities are evaluated to ensure equivalency.

Tuition, Fees, and Aid: $335 per credit. A limited number of graduate assistantships are available.

General: The MA degree facilitates a cross-endorsement in TESOL for teachers who are already certified. Initial certification in TESOL is also offered.
Seven students completed the program in 1996–1997.

Summer Session: Yes

Further Information: Sr. M. Julianna Poole, SSND, EdD, Chair
Department of TESOL, Foreign Language, and Bilingual/Multicultural Education
Canisius 225
Fairfield University
North Benson Road
Fairfield, CT 06430

Telephone: (203) 254-4000 extension 2873
Fax: (203) 254-4047
E-mail: jpoole@fairi.fairfield.edu

◆ FAIRFIELD UNIVERSITY, Graduate School of Education and Allied Professions, Department of TESOL, Foreign Language, and Bilingual/Multicultural Education

Degree Offered: Certificate of advanced study in TESOL.

Length of Program: 4 semesters. Students may be full-time or part-time and may begin their study at the beginning of any semester. Rolling admissions are in effect.

Program Requirements: 30 credits. Competence in a language other than English is not required. Practice teaching is required only for initial certification. Neither a thesis nor a comprehensive examination is required.

Courses Offered: (*required) *Comparative Philosophies of Education; *Theories of Learning; *Principles of Curriculum Development and Evaluation *or* Second Language Curriculum Development; *Testing and Assessment in Foreign Language, ESL, and Bilingual Programs; *Certificate of Advanced Study Practicum in Teaching; Special Learners in the Bilingual/ESL Classroom; Teaching Grammar in Second Language Settings; Comprehending and Communicating in a Second Language; Content Area Instruction in Bilingual/ESL Classrooms; Reading and Writing in a Second Language; Culture and Second Language Acquisition; Practicum in Bilingual Programs; Thesis Seminar; The English Language Learner in the Regular Classroom; Historical and Sociopolitical Issues in Bilingual/Multicultural Education; Directed Observation and Supervised Student Teaching; Student Teaching Seminar.

Full-Time Staff: Sr. M. Julianna Poole (chair).

Requirements for Admission: The university's requirement for admission is an MA from an accredited college or university with a 3.0 cumulative quality point average. The program requires proficiency in English. Credits obtained from foreign universities are evaluated to ensure equivalency.

Tuition, Fees, and Aid: See MA in TESOL program description.

General: For students who are not already certified, 21 of the 30 required credits count for state certification or cross-endorsement in TESOL.

Four students completed the program in 1996–1997.

Summer Session: Yes

Further Information: Sr. M. Julianna Poole, SSND, EdD, Chair
Department of TESOL, Foreign Language, and Bilingual/
Multicultural Education
Canisius 225
Fairfield University
North Benson Road
Fairfield, CT 06430

Telephone: (203) 254-4000 extension 2873
Fax: (203) 254-4047
E-mail: jpoole@fairi.fairfield.edu

◆ FAIRLEIGH DICKINSON UNIVERSITY, School of Education

Degree Offered: MAT in ESL (first certification).

Length of Program: 3 semesters. Students may be full-time or part-time and may begin their study at the beginning of any semester. Application deadlines are fall semester, August 15; spring semester, December 15; summer semester, May 15.

Program Requirements: 36 credits. Competence in a language other than English is not required. Practice teaching and a final project in curriculum development are required. A comprehensive examination is not required.

Courses Offered: *Instructional Theory and Practice; *Effective Reading Instruction; *Effective Teaching/Effective Schools; *Internship and Seminar I; *Internship and Seminar II; *Evaluation and Testing in the Language Classroom; *Teaching Reading and Composition for ESL Teachers; *Linguistics for Teachers: Comparative Phonology; *Applied Linguistics for Teachers; *Language and Culture; *Methods, Materials, and Curriculum for EFL/ESL Teachers; *The Multicultural Classroom; *Final Project.

Full-Time Staff: Liliane Gaffney (director), Rosemary Rowlands, Paul Franklin.

Requirements for Admission: The university's requirements for admission are a baccalaureate degree with a minimum cumulative GPA of 2.5 and a minimum GPA of 3.0 in the major, an official transcript, and two letters of recommendation. International students must have a TOEFL score of 530 or higher. In-service teachers must have a bachelor's degree, certification to teach a specific discipline, and a Miller Analogies Test score or a passing Praxis Series score in the area of teacher certification. The program leads to a New Jersey credential in ESL.

Tuition, Fees, and Aid: $496 per credit. Assistantships and scholarships are available.

General: After an intensive practicum in the spring or summer semester, the interns may accept a paid teaching position and satisfy the 3 credits of internship. MAT interns are encouraged to take the practicum early in their course of study.

Nineteen students completed the program in 1996–1997.

The university has an intensive English language program for nonnative speakers of English.

Summer Session: Yes

Further Information: Director, MAT Program
School of Education
Bancroft Hall T-200-B
Fairleigh Dickinson University
1000 River Road
Teaneck, NJ 07666

Telephone: (201) 692-2603

◆ FAIRLEIGH DICKINSON UNIVERSITY, School of Education

Degree Offered: MAT in ESL (second certification).

Length of Program: Variable. Students must be part-time. There are no application deadlines.

Program Requirements: 15 credits. Competence in a language other than English is not required. Neither practice teaching, nor a thesis, nor a comprehensive examination is required.

Courses Offered: (*required) *Linguistics for Teachers: Comparative Phonology; *Applied Linguistics for Teachers; *Language and Culture; *Methods, Materials, and Curriculum for EFL/ESL Teachers; *The Multicultural Classroom; Evaluation and Testing in the Language Classroom; Teaching Reading and Composition for ESL Teachers; Discourse Analysis; Final Project; Instructional Theory and Practice; Internship and Seminar I; Seminar in Language Acquisition; Teaching Culture Through Literature and Film; Workshop in Curriculum Development the Language Classroom; Teaching ESL Through Content Areas; Grammar for English and ESL.

Full-Time Staff: See program description for MAT (first certification).

Requirements for Admission: The program requires certification in a teaching field.

General: The program leads to a New Jersey credential in ESL.

Tuition, Fees, and Aid: See program description for MAT (first certification).

Summer Session: Yes

Further Information: Director, MAT Program
School of Education
Bancroft Hall T-200-B
Fairleigh Dickinson University
1000 River Road
Teaneck, NJ 07666

Telephone: (201) 692-2603

◆ FAIRLEIGH DICKINSON UNIVERSITY, School of Education

Degree Offered: Multilingual MA.

Length of Program: Variable. Students may be full-time or part-time and may begin their study at the beginning of any semester. Application deadlines are fall semester, August 15; spring semester, December 15; summer semester, May 15.

Program Requirements: 33 credits. Competence in a language other than English is not required. A final project in curriculum development is required. Neither practice teaching, nor a thesis, nor a comprehensive examination is required.

Courses Offered: (*required) *Comparative Phonology; *Applied Linguistics; *Evaluation and Testing in the Language Classroom; *Teaching Culture Through Literature and Film; *Introduction to U.S. Culture; *Methods, Materials, and Curriculum for EFL/ESL Teachers; *Clinical Practice in Language Instruction; *Final Project; Language and Culture; Vocabulary Expansion; Techniques of Literary Analysis; Advanced Aural/Oral Practice and Public Speaking; Grammar; Teaching Reading and Composition for ESL Teachers; Whole Language.

Full-Time Staff: See program description for MAT (first certification).

Requirements for Admission: See program description for MAT (first certification).

Tuition, Fees, and Aid: $496 per credit.

General: U.S. culture and the relationship of language to culture are strongly emphasized. International students have an opportunity to observe and assist in an area public school.

Eighteen students completed the program in 1996–1997.

The university has an intensive English language program for nonnative speakers of English.

Summer Session: Yes

Further Information: Chair
School of Education
Bancroft Hall T-200-B
Fairleigh Dickinson University
1000 River Road
Teaneck, NJ 07666

Telephone: (201) 692-2838, 2631, 2079
Fax: (201) 692-2603

◆ FINDLAY, THE UNIVERSITY OF, International Center

Degree Offered: MA in TESOL and bilingual education.

Length of Program: 4 semesters. Students may be full-time or part-time and may begin their study at the beginning of any semester. There are no application deadlines.

Program Requirements: 36 semester hours. Competence in a language other than English is not required. Neither practice teaching, nor a thesis, nor a comprehensive examination is required.

Courses Offered: (*required) *Methods and Materials for TESL; *Advanced Methods and Materials for TESL; *Linguistics for Teachers; *Second Language Acquisition; *Assessment of English Language Learners; *Sociolinguistics and the Classroom; *Practicum in Bilingual/ESL Education; Foundations of Multicultural Education; Principles, Practices, and Curriculum of Bilingual Education; Bilingual/ESL Instruction in the Content Areas; Teaching Language Arts in Bilingual/ESL Classrooms; Advanced Linguistics; English Grammar in the ESL Classroom; Advanced Topics in Bilingual/ESL Education; Reading in a Second Language; International Experience Abroad; Special Topics in Bilingual/ESL Education.

Full-Time Staff: Irma Hanson (chair), Fumiko Harada, Michael Reed, Jian Yang.

Requirements for Admission: The university's requirements for admission are a bachelor's degree from an accredited institution, a GPA of 3.0, and three letters of recommendation. The program requires an affidavit of financial support, a copy of the teaching certificate (if applicable), official transcripts, and, for nonnative speakers of English, a TOEFL score of 550 or higher.

Tuition, Fees, and Aid: $227 per semester hour. Teaching assistantships are available.

General: The program fulfills the requirements for validations in bilingual education and TESOL. It is the only program of its kind in Ohio.

Summer Session: Yes

Further Information: Director, MA in TESOL
International Center
The University of Findlay
1000 North Main Street
Findlay, OH 45840

Telephone: (419) 424-4474 or 424-4826
E-mail: ihanson@hewey.findlay.edu

◆ FLORIDA, UNIVERSITY OF, Program in Linguistics

Degree Offered: Undergraduate minor in TESL.

Length of Program: 2 semesters. Students may be full-time or part-time and may begin their study at the beginning of any semester. Application deadlines vary according to year in school and intended undergraduate major.

Program Requirements: 18 semester hours. Competence in a language other than English is not required. Practice teaching is required. Neither a thesis nor a comprehensive examination is required.

Courses Offered: (*required) *Introduction to Linguistics; *Modern English Structure; *Introduction to TESL; *an elective from each of three categories: Understanding the English Language, Understanding English Language Materials, and Understanding English Language Culture.

Full-Time Staff: Roger M. Thompson (coordinator), Diana Boxer, Anne Wyatt-Brown, Kevin McCarthy, Marie Nelson (chair), Clemons Hallman.

Requirements for Admission: The university's requirement for admission is graduation from an accredited high school and SAT scores. The average GPA for incoming freshmen is 3.8.

Tuition, Fees, and Aid: For in-state students, $1,926 per year; for out-of-state students, $7,842 per year. No financial aid is available.

General: The minor, awarded only on completion of a major, is designed for students who wish to go overseas after graduation to teach English. It is popular with English, linguistics, foreign language, and anthropology majors.

Twenty students completed the program in 1996–1997

The university has an intensive English language program for nonnative speakers of English.

Summer Session: Yes

Further Information: TESL Coordinator
Program in Linguistics
112 Anderson Hall
University of Florida
Gainesville, FL 32611

Telephone: (352) 392-0639
Fax: (352) 392-8480
E-mail: rthompso@english.ufl.edu
http://web.nwe.efl.edu

◆ FLORIDA, UNIVERSITY OF, Program in Linguistics

Degree Offered: TESL certificate (graduate or postbaccalaureate).

Length of Program: 2 semesters. Students may be part-time or full-time and may begin their study at the beginning of any semester. Teaching assistants must complete TESOL Methods, which is offered only in the fall. Application deadlines are flexible.

Program Requirements: 15 semester hours. Competence in a language other than English is not required. Either a 1-semester experience living in a cultural setting on the student's own or 1 semester of a non–Western European language is required. Practice teaching and a presentation at a professional meeting are required. Neither a thesis nor a comprehensive examination is required.

Courses Offered: (*required) *TESL Methods and Materials; *Second Language Acquisition; *Modern English Structure; electives in sociolinguistics, language testing, writing theory, problems in literacy, ESL/EFL curriculum development, intercultural communication, and bilingualism.

Full-Time Staff: Roger M. Thompson (coordinator), Diana Boxer, Anne Wyatt-Brown, Robert Scholes, Florencia Cortes-Conde, Kathy Kidder, Marie Nelson (chair), Clemons Hallman, Kevin McCarthy.

Requirements for Admission: Students may begin taking courses upon acceptance by any graduate program.

Tuition, Fees, and Aid: For in-state students, $3,096 per year; for out-of-state students, $10,428 per year. Teaching assistantships in the English Language Institute and fellowships are available.

General: The graduate TESL certificate is open to graduate students of any major or level or may be taken as a postbaccalaureate program.

Twelve students completed the program in 1996–1997.

The university has an intensive English language program for nonnative speakers of English.

Summer Session: Yes

Further Information: TESL Coordinator
Program in Linguistics
112 Anderson Hall
University of Florida
Gainesville, FL 32611

Telephone: (352) 392-0639
Fax: (352) 392-8480
E-mail: rthompso@english.ufl.edu
http://web.nwe.ufl.edu

◆ FLORIDA ATLANTIC UNIVERSITY, Department of Teacher Education

Degree Offered: BA in elementary education with ESOL endorsement.

Length of Program: 4 semesters after completion of first 2 years of university. Students may begin their study at the beginning of any semester.

Program Requirements: 60 credits. Competence in a language other than English is not required. Practice teaching and a comprehensive examination are required. A thesis is not required.

Courses Offered: (*required) *Multicultural Education; *Introduction to TESOL; *Language Arts/Children's Literature; *Science: Elementary and Middle; *Social Studies: Elementary and Middle; *Math: Elementary and Middle; *Survey of Exceptionalities; *Reading I and II; *General Teaching Practices I and II; *Art; *Music; *Physical Education; *Measurement and Evaluation; *Applied Learning Theory; *Educational Technology; *Practices in Teaching ESOL; *Student Teaching.

Full-Time Staff: Valerie Bristol (chair), Carmen Gonzalez-Jones, Eileen Airiza, Noorshaya Yahyha, Gloria M. Pelaez (coordinator).

General: This is the only undergraduate degree in the state of Florida that combines an elementary education degree with a state-approved ESOL endorsement.

Summer Session: Yes

Further Information: Gloria M. Pelaez, Coordinator
Department of Teacher Education
College of Education, Room 329
Florida Atlantic University
777 Glades Road
Boca Raton, FL 33431

Telephone: (561) 297-3583
E-mail: Gpelaez@fau.edu

◆ FLORIDA INTERNATIONAL UNIVERSITY, College of Education–TESOL

Degree Offered: BA certification.

Length of Program: Students may be full-time or part-time and may begin their study at the beginning of any semester. Open enrollment is in effect.

Program Requirements: 15 semester hours. Competence in a language other than English is not required. Practice teaching and the Florida State ESOL Certification Examination are required. A thesis is not required.

Courses Offered: (*required) *Curriculum Development; *Special Methods of TESOL; *Principles of ESOL Testing; *Cross-Cultural Studies; *Developing ESOL Language and Literacy.

Full-Time Staff: Patricia Killian, Rosa Castro Feinberg, Jodi Reiss coordinator), Deborah Hassan.

Requirements for Admission: Students must be fully enrolled in the College of Education or be a special student; special students must have a BA or BS in elementary education, foreign language education, or English education.

Tuition, Fees, and Aid: For in-state students, $60 per credit (undergraduate), $115 per credit (graduate); for out-of-state students, $385 per credit (graduate). Various types of aid, though limited, are available.

General: This add-on certification/endorsement is valid only for these four degrees: elementary education, English education, foreign language education, and special education. Endorsement in other education areas requires a master's in TESOL.

The university has an intensive English language program for nonnative speakers of English.

Summer Session: Yes

Further Information: TESOL Coordinator
EFPS-TESOL Program
College of Education
UP Campus ZEB 311
Florida International University
Miami, FL 33199

Telephone: (305) 348-3418
Fax: (305) 348-1515
E-mail: Killianp@fiu.edu or Reissj@fiu.edu

◆ FLORIDA INTERNATIONAL UNIVERSITY, College of Education–TESOL

Degree Offered: MS-TESOL.

Length of Program: 3–4 semesters. Students may be full-time or part-time and may begin their study at the beginning of any semester. Open enrollment is in effect for U.S. students and special students. Application deadlines for matriculating international students are summer, January 30; fall semester, April 1; spring semester, August 30.

Program Requirements: 36 semester hours plus prerequisite. Competence in a language other than English is not required. Neither practice teaching, nor a thesis, nor a comprehensive examination is required.

Courses Offered: (*required) *Analysis and Application of Educational Research; *Social, Philosophical, and Historical Foundations of Education; *Psychological Foundations of Education *or* Educational Psychology: Principles and Applications; *Curriculum Development; *Special Methods of TESOL; *Principles of ESOL Testing; *Field Component; *English Syntax; *Applied Phonetics; Cross-Cultural Studies; Developing ESOL Language and Literacy; Troublesome English: Grammar for ESOL Teachers; History of the English Language; General Morphology and Syntax; Studies in Bilingualism; Language Acquisition; Methods of Teaching Accent Reduction; Instruction for Thinking Strategies; Languages of the World; Sociolinguistics; General Phonology; Pragmatics; Semantics; Discourse Analysis.

Full-Time Staff: See program description for BA certification.

Requirements for Admission: The university's requirement for admission is a bachelor's degree from an accredited college or university with either a minimum GPA of 3.0 in the last 60 credits or a minimum GRE score of 1000.

Tuition, Fees, and Aid: See program description for BA certification.

General: The university has an intensive English language program for nonnative speakers of English.

Summer Session: Yes

Further Information: TESOL Coordinator
EFPS-TESOL Program
College of Education
UP Campus ZEB 311
Florida International University
Miami, FL 33199

Telephone: (305) 348-3418
Fax: (305) 348-1515
E-mail: Killianp@fiu.edu or Reissj@fiu.edu

◆ FLORIDA STATE UNIVERSITY, Department of Curriculum and Instruction

Degree Offered: MS in education with a TESOL specialization.

Length of Program: 1 year. Students may be full-time or part-time and must begin their study at the beginning of the fall semester. The application deadline is May 15.

Program Requirements: 33 semester hours. Competence in a language other than English is not required. Practice teaching and a comprehensive examination are required. A thesis is optional.

Courses Offered: (*required) *Introduction to Teaching ESL/EFL; *Introduction to Second Language Research; *Introduction to Applied Linguistics; *Testing and Evaluation in Second Languages; *Development of Second Language Curriculum and Materials; *Teaching of Culture; Second Language Reading: Teaching/Learning; Psycholinguistic Perspectives on Second Language Acquisition; Current Issues in TESOL; Special Topics in Applied Linguistics; Teaching ESL in Content Areas.

Full-Time Staff: Frank Brooks, Frederick L. Jenks, Elizabeth Platt.

Requirements for Admission: The university's requirements for admission are a bachelor's degree with a minimum GPA of 3.0 for the last 2 years of undergraduate study and minimum combined verbal and quantitative GRE scores of 1000. The program requires three letters of recommendation and a statement of educational goals.

Tuition, Fees, and Aid: For in-state students, $120 per semester hour; for out-of-state students, $300 per semester hour. Fees are $85 per semester. University and College of Education fellowships are available.

General: The program may be completed in 1 year (fall, spring, and summer semesters) and meets the TESOL course requirements for Florida state teacher certification.

Practice teaching has been arranged in Colombia, Costa Rica, and other countries. The university has a postdegree exchange program with a Costa Rican university, and fieldwork has been approved in Japan, Saudi Arabia, Taiwan, and Korea, among other countries.

Fifteen students completed the program in 1996–1997.

The university has an intensive English language program for nonnative speakers of English.

Summer Session: Yes

Further Information: Coordinator
Department of Multilingual/Multicultural Education
209 Carothers
Florida State University
Tallahassee, FL 32306-4490

Telephone: (850) 644-6553
Fax: (850) 644-1880
E-mail: fbrooks@garnet.acns.fsu.edu

◆ THE FLORIDA STATE UNIVERSITY, Department of Curriculum and Instruction

Degree Offered: PhD in multilingual/multicultural education with a specialization in TESOL.

Length of Program: 7–10 semesters. Students may be part-time or full-time and must begin their study at the beginning of the fall semester. The application deadline is May 15.

Program Requirements: 60 hours minimum, including dissertation hours. Competence in a language other than English is recommended. Practice teaching is optional. A dissertation and a comprehensive examination are required.

Courses Offered: (*required) *Teaching ESL/EFL; *Second Language Research Design; *Applied Linguistics; *L2 Psycholinguistics; *L2 Testing and Evaluation; *L2 Curriculum and Materials Development; *Learning/Teaching of Culture; *L2 Reading; *Discourse Analysis; *Current Issues in TESL; *ESL Administration; *12 hours of research tools course work; Teaching ESL in Content Areas; Survey and Qualitative Research Methods; Basic Descriptive and Inferential Statistics; General Linear Model or Analysis of Variance Applications; 12 hours in a minor/related field.

Full-Time Staff: See program description for MS in education with a TESOL specialization.

Requirements for Admission: The university's requirements for admission are a master's degree in TESOL or a related field, a GPA of 3.25 in the graduate degree program, and minimum combined verbal and quantitative GRE scores of 1000. Nonnative speakers of English must have a minimum TOEFL score of 600. The program requires a statement of educational and research goals, three letters of recommendation, and 3 years' full-time teaching experience.

Tuition, Fees, and Aid: For in-state students, $120 per semester hour; for out-of-state students, $300 per semester hour. Fees are $85 per semester. Teaching assistantships and university and College of Education fellowships are available.

General: The program emphasizes social contexts as factors in L2 learning, classroom-based research, L2 learning in multicultural school contexts, and EFL. The doctoral student body is tightly knit. The program is the major TESL graduate program in the southeastern United States. Practice teaching and internships have been offered at the university in the state department of education and in regional schools.

Annual opportunities are available for teaching and research in Panama and Costa Rica. In the past 5 years, four students have won Fulbright lectureships in

Eastern Europe and the Middle East. Fieldwork options have been organized in Costa Rica, Japan, Taiwan, England, and Italy at the dissertation stage.

Four students completed the program in 1996–1997.

The university has an intensive English language program for nonnative speakers of English.

Summer Session: Yes

Further Information: Coordinator
Department of Multilingual/Multicultural Education
209 Carothers
Florida State University
Tallahassee, FL 32306-4490

Telephone: (850) 644-6553
Fax: (850) 644-1880
E-mail: fbrooks@garnet.acns.fsu.edu

◆ FORDHAM UNIVERSITY, Graduate School of Education, Curriculum and Teaching Division

Degree Offered: MS in education.

Length of Program: Variable. Students may be full-time or part-time and may begin their study at the beginning of any semester. Admission is ongoing.

Program Requirements: 33–45 credits. Competence in a language other than English is not required. Practice teaching and a comprehensive examination are required. A thesis is not required.

Courses Offered: Issues and Trends in American Education; Race and Multicultural Education in American Society; Introduction to Research; TESOL; Teaching the Structure of the English Language; Bilingual/ESL Curriculum Development; Sociolinguistics: Language and Reading Analysis; Principles of Bilingual Education.

Full-Time Staff: Drs. Antonacci, Baratta, Barnhardt, Bates, Baecher, Bologna, Brause, Carrasquillo (chair), Cicchelli, Ellsworth, Freedman, George, Hicks, Hughes, King, Kucer, London, Mello, Sheinmel, Strear, Uhry.

Requirements for Admission: The university's requirements for admission are a baccalaureate in a liberal arts or science discipline with a GPA of 3.0, two reference reports, and proof of immunization.

Tuition, Fees, and Aid: $462 per credit. Graduate assistantships, alumni scholarships, New York State tuition assistance, and deferred payment programs are available.

General: The program leads to a New York State credential in TESOL.

Summer Session: Yes

Further Information: Dr. Angela Carrasquillo, Chair
Curriculum and Teaching Division
Lowenstein Building, Room 1102-A
Fordham University Graduate School of Education
113 West 60th Street
New York, NY 10023

Telephone: (212) 636-6450
Fax: (212) 636-7826

◆ FRESNO PACIFIC UNIVERSITY, School of Graduate Studies

Degree Offered: TESOL certificate.

Length of Program: 2 semesters. Students may be full-time or part-time and may begin their study at the beginning of any semester. Application deadlines are fall semester, September 3; spring semester, January 7; summer semester, May 5.

Program Requirements: 18 semester units. Competence in a language other than English is optional. Practice teaching is required. A comprehensive examination and a thesis are not required.

Courses Offered: (*required) *Reading Process and Practice; *Language Acquisition and Cross-Cultural Communication; *Current Theories, Methods, and Materials for Teaching a Second Language; *Practicum in TESOL; *Introduction to Linguistics; *Linguistics for Second Language Teaching.

Full-Time Staff: David E. Freeman (chair), Yvonne S. Freeman, Jean Fennacy, Doreen Myovich.

Requirements for Admission: The university's requirements for admission are a baccalaureate degree, three letters of recommendation, GRE or Miller Analogies Test scores, official transcripts, a statement of intent, and two writing samples.

Tuition, Fees, and Aid: $240 per semester unit. Some research assistantships and grants are available.

General: The program emphasizes practical application of theory and content-based ESL and EFL instruction. It qualifies students for California's CLAD certificate.

Four students completed the program in 1996–1997.

The university has an intensive English language program for nonnative speakers of English.

Summer Session: No

Further Information: Dr. David Freeman, Director
TESOL Program
Fresno Pacific University
1717 South Chestnut
Fresno, CA 93702

Telephone: (209) 453-2201
Fax: (209) 453-2001
E-mail: defreema@fresno.edu

◆ FRESNO PACIFIC UNIVERSITY, School of Graduate Studies

Degree Offered: MA in TESOL.

Length of Program: Variable. Students may be full-time or part-time and may begin their study at the beginning of any semester. Application deadlines are fall semester, September 3; spring semester, January 7; summer semester, May 5.

Program Requirements: 37 semester units. Competence in a language other than English is optional. Practice teaching and a thesis are required. A comprehensive examination is not required.

Courses Offered: (*required) *Reading Process and Practice; *Language Acquisition and Cross-Cultural Communication; *Current Theories, Methods, and Materials for Teaching a Second Language; *Writing Process and Practice *or* Reading/Writing in the Content Areas; *Practicum in TESOL; *Current Theories, Methods, and Materials for Bilingual Education; *Cultural Diversity and Education; *Introduction to Linguistics; *Linguistics for Second Language Teaching; *Research in Language,

Literacy, and Culture; *Values in School and Society; *Project/Thesis Proposal; *Project/Thesis.

Full-Time Staff: David E. Freeman (chair), Yvonne S. Freeman, Jean Fennacy, Mary Ann Larsen-Pusey, Doreen Myovich.

Requirements for Admission: See TESOL certificate program description.

Tuition, Fees, and Aid: See TESOL certificate program description.

General: See TESOL certificate program description. The program leads to a California credential in TESOL.

Three students completed the program in 1996–1997.

The university has an intensive English language program for nonnative speakers of English.

Summer Session: No

Further Information: Dr. David Freeman, Director
TESOL Program
Fresno Pacific University
1717 South Chestnut
Fresno, CA 93702

Telephone: (209) 453-2201
Fax: (209) 453-2001
E-mail: defreema@fresno.edu

◆ GEORGE MASON UNIVERSITY, Department of English

Degree Offered: Certificate in TESL.

Length of Program: 2 semesters. Students may be full-time or part-time and may begin their study at the beginning of any semester.

Program Requirements: 18 credit hours. Competence in a language other than English is not required. Neither practice teaching, nor a thesis, nor a comprehensive examination is required.

Courses Offered: (*required) *Descriptive Linguistics; *Modern English Grammar; *Descriptive Aspects of English Phonetics and Phonology; *Second Language Acquisition; *Applied Linguistics; electives.

Full-Time Staff: Dee Ann Holisky, Charles Jones, Anne Lazaraton, Steven Weinberger.

Requirements for Admission: The university's requirement for admission is a baccalaureate degree with a GPA of 3.0 or higher in the last 60 hours of undergraduate work. Nonnative speakers of English must have a TOEFL score of 575 or higher.

Tuition, Fees, and Aid: For in-state students, $139 per credit hour; for out-of-state students, $358.50 per credit hour.

General: The program offers a primarily linguistics-oriented approach to TESL. Internships are available.

Twenty-four students completed the program in 1996–1997.

The university has an intensive English language program for nonnative speakers of English.

Summer Session: Yes

Further Information: Charles Jones
English Department, 3E4
George Mason University
4400 University Drive
Fairfax, VA 22030

Telephone: (703) 993-1182

◆ GEORGETOWN UNIVERSITY, Department of Linguistics

Degrees Offered: Certificate in TESL; certificate in TESL and bilingual education.

Length of Program: 2 semesters. Students may be full-time or part-time and may begin their study at the beginning of any semester. Application deadlines are fall semester, February 1; spring semester, October 15; summer semester, February 1.

Program Requirements: 24 credits. Competence in a language other than English is optional. Neither practice teaching, nor a thesis, nor a comprehensive examination is required.

Courses Offered: (*required) *General Linguistics; *General Phonology; *General Syntax; *Language Acquisition; *Methodology of Language Teaching; *Language Testing; *(for certificate in bilingual education) Bilingualism; EFL Materials Preparation; History of the English Language; Cross-Cultural Communication; Introduction to Sociolinguistics.

Full-Time Staff: James E. Alatis (director), S. Biesenbach-Lucas, J. Connor-Linton, C. Doughty, D. Lardiere, A. Tyler (concentration head).

Requirements for Admission: The university's requirements for admission are a baccalaureate degree from an accredited institution with a better-than-B average, including 18–24 semester hours of credit in the proposed field of study. The program requires a B+ undergraduate average, an autobiographical statement of purpose, and a professional or academic writing sample showing analytic skills. Nonnative speakers of English must have a minimum TOEFL score of 600.

Tuition, Fees, and Aid: $751 per credit hour. Fees are application, $50 or $55; recreational facility, $94.50. No financial aid is available.

General: Students wishing a program less extensive than that of the MAT may pursue the certificate (not to be interpreted as certification or accreditation to teach in any state or region of the United States). The program can serve as a theoretical enhancement of skills of working teachers.

Participants may be eligible for the university's summer session with the Universidad Católica de Ecuador in Quito, studying Spanish linguistics, cross-cultural communication, and immersion in a nonnative culture.

The university has an English language program for nonnative speakers of English.

Summer Session: Yes

Further Information: Director, MAT Program
Department of Linguistics
ICC 479
Georgetown University
37th and Q Streets, NW
Washington, DC 20057

Telephone: (202) 687-5956
Fax: (202) 687-7083

◆ GEORGETOWN UNIVERSITY, Department of Linguistics

Degrees Offered: MAT in TESL; MAT in TESL and bilingual education.

Length of Program: 3–4 semesters. Students may be full-time or part-time and may begin their study at the beginning of any semester. Application deadlines are fall semester, February 1; spring semester, October 15; summer semester, February 1.

Program Requirements: 36 credits. Competence in a language other than English is required; English meets the requirement for nonnative speakers of English. Practice teaching and a thesis are required. A comprehensive examination is not required.

Courses Offered: (*required) *General Linguistics; *General Phonology *or* General Syntax *or* Generative Syntax I; *General Semantics *or* Phonology I; *General Semantics *or* Formal Semantics I *or* Pragmatics; *Language Acquisition; *Methodology of Language Teaching; *Language Testing; *Teaching Practicum; *(for MAT in bilingual education) Bilingualism; foreign linguistics; analyses; language history; communications; seminars; materials preparation.

Full-Time Staff: See program description for certificate in TESL or TESL and bilingual education.

Requirements for Admission: The university's requirements for admission are a bachelor's degree with a better-than-B average, including 18–24 semester hours of credit in the proposed field of study; academic credentials indicating the ability to pursue graduate work; letters of recommendation; and transcripts. The program requires a B+ undergraduate average, a professional or academic writing sample showing analytic skills, and knowledge of one nonnative language. Nonnative speakers of English must have a TOEFL score of at least 600.

Tuition, Fees, and Aid: $751 per credit hour. Fees are application, $50 or $55; recreational facility, $94.50. Federal need-based student loans and U.S. Department of Education Title VII traineeships are sometimes available.

General: The program offers a balance between theory and practice through a combination of linguistics, English language, methodology, and foreign language studies, plus some student teaching. The practicum is waived for experienced teachers.

Participants may be eligible for the university's summer session with the Universidad Católica de Ecuador in Quito, studying Spanish linguistics, cross-cultural communication, and immersion in a nonnative culture. Students in the joint Georgetown University–Kawaijuku ESL program may transfer 12 credits to the MAT degree.

The university has an English language program for nonnative speakers of English.

Summer Session: Yes

Further Information: Director, MAT Program
Department of Linguistics
ICC 479
Georgetown University
37th and Q Streets, NW
Washington, DC 20057

Telephone: (202) 687-5956
Fax: (202) 687-7083

◆ GEORGETOWN UNIVERSITY, Department of Linguistics

Degree Offered: PhD in applied linguistics.

Length of Program: 8–10 semesters. Students may be full-time or part-time and may begin their study at the beginning of any semester. Application deadlines are fall semester, February 1; spring semester, October 15; summer semester, February 1.

Program Requirements: 36 credits (30 credits for holders of a master's degree in linguistics from Georgetown University). Competence in a language other than English is required; English meets the requirement for nonnative speakers of English. Students are reviewed in their first or second semester of study for advancement to PhD candidacy. A comprehensive examination and a thesis are required. Practice teaching is optional.

Courses Offered: (*required) *Statistics for Linguistic Research; *Research Design and Methodology *or* Seminar: Research Planning and Preparation; *Language Acquisition; *three seminars, two in applied linguistics; *Syntax; General Phonology; General Morphology; Bilingualism; *foreign language course work; language teaching; program administration; electives in theoretical linguistics, computational linguistics, and sociolinguistics.

Full-Time Staff: See program description for certificate in TESL or TESL and bilingual education.

Requirements for Admission: The university's requirements for admission are a master's degree from an accredited college or university in the same or a related field, academic credentials indicating an ability to pursue further graduate work, letters of recommendation, and transcripts. The program requires an autobiographical statement of purpose and linguistic knowledge of two nonnative languages, at least one of which is known in depth. Nonnative speakers of English must have a TOEFL score of 600 or higher.

Tuition, Fees, and Aid: See program description for MAT in TESL or TESL and bilingual education.

General: The university's applied linguistics program emphasizes using linguistic theory to solve language-related problems in learning and teaching. It asks, "How can theoretical research help to improve teaching?" and "How do language users understand spoken and written texts?"

Participants may be eligible for the university's summer session with the Universidad Católica de Ecuador in Quito, studying Spanish linguistics, cross-cultural communication, and immersion in a nonnative culture.

The university has an English language program for nonnative speakers of English.

Summer Session: Yes

Further Information: Concentration Head, Applied Linguistics
Department of Linguistics
ICC 480
Georgetown University
37th and O Streets, NW
Washington, DC 20057

Telephone: (202) 687-5956
Fax: (202) 687-7083

◆ UNIVERSITY OF GEORGIA, Department of Language Education

Degree Offered: MEd in TESOL.

Length of Program: 4 quarters. Students may be full-time or part-time and may begin their study at the beginning of any quarter. Application deadlines are summer/fall quarters, February 1; spring quarter, November 15; summer quarter, April 1.

Program Requirements: 36 quarter hours. Nine credits of a language other than English are required for native speakers of English. A research project and a portfolio are required. A comprehensive examination is required. Practice teaching is optional.

Courses Offered: (*required) *one course in the social and cognitive foundations of education; *four courses in TESOL curriculum, materials, and methods; *six courses in languages and linguistics; *one course in language research.

Full-Time Staff: Thomas C. Cooper, Joan Kelly Hall, Linda Harklau, Donald Rubin.

Requirements for Admission: For native speakers of English, the program requires at least 6 credits in English, 6 credits in English linguistics, and a combined GRE score of 900 or above. Nonnative speakers of English must have either (a) an undergraduate degree in English, 6 of which must be in English linguistics, and a minimum TOEFL score of 550; or (b) 18 credits in English, 6 of which must be in English linguistics, and a minimum TOEFL score of 600.

Tuition, Fees, and Aid: For in-state students, $1,500 per semester; for out-of-state students, $4,700 per semester. A limited number of graduate assistantships are available to students who apply in the February admissions cycle.

General: The program takes a sociocultural perspective on second language acquisition. It emphasizes learners' development of English language and literacy in classroom contexts. Two tracks (K–12 and adult ESL/EFL) and a broad range of electives in education and linguistics are available to students. With three additional courses, the program leads to a Georgia credential in TESOL.

Ten students completed the program in 1996–1997.

The university has an intensive English language program for nonnative speakers of English.

Summer Session: Yes

Further Information: Linda Harklau
Department of Language Education
125 Aderhold Hall
University of Georgia
Athens, GA 30602

Telephone: (706) 542-5674
Fax: (706) 542-4509
E-mail: lharklau@coe.uga.edu

◆ UNIVERSITY OF GEORGIA, Department of Language Education

Degree Offered: PhD in language education with a specialization in TESOL.

Length of Program: 4 years. Students may be full-time or part-time and must begin their study at the beginning of the fall quarter. The application deadline is February 1.

Program Requirements: 36 quarter hours beyond the master's. Competence in a language other than English is required; English meets the requirement for nonnative speakers of English. A thesis and a comprehensive examination are required. Practice teaching is not required.

Courses Offered: Students must satisfy minimum credit-hour requirements in common core, area of specialization, foundations of education, curriculum and teaching, and research.

Full-Time Staff: See MEd program description.

Requirements for Admission: The program requires a minimum GRE score of 1100, a minimum GPA of 3.0 in undergraduate work, and a minimum GPA of 3.5 in graduate work.

Tuition, Fees, and Aid: See MEd program description.

General: See MEd program description.
   Two students completed the program in 1996–1997.
   The university has an intensive English language program for nonnative speakers of English.

Summer Session: Yes

Further Information: Linda Harklau
                        Department of Language Education
                        125 Aderhold Hall
                        University of Georgia
                        Athens, GA 30602

                        Telephone: (706) 542-5674
                        Fax: (706) 542-4509
                        E-mail: lharklau@coe.uga.edu

◆ GEORGIA STATE UNIVERSITY, Department of Applied Linguistics and ESL

Degree Offered: MS in TESL.

Length of Program: 1½–2 years. Students may be full-time or part-time and may begin their study at the beginning of any semester. Application deadlines are fall semester, June 1; winter semester, October 1; summer semester, March 1.

Program Requirements: 36 semester hours. Native speakers of English must have studied a language other than English; English meets the requirement for nonnative speakers. Practice teaching and a portfolio containing documentation of teaching experience, documentation of professional development, and a master's paper or project are required. A comprehensive examination is not required.

Courses Offered: (*required) *Approaches to Teaching ESL; *English Grammar/Pedagogical Grammar; *Intercultural Communication; *General Linguistics; *Practicum; *Second Language Acquisition; *Sound System of English; Sociolinguistics; Classroom Practices; Second Language Evaluation and Assessment; Second Language Writing; Second Language Reading; Second Language Materials Adaptation and Development; Teaching and Testing Second Language Listening Comprehension.

Full-Time Staff: Patricia H. Byrd, Patricia L. Carrell, Joan C. Carson (chair), Patricia Dunkel, John M. Murphy, Gayle L. Nelson, Sarah Weigle.

Requirements for Admission: The department's requirements for admission are an undergraduate degree from an accredited program, an acceptable and current (within 5 years) GRE score, three letters of recommendation, transcripts, and a statement of professional goals. Nonnative speakers of English must have a minimum TOEFL score of 600.

Tuition, Fees, and Aid: For in-state students, $82.50 per credit hour; for out-of-state students, $247.50 per credit hour. Teaching assistantships are available after students have taken six courses. Graduate research assistantships are available to all full-time students.

General: The program combines theoretical study with practical application. Both theoretical and practical aspects of the program focus on the needs of adolescent and adult learners of ESL/EFL. Atlanta offers graduate students many opportunities for paid and volunteer teaching of ESL.

The university has an intensive English language program for nonnative speakers of English.

Summer Session: Yes

Further Information: Gayle Nelson, Director of Graduate Studies
Department of Applied Linguistics and ESL
Urban Life Building 1026
Georgia State University
Atlanta, GA 30303

Telephone: (404) 651-3650, 2940
Fax: (404) 651-3652
E-mail: gnelson@gsu.edu
http://www.gsu.edu/ ~ wwwesl/alesl

◆ GONZAGA UNIVERSITY, English Language Center

Degree Offered: MA in TESL.

Length of Program: 3 semesters. Students may be full-time or part-time and may begin their study at the beginning of any semester. Application deadlines are fall semester, August 1; winter semester, December 1; summer semester, April 15.

Program Requirements: 30 semester hours. Competence in a language other than English is required; English meets the requirement for nonnative speakers. Practice teaching and either a thesis or a research project are required. A comprehensive examination is not required.

Courses Offered: (*required) *ESL Methods and Materials; *Pedagogical Grammar; *Theories of Communication; *Principles of Second Language Acquisition; *Testing and Evaluation in ESL; *Research Perspectives in Second Language Education; *MA-TESOL Practicum; *Research Thesis *or* Research Project; Multicultural Curriculum Development; Ethnographic Study of Nonnative Communication; Research in Reading and Writing; Technology in Second Language Education; History of the English Language; Communication and Cultural Dissonance; Leadership Theory.

Full-Time Staff: Mary Jeannot (chair), Ronald Harris, James Hunter, Lucia Huntington, Doss Mellon, Marilyn Runyan, Janet Streyer, Dina Tanners.

Requirements for Admission: The university's requirements for admission are a bachelor's degree or the equivalent with a GPA of at least 3.0 or the equivalent, a satisfactory GRE or Miller Analogies Test score, and two letters of recommendation. Nonnative speakers of English must have a minimum TOEFL score of 550. The program requires 2 years of successful university-level study of a foreign language or other satisfactory evidence of foreign language competence.

Tuition, Fees, and Aid: $396 per credit. No financial aid is available.

General: The program, first offered in September 1998, features a 12-week practicum. Theory and practice are integrated rather than sequenced. Relationships with other institutions permit a variety of exchanges.

The university has an intensive English language program for nonnative speakers of English.

Summer Session: No

Further Information: Director, MA-TESOL Program
English Language Center
AD Box 68
Gonzaga University
Spokane, WA 99258

Telephone: (509) 328-4220 extension 6284
Fax: (509) 324-5814
E-mail: fadeley@gonzaga.edu

◆ GOSHEN COLLEGE, Department of English

Degree Offered: BA with a minor in TESOL.

Length of Program: 1 year. Students may be either full-time or part-time and may begin their study at the beginning of any semester. Application deadlines are fall semester, August 15; spring semester, December 15; May term, April 15.

Program Requirements: 20 credit hours. Beginning-level competence in a language other than English is required for native speakers of English; English meets the requirement for nonnative speakers of English. Practice teaching is required. Neither a thesis nor a comprehensive examination is required.

Courses Offered: (*required) *Linguistics; *English Language Problems; *TESOL Methods; *TESOL Field Experience; communications courses, anthropology courses.

Full-Time Staff: Carl Barnett (director), Ervin Beck, Ronald Stutzman.

Requirements for Admission: The university's requirements for admission are graduation from high school in the top half of the class, a minimum GPA of 2.0, and SAT scores of 920 or better. Nonnative English speakers must present a minimum TOEFL score of 550. The program requires sophomore status in college.

Tuition, Fees, and Aid: $5,725 per semester; 3 credits only, $550; 4 credits only, $730. Federal and state aid, academic scholarships, college need-based grants, and on-campus employment are available. Ninety percent of the students receive some form of financial aid.

General: The program helps students acquire both theoretical and practical knowledge and experience in the teaching of English. With 20 years' experience, the program has graduates teaching children and adults all over the world.

Field experience may be pursued outside the United States. Students who want to teach overseas may work with the program director to find a suitable location.

Six students completed the program in 1996–1997.

The college has an intensive English language program for nonnative speakers of English.

Summer Session: Yes

Further Information: Carl Barnett
English Department
Goshen College
1700 South Main Street
Goshen, IN 46526

Telephone: (219) 535-7535, (800) 348-7422
Fax: (219) 535-7609
E-mail: carleb@goshen.edu

◆ GOSHEN COLLEGE, Department of English

Degree Offered: 1-year certificate in TESOL.

Length of Program: 1 year. Students may be either full-time or part-time and may begin their study at the beginning of any semester. Application deadlines are fall semester, August 15; spring semester, December 15; May term, April 15.

Program Requirements: 30 credit hours. Beginning-level competence in a language other than English is required; English meets the requirement for nonnative speakers of English. Practice teaching is required. Neither a thesis nor a comprehensive examination is required.

Courses Offered: (*required) See program description for BA with a minor in TESOL; *any Bible or religion course.

Full-Time Staff: See program description for BA with a minor in TESOL.

Requirements for Admission: See program description for BA with a minor in TESOL.

Tuition, Fees, and Aid: See program description for BA with a minor in TESOL.

General: See program description for BA with a minor in TESOL.
Three students completed the program in 1996–1997.

Summer Session: Yes

Further Information: Carl Barnett
English Department
Goshen College
1700 South Main Street
Goshen, IN 46526

Telephone: (219) 535-7535, (800) 348-7422
Fax: (219) 535-7609
E-mail: carleb@goshen.edu

◆ GOSHEN COLLEGE, Department of English

Degree Offered: State teaching endorsement in ESL.

Length of Program: 1 year. Application deadlines are fall semester, August 15; spring semester, December 15; May term, April 15.

Program Requirements: 34 credit hours. Beginning-level competence in a language other than English is required; English meets the requirement for nonnative speakers of English. Practice teaching is required. Neither a thesis nor a comprehensive examination is required.

Courses Offered: (*required) See program description for BA with a minor in TESOL. *Developmental Reading; *Reading in Content Areas; *Reading Problems; *Children's Literature.

Full-Time Staff: See program description for BA with a minor in TESOL.

Requirements for Admission: See program description for BA with a minor in TESOL.

Tuition, Fees, and Aid: See program description for BA with a minor in TESOL.

General: See program description for BA with a minor in TESOL.
Two students completed the program in 1996–1997.

Summer Session: Yes

Further Information: Carl Barnett
English Department
Goshen College
1700 South Main Street
Goshen, IN 46526

Telephone: (219) 535-7535; (800) 348-7422
Fax: (219) 535-7609
E-mail: carleb@goshen.edu

◆ GRAND CANYON UNIVERSITY, College of Education

Degree Offered: MA with a major in TESL.

Length of Program: 4 semesters. Students may be full-time or part-time and may begin their study at the beginning of any semester. Applications are considered continuously.

Program Requirements: 38 semester hours. The equivalent of 6 hours of a language other than English is required for native speakers of English; English meets the requirement for nonnative speakers. A teaching internship required. A thesis is optional. A comprehensive examination is not required.

Courses Offered: (*required) *Language and Culture; *English Linguistics; *English Language Teaching: Foundations and Methodology; *Advanced Grammar for English Language Teaching; *Advanced Language Teaching: Methodologies and Assessment; *Language Teaching: Curriculum and Materials Design; *Internship in TESL; *Psychological Issues; *Curriculum Issues and Innovations *or* Philosophical/Social Issues (both required for certification track).

Full-Time Staff: Patricia Bringaze, Janet Johnson, Bethyl Pearson (coordinator).

Requirements for Admission: The university's requirement for admission is an undergraduate GPA of at least 2.8. The program requires a GRE or Miller Analogies Test score (waived for applicants with a GPA of at least 3.0), a current teaching certificate (for certification track), and three references. A TOEFL score of 575 is required for nonnative speakers of English.

Tuition, Fees, and Aid: $289 per credit. Graduate fellowships are available.

General: The program has a certification track (leading to an Arizona credential in TESOL) and a noncertification track. Practicum experience is offered in kindergarten through adult education contexts.
Three students completed the program in 1996–1997.
The program has an intensive English language program for nonnative speakers of English.

Summer Session: Yes

Further Information: Prof. Bethyl A. Pearson
College of Education
Grand Canyon University
3300 West Camelback Road
Phoenix, AZ 85308

Telephone: (602) 589-2747
Fax: (602) 589-2447
E-mail: bpearso@grcanuniv.k12.az.us

◆ HAMLINE UNIVERSITY, Graduate Education, Second Language Teaching and Learning

Degree Offered: First state licensure in ESL (postbaccalaureate).

Length of Program: Variable. Students may be full-time or part-time and may begin their study at the beginning of any quarter. Application deadlines are fall quarter, August 1; winter quarter, December 1; summer quarter, May 1.

Program Requirements: Competence in a language other than English is required; English meets the requirement for nonnative speakers of English. Practice teaching and a portfolio assessment are required. Neither a thesis nor a comprehensive examination is required.

Courses Offered: (*required) *The Ethnography of Language; *Introduction to Linguistics; *Basics of Modern English for ESL Teachers; *Second Language Acquisition; *Development of Literacy Skills; *Special Methods in ESL; *Language and Society; *The History and Pattern of English; *Introduction to Teaching; *Educational Psychology; *Education and Cultural Diversity; *Literacy in the Middle and High School; *Exceptionality in the Classroom; *Teaching in the Secondary School; *Personal and Community Health; *Practicum Seminar; *Practicum.

Full-Time Staff: Kathryn Heinze, Ann Mabbott (chair), Betsy Parrish, Julia Reimer, Colleen Bell, Steven Jongewaard, George Redman, Sandra Tutweiler, Dwight Watson.

Requirements for Admission: The university's requirement for admission is a bachelor's degree with a GPA of 2.5. The program requires an essay and a letter of recommendation.

Tuition, Fees, and Aid: $200 per quarter credit. Loans are available.

General: This program provides both the education and the ESL course work required for ESL teacher licensure, K–12. Equivalencies are granted for previous work. Some courses are offered on-line.

Ten students completed the program in 1996–1997.

The university has an intensive English language program for nonnative speakers of English.

Summer Session: Yes

Further Information: Program Assistant
Second Language Teaching and Learning
Hamline University
1536 Hewitt Avenue
Saint Paul, MN 55104

Telephone: (612) 523-2964
Fax: (612) 523-2489
E-mail: amabbott@gw.hamline.edu

◆ HAMLINE UNIVERSITY, Graduate Education, Second Language Teaching and Learning

Degree Offered: Second state licensure in ESL.

Length of Program: Variable. Students may be full-time or part-time and may begin their study at the beginning of any quarter. Rolling admissions are in effect.

Program Requirements: 40 quarter credits. Two years of high school or 1 year of college courses in a language other than English is required; English meets the requirement for nonnative speakers of English. Practice teaching and a portfolio assessment are required. Neither a thesis nor a comprehensive examination is required.

Courses Offered: (*required) *Introduction to Linguistics; *Basics of Modern English for ESL Teachers; *Language and Society; *The History and Pattern of English; *Second Language Acquisition; *Introduction to ESL Methods; *Development of Literacy Skills; *The Ethnography of Language; *Human Relations and Cross-Cultural Communication; *Practicum Seminar; *Practicum.

Full-Time Staff: Kathryn Heinze, Ann Mabbott (chair), Betsy Parrish, Julia Reimer.

Requirements for Admission: The university's requirement for admission is a bachelor's degree with a GPA of 2.5. The program requires first licensure in K–12.

Tuition, Fees, and Aid: $125 per quarter credit. Loans are available.

General: This program prepares participants to teach ESL in K–12 schools. Individualized learning programs are developed for each participant through a portfolio process. Some courses are offered on-line.

Forty students completed the program in 1996–1997.

The university has an intensive English language program for nonnative speakers of English.

Summer Session: Yes

Further Information: Program Assistant
Second Language Teaching and Learning
Hamline University
1536 Hewitt Avenue
Saint Paul, MN 55104

Telephone: (612) 523-2964
Fax: (612) 523-2489
E-mail: amabbott@gw.hamline.edu

◆ HAMLINE UNIVERSITY, Graduate Education, Second Language Teaching and Learning

Degree Offered: Bilingual/bicultural state endorsement.

Length of Program: Variable. Students may be full-time or part-time and may begin their study at the beginning of any quarter. Rolling admissions are in effect.

Program Requirements: 30 quarter credits. Competence in a language other than English is required; English meets the requirement for nonnative speakers of English. Practice teaching and a portfolio assessment are required. Neither a thesis nor a comprehensive examination is required.

Courses Offered: (*required) *Introduction to Linguistics; *Second Language Acquisition; *Testing and Evaluation of ESL Students; *Development of Literacy Skills; *Principles of Bilingual Education; *Methods and Materials of Bilingual Education.

Full-Time Staff: Kathryn Heinze, Ann Mabbott (chair), Betsy Parrish, Julia Reimer.

Requirements for Admission: The university's requirement for admission is a bachelor's degree with a GPA of 2.5. The program requires first licensure in K–12 and fluency in English and another language.

Tuition, Fees, and Aid: $125 per quarter credit. Loans are available.

General: This program prepares elementary and secondary teachers to teach in a bilingual setting. Assessment of previous experience occurs through a portfolio process. Some courses are offered on-line.

Three students completed the program in 1996–1997.

The university has an intensive English language program for nonnative speakers of English.

Summer Session: Yes

Further Information: Program Assistant
Second Language Teaching and Learning
Hamline University
1536 Hewitt Avenue
Saint Paul, MN 55104

Telephone: (612) 523-2964
Fax: (612) 523-2489
E-mail: amabbott@gw.hamline.edu

◆ HAMLINE UNIVERSITY, Graduate Education, Second Language Teaching and Learning

Degree Offered: Certificate for teachers of adult ESL.

Length of Program: Students are part-time only and may begin their study at the beginning of any term. There are no application deadlines.

Program Requirements: 12 credits. Competence in a language other than English is optional. Neither practice teaching, nor a thesis, nor a comprehensive examination is required.

Courses Offered: One 2-credit course is offered per term: *Introduction to the Adult Limited English Proficient Student; *Building Reading and Writing Skills With Adult Learners; *Teaching English to the Adult Learner: Oral Skills; *Course Design for Adult ESL Classes; *The Assessment of Adult ESL Students; What Works in Adult ESL Education; An Introduction to Hmong Culture and Language; An Introduction to Hispanic Culture; other electives.

Full-Time Staff: Ann Mabbott, Betsy Parrish (coordinator), Julia Reimer.

Requirements for Admission: The university's requirement for admission is a bachelor's degree.

Tuition, Fees, and Aid: $225 per course.

General: This certificate is intended for practicing teachers working with adult ESL learners.

The university has an intensive English language program for nonnative speakers of English.

Summer Session: Yes

Further Information: Betsy Parrish, Coordinator
Adult Certificate Programs
Graduate Education
195 Drew Hall
Hamline University
1536 Hewitt Avenue
Saint Paul, MN 55104

Telephone: (612) 523-2853
Fax: (612) 523-2489
E-mail: bparrish@gw.hamline.edu

◆ HAMLINE UNIVERSITY, Graduate Education, Second Language Teaching and Learning

Degree Offered: TEFL certificate.

Length of Program: One-month, 10-week, and 6-month courses are offered. Application deadlines are September–March evenings, June 20; January–March 10-week, October 20; April intensive, February 15; July and August intensives, April 20.

Program Requirements: Competence in a language other than English is preferred for native English-speaking students. Practice teaching and a comprehensive examination are required. A thesis is not required.

Courses Offered: Participants attend an entire session as a cohort. Topics include lesson planning; practice techniques; classroom management; teaching reading, writing, speaking, and listening; English for special purposes; phonetics; and language awareness.

Full-Time Staff: Betsy Parrish (coordinator), Kathryn Heinze, Julia Reimer.

Requirements for Admission: A bachelor's degree is preferred, and it is required for those seeking graduate credit.

Tuition, Fees, and Aid: $1,960 per 1-month intensive; $2,280 per 6-month and 10-week program. Loans are available.

General: The certificate is internationally recognized. Graduates are teaching in over 25 countries. The emphasis is on teaching adults overseas.

Seventy-two students completed the program in 1996–1997.

The university has an intensive English language program for nonnative speakers of English.

Summer Session: Yes

Further Information: Betsy Parrish, Coordinator
TEFL Certificate Program
Graduate Education
195 Drew Hall
Hamline University
1536 Hewitt Avenue
Saint Paul, MN 55104

Telephone: (800) 888-2182; (612) 523-2853
Fax: (612) 523-2489
E-mail: bparrish@gw.hamline.edu

◆ HAWAI'I, UNIVERSITY OF, AT MANOA, Department of ESL

Degrees Offered: BA in liberal studies with a specialization in ESL; BEd in ESL.

Length of Program: Students may be full-time or part-time and may begin their study at the beginning of any semester. Application deadlines are fall semester, December 1–May 1; spring semester, June 1–November 1.

Program Requirements: Competence in a language other than English is required for native speakers of English. Neither practice teaching, nor a thesis, nor a comprehensive examination is required.

Courses Offered: Second Language Learning; Second Language Teaching; Techniques in TESOL: Reading and Writing; Techniques in TESOL: Listening and Speaking; Bilingual Education; Pidgin and Creole English in Hawai'i; Language Concepts for ESL; English Phonology; Second Language Testing.

Full-Time Staff: Robert Bley-Vroman, J. D. Brown, Craig Chaudron, Graham Crookes, Kathryn A. Davis, Richard R. Day, D. Eades, Thom Hudson, Roderick Jacobs (chair), Gabriele Kasper, Michael H. Long, Richard W. Schmidt, Kathryn Wolfe-Quintero.

Requirements for Admission: The university's requirements for admission are a minimum GPA of B–B +, graduation in the upper 40% of the high school graduating class for Hawai'i residents, and SAT or ACT scores.

Tuition, Fees, and Aid: For in-state students, $1,512 per semester; for out-of-state students, $4,752 per semester. Fees are $55. Some university work-study is available.

General: Although the Department of ESL does not offer a bachelor's degree, undergraduates may elect to have an ESL emphasis in their program of study through either the BA program in liberal studies or the BEd program in ESL. In the liberal studies option, students construct their own undergraduate major equivalent with the guidance of an ESL faculty member. In the BEd option, students follow a program set by the Department of Curriculum and Instruction of the College of Education.

Sixteen students completed the programs in 1996–1997.

The university has an intensive English language program for nonnative speakers of English.

Summer Session: Yes

Further Information: Liberal Studies in ESL Advisor
Department of ESL
Moore Hall, Room 570
University of Hawai'i at Manoa
1890 East-West Road
Honolulu, HI 96822

Telephone: (808) 948-8610
Fax: (808) 956-2802

◆ HAWAI'I, UNIVERSITY OF, AT MANOA, Department of ESL

Degrees Offered: MA in ESL.

Length of Program: 4 semesters. Students may be full-time or part-time and must begin their study at the beginning of the fall semester. The application deadline is March 1.

Program Requirements: 39 credits. Competence in a language other than English is required. Practice teaching is required. A thesis is optional. A comprehensive examination is not required.

Courses Offered: (*required) *Language Concepts for ESL; *Second Language Testing; *Introduction to Second Language Studies; *English Syntax; *Second Language Acquisition; *Sociolinguistics and ESL; *ESL Teaching Practicum; *TESL; Seminar in ESL; Seminar in Second Language Acquisition; Seminar in Second Language Use; Bilingual Education; Pidgin and Creole English in Hawai'i; English Phonology; Innovative Approaches to ESL; ESL Listening and Speaking; ESL Writing; Instructional Media; ESL Reading; Program Development in ESL; Comparative Grammar and Second Language Acquisition; Second Language Research Methods; Research in Language Testing; Second Language Classroom Research; Applied Psycholinguistics and Second Language Acquisition; Micro Analysis in Second Language Research; Second Language Learning; Second Language Analysis;

Second Language Pedagogy; Second Language Research; Second Language Use; Directed Reading/Research; Thesis Research.

Full-Time Staff: Robert Bley-Vroman, J. D. Brown, Craig Chaudron, Graham Crookes, Kathryn Davis, Richard R. Day, Diana Eades, Thom Hudson, Roderick Jacobs (chair), Gabriele Kasper, Michael H. Long, Richard W. Schmidt, Kathryn Wolfe-Quintero.

Requirements for Admission: The university's requirements for admission are a minimum GPA of 3.0 and a GRE score (a TOEFL score for nonnative speakers of English). The program requires high scores and grades and a writing sample.

Tuition, Fees, and Aid: For in-state students, $2,016 per semester; for out-of-state students, $4,980 per semester. Fees are $55. Financial aid has traditionally been strong.

General: The MA program has been in existence since 1961, and the Department of ESL, the first and still the largest such department at a U.S. university, was established in 1968. The MA program strives to maintain a balance between theoretical and practical concerns by requiring courses that are concerned with linguistic, psychological, and sociocultural aspects of language as well as those which treat the methodological and practical aspects of language learning and teaching. By stressing the interdependence of theory and practice, the program cultivates in students the intellectual basis for an understanding of principles that will help guide them in their future careers. The department has attained top-ranked recognition as a result of the diverse expertise and professional activities of its faculty, the breadth and depth of its curriculum, and its research productivity.

Nineteen students completed the program in 1996–1997.

The university has an intensive language program for nonnative speakers of English.

Summer Session: Yes

Further Information: Chair
Department of ESL
Moore Hall 570
University of Hawai'i at Manoa
1890 East-West Road
Honolulu, HI 96822

Telephone: (808) 948-2786
Fax: (808) 956-2802
http://www.lll.hawaii.edu.esl

◆ HAWAI'I, UNIVERSITY OF, AT MANOA, Department of ESL

Degree Offered: PhD in second language acquisition.

Length of Program: 6–8 semesters. Students must be full-time and must begin their study at the beginning of the fall semester. The deadline for application is March 1.

Program Requirements: 3 semesters of residency. Competence in two foreign languages is required. A dissertation, qualifying examinations in four areas, and comprehensive examinations in three areas are required. Practice teaching is not required.

Courses Offered: (*required) *At least two graduate courses in three of the four program subfields: second language analysis, second language use, second language learning, and second language pedagogy; *two courses in research methods.

Full-Time Staff: David Ashworth, Frederick Bail, Ann Bayer, Jacob M. Bilmes, Robert Bley-Vroman (chair), J. D. Brown, Craig Chaudron, Haruko Cook, Graham Crookes, Kathryn Davis, Richard R. Day, Diana Eades, Thom Hudson, Roderick Jacobs, Gabriele Kasper, Ying-Che Li, Michael H. Long, Raymond Moody, William O'Grady, Ann Peters, Teresita Ramos, Kenneth Rehg, Herbert Roitblat, Richard W. Schmidt, Kathryn Wolfe-Quintero, Shuqiang Zhang.

Requirements for Admission: The requirements for admission are completion of an MA in ESL, applied linguistics, second or foreign language education, or a related discipline with appropriate course work; a GRE score; a statement of purpose; and strong evidence of research potential.

Tuition, Fees, and Aid: See program description for MA in ESL.

General: See program description for MA in ESL. The goal of the program is to promote significant doctoral-level research into major areas of second language acquisition and use, such as how second languages are learned, how they should be taught, and what psychological and sociological factors influence their acquisition. Other areas of research include language styles and dialect variation. Knowledge in this field has a significant impact on such matters as proficiency assessment, program organization, teaching methodologies, legal and social policy issues concerning language, and the understanding of the nature of language.

The university has an intensive language program for nonnative speakers of English.

Summer Session: No

Further Information: Chair, Program in Second Language Acquisition
Department of ESL
Moore Hall 570
University of Hawai'i at Manoa
1890 East-West Road
Honolulu, HI 96822

Telephone: (808) 948-2786
Fax: (808) 956-2802
http://www.lll.hawaii.edu.esl

◆ HAWAII PACIFIC UNIVERSITY, Department of TESL

Degree Offered: BA with a major in TESL.

Length of Program: 8 semesters. Students may be full-time or part-time and may begin their study at the beginning of any semester. Rolling admissions are in effect.

Program Requirements: 124 semester hours. Four semesters (or courses through the intermediate level) of a language other than English are required for native speakers of English; nonnative speakers must take one course in a new language. Practice teaching is required. Neither a thesis nor a comprehensive examination is required.

Courses Offered: (*required) *Introduction to Linguistics; *Phonetics and English Phonology; *English Syntax; *Methods, Materials, Testing: Spoken English; *Methods, Materials, Testing: Written English; *Psycholinguistics; *Sociolinguistics; *Language Classroom Experience; *Practice Teaching; Semantics; History of the English Language; ESL Evaluation Methods; Methods of Teaching Writing in ESL; Technology in the Language Classroom; Selected Topics in Applied Linguistics; Translation and Second Language Acquisition.

Full-Time Staff: Jean Coffman, Kenneth Cook, Irene Gordon, Jean Kirschenmann, Edward F. Klein (chair), Teresa Lane, Carol Perrin.

Requirements for Admission: The university's requirement for admission is a high school diploma with a minimum GPA of 2.5. The program requires completion of English Composition and Introduction to Linguistics with a grade of at least C.

Tuition, Fees, and Aid: $3,750 per semester, or $135 per credit. Federal, state, and private financial aid is available.

General: The university is by far the largest independent college or university in Hawaii. Its English Foundations Program, in which TESL majors do their language classroom experience and practice teaching, is one of the largest ESL programs in the United States and enrolls students from over 40 different nations. TESL courses are offered both during the day and in the evening. The major is very practically oriented, and graduates have been very successful at finding positions.

The university has several exchange programs in place with Japanese universities.

Twelve students completed the program in 1996–1997.

The university has an intensive English language program for nonnative speakers of English.

Summer Session: Yes

Further Information: Edward F. Klein
Department of TESL
MP-132
Hawaii Pacific University
1188 Fort Street Mall
Honolulu, HI 96813

Telephone: (808) 544-0275
Fax: (808) 544-1142
E-mail: eklein@hpu.edu

◆ HAWAII PACIFIC UNIVERSITY, Department of TESL

Degree Offered: TESL certificate.

Length of Program: 2 semesters minimum. Students may be full-time or part-time and may begin their study at the beginning of any semester. Rolling admissions are in effect.

Program Requirements: 24 semester hours. Competence in a language other than English is not required. Practice teaching is required. Neither a thesis nor a comprehensive examination is required.

Courses Offered: (*required) *Introduction to Linguistics; *Phonetics and English Phonology; *English Syntax; *Methods, Materials, Testing: Spoken English *or* Methods, Materials, Testing: Written English; *Language Classroom Experience; *Practice Teaching; Semantics; History of the English Language; Sociolinguistics; Psycholinguistics; Methods of Teaching Writing in ESL; Technology in the Language Classroom; Selected Topics in Applied Linguistics; Translation and Second Language Acquisition.

Full-Time Staff: See program description for BA in TESL.

Requirements for Admission: The program's requirement for admission is an undergraduate degree from an accredited institution. Nonnative speakers of English not exiting a U.S. institution must have a TOEFL score of 550 and a TWE score of 5 or must finish the university's ESL program and complete English Composition.

Tuition, Fees, and Aid: See program description for BA in TESL.

General: The university has one of the largest ESL programs in the United States, the English Foundations Program (EFP), in which TESL students do their language classroom experience and practice teaching. EFP students come from over 40 different countries. TESL courses are offered both during the day and in the evening. The program has been developed to provide a very practical teacher education, and graduates have been successful at finding positions, especially in Asia. The university is located in a vibrant part of the semitropical city of Honolulu.

The university has several exchange programs in place with Japanese universities. Fifteen students completed the program in 1996–1997.

The university has an intensive English language program for nonnative speakers of English.

Summer Session: Yes

Further Information: Edward F. Klein
Department of TESL
MP-132
Hawaii Pacific University
1188 Fort Street Mall
Honolulu, HI 96813

Telephone: (808) 544-0275
Fax: (808) 544-1142
E-mail: eklein@hpu.edu

◆ HOBE SOUND BIBLE COLLEGE, Missions Department

Degree Offered: Minor in TESOL.

Length of Program: 4 years. Students may be either full-time or part-time and may begin their study at the beginning of any semester. There are no application deadlines for U.S. citizens; for non-U.S. applicants, the deadline is March 1 for the fall semester.

Program Requirements: 18 credit hours. Competence in a language other than English is not required. Neither practice teaching, nor a thesis, nor a comprehensive examination is required.

Courses Offered: A missions major may choose 18 hours in TESOL for a minor or professional concentration.

Full-Time Staff: Joy Budensiek (chair), Ignacio Palacios, interdepartmental staff.

Requirements for Admission: The college's requirements for admission are an SAT or ACT score; graduation from high school (or GED diploma); and transcripts showing at least 4 units in English, 3 units in science, 3 units in mathematics, 3 units in social studies, and additional units in electives. For those who are not U.S. citizens, the program requires proof of proficiency in English, transcripts of secondary or previous university-level work, and proof of financial responsibility.

Tuition, Fees, and Aid: $1,970 per 12–17 hours. For U.S. citizens, Pell grants, Federal Family Education Loans, federal SEOC, and work study are available.

General: This program is ideal professional preparation for missionaries within a conservative Christian college atmosphere with a strong biblical foundation. Opportunities for work and ministry with internationals in South Florida are available, as are short-term summer missions around the world.

The college has an intensive English language program for nonnative speakers of English.

Summer Session: No

Further Information: Admissions Director
Hobe Sound Bible College
PO Box 1065
Hobe Sound, FL 33275

Telephone: (561) 546-5534
Fax: (561) 545-1422
E-mail: HSBCUWIN@aol.com

◆ HOBE SOUND BIBLE COLLEGE, Department of Christian Teacher Education

Degree Offered: BA in TESOL.

Length of Program: 8 semesters. Students may be either full-time or part-time and may begin their study at the beginning of any semester. There are no application deadlines for U.S. citizens; for non-U.S. applicants, the deadline is March 1 for the fall semester.

Program Requirements: 128 credit hours. Competence in a language other than English is not required. Practical training in tutorials or observations are required throughout the program. Neither a thesis nor a comprehensive examination is required.

Courses Offered:(*required) *Theory in TESOL; *Methods in TESOL; *Descriptive Linguistics; *Grammar for TESOL I and II; *Language and Culture *or* Cultural Communication; *Practicum in TESOL; *Advanced Composition; *English Literature; *American Literature; *30 hours in Bible and theology; *39 hours in general studies; *22 hours in professional education.

Full-Time Staff: Ignacio Palacios, interdepartmental staff.

Requirements for Admission: See program description for minor in TESOL.

Tuition, Fees, and Aid: See program description for minor in TESOL.

General: The major is designed to prepare Christian teachers, both U.S. and non-U.S., to teach ESL/EFL to child and adult speakers of other languages within a conservative Christian college atmosphere with a strong biblical foundation. Opportunities are available for tutorials and a practicum with international students and Spanish-speaking residents. The program leads to a Florida credential in TESOL.

One student completed the program in 1996–1997.

The college has an intensive English language program for nonnative speakers of English.

Summer Session: No

Further Information: Admissions Director
Hobe Sound Bible College
PO Box 1065
Hobe Sound, FL 33275

Telephone: (561) 546-5534
Fax: (561) 545-1422
E-mail: HSBCUWIN@aol.com

◆ HOBE SOUND BIBLE COLLEGE, Department of General Christian Studies

Degree Offered: BA in Bible–Christian studies with a concentration in TESOL.

Length of Program: 8 semesters. Students may be either full-time or part-time and may begin their study at the beginning of any semester. There are no application deadlines for U.S. citizens; for non-U.S. applicants, the deadline is March 1 for the fall semester.

Program Requirements: 128 credit hours. Competence in a language other than English is not required. Neither practice teaching, nor a thesis, nor a comprehensive examination is required.

Courses Offered: Students choose 30 hours of TESOL courses or other possible Christian studies courses in consultation with their adviser.

Full-Time Staff: Ignacio Palacios, interdepartmental staff.

Requirements for Admission: See program description for minor in TESOL.

Tuition, Fees, and Aid: See program description for minor in TESOL.

General: This program provides and in-depth understanding of the Bible, the broad range of a general education with a Christian world view, and a major in TESOL. A practicum is an option in this major. Opportunities for tutorials with international students are available.

Six students completed the program in 1996–1997.

The college has an intensive English language program for nonnative speakers of English.

Summer Session: No

Further Information: Admissions Director
Hobe Sound Bible College
PO Box 1065
Hobe Sound, FL 33275

Telephone: (561) 546-5534
Fax: (561) 545-1422
E-mail: HSBCUWIN@aol.com

◆ HOFSTRA UNIVERSITY, Department of Curriculum and Teaching

Degrees Offered: MS in education: TESL.

Length of Program: 3 semesters. Students may be full-time or part-time and may begin their study at the beginning of any semester. Revolving admissions are in effect.

Program Requirements: 36 semester hours. Competence in a language other than English is required; English meets the requirement for nonnative speakers of English. Practice teaching is required. A thesis is optional. A comprehensive examination is not required.

Courses Offered: (*required) *The Learner and the School; *TESL (K–8); *Teaching English to Adolescent and Adult Speakers of Other Languages; *Approaches to English Grammar; *Second Language Acquisition; *Reading, Writing, and Cognition; *Testing and Evaluation of Bilingual Students; *Internship Practicum; electives in language and culture.

Full-Time Staff: Nancy L. Cloud, Mustafa Masrour, Scott Harschbarger, Cynthia McAllister.

Requirements for Admission: The university's requirements for admission are a baccalaureate degree from an accredited college or university with an undergraduate GPA of 2.5 or higher and letters of recommendation. The program requires 12 semester hours of foreign language study at the college level.

Tuition, Fees, and Aid: $429 per credit. Fees are $107. Limited departmental scholarships are available.

General: The program, which leads to a New York State credential in TESOL, provides many opportunities to be in classrooms (field experiences) before student teaching.

Twenty students completed the program in 1996–1997.

The university has an intensive English language program for nonnative speakers of English.

Summer Session: Yes

Further Information: Dr. Nancy L. Cloud
Department of Curriculum and Teaching
243 Gallon Wing, Mason Hall
Hofstra University
Hempstead, NY 11549

Telephone: (516) 463-5768, 5769
Fax: (516) 463-6503
E-mail: catnlc@hofstra.edu

◆ HOUSTON, UNIVERSITY OF, Department of Curriculum and Instruction

Degree Offered: MEd in TESL.

Length of Program: 3 semesters. Students may be full-time or part-time and may begin their study at the beginning of any semester. Application deadlines are fall semester, July 7; spring semester, December 1; summer semester, April 7.

Program Requirements: 36 semester hours. Competence in a language other than English is not required but strongly encouraged. Practice teaching or evidence of teaching experience, and a comprehensive examination, are required. A thesis is not required.

Courses Offered: (*required) *Instructional Evaluation; *Principles of Curriculum Development; *Principles of Human Learning; *Educational Principles of Second Language Acquisition; *Techniques of Second Language Teaching; *Instructional Design in Second Language Education; *Descriptive and Contrastive Linguistics; at least four electives.

Full-Time Staff: Irma Guadarrama, Yolanda Padron, Henry Trueba, Kip Téllez (coordinator).

Requirements for Admission: Admission is based on GPA in previous graduate work, GRE score, and, for international students, TOEFL score.

Tuition, Fees, and Aid: For in-state students, $504 per 9 semester hours (three courses); for out-of-state students, $2,214 per 9 semester hours (three courses). Fees are $350. Occasional teaching and research assistantships are available.

General: The program has a strong focus on K–12 English learners, both U.S. and international, and leads to a Texas credential in TESOL.

Limited international field experience is available.

Twenty-five students completed the program in 1996–1997.

The university has an intensive English language program for nonnative speakers of English.

Summer Session: Yes

Further Information: Kip Téllez
Department of Curriculum and Instruction
Farish Hall
University of Houston
4800 Calhoun
Houston, TX 77204-5872

Telephone: (713) 743-4968
Fax: (713) 743-4990
E-mail: ktellez@uh.edu

◆ HOUSTON, UNIVERSITY OF, Department of Curriculum and Instruction

Degree Offered: EdD.

Length of Program: 6 semesters. Students may be full-time or part-time and may begin their study at the beginning of any semester. Application deadlines are fall semester, July 7; spring semester, December 1; summer semester, April 7.

Program Requirements: 66 semester hours. Competence in a language other than English is strongly encouraged. A dissertation, a comprehensive examination, and evidence of teaching experience are required. Practice teaching is not required.

Courses Offered: (*required) *Five of the following: Educational Principles of Second Language Acquisition, Techniques of Second Language Teaching, Instructional Design in Second Language Education, Teaching the Language Minority Student, Principles and Issues in Multilingual Education, Research in Second Language Acquisition, Theoretical Models of Multilingual Education, Survey of Research in Multilingual Education; *18 semester hours of research; electives in linguistics and cultural studies.

Full-Time Staff: See program description for MEd in TESL.

Requirements for Admission: See program description for MEd in TESL.

Tuition, Fees, and Aid: For in-state students, $504 per 9 semester hours (three courses); for out-of-state students, $2,214 per 9 semester hours (three courses). Fees are $350. Research fellowships are often available.

General: The program has a strong focus on culturally diverse English learners in the United States and throughout the Western hemisphere. It is also specialized for EFL in elementary school.

Five students completed the program in 1996–1997.

The university has an intensive English language program for nonnative speakers of English.

Summer Session: Yes

Further Information: Kip Téllez
Department of Curriculum and Instruction
Fairish Hall 256
University of Houston
4800 Calhoun
Houston, TX 77204-5872

Telephone: (713) 743-4968
Fax: (713) 743-4990
E-mail: ktellez@uh.edu

◆ HOUSTON, UNIVERSITY OF, Department of English

Degree Offered: MA in applied English linguistics.

Length of Program: 4 semesters. Students may be full-time or part-time and may begin their study at the beginning of any semester. Application deadlines are fall semester, February 1; spring semester, November 1.

Program Requirements: 36 semester hours. Competence in a language other than English is required for native speakers of English. Either a thesis or a master's examination is required. Practice teaching is not required.

Courses Offered: (*required) *Syntax; *Phonology; *Sociolinguistics; *Theories of ESL; *Background Studies in Language Acquisition *or* Second Language Acquisition; *Linguistic Bases of Materials Development; *Language Assessment; General Linguistics; Descriptive and Contrastive Linguistics; History of the English Language; First Language Acquisition; Discourse Analysis; Computers in Composition; Applied Phonology.

Full-Time Staff: Harmon S. Boertien (chair), Marianne Cooley, Peter J. Gingiss, Dudley W. Reynolds, Thomas M. Woodell II.

Requirements for Admission: The university's requirements for admission are a bachelor's degree from an accredited institution with an overall GPA of 3.0 or higher in the last 60 hours of course credit and a GPA of at least 3.0 in the discipline, and an acceptable score on the GRE General Test. The program requires a minimum of 18 semester hours in literature, writing, or linguistics, at least 12 hours of which must be upper division, with at least a 3.0 GPA; of the 12 upper-division credits, 6–9 in linguistics (may be taken in residence); at least 12 semester hours in a single foreign language or demonstration of a reading knowledge of a single foreign language; a statement of intent; three letters of recommendation; and official transcripts of all academic work. Nonnative speakers of English must have a TOEFL score of 620 and a passing score on the department's English proficiency exam.

Tuition, Fees, and Aid: For in-state students, $720 per semester (12 hours); for out-of-state students, $2,976 per semester. Fees are $564.50. A limited number of teaching assistantships are available.

General: Building on the rich, multicultural environment of the Houston metropolitan area, the program combines foundation courses in general and theoretical linguistics with practical courses on the acquisition and teaching of ESL. The program leads to a state ESL endorsement.

Four students completed the program in 1996–1997.

The university has an intensive English language program for nonnative speakers of English.

Summer Session: Yes

Further Information: Dr. Dudley W. Reynolds
Department of English
Roy G. Cullen Building 205
University of Houston
Houston, TX 77204-3012

Telephone: (713) 743-2946
Fax: (713) 743-3215
E-mail: Dreynolds@uh.edu

◆ HOUSTON–CLEAR LAKE, UNIVERSITY OF, Studies in Language and Culture

Degree Offered: MS in multicultural studies with an ESL endorsement.

Length of Program: 2 years including summers. Students may be full-time or part-time and may begin their study at the beginning of any semester. Deadlines for application are summer semester, March 1; fall semester, June 1; spring semester, October 1.

Program Requirements: 36 semester hours. Competence in a language other than English is not required. One year of teaching in an approved ESL classroom is required for state certification. A thesis or master's project is required. A comprehensive examination is not required.

Courses Offered: (*required) *Developing Skills for Transcultural Communication; *Applications of Technology; *Statistics and Measurement; *Research Design and Analysis; *Second Language Teaching; *Applied Linguistics; Language Skills of Culturally Different Learners; *Models of Language; *Thesis or Project; Social and Cultural Diversity in Schools and Communities; Understanding Issues of Diversity; Research.

Full-Time Staff: Andrea Bermudez, Judith Márquez (chair), Laurie Weaver.

Requirements for Admission: The university's requirements for admission are a bachelor's degree, a GRE or Miller Analogies Test score, and a GPA of 3.0 in the last 60 hours of course work.

Tuition, Fees, and Aid: For in-state students, $240 per 3-hour course; for out-of-state students, $744 per 3-hour course. Fees are $203.50. Scholarships are available.

General: The program emphasizes teaching ESL in a public school setting and leads to a Texas credential in TESOL.

Five students completed the program in 1996–1997.

The university has an intensive English language program for nonnative speakers of English.

Summer Session: Yes

Further Information: Dr. Judith A. Márquez
Studies in Language and Culture
Bayou Building, Suite 1325
University of Houston–Clear Lake
2700 Bay Area Boulevard
Houston, TX 77058

Telephone: (281) 283-3591
Fax: (281) 283-3599
E-mail: marquez@uhcl.cl.uh.edu

◆ HUNTER COLLEGE OF THE CITY UNIVERSITY OF NEW YORK, Department of Curriculum and Teaching

Degree Offered: MA in education (TESOL).

Length of Program: 1–2 years. Students may be full-time or part-time and may begin their study at the beginning of the fall semester. The application deadline is April 30.

Program Requirements: 37 credits (New York State certification track) or 36 credits (adult education). Competence in a language other than English is required. Practice teaching plus either a thesis or a comprehensive examination is required.

Courses Offered: Introduction to General Linguistics; Methodology of TESOL; Second Language Acquisition: Theory and Research; Language and Culture; Workshop in Curriculum and Materials; Workshop in Teaching Children; Evaluation and Assessment; Practicum in Pre-K–12; Workshop in Teaching Adults; Technology in TESOL; Current Topics in TESOL; Bilingual Education; two courses in education foundations; Master's Essay; Phonetics of American English; Practicum With Adults.

Full-Time Staff: Donald R. H. Byrd (head), Angela Parrino.

Requirements for Admission: The program's requirements for admission are a B average on undergraduate work, 12 credits of study in a language other than English, and demonstrated proficiency in English.

Tuition, Fees, and Aid: For in-state students, $185 per credit ($2,175 full-time); for out-of-state students, $320 per credit ($3,800 full-time). No financial aid is available.

General: The curriculum is a unique balance of theory and practice that addresses the needs of women and men who wish to teach students in the public schools or adults in postsecondary settings. The program can lead to New York State certification in TESOL.

Plans are under consideration for international sites in Brazil and Greece.

Sixty students completed the program in 1996–1997.

The college has an intensive English language program for nonnative speakers of English.

Summer Session: Yes

Further Information: Dr. Donald R. H. Byrd, Head
MA Program in TESOL
Department of Curriculum and Teaching
1011 West Building
Hunter College of the City University of New York
695 Park Avenue
New York, NY 10021

Telephone: (212) 772-4691
Fax: (212) 772-4666
E-mail: drhbyrd@aol.com

◆ IDAHO, UNIVERSITY OF, Department of English

Degree Offered: MA-TESL.

Length of Program: 4 semesters. Students may be full-time or part-time and may begin their study at the beginning of any semester. Application deadlines are fall and summer semesters, February 15; spring semester, October 15.

Program Requirements: 33 credits. Competence in a language other than English is required; English meets the requirement for nonnative speakers. A comprehensive examination is required. Practice teaching is strongly encouraged. A thesis is optional.

Courses Offered: (*required) *12 credits from Introduction to English Syntax, Phonetics and Phonology, Semantics, Contrastive Linguistics, Linguistic Analysis, Typology, Advanced English Grammar, Topics in English Linguistics; *9 credits from TESL Methods I, TESL Methods II, Current Issues in ESL, TESL Teaching Practicum; 12 elective credits from the preceding lists or from other approved courses in linguistics and education.

Full-Time Staff: Douglas Q. Adams (chair), Steve Chandler, Richard Penticoff, Gordon Thomas.

Requirements for Admission: The university's requirement for admission is a bachelor's degree. The program requires a GPA of at least 3.0. Nonnative speakers of English must have a minimum TOEFL score of 560.

Tuition, Fees, and Aid: For in-state students, $810 per semester; for out-of-state students, $2,690 per semester. Teaching assistantships and English scholarships are available.

General: The program includes cooperative courses with Washington State University. Students have an opportunity to emphasize composition and writing instruction and to obtain practice-teaching experience with the three intensive English programs within 30 miles of the campus.

The university has agreements with Nagasaki Junior College in Japan, Shanxi University in China, Patagonia University in Argentina, and the University of Cuenca in Ecuador for the provision of ESL teachers and practice teachers.

Fourteen students completed the program in 1996–1997.

The university has an intensive English language program for nonnative speakers of English.

Summer Session: No

Further Information: Director of Graduate Studies
Department of English
University of Idaho
Moscow, ID 83844-1102

Telephone: (208) 885-6156
Fax: (208) 885-5944
E-mail: englishdept@uidaho.edu
http://www.uidaho.edu/LS/Eng/

◆ ILLINOIS, UNIVERSITY OF, AT CHICAGO, Department of English

Degree Offered: MA in linguistics with a concentration in TESOL.

Length of Program: 4 semesters. Students may be full-time or part-time and must begin their study at the beginning of the fall semester. The application deadline is May 15 (March 15 for international applicants).

Program Requirements: 49 credits. Competence in a language other than English is required for native speakers of English and optional for nonnative speakers. Practice teaching and a comprehensive examination are required. A thesis is optional.

Courses Offered: (*required) *Methodology of TESOL; *Curriculum and Materials Development in TESOL; *Second Language Learning; *Classroom Testing in TESOL; Grammatical Structures of American English for TESOL; *Linguistic Analysis I;

*Linguistic Analysis II; *Sociolinguistics; *TESOL Internship; *one elective in TESOL or a related area.

Full-Time Staff: Richard Cameron, Marcia Farr, Kyoko Inoue, Elliot Judd (chair), Adam Makkai, Valerie B. Makkai, John Rohsenow, Jessica Williams.

Requirements for Admission: The university's requirements for admission are a B average in the undergraduate program, three letters of recommendation, and a 250-word personal statement. Nonnative speakers of English must have a TOEFL score of 590 and a TSE score of 50.

Tuition, Fees, and Aid: For in-state students, $2,155 per semester; for out-of-state students, $5,111 per semester. Teaching assistantships, graduate assistantships, fellowships, and tuition and fee waivers are available.

General: The program combines academic course work with practical teaching experience.

Twenty students completed the program in 1996–1997.

The university has an intensive English language program for nonnative speakers of English.

Summer Session: No

Further Information: Elliott L. Judd, Director
MA TESOL Program
Department of English (M/C 162)
University of Illinois at Chicago
601 South Morgan
Chicago, IL 60605

Telephone: (312) 413-1559
Fax: (312) 413-1005
E-mail: ejudd@uic.edu

◆ ILLINOIS, UNIVERSITY OF, AT URBANA-CHAMPAIGN, Division of English as an International Language

Degree Offered: MA in TESL.

Length of Program: 4 semesters. Students may be full-time or part-time and usually begin their study at the beginning of the fall semester. Summer entry is also possible. Deadlines for application are fall semester, June 15; summer session, April 15.

Program Requirements: 12 units (approximately 48 semester hours). Competence in a language other than English is required for native speakers of English; English meets the requirement for nonnative speakers. Practice teaching is required. A thesis is required for the research track. For the pedagogical track, either a comprehensive examination or thesis is required.

Courses Offered: (*required) Pedagogical and research tracks: *Descriptive English Grammar for ESL Teachers; *Theoretical Foundations of Second Language Acquisition; *English Phonology and Morphology for ESL Teachers. Pedagogical track: *ESL Methods and Materials; *ESL for Beginning-Level Adult Learners; *Reading and Writing in a Second Language; *Impact of Cultural Differences in TESL *or* Sociolinguistics; *Principles of Language Testing; *Communicative Approaches to Second and Foreign Language Teaching; *Pedagogical Grammar. Research track: *Research Methods in Language Learning; *Thesis Research.

Full-Time Staff: Lawrence F. Bouton (chair), J. Ronayne Cowan, Fred Davidson, Wayne B. Dickerson, Thomas M. Gould, Molly Mack, Numa Markee, Eyamba G.

Bokamba, C. C. Cheng, Donald Cruickshank, Gary Cziko, Susan Gonzo, Hans H. Hock, Braj B. Kachru, Yamuna Kachru, Chin-woo Kim, Howard Maclay, Erica McClure.

Requirements for Admission: The university's requirements for admission are a baccalaureate degree or the equivalent, a minimum GPA of 3.0 for the last 60 hours of undergraduate course work, and a statement of purpose. Nonnative speakers of English must have a TOEFL score of 600. The program requires a TWE score of 4 for nonnative speakers of English, 2 years of formal instruction in a second or foreign language, completion of an introduction to general linguistics and, for those applying for the research track, an introduction to applied linguistics. These prerequisites may be fulfilled on campus concurrently with regular course work.

Tuition, Fees, and Aid: For in-state students, $1,885 per semester; for out-of-state students, $5,222 per semester. Fees are $532 per semester. The division offers several part-time teaching assistantships, usually awarded to students who have completed their first semester's work. A few tuition and partial fee waivers are available.

General: This program enables students to carry out studies in interdisciplinary theory and practice in descriptive linguistics, language acquisition, classroom teaching, and materials development. Core and cooperating faculty have area specializations in Africa, Europe, and South America as well as South, West, and Southeast Asia. Students have access to the third largest university academic library in the U.S. as well as a specialized TESL library. Special features of the Division of EIL include experimental classes in English for international members of the local community, state-of-the-art computer-based instructional and research equipment and program, liaison with public school ESL programs, and a laboratory suitable for conducting experiments in speech perception and production. The division publishes an international journal, *IDEAL*, organizes an annual international conference on pragmatics and language learning, and provides intensive English language instruction through selected courses and through the Intensive English Institute.

The division offers internship programs in Costa Rica and Finland.

Thirty-four students completed the program in 1996–1997.

The university has an intensive English language program for nonnative speakers of English.

Summer Session: Yes

Further Information: Lawrence F. Bouton
Division of English as an International Language
3070 Foreign Languages Building
University of Illinois at Urbana-Champaign
707 South Mathews Avenue
Urbana, IL 61801

Telephone: (217) 333-1506
Fax: (217) 244-3050
E-mail: deil@uiuc.edu

◆ ILLINOIS STATE UNIVERSITY, Department of English

Degree Offered: BA minor in TESOL.

Length of Program: 3–4 semesters. Students may be full-time or part-time and may begin their study at the beginning of any semester. The application deadline for the fall semester is June 30.

Program Requirements: 18 semester hours. Competence in a language other than English is required; English meets the requirement for nonnative speakers. Practice teaching is required. A thesis and a comprehensive examination are optional.

Courses Offered: (*required) *Introduction to Descriptive Linguistics; *Cross-Cultural Aspects in TESOL; *Theoretical Foundations in TESOL; *Methods and Materials in TESOL; *Assessment and Testing in ESL; *TESOL Practicum; Traditional and Nontraditional Grammars of English; Growth and Structure of the English Language; Semantics; Psychology of Language.

Full-Time Staff: Irene Brosnahan, Leger Brosnahan, Mahide Demirci, Bruce Hawkins, Lorie Heggie, Sandra Metz, Kasia Stadnik, Margaret Steffensen.

Requirements for Admission: Admission is based on all aspects of a student's high school academic record, including high school course credits, class rank, standardized test scores, and any completed college credit.

Tuition, Fees, and Aid: For in-state students, $98.40 per credit hour; for out-of-state students, $295.20 per credit hour. Fees are $35.05 per credit hour plus $88 per semester.

General: The program can lead to an Illinois credential in TESOL if the student satisfies requirements in K–12 certification.

Four students completed the program in 1996–1997.

The university has an intensive English language program for nonnative speakers of English.

Summer Session: Yes

Further Information: Ronald Fortune, Chair
Department of English
Stevenson Hall 409
Campus Box 4240
Illinois State University
Normal, IL 61790-4240

Telephone: (309) 438-3667
Fax: (309) 438—5414
E-mail: rfortune@rs6000.cmp.ilstu.edu

◆ ILLINOIS STATE UNIVERSITY, Department of English

Degree Offered: MA in writing with a concentration in TESOL.

Length of Program: 4 semesters. Students may be full-time or part-time and may begin their study at the beginning of any semester. Application deadlines are fall semester, February 1; spring semester, October 1.

Program Requirements: 37 semester hours. Competence in a language other than English is strongly recommended. Practice teaching, a thesis, and a comprehensive examination are required.

Courses Offered: (*required) *Introduction to Graduate Study; *Introduction to the Composing Process; *Introduction to Descriptive Linguistics; *three courses in literature; *TESOL Practicum; History and Development of the English Language; Studies in English Linguistics; Cross-Cultural Aspects in TESOL; Theoretical Foundations in TESOL; Methods and Materials in TESOL; Assessment and Testing in ESL; (*for state certification) six courses in linguistics and TESOL in five core areas.

Full-Time Staff: Irene Brosnahan, Leger Brosnahan, Mahide Demirci, Ronald Fortune (chair), Bruce Hawkins, Lorie Heggie, Douglas Hesse, Kenneth Lindblom,

Janice Neuleib, Kasia Stadnik, Margaret Steffensen, Rodger Tarr, Ray Lewis White, William Woodson.

Requirements for Admission: The university's requirement for admission is a baccalaureate degree or the equivalent from an accredited institution. Nonnative speakers of English must submit TOEFL scores, a financial statement, and proof of freedom from tuberculosis. The program requires nonnative speakers of English to submit a TOEFL score of 600 and, for teaching assistantships, a TSE score of at least 50.

Tuition, Fees, and Aid: For in-state students, $99.40 per credit hour; for out-of-state students, $298.20 per credit hour. Fees are $35.03 per semester hour plus $88 per semester. A substantial number of teaching assistantships (including a tuition waiver) are available.

General: All writing classes in the department are taught on networked computers, and all students receive training on and have access to computers. Technical writing classes also include desktop publishing. The program has a strong commitment to the integration of theory and pedagogy, including TESL. The program can lead to an Illinois credential in TESOL if the student satisfies requirements in K–12 certification.

The program has arrangements with several colleges in Korea and one university in Thailand, where students can do their teaching internships while enrolled as candidates and teach on a regular appointment when their studies are completed.

Four students completed the program in 1996–1997.

The university has an intensive English language program for nonnative speakers of English.

Summer Session: Yes

Further Information: Douglas Hesse, Director of Graduate Studies
Department of English
Stevenson Hall 409
Illinois State University
Campus Box 4240
Normal, IL 61790-4240

Telephone: (309) 438-3667
Fax: (309) 438-5414
E-mail: ddhesse@rs6000.cmp.ilstu.edu

◆ ILLINOIS STATE UNIVERSITY, Department of English

Degree Offered: PhD in English studies (with linguistics and TESOL as cognate areas).

Length of Program: Students may be full-time or part-time and may begin their study at the beginning of any semester. Application deadlines are fall semester, February 1; spring semester, October 1.

Program Requirements: 43 semester hours. Competence in a language other than English is strongly recommended. Practice teaching, a comprehensive examination, and a thesis are required.

Courses Offered: (*required) *Introduction to Descriptive Linguistics; *Seminar in Language; *Seminar in Composition; *Seminar in Selected Areas in Literature; *Professional Seminar in the Teaching of English; *Practicum (Internship) in College Teaching; Studies in English Linguistics; Cross-Cultural Aspects in TESOL; Theoretical Foundations in TESOL; Methods and Materials in TESOL; Assessment and Testing in ESL; Research Methods in Composition Studies; Teaching of Composition in the Community College; Classical and Modern Theories of Rhetoric; History and Development of the English Language.

Full-Time Staff: Irene Brosnahan, Leger Brosnahan, Mahide Demirci, Ronald Fortune (chair), Charles Harris, Bruce Hawkins, Douglas Hesse, Kenneth Lindblom, Janice Neuleib, Maurice Scharton, Ronald Strickland, Kasia Stadnik, Margaret Steffensen.

Requirements for Admission: The university's requirements for admission are a level of preparation equivalent to a master's degree in an appropriate discipline from an accredited institution, letters of recommendation, and a GRE score. The program requires a master's degree and prior teaching experience. Nonnative speakers of English must submit a TOEFL score of 600 and, for a teaching assistantship, a TSE score of at least 50.

Tuition, Fees, and Aid: See program description for MA in writing.

General: The program is unusual in being an integrated English studies program. The students are required and encouraged to integrate their course work in literature, language, composition, and rhetorical theories and to relate theory and pedagogy. Students with a cognate in TESOL are prepared to teach not only ESL but also related courses in composition. The program can lead to an Illinois credential in TESOL if the student satisfies requirements in K–12 certification.

The program has arrangements with several colleges in Korea and one university in Thailand, where students can do their teaching internships while enrolled as candidates and teach on a regular appointment when their studies are complete.

The university has an intensive English language program for nonnative speakers of English.

Summer Session: Yes

Further Information: Douglas Hesse, Director of Graduate Studies
Department of English
Stevenson Hall 409
Illinois State University
Campus Box 4240
Normal, IL 61790-4240

Telephone: (309) 438-3667
Fax: (309) 438-5414
E-mail: ddhesse@rs6000.cmp.ilstu.edu

◆ INDIANA STATE UNIVERSITY, Department of English

Degree Offered: Minor in linguistics/TESL.

Length of Program: 2 semesters. Students may be full-time or part-time and may begin their study at the beginning of any semester.

Program Requirements: 24 semester hours. Competence in a language other than English is required; English meets the requirement for nonnative speakers of English. Practice teaching is required. A thesis is optional. A comprehensive examination is not required.

Courses Offered: (*required) *Introduction to Linguistics; *Children's Literature; *English Grammar; *TESL; *Varieties of American English; *Language Differences and Linguistic Universals; *6 hours in language teaching and linguistics, such as History of English and Lexicology.

Full-Time Staff: Leslie Barratt, Cecil Nelson, Betty Phillips, Lewis Sego.

Requirements for Admission: The university's requirements for admission are ranking in the upper 50% of the high school graduating class and completion of course work equivalent to the Indiana Core 40 curriculum. Freshman applicants and transfers with fewer than 24 transfer hours must submit an SAT or ACT score.

Tuition, Fees, and Aid: For in-state students, $1,925 per 18 semester hours or more; for out-of-state students, $4,755 per 18 semester hours or more.

General: This program allows students to receive the training required to teach ESL in the Indiana public schools. Students may vary the program to some extent to fit their interests.

The university offers a limited number of international exchange programs.

Two students completed the program in 1996–1997.

Summer Session: No

Further Information: Director of Undergraduate Studies
Department of English
Indiana State University
Terre Haute, IN 47809

Telephone: (812) 237-3021
Fax: (812) 237-3156
E-mail: ejengl@root.indstate.edu

◆ INDIANA STATE UNIVERSITY, Department of English

Degree Offered: MA in English with a concentration in applied linguistics.

Length of Program: 4 semesters. Students may be full-time or part-time and may begin their study at the beginning of any semester.

Program Requirements: 32 semester hours. Competence in a language other than English is required for native speakers of English. Practice teaching, a thesis, and a comprehensive examination are optional.

Courses Offered: (*required) *Bibliography and Research Methods in English; *Advanced Seminar in Teaching English: English Language and Linguistics; *one 600-level course each in American literature, English literature, and English language and linguistics; *11 hours in applied linguistics; *6 hours outside the Department of English.

Full-Time Staff: See program description for minor in linguistics/TESL.

Requirements for Admission: The university's requirements for admission are a bachelor's degree from an accredited college or university; a GPA of 3.0 at all graduate schools attended; and an undergraduate major, minor, or strength in a related field.

Tuition, Fees, and Aid: For in-state students, $137.50 per credit hour; for out-of-state students, $311.50 per credit hour. Teaching assistantships are available in composition, ESL, and foreign languages.

General: This flexible program allows students to pursue their own area of interest, such as lexicology, through independent course work in addition to the course offerings.

The university has an exchange program with institutions in China and Japan for faculty.

Two students completed the program in 1996–1997.

Summer Session: No

Further Information: Director of Graduate Studies
Department of English
Indiana State University
Terre Haute, IN 47809

Telephone: (812) 237-3139
Fax: (812) 237-3156
E-mail: ejhudsn@root.indstate.edu

◆ INDIANA UNIVERSITY, Program in TESOL and Applied Linguistics

Degrees Offered: Certificate in applied linguistics with a minor in TESOL; MA in applied linguistics with a minor in TESOL.

Length of Program: 3 semesters. Students may be full-time or part-time and may begin their study at the beginning of the fall or spring semester. Application deadlines are fall semester, January 15 (December 15 for international students); spring semester, September 1 (August 1 for international students).

Program Requirements: 30 credits. Competence in a language other than English is required; English meets the requirement for nonnative speakers of English. Practice teaching is required. Neither a thesis nor a comprehensive examination is required.

Courses Offered: (*required) *Traditional and Structural English Grammar; *Applied Transformational English Grammar; *Second Language Acquisition; *Linguistic Resources and TESOL; *TESOL Practicum; *Language Testing; Phonology and Second Language Learning and Teaching; Survey of Applied Linguistics; Second Language Writing; The Language Laboratory: Hardware and Software; American Culture; English Dialects; Advanced Second Language Acquisition; Contrastive Analysis; Readings; Thesis; Language and Society; Sociolinguistics; Bilingualism and Language Contact; Topical Seminar; Seminar in Sociolinguistics.

Full-Time Staff: Kathleen Bardovi-Harlig, Richard R. Bier, Harry L. Gradman (chair), Susan E. Greer, Scott Jarvis, Beverly S. Hartford, Marlin G. Howard, Bruce L. Leeds.

Requirements for Admission: The program requires a baccalaureate degree from an accredited institution of higher education, a GRE score, three letters of recommendation, and a statement of purpose. Nonnative speakers of English must have a minimum TOEFL score of 573.

Tuition, Fees, and Aid: For in-state students, $147 per credit hour; for out-of-state students, $428 per credit hour. Fees are $21.95 per credit hour. One recruitment fellowship plus tuition waiver, foreign language and area studies fellowships, associate instructorships, research assistantships, and other forms of financial aid are available.

General: The program currently has approximately 50 students enrolled in the certificate and MA programs from all over the United States and many foreign countries. The core faculty has strengths in second language acquisition, sociolinguistics, interlanguage pragmatics, language testing, language learning backgrounds, and language program development and evaluation. The program maintains close contacts with cooperating faculty in such areas as Africa studies, anthropology, classical studies, computer science, East Asian languages, folklore, French, Italian, Germanic studies, Near Eastern languages and cultures, philosophy, psychology, Slavic languages and literatures, sociology, Spanish, Portuguese, speech and hearing sciences, Uralic and Altaic studies, and the School of Education.

Twenty-one students completed the program in 1996–1997.

The university has an intensive English language program for nonnative speakers of English.

Summer Session: Yes

Further Information: Karla J. Bastin
Program in TESOL and Applied Linguistics
Memorial Hall 313
Indiana University
Bloomington, IN 47405

Telephone: (812) 855-7951
Fax: (812) 855-5605
E-mail: kjbastin@indiana.edu

◆ INDIANA UNIVERSITY OF PENNSYLVANIA, Graduate Studies in Rhetoric and Linguistics

Degree Offered: MA in English (TESOL).

Length of Program: Minimum of 1 academic year; 2 years recommended. Students may be full-time or part-time and may begin their study at the beginning of any semester. Application deadlines are fall semester, July 15; spring semester, November 15; summer semester, April 15.

Program Requirements: 36 semester hours. Competence in a language other than English is not required. An internship in ESL is required. A thesis is optional. A comprehensive examination is not required.

Courses Offered: (*required) *Topics in ESL Pedagogy; *American English Grammar; *Observation of English Teaching; *TESL/TEFL Methodology; *Cross-Cultural Communication; *Internship in ESL; Second Language Acquisition; ESL Media and Materials; Linguistics and the English Teacher; Psycholinguistics; Sociolinguistics; College Reading Theory; 9 elective semester hours.

Full-Time Staff: Dan J. Tannacito (director), Jerry G. Gebhard (coordinator), Ali A. Aghbar, Jeanine L. Heny, Lilia Savova, Barbara Hill Hudson, Carole Bencich, Bennett A. Rafoth.

Requirements for Admission: The university's requirements for admission are a bachelor's degree in a related discipline, two letters of recommendation from academic sources, and official transcripts from all undergraduate and graduate work. Nonnative speakers of English must submit a TOEFL score. The program requires a goal statement.

Tuition, Fees, and Aid: For in-state students, $1,734 per semester; for out-of-state students, $3,118 per semester. Fees are $302.50. A few graduate assistantships are available.

General: This program offers students professional preparation for ESL/EFL teaching while grounding them in applied linguistics. The degree is appropriate for doctoral study in English or a related discipline as well as for teaching.

Nineteen students completed the program in 1996–1997.

The university has an intensive English language program for nonnative speakers of English.

Summer Session: Yes

Further Information: Dr. Dan J. Tannacito, Director
Graduate Studies in Rhetoric and Linguistics
111 Leonard Hall
Indiana University of Pennsylvania
Indiana, PA 15705

Telephone: (412) 357-2263
Fax: (412) 357-3056
E-mail: djt@grove.iup.edu
http://gradeng.en.iup.edu

◆ INDIANA UNIVERSITY OF PENNSYLVANIA, Graduate Studies in Rhetoric and Linguistics

Degree Offered: PhD in English (rhetoric and linguistics).

Length of Program: 8 semesters (4–5 years). Students may be part-time except when fulfilling the residency requirement and may begin their study at the beginning of any semester. Application deadlines are fall semester, July 15; spring semester, November 15; summer semester, April 15.

Program Requirements: 48 semester hours. Competence in a language other than English is not required, but foreign language course work may be used to fulfill the research skills requirement. Practice teaching is not required. A thesis and comprehensive examinations are required.

Courses Offered: (*required) *Research Methodology in Rhetoric and Linguistics; *Linguistics and the English Teacher; *Psycholinguistics *or* Sociolinguistics; *Teaching Writing; *Orientation and Field Experience in the Community College; Rhetorical Traditions; Second Language Acquisition; TESL/TEFL Methodology; Observation of English Teaching; Cross-Cultural Communication; Advanced Seminar in Composition; Qualitative Research Methods; American English Grammar; College Reading Theory.

Full-Time Staff: Dan J. Tannacito (director), Ali A. Aghbar, Carole Bencich, Lynne Alvine, Jerry Gebhard, Patrick Hartwell, Jeanine L. Heny, Mark Hurlbert, Donald McAndrew, Bennett A. Gian Pagnucci, Rafoth, Michael Williamson.

Requirements for Admission: The university's requirements for admission are a goal statement, two letters of recommendation, official transcripts for undergraduate and graduate work, a $20 application fee, an affirmative action verification, and, for international students, a financial statement and an official TOEFL score of at least 520. The program requires teaching experience and a master's degree in a related field.

Tuition, Fees, and Aid: See MA program description. A limited number of graduate assistantships and several teaching associateships are available to advanced PhD candidates.

General: Students can fulfill residency through three consecutive summers of 12 semester hours each. Students are offered a balance of TESOL and composition courses.

Fourteen students completed the program in 1996–1997.

The university has an intensive English language program for nonnative speakers of English.

Summer Session: Yes

Further Information: Dr. Dan J. Tannacito, Director
Graduate Studies in Rhetoric and Linguistics
111 Leonard Hall
Indiana University of Pennsylvania
Indiana, PA 15705

Telephone: (412) 357-2263
Fax: (412) 357-3056
E-mail: djt@grove.iup.edu
http://gradeng.en.iup.edu

◆ INTER AMERICAN UNIVERSITY OF PUERTO RICO— SAN GERMÁN CAMPUS, Department of English

Degree Offered: MA in TESL.

Length of Program: 2 years. Students may be full-time or part-time and may begin their study at the beginning of any semester. Application deadlines are 1 month before the beginning of the semester.

Program Requirements: 36 credits. Knowledge of Spanish is helpful for native speakers of English. A comprehensive examination is required. Neither practice teaching nor a thesis is required.

Courses Offered: (*required) *Principles of Linguistics; *English and Spanish Phonological Systems; *English Syntax and Morphology; *Writing Theories and Application; *Reading in a Second Language; *Theory and Principles of TESL; *Techniques and Materials in TESL; *Research Methods; Historical Development of English; Literary Analysis and Interpretation; Language and Communication; Dramatic Literature; Psycholinguistics; Sociolinguistics; First and Second Language Acquisition; Sociocultural Aspects of Puerto Rico and the United States; Fundamentals of Bilingual Education; Translation.

Full-Time Staff: Glenn Ayres, Arlene Clachar, Ralph Deschler, Ahmad Fassihian, Aurora Meléndez, Aurora Rodríguez, Olena H. Saciuk.

Requirements for Admission: The university's requirements for admission are a BA from an accredited institution with a minimum GPA of 2.5 in the last 60 credits of academic work, a GRE score from within the last 5 years or during the first semester of the MA program, and the ability to express oneself correctly in writing in English at the university level.

Tuition, Fees, and Aid: $130 per credit hour. Fees are $150 per semester. Teaching assistantships and federal loans are available.

General: The program provides the opportunity to live in a Hispanic culture in a small, picturesque university town. Students can apply theories learned in class to the teaching of ESL students at the university level. Courses are offered at night. The island-wide Puerto Rico TESOL convention and the conferences of Western and Southern Puerto Rico TESOL provide additional professional and academic development. Students can take Spanish courses for nonnative speakers during the day if they wish. The program leads to a Puerto Rico credential in TESOL.

Six students completed the program in 1996–1997.

Summer Session: No

Further Information: Dr. Olena H. Saciuk
Department of Languages and Literatures—English
PO Box 5100
Inter American University of Puerto Rico
San Germán, PR 00683

Telephone: (787) 264-1912 extension 7540
Fax: (787) 892-6350

◆ IOWA, THE UNIVERSITY OF, Department of Linguistics

Degree Offered: MA in linguistics with a TESL focus.

Length of Program: 4 semesters. Students may be full-time or part-time and must begin their study at the beginning of the fall semester. The financial aid application deadline is March 15; there are no other application deadlines.

Program Requirements: 36 semester hours. Competence in a language other than English is not required. Practice teaching and a comprehensive examination are required. A thesis is not required.

Courses Offered: (*required) *Phonetics; *Syntactic Analysis; *Syntactic Theory; *Phonological Analysis and Theory; *Phonological Theory; *Structure of English; *Methods in TESL; *Practicum in TESL; *Applied Linguistics; *Historical and Comparative Linguistics; *Field Methods *or* Linguistic Structures *or* Language Universals and Linguistic Typology; one or two electives in areas such as theoretical linguistics, anthropological linguistics, and psychology of language.

Full-Time Staff: Jull Beckman, Maureen Burke, Christopher Culy, William D. Davies (chair), Alice L. Davison, Nora England, Tamar I. Kaplan, Catherine O. Ringen, Jerzy Rubach, Robert S. Wachal.

Requirements for Admission: Admission to the university is based on acceptance by the department with a minimum undergraduate GPA of 2.3 (or foreign equivalent) and a combined quantitative and verbal GRE score of approximately 1000 for native speakers of English. The minimum TOEFL score for nonnative speakers of English is 600. All nonnative speakers of English must have their English competency evaluated.

Tuition, Fees, and Aid: For in-state students, $1,621 per semester; for out-of-state students, $5,511 per semester. Teaching assistantships, research assistantships, and fellowships are available.

General: The program emphasizes core linguistics. Students generally have the opportunity to teach ESL during their second year.
Seven students completed the program in 1996–1997.

Summer Session: Yes

Further Information: Prof. William D. Davies
Department of Linguistics
553 EPB
The University of Iowa
Iowa City, IA 52242-1408

Telephone: (319) 335-0215
Fax: (319) 335-3971
E-mail: william-davies@uiowa.edu

◆ IOWA STATE UNIVERSITY, Department of English

Degree Offered: MA in TESL/applied linguistics.

Length of Program: 4 semesters. Students may be full-time or part-time and must begin their study at the beginning of the fall semester. The application deadline is February 1.

Program Requirements: 30 credits. Competence in a language other than English is required; English meets the requirement for nonnative speakers of English. Practice teaching and a thesis are required. A comprehensive examination is not required.

Courses Offered: (*required) *Introduction to Linguistics; *Introduction to Computers; *Grammar; *Sociolinguistics; *Grammatical Analysis; *Second Language Acquisition; *Second Language Teaching Methods; *Second Language Testing; *Practicum in ESL; Literacy; Teaching ESL Listening and Speaking; Discourse Analysis; English for Special Purposes; Computer-Assisted Language Learning; Practicum in Assessment.

Full-Time Staff: Janet Anderson-Hsieh, Carol Chapelle, Susan Conrad, Dan Douglas, Barbara Schwarte, Roberta Vann.

Requirements for Admission: The university's requirements for admission are an undergraduate degree from an accredited university and official transcripts. The program requires GRE General Test scores, three letters of recommendation, an expository writing sample, a résumé, and a cover letter. Nonnative speakers of English must submit a TOEFL score of 600, a TWE score of 5, and an audiotape or videotape demonstrating competence in spoken English.

Tuition, Fees, and Aid: For in-state students, $3,048 per year; for out-of-state students, $8,974 per year. Teaching assistantships and PACE awards are available.

General: The program offers concentrations in literacy, computer-assisted language learning, English for special purposes, assessment, and literature in ESL. It can lead to Iowa add-on certification in ESL.

Twelve students completed the program in 1996–1997.

The university has an intensive English language program for nonnative speakers of English.

Summer Session: Yes

Further Information: TESL Coordinator
Department of English
203 Ross Hall
Iowa State University
Ames, IA 50011

Telephone: (515) 294-2477
Fax: (515) 294-6814
E-mail: englgrad@iastate.edu

◆ JERSEY CITY STATE COLLEGE, Multicultural Center

Degrees Offered: ESL initial certification; ESL second certification.

Length of Program: 3 semesters. Students may be full-time or part-time and may begin their study at the beginning of any semester.

Program Requirements: 39 credits for initial certification; 21 credits for second certification. Competence in a language other than English is not required. Practice teaching is required for initial certification. Neither a thesis nor a comprehensive examination is required.

Courses Offered: (*required) For initial and second certification: *Historical and Cultural Backgrounds of Limited English Proficient Students; *General Linguistics and Multicultural Education; *Applied Linguistics With Emphasis on Second Language Experience; *Phonology and Structure of American English; *Theories of Language Teaching; *Observation of ESL; *Methods of Teaching ESL; *Field Experience in ESL/Bilingual Education. For initial certification only: *Learning Theories and Instruction; *Human Relations and Multicultural Education; *Solving the Reading Problems of the Urban Learner; *Internship and Seminar.

Full-Time Staff: Elba Herrero, John Klosek, Mihri Napoliello (chair).

Requirements for Admission: The college's requirements for admission are official transcripts from all colleges attended, an undergraduate cumulative average of 2.75, two letters of recommendation, and either a GRE or a Miller Analogies Test score.

Tuition, Fees, and Aid: For in-state students, $170 per credit; for out-of-state students, $213 per credit. Fees are $30 per credit. Graduate assistantships, veterans benefits, and other types of financial assistance and loans are available.

General: Nine students completed initial certification and 65 students completed second certification in 1996–1997.

The college has an intensive English language program for nonnative speakers of English.

Summer Session: Yes

Further Information: Mihri Napoliello
Multicultural Center
Hepburn Hall 114
Jersey City State College
2039 Kennedy Boulevard
Jersey City, NJ 07305-1597

Telephone: (201) 200-3380
Fax: (201) 200-3238
E-mail: MihriN@JCS1.JCState.edu

◆ JERSEY CITY STATE COLLEGE, Multicultural Center

Degree Offered: MA in urban education with a concentration in ESL.

Length of Program: 3–4 semesters. Students may be full-time or part-time and may begin their study at the beginning of any semester.

Program Requirements: 42 credits. Competence in a language other than English is not required. Practice teaching is required if needed for certification. Neither a thesis nor a comprehensive examination is required.

Courses Offered: (*required) *Historical and Cultural Backgrounds of Limited English Proficient Students; *General Linguistics and Multicultural Education; *Applied Linguistics With Emphasis on Second Language Experience; *Phonology and Structure of American English; *Theories of Language Teaching; *Observation of ESL; *Methods of Teaching ESL; *Field Experience in ESL/Bilingual Education; *Multicultural Education and Psycholinguistics; *Multicultural Education and Sociolinguistics; *Introduction to Bilingual Education; *Language, Culture, and Communication; *Contemporary Issues in Bilingual Curriculum Development; *Human Relations and Multicultural Education; *Americans in the World Community; *Multicultural Values in the Urban Community; *Learning Theories and Instruction; *Solving the Reading Problems of the Urban Learner; *Research in ESL/Bilingual Education; *Survey and Development of ESL Materials.

Full-Time Staff: See program description for ESL initial and second certification.

Requirements for Admission: See program description for ESL initial and second certification.

Tuition, Fees, and Aid: See program description for ESL initial and second certification.

General: The program leads to a New Jersey credential in TESOL.
Thirty-five students completed the program in 1996–1997.

Summer Session: Yes

Further Information: Mihri Napoliello
Multicultural Center
Hepburn Hall 114
Jersey City State College
2039 Kennedy Boulevard
Jersey City, NJ 07305-1597

Telephone: (201) 200-3380
Fax: (201) 200-3238
E-mail: MihriN@JCS1.JCState.edu

◆ KANSAS, UNIVERSITY OF, Department of Linguistics

Degrees Offered: BA, MA, and PhD in linguistics.

Length of Program: Students may be full-time or part-time and may begin their studies at the beginning of any semester. Application deadlines for international students are fall semester, June 1; spring semester, October 1. Domestic deadlines are flexible.

Program Requirements: 30 credits. Competence in a language other than English is required. A thesis and a comprehensive examination are required. Practice teaching is optional.

Courses Offered: Introduction to Linguistics; Phonetics I; Contrastive Phonetics; Problems in Linguistic Analysis; Language Acquisition; Phonology I and II; Linguistics and Second Language Acquisition; Syntax I and II; Discourse Analysis; Linguistics in Anthropology; Semantics I; North American Indian Languages; Comparative/Historical Linguistics; Indo-European Language Family; Field Methods; Computational Linguistics; Proseminar; Proseminar in Child Language; Seminar in Ethnolinguistics; Non-Linear Phonology; Seminar in Acquisition; Pragmatics; Advanced Comparative-Historical Linguistics; Seminar in Second Language Acquisition; Topics in Applied Linguistics; Acoustic Phonetics; Seminar in Syntax; Seminar in Amerindian Linguistics; Seminar in Comparative-Historical Linguistics; Seminar in Applied Linguistics.

Full-Time Staff: Naomi Bolotin, Michael Henderson, Frances Ingemann, Fiona McLaughlin, Kenneth Miner, Clifton Pye, Robert Rankin, Sara Rosen, Donald Watkins, Akira Yamamoto.

Requirements for Admission: The university's requirements for admission are a 3.0 GPA in previous work, a GRE score for native speakers of English, and a TOEFL score (58-58-58 minimum) for nonnative speakers (600 total also required for PhD). The program requires 6 hours of prerequisites for the MA, and, for the PhD, the 18 hours required in the general MA; a statement of purpose, a curriculum vitae, three letters of recommendation, and transcripts

Tuition, Fees, and Aid: For in-state students, $97.80 per credit; for out-of-state students, $321.75 per credit. Fees are $30 per credit up to 6 credits and $210 for more than 6 credits. Very little financial aid is available. ESOL teachers with experience may apply for teaching assistantships.

General: The program emphasizes first and second language acquisition, seeking to prepare students in both areas. Students may take methodology courses in the School of Education.

Four students completed the program in 1996–1997.

Summer Session: No

Further Information: Chair
Linguistics Department
427 Blake Hall
University of Kansas
Lawrence, KS 66045-2140

Telephone: (785) 864-3450
Fax: (784) 864-5724
E-mail: linguistics@ukans.edu

◆ KANSAS, UNIVERSITY OF, Department of Teaching and Leadership

Degrees Offered: MA TESL; PhD TESL.

Length of Program: 4 semesters (MA). Students may be full-time or part-time and may begin their study at the beginning of any semester. Application deadlines are fall and summer semesters, April 15; spring semester, October 15.

Program Requirements: 36 credits (MA). Competence in a language other than English is highly recommended. Practice teaching is required for students without prior experience. A comprehensive examination is required. A thesis is not required.

Courses Offered: (*required for MA) *Methods of TESOL; *Second Language Acquisition; *Second Language Testing; *ESL/Bilingual Education Practicum; *Foundations of Curriculum and Instruction; *Introduction to Educational Research; *12 credit hours of linguistics course work.

Full-Time Staff: Paul Garcia, Manuela Gonzalez-Bueno, Paul Markham (chair).

Requirements for Admission: The university's requirements for admission are a minimum undergraduate GPA of 3.0 and a minimum graduate GPA of 3.5. The program requires official transcripts and three letters of recommendation. Nonnative speakers of English must have a minimum TOEFL score of 590.

Tuition, Fees, and Aid: For in-state students, $125 per credit hour; for out-of-state students, $325 per credit hour. Some graduate teaching assistantships, mostly for doctoral students, and competitive fellowships are available.

General: The program is quite multicultural and has a good mixture of adult ESL and K–12 ESL teachers.

Faculty and students exchanges take place with the University of Costa Rica and with Kanagawa University in Yokohama, Japan.

Twenty-two students completed the program in 1996–1997.

Summer Session: Yes

Further Information: Paul L. Markham
Department of Teaching and Leadership
202 Bailey Hall
University of Kansas
Lawrence, KS 66045

Telephone: (785) 864-9677
Fax: (785) 864-5076
E-mail: markham@kuhub.cc.ukans.edu

◆ LAMAR UNIVERSITY, Department of English and Foreign Languages

Degree Offered: ESL endorsement.

Length of Program: Approximately 2 years. Students may be full-time or part-time and may begin their study at the beginning of any semester. Application deadlines are fall semester, August 1; spring semester, January 2; summer I, May 25; summer II, July 1.

Program Requirements: 12 semester hours. Competence in a language other than English is recommended for native speakers of English. Neither practice teaching, nor a thesis, nor a comprehensive examination is required.

Courses Offered: (*required) *Methodology for TESL; *Cross-Cultural Foundations for TESL; *Psycholinguistics; *Introduction to Linguistics.

Full-Time Staff: Pamela Saur.

Requirements for Admission: The university's requirements for admission are graduation from an accredited high school and an SAT or ACT score. Students who fail to qualify for unconditional admission may petition for individual approval for admission. Any applicant over 25 years of age will be admitted with proof of high school graduation and presentation of an SAT or ACT score.

Tuition, Fees, and Aid: $480 per academic year. Fees are $418 per semester. Grants and loans are available for undergraduates; teaching assistantships are available for graduate students.

General: The course work meets ESL endorsement requirements in the state of Texas.

Summer Session: Yes

Further Information: Chair
Department of English and Foreign Languages
Lamar University
PO Box 10023
Beaumont, TX 77710

Telephone: (409) 880-8558
Fax: (409) 880-8591

◆ LONG ISLAND UNIVERSITY, BROOKLYN CAMPUS, Department of Teaching and Learning

Degree Offered: MS in education with a concentration in TESL.

Length of Program: 3 semesters. Students may be full-time or part-time and may begin their study at the beginning of any semester.

Program Requirements: 36 semester hours. Competence in a language other than English is required; English meets the requirement for nonnative speakers of English. Practice teaching and a comprehensive examination are required. A thesis is not required.

Courses Offered: (*required) *Systems of Orthography; *Articulatory Phonetics; *Linguistics and Reading; Introduction to Linguistics; Modern English Structure; Psycholinguistics and Language Learning; Sociolinguistics; Multicultural Perspectives in Education; Theory and Practice of Bilingual Education; Assessment of Limited English Proficient Students; Methods and Materials 1 and 2; Second Language Learning for Students With Special Needs; Practicum/Student Teaching; Advanced Teaching in TESOL.

Full-Time Staff: Gurprit S. Bains (chair), Nancy Lemburger, Carole Kazlow.

Requirements for Admission: The university's requirement for admission is a bachelor's degree in liberal arts and sciences.

Tuition, Fees, and Aid: $475 per credit hour. Teaching assistantships are occasionally available.

General: The program provides thorough training in general and applied linguistics. A New York State certification and an adult track are available. Adult-track students do their practicum at the university's 2,000-student English Language Institute.

Twenty students completed the program in 1996–1997.

The university has an intensive English language program for nonnative speakers of English.

Summer Session: Yes

Further Information: Graduate Admissions
Department of Education
M202
Long Island University, Brooklyn Campus
University Plaza
Brooklyn, NY 11201

Telephone: (718) 488-1103
Fax: (718) 488-3472
E-mail: gbains@hornet.liunet.edu

◆ MANHATTANVILLE COLLEGE, School of Education, Department of Second Languages

Degree Offered: Master of professional studies in TESOL/TEFL.

Length of Program: Students may be full-time or part-time and may begin their study at the beginning of any semester. Rolling admissions are in effect.

Program Requirements: 36 credits. Competence in a language other than English is not required. Practice teaching is required for state certification only. Either a comprehensive examination or a thesis is required.

Courses Offered: (*required) *Structure of English/Introduction to Linguistics; *Methods and Materials for TESOL; *Teaching ESL Through Content; *Integrating Culture and Literature in ESL; *Foundations of Bilingual Education; *Principles of Language Learning; workshops and electives.

Full-Time Staff: Karen Kolbert, Laurence Krute (chair).

Requirements for Admission: The university's requirements for admission are a bachelor's degree from an accredited institution and a GPA of 3.0. Nonnative speakers of English must have a TOEFL score of 550.

Tuition, Fees, and Aid: $406 per credit. Graduate assistantships and internships with local programs are available.

General: The program offers a balanced mix of theory and practice leading to self-aware, reflective teaching emphasizing a variety of teaching tools. Option I leads to a New York State credential in TESOL; Option II, adult and international TESOL, does not.

Possibilities exist for teaching in Korea or Mexico.

Twenty-two students completed the program in 1996–1997.

The college has an intensive English language program for nonnative speakers of English.

Summer Session: Yes

Further Information: Dr. Laurence Krute
School of Education
Manhattanville College
2900 Purchase Street
Purchase, NY 10577

Telephone: (914) 323-5141
Fax: (914) 323-5493
E-mail: Lkrute@mville.edu

◆ MANKATO STATE UNIVERSITY, Department of Modern Languages

Degree Offered: BS in teaching with licensure minor in TESL.

Length of Program: 2 semesters plus student teaching. Students may be full-time or part-time and may begin their study at the beginning of any quarter. Application deadlines are fall semester, August 1; spring semester, December 1.

Program Requirements: 24 semester hours plus student teaching. Two years of study of a language other than English is required; English meets the requirement for nonnative speakers of English. Practice teaching at both the elementary and the secondary levels is required for K–12 certification. Neither a thesis nor a comprehensive examination is required.

Courses Offered: (*required) *English Linguistics; *Phonetics and Grammar for TESL; *Theory and Methods I; *Theory and Methods II; *Second Language Cultures; *Reading in the Elementary School; *Reading in the Content Areas.

Full-Time Staff: Pat Wilcox Peterson, Harry Solo, Stephen Stoynoff.

Requirements for Admission: The university's requirement for admission is high school graduation in the top 50% of the graduating class.

Tuition, Fees, and Aid: For in-state students, $96 per semester credit; for out-of-state students, $195 per semester credit.

General: Occasional international internships are available.

Ten native students completed the program in 1996–1997.

Summer Session: Yes

Further Information: Pat Wilcox Peterson
Department of Modern Languages
Armstrong Hall, Box 87
Mankato State University
Mankato, MN 56002-8400

Telephone: (507) 389-2116
Fax: (507) 389-5887
E-mail: PWP@vax1.mankato.msus.edu

◆ MANKATO STATE UNIVERSITY, English Department

Degree Offered: MA in English (TESL track).

Length of Program: 4 semesters. Students may be full-time or part-time and may begin their study at the beginning of any quarter. Application deadlines are fall semester, August 1; spring semester, December 1.

Program Requirements: 34 semester hours. Two years of college study of a language other than English is required; English meets the requirement for nonnative speakers of English. A comprehensive examination and a thesis are required. Practice teaching is not required.

Courses Offered: (*required) *English Grammar and Phonetics for TESL; *Theories and Methods of TESL (two courses); *Bibliography and Research in TESL; *two of the following: History of the English Language, Language and Culture in TESL, Language and the Teaching of English, Language Planning and Language Policy, Bilingualism and Language Contact, Psycholinguistics and Second Language Learning, Topics in TESL, English Grammar, Sociolinguistics, Theory and Practice of Translation, Studies in English Linguistics.

Full-Time Staff: See program description for BS in teaching with licensure minor in TESL.

Requirements for Admission: The requirement for admission is an undergraduate degree with an undergraduate GPA of at least 3.0. Candidates whose native language is not English must have a minimum TOEFL score of 550.

Tuition, Fees, and Aid: For in-state students, $140 per semester hour; for out-of-state students, $21 per semester hour. Assistantships are available in the English and modern languages departments in teaching composition, Spanish, and occasionally German, French, and ESL. Various grants and loans are available.

General: Occasional international internships are available.
Seven students completed the program in 1996–1997.

Summer Session: Yes

Further Information: Harry Solo
English Department
Mankato State University
PO Box 8400
Mankato, MN 56001-8400

Telephone: (507) 389-2117
Fax: (507) 389-5362
E-mail: SOLO@vax1.mankato.msus.edu

◆ MARYLAND, UNIVERSITY OF, BALTIMORE COUNTY, Department of Education

Degree Offered: MA in ESOL/bilingual instructional systems development.

Length of Program: 2–3 semesters. Students may be full-time or part-time and may begin their study at the beginning of any semester. Application deadlines are fall semester, July 1; spring semester, November 1.

Program Requirements: 36 credits. Competence in a language other than English is optional. An internship in an ESL setting is required. A thesis or a comprehensive examination is required.

Courses Offered: (*required) *Methods and Techniques in TESL; *Teaching Reading to the Bilingual/ESOL Student; *Linguistics and Bilingualism; *Intercultural–Cross-Cultural Communication; *Human Learning and Cognition; *Instructional Systems Development I and II; *Instructional Systems Development Internship in ESOL; *(for nonthesis option) Instructional Systems Development Project Seminar in ESOL; *Research Designs in Education; *(for thesis option) Master's Thesis Research; Teaching Writing to ESOL/Bilingual Students; American English Structure for ESL/EFL Teachers; ESL/EFL Testing and Evaluation; Language Learning; The Immigrant Experience.

Full-Time Staff: Jodi Crandall (codirector), Ron Schwartz (codirector), Stanley McCray, Ana Maria Schwartz, Zane Berge, Diane Lee, Signithia Fordham.

Requirements for Admission: The university's requirements for admission are a minimum undergraduate GPA of 3.0; scores on the GRE verbal, quantitative, and analytical sections; and three letters of recommendation. Nonnative English-speaking students must have a minimum TOEFL score of 550.

Tuition, Fees, and Aid: For in-state students, $253 per credit hour; for out-of-state students, $455 per credit hour. Fees are $65 per semester. Graduate assistantships are available in the Department of Education. Fellowships and other assistance are available through the Graduate School.

General: The program is designed to train both prospective and experienced teachers, administrators, and program developers in ESL and EFL. Theory to practice is emphasized in all classes. The instructional system design core prepares students for the analysis, design, and development, administration, and evaluation of instructional programs. The program features a strong cross-cultural component and field-oriented internships either in the U.S. or abroad. Graduates work as ESL/EFL teachers, program developers, administrators, teacher trainers, and cross-cultural trainers in K–12 education, English language programs, government agencies, and business. MA study may be combined with the PhD program in language, literacy, and culture.

International fieldwork is encouraged as part of the internship or thesis. Opportunities exist for work in EFL programs, binational centers, and universities in Mexico, Uruguay, Ecuador, Korea, and other countries. The program collaborates with a graduate-level TEFL certificate program at a Korean university.

Five students completed the program in 1996–1997.

The university has an intensive English language program for nonnative speakers of English.

Summer Session: Yes

Further Information: Jodi Crandall/Ron Schwartz
Department of Education
1000 Hilltop Circle
University of Maryland, Baltimore County
Baltimore, MD 21250

Telephone: (410) 455-3061
Fax: (410) 455-3986
E-mail: crandall@umbc.edu;
rschwartz@umbc7.umbc.edu
http://www.umbc.edu.esol

◆ MARYLAND, UNIVERSITY OF, BALTIMORE COUNTY, Department of Education

Degree Offered: MA in ESOL/bilingual instructional systems development with K–12 certification.

Length of Program: 4 semesters. Students may be full-time or part-time and may begin their study at the beginning of any semester. Application deadlines are fall semester, June 1; spring semester, November 1.

Program Requirements: 42 credits. Two years of undergraduate foreign language study are required for certification. Practice teaching is required. Either a thesis or a comprehensive examination is required.

Courses Offered: (*required) *Methods and Techniques in TESL; *Teaching Reading to the Bilingual/ESOL Student; *Linguistics and Bilingualism; *Intercultural–Cross-Cultural Communication; *Human Learning and Cognition; *Instructional Systems Development I and II; *ESOL Practicum (field experience) in K–12; *Instructional Systems Development ESOL Internship; *(for nonthesis option) Instructional Systems Development Project Seminar in ESOL; *Research Designs in Education; *(for thesis option) Master's Thesis Research; *Teaching Writing to ESOL/Bilingual Students; *American English Structure for ESL/EFL Teachers; *ESL/EFL Testing and Evaluation; Language Learning; The Immigrant Experience.

Full-Time Staff: See program description for MA in ESOL/bilingual instructional systems development.

Requirements for Admission: See program description for MA in ESOL/bilingual instructional systems development.

Tuition, Fees, and Aid: See program description for MA in ESOL/bilingual instructional systems development.

General: See program description for MA in ESOL/bilingual instructional systems development. The program collaborates closely with local and international K–12 ESOL programs. Student teaching can be done at accredited international schools abroad.

Twenty students completed the program in 1996–1997.

The university has an intensive English language program for nonnative speakers of English.

Summer Session: Yes

Further Information: Jodi Crandall/Ron Schwartz
Department of Education
1000 Hilltop Circle
University of Maryland, Baltimore County
Baltimore, MD 21250

Telephone: (410) 455-3061
Fax: (410) 455-3986
E-mail: crandall@umbc.edu;
rschwartz@umbc7.umbc.edu
http://www.umbc.edu.esol

◆ MARYLAND, UNIVERSITY OF, COLLEGE PARK,
Department of Curriculum and Instruction.

Degrees Offered: MEd and EdD/PhD in TESOL with or without certification.

Length of Program: MEd: 1½–2 years with summer courses. Students may be full-time or part-time and may begin their study at the beginning of any semester. Application deadlines are fall semester, March 1 (preferred final deadline is June 1); spring semester, September 1 (preferred final deadline is October 1); summer semester, March 15.

Program Requirements: 30 semester hours for the MEd; 42 with certification. The equivalent of 2 years of a foreign language is required; English meets the requirement for nonnative speakers of English. Practice teaching is required only for those seeking certification. A 6-hour written comprehensive examination is required. A thesis is not required.

Courses Offered: (*required) *Introduction to TESOL Methods; *Testing in the Foreign Language/ESL Classroom; *Trends in Foreign Language Education and TESOL; *Research; *Reading and Writing; *Psycholinguistics; *Cross-Cultural Communication; *English Grammar for ESL Teachers; *Tests and Measurement; *one or two electives in second language acquisition; *(for certification) K–6 Methods, Educational Psychology, Student Teaching.

Full-Time Staff: William E. DeLorenzo (coordinator), Elizabeth Varela.

Requirements for Admission: The university's requirements for admission are a minimum GPA of 3.0 for the MEd and 3.5 for the PhD and a score in the 50th percentile on the GRE. For nonnative speakers of English, the program requires a minimum TOEFL score of 600 and a TWE score of 4. An Oral Proficiency Index score is preferred.

Tuition, Fees, and Aid: For in-state students, $272 per credit; for out-of-state students, $400 per credit. Fees are $146.50 per semester.

General: Students are encourage to do joint research projects with faculty and other students. This leads to joint presentations and publications. All students are required to volunteer some time with local schools or on campus at the Maryland English Institute as part of their course. The program can lead to a Maryland credential in TESOL.

Ten students completed the program in 1996–1997.

The university has an intensive English language program for nonnative speakers of English.

Summer Session: Yes

Further Information: Dr. William E. DeLorenzo
Department of Curriculum and Instruction
Benjamin Building, Room 2304G
University of Maryland, College Park
College Park, MD 20742

Telephone: (301) 405-3130
Fax: (301) 314-9500
E-mail: wd4@umail.umd.edu

◆ MARYMOUNT UNIVERSITY, School of Education and Human Services

Degree Offered: MEd in TESL, K–12.

Length of Program: 4 semesters. Students may be full-time or part-time and may begin their study in January, May, June, or late August. Rolling admissions are in effect.

Program Requirements: 39 credits. Competence in a language other than English is required for state endorsement. Practice teaching is required. Neither a thesis nor a comprehensive examination is required.

Courses Offered: (*required) *Module: Curriculum and Foundations; *Reading, Language Development, and Remedial Strategies; *ESL/English for Specific Purposes: Curriculum, Materials, and Tests; *Cross-Cultural Education and the Language Arts; *Internship: ESL; *Advanced Study of Individuals With Disabilities; *Computers and Technology in the Classroom; *General Linguistics *or* Fundamentals of Language Arts; Module III: Skills Development; Applied Phonology; Applied Grammar: Syntactic Structures; History of the English Language; Teaching Language Pragmatics.

Full-Time Staff: Ana Lado (coordinator), Raja Nasr.

Requirements for Admission: The program's requirements for admission are a bachelor's degree, admission to the university's master's program in education, and an interview.

Tuition, Fees, and Aid: $445 per credit hour. Federal loans, state tuition grants, and graduate Assistantships are available.

General: The program leads to a Virginia credential in TESOL. An additional endorsement in elementary education is also possible, as is international fieldwork in practice teaching.

Twenty students completed the program in 1996–1997.

The university has an intensive English language program for nonnative speakers of English.

Summer Session: Yes

Further Information: Graduate Admissions Coordinator
Marymount University
2807 North Glebe Road
Arlington, VA 22207-9945

Telephone: (703) 284-1500, (800) 548-7638
Fax: (703) 527-3815
E-mail: grad.admissions@marymount.edu
http://www.marymount.edu

◆ MASSACHUSETTS, UNIVERSITY OF, AT AMHERST, School of Education

Degree Offered: MEd with a concentration in ESL.

Length of Program: 3 semesters. Students may be full-time or part-time and may begin their study at the beginning of the fall or spring semester. Application deadlines are fall semester, March 1; spring semester, October 1.

Program Requirements: 33 credits. Intermediate proficiency in a language other than English is required; English meets the requirement for nonnative speakers.

Practice teaching is required for certification. A portfolio and a teacher-research project are required. Neither a thesis nor a comprehensive examination is required.

Courses Offered: Principles of Second Language Learning and Teaching; Language Analysis; Theories of Communication for ESL/Bilingual Education; Review of Research in Language Education for Teacher-Researchers; Curriculum Development for Content-Based ESL; Technology and Language Teaching; Reading and Writing in a Foreign Language; Foreign Language Methodology; Adult Literacy; Bilingual Education; Issues in Special Education; ESL Program Development; Research in Foreign Language Teaching; Writing Workshop; Methods and Materials for ESL/Bilingual Education; Basic Linguistics for ESL/Bilingual Education; International Education.

Full-Time Staff: Sonia Nieto (chair), Theresa Austin, Eileen Kelley, Jerri Willett, Debbie Zacarian.

Requirements for Admission: The university's requirements for admission are a bachelor's degree from an accredited institution, an undergraduate GPA of 2.75, and a graduate GPA of 3.00. Nonnative speakers of English must have a TOEFL score of 560 or higher. The program requires teaching experience, cross-cultural experience or course work, and introductory course work in methods, linguistics, and second language acquisition.

Tuition, Fees, and Aid: For in-state students, $1,320 per semester; for out-of-state students, $4,476 per semester. Fees are $1,458 per semester. A limited number of teaching assistantships, fellowships, tuition waiver awards for top international students, part-time ESL teaching, and work study are available.

General: The program, designed for experienced second/foreign language educators, seeks to create a collaborative, inclusive, and diverse learning community capable of supporting educators to envision new ways of working with second language learners. Fieldwork is integrated into every course, and candidates are encouraged to try out their new ideas in the program's Professional Development Schools. The program leads to a Massachusetts credential in TESOL.

Sixteen students completed the program in 1996–1997.

The university has an intensive English language program for nonnative speakers of English.

Summer Session: Yes

Further Information: Chair, Bilingual/ESL/Multicultural
Department of Teacher Education and Curriculum Studies
School of Education
Furcolo Hall, Room 205
University of Massachusetts at Amherst
Amherst, MA 01003

Telephone: (413) 545-0246
Fax: (413) 545-2875
E-mail: dbrouillet@educ.umass.edu

◆ MASSACHUSETTS, UNIVERSITY OF, AT AMHERST, School of Education

Degree Offered: EdD with a concentration in language, literacy, and culture.

Length of Program: 4–7 years. Students may be full-time or part-time and may begin their study at the beginning of the fall or spring semester. Application deadlines are fall semester, March 1; spring semester, October 1.

Program Requirements: 36 semester credits minimum beyond the master's. Competence in a language other than English is highly desirable for native speakers of English. Practice teaching is not required. A thesis and a comprehensive examination are required.

Courses Offered: The guidance committee and the student jointly put together a program of study based on the academic focus elected by the student. Two doctoral seminars are offered each semester; a year-long ethnographic research course and practica in teacher education, supervision, and program development are offered each year.

Full-Time Staff: Jerri Willett (co-chair), Judy Solsken (co-chair), Sonia Nieto (chair), Theresa Austin, Catherine Luna.

Requirements for Admission: The university's requirements for admission are a bachelor's degree from an accredited institution, an undergraduate GPA of 2.75, and a graduate GPA of 3.00. Nonnative speakers of English must have a TOEFL score of 560 or higher. The program requires a master's degree in a relevant area; interest in sociocultural perspectives on language, literacy, and culture; and evidence of strong writing skills. Teaching experience is highly recommended.

Tuition, Fees, and Aid: See program description for MEd with a concentration in ESL.

General: The program prepares experienced educators for leadership roles in the fields of native and nonnative language, literacy, and multicultural education. The goals of the doctoral area are to develop theoretical understandings of language, literacy, and culture as social and political action; skill in using such perspectives to inform research and scholarship in one's specific area of interest; and skill in using such perspectives to inform the development, implementation, and evaluation of curriculum and educational practice.

Eight students completed the program in 1996–1997.

The university has an intensive English language program for nonnative speakers of English.

Summer Session: Yes

Further Information: Chair
Language, Literacy, and Culture Doctoral Area
Department of Teacher Education and Curriculum Studies
School of Education
Furcolo Hall
University of Massachusetts at Amherst
Amherst, MA 01003

Telephone: (413) 545-0246
Fax: (413) 545-2879
E-mail: dbrouillet@educ.umass.edu

◆ MASSACHUSETTS, UNIVERSITY OF, AT BOSTON, English Department

Degree Offered: MA in bilingual or ESL studies.

Length of Program: Students may be full-time or part-time and may begin their study at the beginning of any semester. Application deadlines are fall semester, March 1; spring semester, October 15.

Program Requirements: 30 credits. Competence in a language other than English is optional. Practice teaching is required. A thesis or a comprehensive examination is required.

Courses Offered: (*required) *Linguistics and Contrastive Analysis; *Psycho-linguistics; *Sociolinguistics; *Cross-Cultural Perspectives. For the bilingual education major: *Methods and Materials in Bilingual Education; *Curriculum Development in Bilingual Education; *Practicum. For the ESL major: *Teaching ESL: Theories and Principles; *Teaching ESL: Methods and Approaches; *Practicum.

Full-Time Staff: Elsa Auerbach, Neal Bruss, Donaldo P. Macedo, Charles Meyer, Conduce Mitchell, Nancy Smith-Hefner, Vivian Zamel.

Requirements for Admission: The program's requirements for admission to the bilingual major are nonnative proficiency in a bilingual target language and, for nonnative speakers of English, a TOEFL score of 575 or higher. Requirements for admission to the ESL major are proficiency in a language other than English at a level equivalent to 2 years of successful college study; evidence of general knowledge of English literature, American literature, and American culture; and, for nonnative speakers of English, a TOEFL score of 575 or higher.

Tuition, Fees, and Aid: For in-state students, $110 per credit; for out-of-state students, $368.50 per credit. Fees are $279–$1,320 per semester. Graduate assistant-ships and grant-funded scholarships are available.

General: The programs provide preservice training and in-service enrichment for teachers instructing limited English proficient students at the elementary, secondary, or university level, or in adult education programs. On-campus classroom work is combined with on-site experience in ESL and bilingual classrooms. Also offered is a concentration in computer-assisted instruction. The programs lead to a Massachusetts credential in TESOL.

An exchange program with Chukyo University, Japan, is available.

One hundred students completed the program in 1996–1997.

The university has an English language program for nonnative speakers of English students.

Summer Session: Yes

Further Information: Donaldo Macedo
Department of Bilingual/ESL Studies
W-6-058
University of Massachusetts at Boston
100 Morrissey Boulevard
Boston, MA 02125-3393

Telephone: (617) 287-5760
Fax: (617) 287-6511
E-mail: macedo@umbsky.cc.umb.edu

◆ MEMPHIS, UNIVERSITY OF, Department of English

Degree Offered: BA in English with a concentration in ESL.

Length of Program: 4 years. Students may be full-time or part-time and may begin their study at the beginning of any semester. Application deadlines are fall semester, August 1; spring semester, December 1; summer semester, May 1.

Program Requirements: 132 credit hours. Competence in a language other than English is required; English meets the requirement for nonnative speakers of English. Practice teaching is recommended. Neither a thesis nor a comprehensive examination is required.

Courses Offered: Modern English Grammar; Introduction to Linguistics; The American Language; History of the English Language; Language and Literature;

Language and Society; Practicum in ESL; Methods and Techniques in ESL; Skills Approaches and Assessment for ESL.

Full-Time Staff: Teresa Dalle, Charles Hall, Emily Thrush.

Tuition, Fees, and Aid: For in-state students, $96 per credit hour (maximum: $1,056); for out-of-state students, $282 per credit hour (maximum: $3,224). Fees are $4 per credit hour (maximum: $34).

General: The program stresses both EFL and ESL teaching for adults and children and works with the professional writing and creative writing programs to provide additional training in skills such as document design, technical editing, or literary publishing.

The program conducts an intensive summer program in the Czech Republic every year and conducts a large internship program in teaching middle and high school students in Shenzhen, China. Organized internships are available in the Czech Republic and Japan.

Two students completed the program in 1996–1997.

The university has an intensive English language program for nonnative speakers of English.

Summer Session: Yes

Further Information: Director of Undergraduate Programs
Department of English
University of Memphis
Memphis, TN 38152

Telephone: (901) 678-4496
Fax: (901) 678-2226
E-mail: cehall@cc.memphis.edu
http://www.people.memphis.edu/ ~ english/esl.htm

◆ MEMPHIS, UNIVERSITY OF, Department of English

Degree Offered: MA in English with a concentration in ESL.

Length of Program: 4 semesters. Students may be full-time or part-time and may begin their study at the beginning of any semester. Application deadlines for international students are fall semester, May 1; spring semester, September 15; summer semester, February 1.

Program Requirements: 33 semester hours. Competence in a language other than English is required; English meets the requirement for nonnative speakers of English. Practice teaching is strongly recommended. A comprehensive examination or a thesis is required.

Courses Offered: Language Skills for Internationals; International Teaching Assistants; History of the English Language; Introduction to Modern English; English Syntax; Dialectology; Sociolinguistics; Language and Literature; English Phonetics and Phonology; Field Experience and Practicum in ESL; Theory and History of ESL; Principles of Skills Assessment in ESL; Methods and Techniques of ESL in K–12; ESL Grammar.

Full-Time Staff: See BA program description.

Requirements for Admission: The program's requirement for admission is 12 hours of upper-division English or related courses.

Tuition, Fees, and Aid: For in-state students, $147 per credit hour (maximum: $1,443); for out-of-state students, $348 per credit hour (maximum: $3,731). Fees are $4 per credit hour (maximum: $34). Graduate assistantships are available.

General: See BA program description
Eighteen students completed the program in 1996–1997.

Summer Session: Yes

Further Information: Director of Graduate Programs
Department of English
University of Memphis
Memphis, TN 38152

Telephone: (901) 678-4496
Fax: (901) 678-2226
E-mail: cehall@cc.memphis.edu
http://www.people.memphis.edu/ ~ english/esl.htm

◆ MEREDITH COLLEGE, Department of Education

Degree Offered: ESL state licensure.

Length of Program: Students may be full-time or part-time and may begin their study at the beginning of any semester. Application deadlines are fall semester, August 1; spring semester, December 1; summer semester, May 1.

Program Requirements: 18 semester hours. Experience as a second language learner is required. A practicum is required. Neither a thesis nor a comprehensive examination is required.

Courses Offered: (*required) *Methods of Teaching ESL; *Second Language Acquisition; *Culture and the Language Teacher; *Teaching ESL in the Public Schools; *Seminar in Advanced Methods of Teaching ESL.

Full-Time Staff: Ellen Collie Graden, Louise Taylor.

Requirements for Admission: The college's requirement for admission is a baccalaureate degree from a regionally accredited college or university with a 2.5 or better GPA. The program requires teaching licensure, a Miller Analogies Test score, and two letters of recommendation. Nonnative speakers of English must submit TOEFL and TSE scores.

Tuition, Fees, and Aid: $250 per semester hour. A tuition grant of $100 for each 3-hour course is available to teachers under contract in a secondary or elementary, public or private North Carolina school.

General: The program prepares teachers to teach nonnative English-speaking students in K–12 classrooms. Because the program is designed to attract professional educators, the times of the classes are matched to their scheduling requirements.

Summer Session: Yes

Further Information: Ellen Collie Graden
Department of Education
Ledford Building
Meredith College
3800 Hillsborough Street
Raleigh, NC 27607-5298

Telephone: (919) 829-7455
Fax: (919) 829-2303
E-mail: gradene@meredith.edu

◆ MEREDITH COLLEGE, Department of Education

Degree Offered: MEd with an ESL specialty.

Length of Program: 2 semesters. Students may be full-time or part-time and may begin their study at the beginning of any semester. Application deadlines are fall semester, August 1; spring semester, December 1; summer semester, May 1.

Program Requirements: 36 semester hours. Experience as a second language learner is required. A thesis or independent study and a comprehensive examination are required.

Courses Offered: (*required) *Curriculum Development; *Advanced Educational Psychology; *Philosophy of Education; *Educational Research; *Methods of Teaching ESL; *Second Language Acquisition; *Culture and the Language Teacher; *Teaching ESL in the Public Schools; *Seminar in Advanced Methods of Teaching ESL; *Study of Linguistics; *Independent Study or Thesis.

Full-Time Staff: Gwendolyn Clay, Ellen Collie Graden, Mary S. Johnson, Sherry Shapiro, Cheryl Southworth, Louise Taylor, Elizabeth Weir.

Requirements for Admission: See ESL licensure program description.

Tuition, Fees, and Aid: See ESL licensure program description.

General: See ESL licensure program description. The program leads to a North Carolina credential in TESOL.

Summer Session: Yes

Further Information: Ellen Collie Graden
Department of Education
Ledford Building
Meredith College
3800 Hillsborough Street
Raleigh, NC 27607-5298

Telephone: (919) 829-7455
Fax: (919) 829-2303
E-mail: gradene@meredith.edu

◆ MICHIGAN STATE UNIVERSITY, Department of English

Degree Offered: MA in TESOL.

Length of Program: 3–4 semesters. Students may be full-time or part-time and should begin their study at the beginning of any semester. The application deadline for fall semester is January 1.

Program Requirements: 30 credits. Competence in a language other than English is not required. Practice teaching and a comprehensive examination are required. A thesis is optional.

Courses Offered: (*required) *Introduction to Linguistics; *Introduction to TESOL; *Advanced Studies in TESOL; *Introduction to Second Language Acquisition; *Methods of Research in Language Learning and Teaching; *Structures and Functions of English; *Special Topics in Language; *Practicum; *one of the following: Phonology, Syntax, Semantics and Pragmatics; *one of the following: Variation in English, Language and Culture, Sociolinguistics, Discourse Analysis; electives.

Full-Time Staff: Susan Gass, Charlene Polio, Alison Mackey.

Requirements for Admission: The requirements for admission are a strong undergraduate record and a GRE score (for native speakers of English). Nonnative speakers of English must have a minimum TOEFL score of 600.

Tuition, Fees, and Aid: For in-state students: $216 per credit hour; for out-of state students, $437 per credit hour. Fees are $283 per semester. Teaching assistantships at the English Language Center are available.

General: The program presents students with a careful balance between theory and practice.

Twenty students completed the program in 1996–1997.

The university has an intensive English language program for nonnative speakers of English.

Summer Session: No

Further Information: Professor C. Polio
Department of English
A714 Wells Hall
Michigan State University
East Lansing, MI 48864

Telephone: (517) 353-0800
Fax: (517) 432-1149
E-mail: polio@pilot.msu.edu

◆ MINNESOTA, UNIVERSITY OF, College of Education, Department of Curriculum and Instruction

Degree Offered: MEd with a major in teaching and an emphasis in ESL.

Length of Program: 5 quarters. Students must be full-time and must begin their study at the beginning of summer quarter I. The deadline for application is February 1.

Program Requirements: College-level experience in a language other than English is required. Practice teaching is required. Neither a thesis nor a comprehensive examination is required.

Courses Offered: (*required) *School and Society; *Learning and Cognitive Foundations of Education; *Interpersonal and Personality Effects on Learning; *Classroom Assessment Methods; *Biological and Physical Foundations of Education; *Basic Concepts in Personal and Community Health; *Secondary School Teaching; *Second Language Curriculum; *Second Language Instruction; *Clinical Experiences in Second Languages; *Introduction to Linguistics; *The Structure of English; *Introduction to Language Learning.

Full-Time Staff: Helen L. Jorstad, Dale L. Lange, Diane Tedick, Constance L. Walker.

Requirements for Admission: The program's requirements for admission are language competency, a minimum GPA of 2.8, experience with school-aged students, experience with diverse populations, a writing sample, and a baccalaureate degree.

Tuition, Fees, and Aid: For in-state students, $107 per credit; for out-of-state students, $230 per credit. Fees are $140.

General: Most credits for the master's-level program are completed when licensure is completed. The program is heavily school based and uses cohort groups.

Nineteen students completed the program in 1996–1997.

The university has an intensive English language program for nonnative speakers of English.

Summer Session: Yes

Further Information: Department of Curriculum and Instruction
125 Peck Hall
University of Minnesota
Minneapolis, MN 55455

Telephone: (612) 625-6372

◆ MINNESOTA, UNIVERSITY OF, Institute of Linguistics and Asian and Slavic Languages and Literatures

Degree Offered: MA in ESL.

Length of Program: 2 years (6 quarters; 4 semesters as of fall 1999). Students may be full-time or part-time and must begin their study at the beginning of the fall quarter (fall semester) or the first summer session. The deadline for application is March 1.

Program Requirements: 46 quarter credits (33 semester credits). Competence in a language other than English is required; English meets the requirement for nonnative speakers of English. Practice teaching is required. An oral examination, and either two qualifying papers or a thesis, are required.

Courses Offered: (*required) *Introduction to Linguistics; *ESL: Methods; *ESL Practicum; *Linguistic Analysis: *Phonetics; *Linguistic Description of Modern English; *Introduction to Second Language Acquisition; Second Language Acquisition; ESL: Materials; English for Specific Purposes; Research Methods in Language Acquisition; electives in linguistics, foreign languages, speech communication, anthropology, English.

Full-Time Staff: Andrew Cohen (chair), Bruce T. Downing, Jeanette Gundel, Bill Johnston, Dan Reed, Amy Sheldon, Nancy Stenson, Elaine Tarone.

Requirements for Admission: The university's requirements for admission are a baccalaureate degree, official transcripts, a minimum undergraduate GPA of 3.2, a GRE score, TOEFL scores for nonnative speakers of English, three letters of recommendation, and a statement of research interest. The program requires ability and potential as an ESL/EFL teacher.

Tuition, Fees, and Aid: For in-state students, $1,660 per quarter; for out-of-state students, $3,260 per quarter. The student services fee is $158 per quarter. Teaching assistantships are available after completion of the ESL Practicum course. Departmental fellowships and tuition waivers are awarded to eligible applicants.

General: This small, selective program focuses on the teaching of adults in second and foreign language settings. It offers a small, friendly, and dynamic atmosphere; an excellent faculty-student ratio; more teaching assistantships than many comparable programs; world-renowned faculty; and excellent teaching and research opportunities. Graduates have gone on to find excellent jobs both in the United States and abroad. Internships are available at the university's campus in Akita, Japan.

Five students completed the program in 1996–1997.

The university has an intensive English language program for nonnative speakers of English.

Summer Session: Yes

Further Information: Dr. Andrew D. Cohen
Department of ESL
130 Klaeber Court
University of Minnesota
320 16th Avenue, SE
Minneapolis, MN 55455

Telephone: (612) 624-3806
Fax: (612) 624-4579
E-mail: adcohen@ic.umn.edu

◆ MONTANA, THE UNIVERSITY OF, Linguistics Program

Degree Offered: Certificate of accomplishment in ESL teaching.

Length of Program: 1 year. Students may be full-time or part-time and may begin their study at the beginning of any semester. Deadlines for application are fall semester, September 1; spring semester, January 20; summer, May 23.

Program Requirements: 21 credits. Competence in a language other than English is required for native speakers of English. Practice teaching is required. Neither a thesis nor a comprehensive examination is required.

Courses Offered: (*required) *Introduction to Linguistics; *Morphophonology; *Syntax and Semantics; *two of the following: Language and Culture, Child Language Acquisition, Bilingualism, Pragmatics, Second Language Acquisition, Computer-Assisted Language Instruction; *TESL; *Internship in TESL.

Full-Time Staff: Deirdre Black, Julie Eels, Robert Hausmann (chair), Istvan Keeskes, Anthony Mattina, Nancy Mattina.

Requirements for Admission: The program is open to undergraduates, graduate students (a GRE score is required), and nondegree graduate students.

Tuition, Fees, and Aid: For in-state students, $1,500 per term; for out-of-state students, $3,400 per term. Fees are $350.

General: The program leads to a Montana credential in TESOL.
There are opportunities to teach in the Soros Professional English Language Teaching Program and in several Japanese universities.

Summer Session: Yes

Further Information: Robert B. Hausmann
Linguistics Program
Fine Arts 201
University of Montana
Missoula, MT 59812

Telephone: (406) 243-4751
Fax: (406) 243-2016
E-mail: hausmann@selway.umt.edu

◆ MONTANA, THE UNIVERSITY OF, Linguistics Program

Degree Offered: MA in English linguistics and TESOL.

Length of Program: 1–1½ years. Students must be full-time and may begin their study at the beginning of any semester. Deadlines for application are fall semester, September 1; spring semester, January 20; summer, May 23.

Program Requirements: 9 credits. Competence in a language other than English is required for native speakers of English. Practice teaching and a comprehensive examination are required. A thesis is not required.

Courses Offered: Introduction to Linguistics; Morphology and Phonology; Syntax and Semantics; Second Language Acquisition; Pragmatics; TEFL.

Full-Time Staff: See certificate program description.

Requirements for Admission: The university's requirements for admission are an undergraduate degree and a GRE score.

Tuition, Fees, and Aid: See certificate program description. Teaching assistantships are available.

General: See certificate program description.
Seven students completed the program in 1996–1997.

Summer Session: Yes

Further Information: Robert B. Hausmann
Linguistics Program
Fine Arts 201
University of Montana
Missoula, MT 59812

Telephone: (406) 243-4751
Fax: (406) 243-2016
E-mail: hausmann@selway.umt.edu

◆ MONTCLAIR STATE UNIVERSITY, Department of Linguistics

Degree Offered: BA in linguistics.

Length of Program: 8 semesters. Students may be full-time or part-time and may begin their study at the beginning of the fall or spring semester. Deadlines for application are fall semester, March 1; spring semester, November 15.

Program Requirements: 128 semester hours. Competence in a language other than English is not required. Practice teaching is required. Neither a thesis nor a comprehensive examination is required.

Courses Offered: (*required) *Introduction to General Linguistics; *Structure of American English; *Language in Society; *Language and Culture; *Syntax; *Semantics *or Pragmatics; *Phonetics; *Phonology; electives.

Full-Time Staff: Mary Call (chair), Eileen Fitzpatrick, Alice F. Freed, Toshihide Nakayama, Steven Seegmiller, Susana M. Sotillo, Longxing Wei.

Requirements for Admission: The university's requirements for admission are a high school diploma and an SAT score. The program requires a GPA of at least 3.0 in linguistics.

Tuition, Fees, and Aid: For in-state students, $117.58 per semester hour; for out-of-state students, $166.33 per semester hour. Work study is available.

General: Located in the Greater New York metropolitan area with its richly diverse demography, the university offers unique opportunities for students pursuing New Jersey TESL certification to work with ESL students from a variety of language backgrounds who differ in proficiency, age, educational level, and aspirations. This diversity of experience benefits graduates of the program as they seek employment as ESL teachers throughout the world.

The university has a student exchange agreement with the Universidad del Valle de Atemajac in Guadalajara, Mexico.

Six students completed the program in 1996–1997.

The university has an intensive English language program for nonnative speakers of English.

Summer Session: No

Further Information: Coordinator of Teacher Education
Department of Linguistics
Dickson Hall Room 124
Montclair State University
Normal Avenue
Upper Montclair, NJ 07043

Telephone: (201) 655-4286

◆ MONTCLAIR STATE UNIVERSITY, Department of Linguistics

Degree Offered: Postbaccalaureate certification in TESL.

Length of Program: 2 semesters. Students may be full-time or part-time and may begin their study at the beginning of any semester. Deadlines for application are fall semester, March 1; spring semester, October 1.

Program Requirements: 18 semester hours. Competence in a language other than English is not required. Practice teaching is required. A thesis and a comprehensive examination are not required.

Courses Offered: (*required) *Language and Linguistics; *Advanced Structure of American English; *Language and Culture; *Methods of TESL; *Current Theory in Second Language Acquisition; *Practicum.

Full-Time Staff: See program description for BA in linguistics.

Requirements for Admission: The program's requirements for admission are undergraduate transcripts, certification in another content area, a statement of objectives, and an interview.

Tuition, Fees, and Aid: For in-state students, $186.30 per semester hour; for out-of-state students, $236.10 per semester hour. No financial aid is available.

General: See program description for BA in linguistics.

Eight students completed the program in 1996–1997.

Summer Session: No

Further Information: Coordinator of Teacher Education
Department of Linguistics
Dickson Hall Room 124
Montclair State University
Normal Avenue
Upper Montclair, NJ 07043

Telephone: (201) 655-4286

◆ MONTCLAIR STATE UNIVERSITY, Department of Linguistics

Degree Offered: MA in applied linguistics with a concentration in TESL.

Length of Program: 4 semesters. Students may be full-time or part-time and may begin their study at the beginning of any semester. Deadlines for application are fall semester, March 1; spring semester, October 1.

Program Requirements: 37 semester hours. Competence in a language other than English is not required. Practice teaching and a comprehensive examination are required. A thesis is not required.

Courses Offered: (*required) *Language and Linguistics; *Sociolinguistics; *Syntax; *Translation Theory; *Semantics and Pragmatics; *Phonetics and Phonology; *Research Design in Applied Linguistics; *Independent Research; electives.

Full-Time Staff: See program description for BA in linguistics.

Requirements for Admission: The university's requirements for admission are official undergraduate transcripts, a GRE score, two letters of reference, and a statement of objectives. The program requires an interview with faculty.

Tuition, Fees, and Aid: See program description for BA in linguistics. Assistantships are available.

General: See program description for BA in linguistics. For candidates who hold certification in another field, the program leads to a New Jersey credential in TESOL. Two students completed the program in 1996–1997.

Summer Session: No

Further Information: Graduate Adviser
Department of Linguistics
Dickson Hall Room 124
Montclair State University
Normal Avenue
Upper Montclair, NJ 07043

Telephone: (201) 655-4286
E-mail: CallM@Saturn.Montclair.edu

◆ MONTEREY INSTITUTE OF INTERNATIONAL STUDIES, Department of TESOL

Degrees Offered: MA in TESOL; certificate in TESOL; certificate in language program administration.

Length of Program: 3 semesters or 2 semesters and two summers. Students may be full-time or part-time and may begin their study at the beginning of any semester. Rolling admissions are in effect.

Program Requirements: 37 semester hours. Competence in a language other than English is optional. Practice teaching and a portfolio are required. Neither a thesis nor a comprehensive examination is required.

Courses Offered: (*required) *Language Analysis; *Introduction to Observation; *Principles and Methods of Teaching; *Educational Research Methods; *Sociolinguistics; *Curricula and Materials in Language Teaching; *Language Testing; *Structure of English; *Second Language Acquisition; *Applied Linguistics Research; *Portfolio; *Practicum; Teaching Reading; Teaching Writing; Bilingual Education; Teacher Supervision; Computer-Assisted Instruction; Teaching Literature; Cross-Cultural Consulting; Teaching Culture.

Full-Time Staff: Kathleen M. Bailey, Lynn Goldstein, John Hedgcock, Ruth Larimer (chair), Bob Oprandy, Peter Shaw, Jean Turner, Leo van Lier.

Requirements for Admission: The Institute requires a bachelor's degree or the equivalent with a GPA of 3.0, two letters of recommendation, and a statement of purpose. A TOEFL score of 600 is required for nonnative speakers of English.

Tuition, Fees, and Aid: $9,100 per semester. Tuition scholarships, work-study, loans, and grants are available.

General: The Institute, a small school with an international character, provides an excellent mix of theory and practice and has a large, well-known, active, and caring faculty. Specialties in language program administration and computer-assisted instruction are also available.

Internships are available in Panama, China, and Mexico, and overseas summer language study is possible in China, France, Germany, Japan, Russia, and Mexico.

Sixty-five students completed the program in 1996–1997.

The Institute has an intensive English language program for nonnative speakers of English.

Summer Session: Yes

Further Information: Admissions Office
Monterey Institute of International Studies
425 Van Buren Street
Monterey, CA 93940

Telephone: (408) 647-4123

◆ MOUNT VERNON COLLEGE, Department of Arts and Humanities

Degrees Offered: Certificate in TESOL; MA in TESOL.

Length of Program: Students may be full-time or part-time and may begin their study at the beginning of any semester. The deadline for application is June 15.

Program Requirements: Certificate, 18 credits; MA, 30 credits. Competence in a language other than English is optional. Practice teaching is required for the MA. Neither a comprehensive examination nor a thesis is required.

Courses Offered: (*required) Certificate and MA: *English Grammar for ESL; *Methodology of Language Teaching; *Methodology of Language Testing; *Methodology of Teaching Reading and Writing; *Methodology of Teaching Listening and Speaking. Certificate: *ESL Methodology for Elementary School Teaching or *ESL Methodology for Secondary School Teaching. MA: *Advanced Principles of Linguistic Research; *Psychological and Sociological Theory of Language Acquisition; *Language Acquisition and Development in Children or ESL Methodology for Elementary School Teaching or ESL Methodology for Secondary School Teaching; *Language and Culture Seminar; *Practicum in TESOL.

Full-Time Staff: Sharon Ahern Fechter (chair), Ann Kennedy.

Requirements for Admission: The college's requirement for admission is a BA with a GPA of 3.0. The program requires students to take the GRE before completion of the degree. A TOEFL score of 600 is required for nonnative speakers of English.

Tuition, Fees, and Aid: $478 per credit. Federal financial aid is available.

General: The program is characterized by a strong practical orientation. International students may complete their practicum overseas.

Five students completed each program in 1996–1997.

Summer Session: Yes

Further Information: Sharon Ahern Fechter, PhD
MA TESOL Program
Mount Vernon College
2100 Foxhall Road, NW
Washington, DC 20007

Telephone: (202) 625-0400
Fax: (202) 625-4688
E-mail: sfechter@mvc.edu

◆ MURRAY STATE UNIVERSITY, English Department

Degree Offered: MA in TESOL.

Length of Program: 4 semesters. Students may be full-time or part-time and may begin their study at the beginning of any semester. Rolling admissions are in effect.

Program Requirements: 34 credit hours. Competence in a language other than English is required; English fulfills the requirement for nonnative speakers of English. Practice teaching is required. Neither a comprehensive examination nor a thesis is required.

Courses Offered: (*required) *Linguistics and English Grammars; *Applied Linguistics for Second Language Teaching; *Computer-Assisted Language Learning; *Methods and Materials for Teaching ESL; *Course and Syllabus Design in ESL; *Testing and Evaluation in Second Language Teaching; *Developing Intercultural Competence; *Seminar in Teaching ESL Grammar; *TESOL Practicum; *TESOL Internship; *Seminar in Teaching ESL Reading/Writing *or* Seminar in Teaching ESL Listening/Speaking.

Full-Time Staff: Michael Morgan, Mary Sue Sroda (director), Guangming Zou.

Requirements for Admission: The university's requirement for admission is an undergraduate GPA of 2.75, or an undergraduate GPA of 2.00 and a combined score of 800 on the verbal and quantitative sections of the GRE. Conditional admission is granted case by case. For native speakers of English, the program requires an undergraduate major in English or a modern foreign language, or a B average in a set equivalent courses; and at least 12 credit hours in a modern foreign language or demonstrated competence at that level. Nonnative speakers of English must have a TOEFL score of 575 or a degree granted in the United States. Students without the requisite TOEFL score must take the TOEFL after completing the highest level of the university's English Language Institute.

Tuition, Fees, and Aid: For in-state students, $1,150 per semester; for out-of-state students, $3,130 per semester. Instructor support assistantships, and teaching assistantships are available.

General: The linguistics-based curriculum is designed to contribute to competencies in linguistics, language pedagogy, language assessment, professional development, and intercultural communication. The teaching practicum and internship allow students to apply their knowledge in real-world situations. The internship may be individualized for either adult or K–12 situations in ESL or EFL contexts. The program is new.

Eleven students completed the program in fall 1997.

The university has an intensive English language program for nonnative speakers of English.

Summer Session: Yes

Further Information: Director, TESOL Program
English Department
Murray State University
PO Box 9
Murray, KY 42071

Telephone: (502) 762-2401
Fax: (502) 762-4545
E-mail: sue.sroda@murraystate.edu

◆ NATIONAL-LOUIS UNIVERSITY,
Department of Curriculum and Instruction

Degree Offered: MEd with a concentration in ESL, bilingual education, or ESL and bilingual special education.

Length of Program: Students may be full-time or part-time and may begin their study at the beginning of any semester. There are no application deadlines.

Program Requirements: 34 semester hours. Competence in a language other than English is not required. Neither practice teaching, nor a thesis, nor a comprehensive examination is required.

Courses Offered: (*required) *Foundations of Language Minority Education; *Methods and Materials for Teaching ESL; *Assessment of Language Minority Students; *Cross-Cultural Education; *Methods and Materials for Teaching Bilingual Students (bilingual endorsement) *or* Linguistics for TESOL (ESL endorsement); elective.

Full-Time Staff: Darrell Bloom (chair), Grete Roland, Leah D. Miller.

Requirements for Admission: The program's requirements for admission are a teaching certificate, a Miller Analogies Test or TOEFL score, official transcripts showing a bachelor's degree, three letters of recommendation, and written statements of academic and professional goals.

Tuition, Fees, and Aid: $490 per 3-credit-hour language minority education course; $399 per semester hour for all other courses taken as a resident. Fellowships and Stafford loans are available.

General: The program leads to a state of Illinois endorsement in ESL, bilingual education, or both. Courses are taught on five campuses and at selected locations throughout the Chicago area. A rich diversity of field sites and experiences is offered. The highly qualified faculty has practical as well as scholarly experience.

The program offers a summer study program in Mexico in which students can take the two courses required for a Spanish endorsement.

Ninety students completed the MEd degree in 1996–1997; 900 completed the 18-hour endorsement sequence.

The university has an intensive English language program for nonnative speakers of English.

Summer Session: Yes

Further Information: Dr. Darrell Bloom, Coordinator
Department of Curriculum and Instruction, Language
Minority Education
National-Louis University
1000 Capital Drive
Wheeling, IL 60090

Telephone: (800) 443-5522 extension 5622
Fax: (847) 465-5629
E-mail: dblo@wheelingl.nl.edu

◆ NAZARETH COLLEGE OF ROCHESTER, Department of TESOL

Degree Offered: MS in education, TESOL.

Length of Program: 4 semesters or less. Students may be full-time or part-time and may begin their study at the beginning of any semester. Application deadlines for applicants with teaching certificates are fall semester, June 1; spring semester, September 15 or November 1; summer semester, February 1 or March 1. Application deadlines for applicants seeking first-time certification are fall semester, March 1; spring semester, September 15.

Program Requirements: 36 semester credits. Competence in a language other than English is not required. Practice teaching is required but is optional for students who are teaching full-time. A comprehensive examination is required. A thesis is not required.

Courses Offered: (*required) *Foundations of Education; *Linguistics; *English Linguistics; *Cross-Cultural Abilities and Awareness in Curriculum Design; *Advanced Methods of Assessment in TESOL; *Foundations of Bilingual/Multicultural Education; *TESOL Methods and Materials; *Advanced Preadolescent Psychology *or* Adolescent Psychology; *Health Education Workshop (for first-time certification only).

Full-Time Staff: Brett Blake (chair).

Requirements for Admission: The college's requirements for admission are a baccalaureate from an accredited institution with a cumulative index of 2.7 or a B average in the major field, official transcripts, two letters of recommendation specifying ability to do graduate-level work and commitment to teacher education, and copies of teacher certification, if applicable. Applicants seeking first-time certification must undergo a complete transcript review to see if prerequisites have been met.

Tuition, Fees, and Aid: $417 per credit hour. Tuition Assistance Program aid (for New York State residents) and loans are available.

General: The program leads to a New York State credential in TESOL
Twenty-one students completed the program in 1996–1997.

Summer Session: Yes

Further Information: Dr. Brett Blake
Department of TESOL
Smith Hall
Nazareth College of Rochester
4245 East Avenue
Rochester, NY 14618-3790

Telephone: (716) 389-2815
E-mail: beblake@naz.edu

◆ NEVADA, UNIVERSITY OF, RENO, College of Education, Department of Curriculum and Instruction

Degree Offered: Interdisciplinary MA in TESOL.

Length of Program: 4 semesters. Students may be full-time or part-time and may begin their study at the beginning of any semester. There are no application deadlines.

Program Requirements: 36 credits. Knowledge of a language other than English is required; English meets the requirement for nonnative speakers of English. A practicum is required if the student has less than 1 year of teaching experience. Written and oral comprehensive examinations are required. A thesis is not required.

Courses Offered: (*required) *ESL Instruction in the Elementary School *or* Second Language Instruction in the Secondary School; *Second Language Acquisition; *Bilingual Education; *one of the following: Research Applications in Curriculum and Instruction, Introduction to Graduate Study, Introduction to Educational Research; *Language and Culture; *Applied Linguistics for Language Teachers; Sociocultural Concerns in Education; The Adolescent Learner and the Secondary Curriculum; The Junior High/Middle School; Literacy Development for ESL Students; Language Assessment; Problems in Teaching; Selection and Development of ESL Texts and Materials; Curriculum Development in Second Language Education; Secondary School Curriculum; Seminar in Multicultural Education; Special Topics; Second Language Practicum; Linguistics; History of the Language; Historical Linguistics; Sociolinguistics; Topics in Linguistics; Evaluation of ESL Textbooks and Materials; Advanced Grammar for ESL Teachers; Problems in Language; Problems in Writing; TEFL; Issues in ESL/EFL; Special Topics in ESL.

Full-Time Staff: John P. Milton, Lee Thomas, Joaquín S. Vilá (coordinator).

Requirements for Admission: The university's requirement for admission is a BA with a minimum last-half undergraduate GPA of 3.0. Nonnative speakers of English must have a minimum TOEFL score of 550. The program requires either 2 years of study of a foreign language at the college level or an equivalent language experience, and an undergraduate major or minor in a relevant field (desirable).

Tuition, Fees, and Aid: For in-state students, $810 per semester; for out-of-state students, $3,527 per semester. Scholarships, fellowships, assistantships, grants, loans, student employment, and deferred payment are available.

General: The program is an interdisciplinary one designed for native and nonnative speakers of English who now work or who wish to work as teachers, program directors, or curriculum consultants or in publishing and materials development. Course work includes the theory and practice of TESL, applied linguistics, the English language, and multicultural education. The program leads to an elementary or secondary Nevada state ESL endorsement.

Six students completed the program in 1996–1997.

The university has an intensive English language program for nonnative speakers of English.

Summer Session: Yes

Further Information: MA in TESL Coordinator
Department of Curriculum and Instruction/282
College of Education Building, Room 3100
University of Nevada, Reno
Reno, NV 89557-0214

Telephone: (702) 784-4961
Fax: (702) 327-5220
E-mail: vila@unr.edu

◆ NEW HAMPSHIRE, UNIVERSITY OF,
   Department of Education

Degree Offered: MAT with a concentration in TESL.

Length of Program: 4 semesters. Students may be full-time or part-time and may begin their study at the beginning of any semester. Application deadlines are fall semester, February 15; spring semester, November 15.

Program Requirements: 32 credits. Competence in a language other than English is required; English meets the requirement for nonnative speakers of English. Practice teaching is required. Neither a thesis nor a comprehensive examination is required.

Courses Offered: (*required) *Exploring Teaching; *Educational Psychology; *Educational Structure and Change; *Perspectives on the Nature of Education; *TESL: Theory and Methods; *Curriculum Design, Materials, and Testing in ESL; *English Grammar *or* Syntax and Semantic Theory *or* Linguistic Field Methods; *Sociolinguistics; *Practicum in TESL; electives in education or linguistic theory.

Full-Time Staff: Mary Clark, Karl Diller, Rochelle Lieber, Naomi Nagy (chair).

Requirements for Admission: The university's requirements for admission are a BA degree or the equivalent, a GRE General Test score, transcripts, and three letters of recommendation. A minimum TOEFL score of 550 for is required for international students.

Tuition, Fees, and Aid: For in-state students, $2,450 per semester; for out-of-state students, $6,880 per semester. Tuition scholarships are available.

General: Students have opportunities for part-time teaching in local public schools or in the Summer Intensive ESL Institute. The program leads to a New Hampshire credential in TESOL.

Two students completed the program in 1996–1997.

The university has an intensive English language program for nonnative speakers of English.

Summer Session: Yes

Further Information: Prof. Mary Clark
Department of English
Hamilton Smith Hall
University of New Hampshire
Durham, NH 03824

Telephone: (603) 862-3990
Fax: (603) 862-3563
E-mail: mmc@christa.unh.edu

◆ NEW HAMPSHIRE, UNIVERSITY OF,
   Department of English

Degree Offered: MA in English language and linguistics with a concentration in TESL.

Length of Program: 3 semesters; 4 semesters for certification. Students may be full-time or part-time and may begin their study at the beginning of any semester. Application deadlines are fall semester, February 15; spring semester, November 15.

Program Requirements: 32 credits. Competence in a language other than English is required; English meets the requirement for nonnative speakers of English.

Practice teaching is required for certification. A thesis is required. A comprehensive examination is not required.

Courses Offered: (*required) *TESL: Theory and Methods; *Curriculum Design, Materials, and Testing in ESL; *Phonetics and Phonology; *Syntax and Semantic Theory; *Master's Paper; Seminar in Linguistics; Seminar in Second Language Acquisition; History of English; Sociolinguistics; Brain and Language; Linguistic Field Methods; Special Topics in Linguistic Theory; English Grammar; Psycholinguistics; Seminar in Teaching Writing; electives from other university departments.

Full-Time Staff: See program description for MAT with a concentration in TESL.

Requirements for Admission: See program description for MAT with a concentration in TESL.

Tuition, Fees, and Aid: For in-state students, $2,450 per semester; for out-of-state students, $6,880 per semester. Teaching assistantships in ESL and tuition waivers for international students are available.

General: Students have considerable freedom in designing their own programs and choosing areas of special research. There are opportunities to teach in the university's Summer ESL Institute. The MA may be combined with course work leading to a New Hampshire credential in TESOL.

Six students completed the program in 1996–1997.

The university has an intensive English language program for nonnative speakers of English.

Summer Session: Yes

Further Information: Prof. Mary Clark
Department of English
Hamilton Smith Hall
University of New Hampshire
Durham, NH 03824

Telephone: (603) 862-3990
Fax: (603) 862-3563
E-mail: mmc@christa.unh.edu

◆ NEW MEXICO, UNIVERSITY OF, Division of Language, Literacy, and Sociocultural Studies

Degrees Offered: BA and MA in elementary or secondary education with a concentration in TESOL.

Length of Program: 4 semesters (MA). Students may be full-time or part-time and may begin their study at the beginning of any semester. Application deadlines are March 1 for the BA in elementary education and continuous for the BA in secondary education. For the MA, the deadlines are March 31 for the summer and fall semesters and October 15 for the spring semester.

Program Requirements: 36 credit hours (MA). Competence in a language other than English is optional. A field experience and a comprehensive examination are required. A thesis is not required.

Courses Offered: Research Applied to Education; Education Across Cultures; Advanced Instructional Strategies; Curriculum Development in Multicultural Education; Linguistics; Seminar: Education of Bilingual Students; Teaching of Writing for ESL; Teaching of Reading for ESL; Methods of TESOL.

Full-Time Staff: Rebecca Benjamin, Federico Carrillo, Holbrook Mahn, Leroy Ortiz, Anita Pfeiffer, William Kline (director).

Requirements for Admission: For the MA, the university's requirements for admission are an application form, a letter of intent, three letters of recommendation, a résumé, and official transcripts. The program requires international students to meet the requirements of the International Admissions Office.

Tuition, Fees, and Aid: MA: For in-state students, $309.30 per 3 credit hours; $1,221 for 12–15 credit hours; for out-of-state students, $4,345.40 per semester. Limited teaching assistantships and occasional scholarships are available.

General: The program is intended to enhance the languages and cultures of the Southwest in a variety of educational settings. The program draws students from many backgrounds from across the United States and other countries.

Summer Session: Yes

Further Information: Coordinator
Division of Language and Literacy
COE/Hokona Hall, Room 140
University of New Mexico
Albuquerque, NM 87131

Telephone: (505) 277-0437
Fax: (505) 2778362
E-mail: pascetti@unm.edu

◆ NEW MEXICO STATE UNIVERSITY, Department of Curriculum and Instruction

Degree Offered: MA in curriculum and instruction with a specialization in TESOL.

Length of Program: 2 long (fall and spring) and 2 short (summer) semesters. Students may be full-time or part-time and may begin their study at the beginning of any semester. Application deadlines are fall semester, July 1; spring semester, November 1; summer semester, April 1.

Program Requirements: 36 credit hours. Competence in a language other than English is not required. Practice teaching and a comprehensive oral examination are required. A thesis is optional.

Courses Offered: (*required) *TESOL Methods; *Second Language Acquisition; *TESOL Practicum; *Introduction to Linguistics; *Sociolinguistics; *Adult/Family Literacy in ESL or Literacy for Bilingual Students; *Technology for TESOL; *Research in Curriculum and Instruction; *Foundations of Curriculum or Curriculum Development; *Evaluation of Instructional Strategies or Classroom Management; Language and Cognition for ESL Learners; Special Topics: TESOL; Issues in Schooling for Bilingual Learners; electives.

Full-Time Staff: Herman Garcia (chair), Ana Huerta-Macias, Robert Gallegos, Marc Druyn.

Requirements for Admission: The university's requirements for admission are a GPA of at least 3.0 in the last half of undergraduate work, of 3.0 for continuing graduate students, and of 3.0 for foreign students. Foreign students must have a TOEFL score of at least 550 and a BA or MA from a U.S. institution.

Tuition, Fees, and Aid: For in-state students, $1,176 per semester; for out-of-state students, $3,672 per semester.

General: The program emphasizes working with Latino students (public school through adult) who are acquiring English. The university is situated in the borderlands, within a bilingual and multicultural area.

Practice teaching may be done in Juarez, Mexico.

Fifteen students completed the program in 1996–1997.

The university has an intensive English language program for nonnative speakers of English.

Summer Session: Yes

Further Information: Ana H. Macias
3CUR
O'Donnell Hall 323
New Mexico State University
PO Box 30001
Las Cruces, NM 88003

Telephone: (505) 646-5637
Fax: (505) 646-5436
E-mail: amacias775@aol.com

◆ NEW ROCHELLE, COLLEGE OF, Graduate School, Division of Education

Degree Offered: MS in TESOL.

Length of Program: 3 academic sessions over 12 months. Students may be full-time, part-time, or nonmatriculated and may begin their study at the beginning of any of the 6 academic sessions. Application deadlines are intersession, December 1997; spring session, January; summer session I, May; summer session II, June; graduate institutes, July; fall, August.

Program Requirements: 36 credits. Competence in a language other than English is required for certification. Practice teaching and guided observation are required. Neither a thesis nor a comprehensive examination is required.

Courses Offered: (*required) *Development of Cultural Awareness; *Bilingual/Multicultural Education; *Second Language Acquisition; *Linguistics I; *Linguistics II; *Teaching in a Multicultural Classroom; *Educational Evaluation of Diverse Groups; TESOL: Methods and Materials, Pre-K–6; TESOL: Methods and Materials, 7–12; *TESOL Across Content Areas; *TESOL Observation and Seminar, Pre-K–12; *TESOL Practicum, Pre-K–12; TESOL: Methods and Materials, Instructional Technology and Learning Centers; TESOL: Methods and Materials, Postsecondary; Management Skills for the TESOL Teacher; TESOL Program Management; TESOL and Psycholinguistics; Practicum in Multicultural Education, Pre-K–12; Practicum in TESOL Through the Content Areas, Pre-K–12; Independent Study; Special Topics in TESOL.

Full-Time Staff: Timothy Ebsworth, Melanie Hannigan (division head).

Requirements for Admission: The college's requirements for admission are a bachelor's degree with a GPA of 2.7 (3.0 for any graduate work), official transcripts, a personal goals statement, two references, an interview with the department head, and a writing sample.

Tuition, Fees, and Aid: $316 per credit. Research assistantships, graduate assistantships, scholarships, good student awards, and community service awards are available.

General: The college seeks to promote social justice through the extension of educational opportunities to both the students it trains and the student populations it serves. By means of close advisement and responsive scheduling of course offerings, the college is able to help students reach their academic and career-related goals in a timely way without compromising the quality of the program. Through the constant development of educational partnerships with urban, suburban, and rural school districts, the college can both train their teachers and place its own student teachers in schools that are actively engaged in recruiting, developing, and retaining new teachers. The MS is a New York State–approved program leading to provisional certification in TESOL, Pre-K–12.

One hundred students completed the program in 1996–1997.

Summer Session: Yes

Further Information: Division Head
Graduate School, Division of Education
College of New Rochelle
29 Castle Place
New Rochelle, NY 10805-2339

Telephone: (914) 654-5330
Fax: (914) 654-5593
E-mail: ebsworth@webspan.net

◆ NEW YORK, STATE UNIVERSITY OF, AT ALBANY, Department of Educational Theory and Practice

Degree Offered: MS in TESOL.

Length of Program: 1½ years. Students may be full-time or part-time and may begin their study at the beginning of any semester. There are no application deadlines.

Program Requirements: 35 (noncertification track)–45 (certification track) credits. Competence in a language other than English is required for native speakers of English. Practice teaching is required. Neither a thesis nor a comprehensive examination is required.

Courses Offered: *TESOL: Elementary, Secondary, and Adult; *Contemporary Patterns in TESOL; *Second Language Acquisition; *Analysis of Research on Teaching; *Perspectives in Bilingual Education; *Educational Psychology *or* Educational Statistics; *Educational Sociology *or* Educational Philosophy; *Language and Culture; *Applied Linguistics; *The Structure of English; *Social Concerns in the Schools (certification only); *Field Experience in TESOL (noncertification only); *Student Teaching (certification only); Reading in a Second Language; Sociocognitive Perspectives on Literacy Using Media in the Second Language Classroom.

Full-Time Staff: Richard Light, Carla Meskill, Judith Langer (chair).

Requirements for Admission: The university's requirements for admission are a GPA of 3.0, three academic letters, and a personal statement. Nonnative speakers of English must have a TOEFL score of 600 or above.

Tuition, Fees, and Aid: For in-state students, $2,550 per semester; for out-of-state students, $4,208 per semester. Teaching assistantships and fellowships are available on a competitive basis.

General: The TESOL program features the federally funded Language Advocacy Project, which offers scholarships and stipends, and the federally funded Center on English Learning and Achievement. Language learning and technology specializations are available. The program optionally leads to New York State certification in TESOL.

Thirty-six students completed the program in 1996–1997.

The university has an English language program for nonnative speakers of English.

Summer Session: Yes

Further Information: Chair
Department of Educational Theory and Practice
ED 115
State University of New York at Albany
Albany, NY 12222

Telephone: (518) 442-5020
Fax: (518) 442-5008
E-mail: meskill@cnsvax.albany.edu

◆ NEW YORK, STATE UNIVERSITY OF, AT BUFFALO, Department of Learning and Instruction

Degree Offered: EdM in TESOL with or without state certification.

Length of Program: 3 semesters without certification; 4 semesters with certification. Students may be full-time or part-time and must begin their study at the beginning of the fall semester. The application deadline is February 1.

Program Requirements: 33 credits. Competence in a language other than English is not required. Practice teaching is required. Either a comprehensive examination or a thesis is required.

Courses Offered: (*required) *TESOL Methods and Materials; *Linguistics for Language Teachers; *Principles of Second Language Acquisition; *History and Structure of English; *two of the following: Writing in the Second Language Context, Reading in the Second Language Context, Teaching Second Language Culture, Developing and Evaluating Proficiency; *(for state certification) ESL in the Content Areas, Foundations of Bilingual/Multicultural Education Cognitive Processes in Second Language Acquisition; Teaching Second Languages at the Elementary Level; Portfolios in the Second Language Classroom; Sociolinguistics; Bilingualism; Phonology; Syntax.

Full-Time Staff: Carol Hosenfeld, Dorothy Rissel (coordinator), Lynne Yang, Lilliam Malavé.

Requirements for Admission: The program's requirements for admission are a baccalaureate degree from an accredited institution with a GPA of 3.5 and two excellent recommendations. Nonnative speakers must have a minimum TOEFL score of 600 and a TWE score of 4.

Tuition, Fees, and Aid: For in-state students, $2,550 per semester; for out-of-state students, $4,208 per semester. Fees are $325 per semester. Financial aid is extremely limited.

General: Twenty-seven students completed the program in 1996–1997.

The university has an English language program for nonnative speakers of English.

Summer Session: Yes

Further Information: Barbara Cracchiolo, Admissions Coordinator
Department of Learning and Instruction
505 Baldy Hall
State University of New York at Buffalo
Buffalo, NY 14260

Telephone: (716) 645-2457
Fax: (716) 645-3161
E-mail: cracchio@acsu.buffalo.edu

◆ NEW YORK, STATE UNIVERSITY OF, AT BUFFALO, Department of Learning and Instruction

Degree Offered: PhD in second language education.

Length of Program: 2 years of course work plus 1–2 years for the dissertation. Students may be part-time or full-time and must begin their study at the beginning of the fall semester. The application deadline is February 1.

Program Requirements: 72 credits. Competence in a language other than English is not required. A conference-quality research paper and a research analysis examination are required. Practice teaching is not required.

Courses Offered: (*required) *24 credits in quantitative and qualitative research methodology; *30 credits in major area, including Second Language Classroom Preparation, Second Language Teacher Preparation, Cognitive Processes I and II, and 12 hours in linguistics, psychology, or another associated area.

Full-Time Staff: Carol Hosenfeld, Dorothy Rissel (coordinator), Lynne Yang, Wolfgang Wolck, Robert Van Valen, Leonard Talmy, Jerry Jaeger.

Requirements for Admission: The requirements for admission are a writing sample and GRE verbal and quantitative scores. Nonnative speakers of English must have a minimum TOEFL score of 600.

Tuition, Fees, and Aid: For in-state students, $2,550 per semester; for out-of-state students, $4,208 per semester. Fees are $325 per semester. A limited number of research assistantships are available, as are some teaching assistantships in the English Language Institute and World Language Institute.

General: The program orients the student toward research from the outset. Research projects are developed in nearly every course. The required research component often serves as a pilot for the dissertation.

The university has an intensive English language program for nonnative speakers of English.

Summer Session: No

Further Information: Barbara Cracchiolo
Department of Learning and Instruction
504 Baldy Hall
State University of New York at Buffalo
Box 601000
Buffalo, NY 14260-1000

Telephone: (716) 645-2457
Fax: (716) 645-3161
E-mail: cracchio@acsu.buffalo.edu

◆ NEW YORK, STATE UNIVERSITY OF, AT STONY BROOK, Department of Linguistics

Degree Offered: MA in TESOL.

Length of Program: 2–3 semesters. Students may be full-time or part-time and must begin their study at the beginning of the fall semester. The application deadline is February 1.

Program Requirements: 30 credits (36 with state certification). Competence in a language other than English is required. Practice teaching is required. Neither a thesis nor a comprehensive examination is required.

Courses Offered: (*required) *Phonetics; *Methods and Materials of TESOL I; *Structure of English; *Introduction to General Linguistics; *Practicum I; *Practicum II; *three of the following: Contrastive Analysis, Analysis of an Uncommonly Taught Language, Methods and Materials of TESOL II, Second Language Acquisition, Bilingualism, Sociolinguistics, Historical Linguistics, Psycholinguistics, Error Analysis, Student Teaching in ESL.

Full-Time Staff: Frank Anshen, Mark Aronoff, John Bailyn, Christina Bethin, Susan Brennan, Ellen Broselow (chair), Daniel Finer, Agnes He, Robert Hoberman, Marie K. Huffman, Dorit Kaufman, Flora Klein-Andreu, Richard Larson, Mikle Ledgerwood, Peter Ludlow, Kamal Sridhar, S. N. Sridhar, Louise Vasvari, David S. Warren.

Requirements for Admission: The requirements for admission are a baccalaureate degree with a minimum GPA of 3.0 from an accredited institution, a GRE score, and proficiency in a foreign language equivalent to 2 years of college work. Nonnative speakers of English must have a minimum TOEFL score of 600.

Tuition, Fees, and Aid: For in-state students, $2,550 per semester; for out-of-state students, $4,208 per semester. A limited number of teaching assistantships and minority fellowships are available.

General: The program combines a thorough grounding in the linguistic analysis of language structure and language acquisition with practical, hands-on experience in the ESL classroom.

The program is affiliated with Adventures in Education, which offers the opportunity to teach in St. Petersburg, Russia.

Fifteen students completed the program in 1996–1997.

The university has an intensive English language program for nonnative speakers of English.

Summer Session: Yes

Further Information: Sandra L. Brennan, Graduate Secretary
Department of Linguistics
S201 Ward Melville Social and Behavioral Sciences
State University of New York at Stony Brook
Stony Brook, NY 11776-4376

Telephone: (516) 632-7774, 7777
Fax: (516) 632-9468
E-mail: slbrennan@notes.cc.sunysb.edu

◆ NEW YORK UNIVERSITY, School of Education, Department of Teaching and Learning

Degree Offered: MA in TESOL with New York State certification.

Length of Program: 4 semesters. Students may be full-time or part-time and may begin their study at the beginning of any semester. Application deadlines are fall semester, March 1; spring semester, December 1; summer semester, May 1.

Program Requirements: 44 credits. Competence in a language other than English is required for native speakers of English; English meets the requirement for nonnative speakers. Student teaching is required. Neither a thesis nor a comprehensive examination is required.

Courses Offered: (*required) *Teaching Second Languages: Theory and Practice; *Bilingual/Multicultural Education: Theory and Practice; *Linguistic Analysis; *Intercultural Perspectives in Multilingual Education; *Structure of American English; *The Second Language Classroom: Elementary and Secondary; *Teaching Second Languages Across Content Areas; *Supervised Student Teaching: K–6 and 7–12; *Inquiries Into Teaching and Learning; *Teaching Second Languages in a Technological Society; *Advanced Individual Project in Multilingual Education *or* Culminating Seminar in Multilingual Education; Linguistics, Literacy, and Bilingualism; Second Language Acquisition Research; Language Evaluation and Assessment; Utilizing Community Resources and Parental Involvement.

Full-Time Staff: Miriam Eisenstein-Ebsworth, Kendall King, Miguel Lopez, John Mayher, Gordon Pradl, Marilyn Sobelman, Frank Tang.

Requirements for Admission: The university's requirement for admission is an accredited baccalaureate degree with a minimum GPA of 2.75. The program requires a bachelor's degree with a concentration in one of the liberal arts or sciences and 2 years of foreign language study.

Tuition, Fees, and Aid: $610 per credit. Scholarships and loans are available.

General: The program's goal is to educate professionals via exploration of current research and classroom practices to enable them to make conscious choices in their classrooms. The program emphasizes the integration of theory with practice. Students have opportunities to visit classes and student teach in New York City public and private schools.

The university has an intensive English language program for nonnative speakers of English.

Summer Session: Yes

Further Information: Frank L. Tang, Director
TESOL Program
Department of Teaching and Learning
School of Education
New York University
239 Greene Street, Room 635
New York, NY 10003

Telephone: (212) 998-5498

◆ NEW YORK UNIVERSITY, School of Education, Department of Teaching and Learning

Degree Offered: MA in TESOL without New York State certification.

Length of Program: 3 semesters. Students may be full-time or part-time and may begin their study at the beginning of any semester. Application deadlines are fall semester, March 1; spring semester, December 1; summer semester, May 1.

Program Requirements: 34 credits. Competence in a language other than English is required for native speakers of English; English meets the requirement for nonnative speakers. Practice teaching is optional. Neither a thesis nor a comprehensive examination is required.

Courses Offered: (*required) *Teaching Second Languages: Theory and Practice; *Linguistic Analysis; *Structure of American English; all courses in program description for MA with certification; Observation and Seminar in Second Language Teaching; Introductory Seminar in Multilingual Education; Internship in Language Teaching; Materials and Curriculum Development in Second Language Teaching; The Second Language Classroom; up to 12 credits of electives.

Full-Time Staff: See program description for MA in TESOL with New York State certification.

Requirements for Admission: The university's requirements for admission are an accredited baccalaureate degree with a minimum GPA of 2.75. Nonnative speakers of English must have a minimum TOEFL score of 600.

Tuition, Fees, and Aid: See program description for MA in TESOL with New York State certification.

General: See program description for MA in TESOL with New York State certification.

Summer Session: Yes

Further Information: Frank L. Tang, Director
TESOL Program
Department of Teaching and Learning
School of Education
New York University
239 Greene Street, Room 635
New York, NY 10003

Telephone: (212) 998-5498

◆ NEW YORK UNIVERSITY, School of Education, Department of Teaching and Learning

Degree Offered: MA in TESOL and foreign language education (French, German, Hebrew, Italian, Latin, Russian, Spanish) with dual New York State certification in ESOL and foreign language.

Length of Program: 4 semesters. Students may be full-time or part-time and may begin their study at the beginning of any semester. Application deadlines are fall semester, March 1; spring semester, December 1; summer semester, May 1.

Program Requirements: 50 credits. Competence in a language other than English is required for native speakers of English; English meets the requirement for nonnative speakers. Student teaching in ESOL and the target foreign language is required. Neither a thesis nor a comprehensive examination is required.

Courses Offered: (*required) *Teaching Second/Foreign Languages: Theory and Practice; *Field Experience Seminar in Teaching Foreign Languages; *Foreign Language Teaching in Elementary/Secondary Schools; *Workshop in Foreign Language Teaching; *Advanced French for Teachers of French; *Advanced Spanish for Teachers of Spanish; *all courses listed in program description for MA with certification; *Supervised Student Teaching in ESL, K–6, and in a target language, 7–12.

Full-Time Staff: See program description for MA in TESOL with New York State certification.

Tuition, Fees, and Aid: See program description for MA in TESOL with New York State certification.

General: See program description for MA in TESOL with New York State certification. This dual certification program is distinctive in that it integrates the teaching and learning of a second language with that of a foreign language. Students have the opportunity to explore the rich resources of second/foreign languages in New York City. Graduates are certified in both ESOL and a target foreign language.

Summer Session: Yes

Further Information: Frank L. Tang, Director
TESOL Program
Department of Teaching and Learning
School of Education
New York University
239 Greene Street, Room 635
New York, NY 10003

Telephone: (212) 998-5498

◆ NEW YORK UNIVERSITY, School of Education, Department of Teaching and Learning

Degree Offered: PhD in TESOL.

Length of Program: Minimum of 5 semesters plus dissertation. Students may be full-time or part-time and must begin their study at the beginning of the fall semester. The application deadline is February 1.

Program Requirements: 54 credits plus 1 credit of doctoral advisement each semester thereafter. Competence in a language other than English is required for native speakers of English; English meets the requirement for nonnative speakers. A dissertation and a comprehensive examination are required. Practice teaching is not required. Certain requirements may be waived based on prior course work.

Courses Offered: (*required) See MA program descriptions; *Doctoral Seminar in Multilingual Multicultural Studies (2 semesters); *Dissertation Proposal Seminar; *Linguistic Analysis; *Language Acquisition and Development; *Pluralistic Approaches to Cultural Literacy; *two courses in educational foundations; *Educational Statistics (2 semesters); *a minimum of four research courses; courses in bilingual or foreign language education and international education.

Full-Time Staff: See program description for MA in TESOL with New York State certification.

Requirements for Admission: The university's requirements for admission are a 3.0 GPA and a GRE score. Nonnative speakers of English must have a TOEFL score of 600 and must take the TWE.

Tuition, Fees, and Aid: See program description for MA in TESOL with New York State certification. Teaching assistantships are also available.

General: The program offers a multilingual, multicultural approach to doctoral study emphasizing research in language acquisition, bilingualism, and pedagogy in linguistically diverse environments for those engaged in research, teaching, materials and curriculum development, and publishing.

The university has an intensive English language program for nonnative speakers of English.

Summer Session: Yes

Further Information: Miriam Eisenstein Ebsworth, Director
Doctoral Program in TESOL
Department of Teaching and Learning
East Building, Room 635
New York University
239 Greene Street
New York, NY 10003

Telephone: (212) 998-5195

◆ NORTH CAROLINA, UNIVERSITY OF, AT CHARLOTTE, Department of Middle, Secondary, and K–12 Education

Degree Offered: MEd.

Length of Program: 3–4 semesters. Students may be full-time or part-time and may begin their study at the beginning of any semester. Rolling admissions are in effect.

Program Requirements: 36 semester hours. Competence in a language other than English is not required. Practice teaching and a thesis are required. A comprehensive examination is not required.

Courses Offered: (*required) *Theories of Human Development and Learning; *Introduction to Linguistics; *Linguistics and Language Learning *or* Language Acquisition; *Language and Culture *or* Intercultural Communication *or* American Ethnic Cultures; *Comparative Language Studies for Teachers; *Second Language Diagnosis and Evaluation; *Curriculum Theory; *TESL; *Language Development and Reading; *Educational Research Methods; *Clinical Experience in TESL; *Seminar and Internship in TESL.

Full-Time Staff: William Britt, Warren DeBiase, Jeanneine Jones, Caroline Linse, Corey Lock, Allen Queen, David Pugalee, Eugene Schaffer (chair).

Requirements for Admission: The university's requirements for admission are a bachelor's degree from an accredited college or university and a satisfactory GRE or Miller Analogies Test score. Nonnative speakers of English must submit a satisfactory TOEFL score.

Tuition, Fees, and Aid: For in-state students, $859 per semester; for out-of-state students, $4,436 per year. Loans and other types of financial aid are available.

General: The master's program is geared to the needs of individuals wishing to teach in U.S. K–12 public schools, U.S. higher education programs, and abroad. Students may specialize in teaching EFL to children, adults, or both. The program can lead to a North Carolina credential in TESOL.

International student teaching or internships may be an option for some students.

Seventeen students completed the program in 1996–1997.

Summer Session: Yes

Further Information: ESL Coordinator
Department of Middle, Secondary, and K–12 Education
University of North Carolina at Charlotte
9201 University City Boulevard
Charlotte, NC 28223-0001

Telephone: (704) 547-2531

◆ NORTH TEXAS, UNIVERSITY OF, Department of English

Degree Offered: MA in English with a concentration in ESL.

Length of Program: 3–4 semesters. Students may be full-time or part-time and may begin their study at the beginning of any semester. Application deadlines are fall semester, August 22; spring semester, January 9; summer 1, June 2; summer 2, July 8.

Program Requirements: 30–36 credit hours. Competence in a language other than English is required. Practice teaching, and either a comprehensive examination or a thesis, are required.

Courses Offered: (*required) *Second Language Acquisition; *Research Methods in ESL; *Methods in Teaching ESL; *Phonology; *Syntax; *Practicum in TESL; Historical Linguistics; Principles of Linguistics; Pedagogical English Grammar; Studies in Applied Linguistics; Sociolinguistics; Language Typology; Studies in Descriptive Linguistics; Linguistics and Composition; Linguistic Field Methods; Psycholinguistics; Linguistics and Literature; Language and the Sexes; World Englishes; Writing in the ESL Classroom; ESL Program Management.

Full-Time Staff: Shobhana Chelliah, Patricia Cukar-Avila, Lynn Eubank, Timothy R. Montler (chair), Haj Ross.

Requirements for Admission: The university's requirements for admission are a bachelor's degree or the equivalent from an accredited institution with a GPA of 3.0 on the last 60 undergraduate hours (or a 2.8 overall GPA) and combined GRE verbal and quantitative scores of 800. The program requires a score in the 50th percentile on verbal section of the GRE. Nonnative speakers of English must have a TOEFL score of 575.

Tuition, Fees, and Aid: For in-state students, $918.65 per semester; for out-of-state students, $2,844.65 per semester. Teaching assistantships, teaching fellowships, and out-of-state fee waivers are available.

General: This program strives for a balance between theory and practice. There are ample opportunities for teaching practice at a variety of age and interest levels. Graduates are trained as ESL professionals in teaching, research, and administration. The program leads to a Texas credential in TESOL.

Select students may do their practicum in the program's overseas intern program. Fifteen students completed the program in 1996–1997.

The university has an intensive English language program for nonnative speakers of English.

Summer Session: Yes

Further Information: Chair
Linguistics/ESL Division, Department of English
Administration Building, Room 112
University of North Texas
PO Box 311307
Denton, TX 76203-1307

Telephone: (940) 565-2050
Fax: (940) 565-4355
http://www.engl.unt.edu/lingall.htm

◆ NORTHEASTERN ILLINOIS UNIVERSITY, Linguistics Program

Degree Offered: MA in linguistics with a concentration in TESL.

Length of Program: 4 semesters. Students may be full-time or part-time and may begin their study at the beginning of any semester. Application deadlines are fall semester, March 15; spring semester, September 13; summer semester, February 5.

Program Requirements: 36 semester hours. Competence in a language other than English is not required. A comprehensive examination is required. A thesis is optional. Practice teaching is not required.

Courses Offered: (*required) *Fundamentals of Modern Linguistics; *Structure of Modern English; *Advanced Linguistic Analysis; *Techniques of TESL; *Sociolinguistics; *Second Language Acquisition; *Seminar in TESL; *Theories of TESL; Linguistics and Literacy; Assessment of Limited English Proficient Students; Psycholinguistics; First Language Acquisition; History of the English Language; Experiential Preparation for TESL; Seminar in Applied Linguistics.

Full-Time Staff: Gary Bevington, Theodora Bofman, Rory Donnelly, Mary Ann Geissal, Judith Kaplan-Weinger, Myrna Knepler, Shahrzad Mahootian, Audrey Reynolds (chair), Marit Vamarasi.

Requirements for Admission: The university's requirement for admission is a baccalaureate degree from an accredited college or university with a minimum GPA of 2.75. The program requires 9 hours of undergraduate study in one language other than English for native speakers of English. Nonnative speakers of English are required to show a minimum TOEFL score of 600 and a minimum TSE score of 50.

Tuition, Fees, and Aid: For in-state students, $92.75 per credit hour; for out-of-state students, $278 per credit hour. Merit tuition waivers and teaching assistantships are available.

General: The program features a strong linguistics component and opportunities for intensive study of literacy acquisition and psycholinguistic studies of bilingualism. It leads to an Illinois credential in TESOL.

Thirty-eight students completed the program in 1996–1997.

Summer Session: Yes

Further Information: Audrey Reynolds
Linguistics Program
Northeastern Illinois University
5500 North Saint Louis Avenue
Chicago, IL 60625-4699

Telephone: (773) 794-2653
Fax: (773) 794-6243
E-mail: A-Reynolds@neiu.edu

◆ NORTHERN ARIZONA UNIVERSITY, Department of English

Degree Offered: MA in TESL.

Length of Program: 4 semesters. Students may be full-time or part-time and must begin their study at the beginning of the fall semester. The application deadline is February 15.

Program Requirements: 37 semester hours. Competence in a language other than English is not required. Practice teaching and a comprehensive examination are required. A thesis is not required; there is an MA writing requirement.

Courses Offered: (*required) *Introduction to Language and Linguistics; *Sociolinguistics; *Grammatical Foundations; *Foundations of ESL and Language Learning; *ESL Methodology; *TESL Practicum; *Assessment for Second Language Skills; *(for teaching concentration) ESL Curriculum and Administration, Topics in ESL; *(for applied linguistics concentration) Research Methods in Applied Linguistics, Second Language Acquisition; Pragmatics; Discourse Analysis; Psycholinguistics; Recent Grammars; Professional Development Seminar; other electives.

Full-Time Staff: Douglas Biber, Susan Fitzmaurice, William Grabe, Joan Jamieson, Mary McGroarty, Dean Mellow, Fredricka Stoller, Jean Zukowski/Faust.

Requirements for Admission: The university's requirements for admission are the graduate admission application form and official undergraduate transcripts. The program requires a statement of purpose.

Tuition, Fees, and Aid: For in-state students, $1,950 per 9-month academic year; for out-of-state students, $7,166 per 9-month academic year. Competitively awarded teaching assistantships are available.

General: The program offers two tracks: applied linguistics and teaching.
Twenty-five students completed the program in 1996–1997.
The university has an intensive English program for nonnative speakers of English.

Summer Session: Yes

Further Information: Coordinator, MA-TESL Program
English Department, Box 6032
Liberal Arts, Room 139
Northern Arizona University
Flagstaff, AZ 86011-6032

Telephone: (520) 523-4911
Fax: (520) 523-7074

◆ NORTHERN ARIZONA UNIVERSITY, Department of English

Degree Offered: PhD in applied linguistics.

Length of Program: About 8 semesters. Students must be full-time for a 2-semester residency period and must begin their study at the beginning of the fall semester. The application deadline is February 15.

Program Requirements: 81 semester hours. Competence in a language other than English is required; English meets the requirement for nonnative speakers of English. A PhD screening process, qualifying examination papers, a dissertation proposal, and a dissertation defense are required. Practice teaching is not required.

Courses Offered: Doctoral seminars: Language Variation and Change; Language Assessment; Second Language Acquisition; Classroom Research; Research Issues in English Language Teaching; Applied Sociolinguistics of Literacy; Linguistic Analysis of Style and Discourse; Language Policy and Planning; Corpus Linguistics; courses in TESL and applied linguistics at the MA level.

Full-Time Staff: See program description for MA in TESL.

Requirements for Admission: The university's requirement for admission is completion of the graduate application form. Nonnative speakers of English must have a minimum TOEFL score of 600. The program requires an MA in TESL, linguistics, applied linguistics, or a related field; a GRE score; three letters of recommendation; transcripts; and a sample publication.

Tuition, Fees, and Aid: See program description for MA in TESL. Depending on annual funding levels, research assistantships may be available.

General: The program offers flexible specializations within a wide range of areas in applied linguistics.

Three students completed the program in 1996–1997.

The university has an intensive English program for nonnative speakers of English.

Summer Session: Yes

Further Information: Coordinator, PhD in Applied Linguistics
English Department, Box 6032
Liberal Arts, Room 139
Northern Arizona University
Flagstaff, AZ 86011-6032

Telephone: (520) 523-4911
Fax: (520) 523-7074

◆ NORTHERN ILLINOIS UNIVERSITY, Department of English

Degree Offered: MA in English with a focus on TESOL.

Length of Program: 4 semesters. Students may be full-time or part-time and may begin their study at the beginning of any semester; fall semester is preferred. Application deadlines are fall semester, June 1 (May 1 for international students); spring semester, November 1 (October 1 for international students); summer semester, April 1.

Program Requirements: 30 semester hours with a foreign language, 36 without. Competence in a language other than English is optional for native speakers of English; English meets the option for nonnative speakers of English. A comprehensive examination is required. Practice teaching is optional. A thesis is not required.

Courses Offered: (*required) * Research Methods in Applied Linguistics; *Descriptive Linguistics; *Phonology; *Morphology and Syntax; *Theories and Methods of TESOL; History of the English Language; Grammars of Modern English; Varieties of English; Semantics; Topics in Linguistics; Second Language Acquisition; Discourse Analysis; Linguistics and Literature; Seminar: English Linguistics.

Full-Time Staff: Edward Callary, Susan Deskis, Donald Hardy, Heather K. Hardy (chair), Doris Macdonald.

Requirements for Admission: The university's requirements for admission are a BA from a 4-year accredited institution, a GPA of 3.0, and an acceptable GRE score. Nonnative speakers of English must submit a TOEFL score of 550. The program requires approval by the departmental admissions committee.

Tuition, Fees, and Aid: For in-state students, $1,150.80 per 12 or more semester hours; for out-of-state students, $3,452 per 12 or more semester hours. Fees are about $410. Departmental teaching assistantships, research assistantships, and a few Graduate School fellowships are available.

General: The university houses the Center for Southeast Asian Studies, which offers some assistantships and support, and also offers an MA in stylistics. Faculty are accessible in a program geared toward individuals.

Overseas experience is encouraged. The university has strong ties to a university in Xian, China, through which students may be able to teach EFL.

Summer Session: No

Further Information: Advisor, MA-TESOL
Department of English
Reavis Hall
Northern Illinois University
DeKalb, IL 60115

Telephone: (815) 753-6622
Fax: (815) 753-0606
E-mail: tb0dnm1@corn.cso.niu.edu

◆ NORTHERN ILLINOIS UNIVERSITY, Department of Leadership and Educational Policy Studies

Degree Offered: MSEd with a major in adult continuing education and a concentration in ESL.

Length of Program: 3 semesters. Students may be full-time or part-time and may begin their study at the beginning of any semester. Application deadlines are fall semester, June 1; spring semester, November 1; summer semester, April 1.

Program Requirements: 30 semester hours. Competence in a foreign language is not required. A comprehensive examination is required. Neither practice teaching nor a thesis is required.

Courses Offered: (*required) *Nature of Adult Continuing Education; *Educational Research; *Adult Learning; *Teaching Adults ESL (12 semester hours); electives in adult continuing education, linguistics, and other related areas.

Full-Time Staff: Richard Orem (chair), Phyllis Cunningham, Paul Ilsey, LaVerne Gyant, Jorge Jeria, Robert Mason, John Niemi, Amy Rose, Gene Roth, Glenn Smith, William Young, Manfred Thullen.

Requirements for Admission: The university's requirements for admission are a baccalaureate degree from an accredited 4-year institution, a minimum undergraduate GPA of 2.5 for the last 2 years of undergraduate work, and a GRE General Test score.

Tuition, Fees, and Aid: For in-state students, $142.82 per semester hour; out-of-state students should contact the bursar's office. Graduate assistantships are available on a limited basis. Other financial aid is available.

General: This program emphasizes methods and materials for teaching adults ESL. The major theme running through all courses is the uniqueness of the adult learner, with a special emphasis on learning in nonformal contexts.

There are opportunities for international fieldwork, internships, and research. The university has agreements with institutes in China, Korea, Chile, and Finland.

Five students completed the program in 1996–1997.

Summer Session: Yes

Richard A. Orem
Graduate Studies in Adult Continuing Education
Gabel 101
Northern Illinois University
DeKalb, IL 60115-2866

Telephone: (815) 753-1448
Fax: (815) 753-9309
E-mail: rorem@niu.edu
http://www.niu.edu

◆ NORTHERN IOWA, UNIVERSITY OF,
Department of English Language and Literature

Degrees Offered: MA in TESOL; MA in TESOL/modern language (Spanish, French, or German).

Length of Program: 3 semesters plus one summer. Students may be full-time or part-time and may begin their study at the beginning of any semester. Application deadlines are fall semester, June 1; spring semester, November 15; summer semester, April 1.

Program Requirements: 33 credits. Competence in a language other than English is required for native speakers of English and optional for nonnative speakers of English. Practice teaching and a comprehensive examination are required. A research paper is required.

Courses Offered: (*required) *Structure of English *or* Introduction to Linguistics; *Phonology; Syntax *or* Semantics *or* Sociolinguistics; *Problems in English Grammar; *TESOL I and II; *Introduction to Graduate Studies in TESOL/Linguistics; *Seminar in Language (Computer-Assisted Language Learning, Language Planning, English for Specific Purposes, Discourse and Pragmatics); *Second Language Acquisition; *Language Testing; *Practicum; *(for the MA in TESOL/modern language) 15 hours in the language emphasis.

Full-Time Staff: Stephen J. Gaies, Michael Janopoulos, Ardith J. Meier, Joyce Milambiling, Cheryl A. Roberts (chair), Carolyn Shields.

Requirements for Admission: The university's requirements for admission are a minimum GPA of 3.0 and three letters of recommendation.

Tuition, Fees, and Aid: For in-state students, $1,583 per semester; for out-of-state students, $3,902 per semester. Teaching assistantships and tuition scholarships are available.

General: The program, which enrolls 60–75 students (50% international) of diverse backgrounds and experiences, presents a balanced program of theory and application, including computer-assisted language learning.
  There is an internship program in Moscow and St. Petersburg, Russia.
  Twenty-five students completed the program in 1996–1997.
  The university has an intensive English language program for nonnative speakers of English.

Summer Session: Yes

Further Information: Dr. Cheryl Roberts, Graduate Coordinator
Department of English Language and Literature
Baker Hall 117
University of Northern Iowa
Cedar Falls, IA 50614-0502

Telephone: (319) 273-2821
Fax: (319) 273-5807
E-mail: kristi.knebel@uni.edu

◆ NORTHWESTERN COLLEGE, Department of Second Languages and Cultures

Degree Offered: BA/BS in ESL education with or without state licensure.

Length of Program: 4 years. Students must be full-time and may begin their study at the beginning of any quarter; fall quarter is preferred. The application deadline for fall semester is August 15.

Program Requirements: 15 quarter hours. Competence in a language other than English is required; English meets the requirement for nonnative speakers of English. Practice teaching is required. Neither a thesis nor a comprehensive examination is required.

Courses Offered: (*required) *Introduction to Linguistics; *Advanced Grammar: Syntax; *Theory of Second Language Acquisition; *Language, School, and Society; *Second Language Literacy Skills; *Language Patterns; *Curriculum and Instruction in ESL; *Methods of TESL K–6; Methods of TESL 7–12; *Child and Adolescent Psychology.

Full-Time Staff: Feng-Ling Margaret Johnson (coordinator), Sally Harris, Kathleen Black.

Requirements for Admission: The college's requirements for admission are evidence of a new birth in Jesus Christ, willingness to follow the ideals and patterns of life and conduct of the college community, likelihood of academic success at the college, a high school or GED diploma, an SAT or ACT score, and the financial capability to meet college expenses. Individuals seeking a teaching license must apply to the Education Department.

Tuition, Fees, and Aid: $4,640 for 12–18 quarter credits. Loans, scholarships, grants, and work study are available.

General: Individuals with a teaching degree in other areas can obtain a Minnesota endorsement or teaching license in ESL. Conversion from the quarter system to the semester system is scheduled to start in fall 1999, at which time application deadlines and courses offered will change slightly.

Six students completed the program in 1996–1997.

Summer Session: No

Further Information: Feng-Ling Margaret Johnson
Education Department
Nazareth Hall, Room 302
Northwestern College
3003 Snelling Avenue N
Saint Paul, MN 55113

Telephone: (612) 628-33721
Fax: (612) 631-5124
E-mail: fmj@nwc.edu

◆ NOTRE DAME COLLEGE, Division of Education

Degree Offered: MEd in TESL.

Length of Program: 2 years. Students may be full-time or part-time or may take accelerated summer courses, and must begin their study at the beginning of the summer semester. The application deadline is May 1.

Program Requirements: 33 credits. Competence in a language other than English is required. Practice teaching and a capstone project are required. Either a thesis or a comprehensive examination is required.

Courses Offered: Issues in Teaching Second Language Children; Language Analysis; The Sociocultural Context of Language Teaching; First and Second Language Acquisition; Curriculum and Assessment; Clinical Experience; Technology in Education; The ESL Professional; Action Research.

Full-Time Staff: Birna Arnbjörnsdottir (director).

Requirements for Admission: The college's requirements for admission are an appropriate undergraduate degree, a GRE or Miller Analogies Test score, three letters of recommendation, a personal essay, and an interview. The program requires teaching experience and, where appropriate, a copy of teacher certification.

Tuition, Fees, and Aid: $1,100 per course. Limited financial aid is available.

General: Completion of the program leads to New Hampshire teacher certification. The program emphasizes application and practice.

Summer Session: Yes

Further Information: Birna Arnbjörnsdottir, PhD, Director
Division of Education
Notre Dame College
2321 Elm Street
Manchester, NH 03104

Telephone: (603) 669-4298
Fax: (603) 644-8316

◆ NOVA SOUTHEASTERN UNIVERSITY, Graduate Teacher Education Program

Degrees Offered: Florida endorsement in TESOL; MS in education with a concentration in TESOL.

Length of Program: 2½ semesters. Students may be full-time or part-time and may begin their study at the beginning of any 8-week session.

Program Requirements: Endorsement, 15 credits; MS, 36 credits. Competence in a language other than English is not required. A practicum is required for the MS. Neither a thesis nor a comprehensive examination is required.

Courses Offered: (*required) *Applied Linguistics; *Methodology of TESOL; *Cultural and Cross-Cultural Communication; *Testing and Evaluation in TESOL; *Curriculum Development; *TESOL Practicum (MS); Foundations of Bilingual Education.

Full-Time Staff: Felicia Guerra.

Requirements for Admission: The university's requirement for admission is a baccalaureate degree from a regionally accredited college or university.

Tuition, Fees, and Aid: $245 per credit. Non–degree-seeking students are not eligible for financial aid.

General: The program is approved for a Florida endorsement in TESOL. On completion of the endorsement, students may continue to complete the MS degree. The program is aimed at the working professional, with classes offered Saturdays or weeknights. The university has satellite sites throughout Florida. Courses are available there through various long-distance technologies.

Summer Session: Yes

Further Information: Director, Graduate Teacher Education Program
Nova Southeastern University
Westport
3301 College Avenue
Fort Lauderdale, FL 33314

Telephone: (800) 986-3223, extension 8635
Fax: (954) 262-3911
E-mail: guerraf@fcae.nova.edu

◆ THE OHIO STATE UNIVERSITY, School of Teaching and Learning

Degree Offered: MA with a concentration in TESOL.

Length of Program: 4 quarters. Students may be full-time or part-time and are encouraged to begin their study at the beginning of the autumn or summer quarter. Application deadlines are autumn quarter, January 1; summer quarter, December 1.

Program Requirements: 50 quarter hours. Competence in a language other than English is highly recommended for native speakers of English. A comprehensive examination or a thesis is optional. Practice teaching is not required.

Courses Offered: (*required) *Second Language Acquisition; *Methods of Teaching English; *Syllabus Design; *Materials of Instruction; *Second Language Testing; electives in areas such as English, linguistics, anthropology, literacy, and elementary school language arts.

Full-Time Staff: Charles Hancock (coordinator), Keiko Samimy, Deborah Wilburn Robinson.

Requirements for Admission: The university's requirements for admission are a bachelor's degree, a GRE score, three letters of reference, and a personal statement of goals and objectives. A minimum TOEFL score of 575 is preferred for nonnative speakers of English; students may be placed in English language courses depending on placement test scores.

Tuition, Fees, and Aid: For in-state students, $1,738 per quarter; for out-of-state students, $4,500 per quarter. Fees are $191 per quarter. Very limited teaching, research, and administrative assistantships are available on a competitive basis.

General: The university, the second largest in the United States, is a state university with 19 different colleges. The TESOL program has been in existence for many years and is considered one of the top second language programs in the nation.

A limited number of slots are available for visiting scholars (faculty) from international institutions.

Thirty students completed the program in 1996–1997.

The university has an intensive English language program for nonnative speakers of English.

Summer Session: Yes

Further Information: Professor Charles R. Hancock
Foreign/Second Language Program
School of Teaching and Learning
Arps Hall, Room 327
The Ohio State University
1945 High Street
Columbus, OH 43210-1172

Telephone: (614) 292-8047
Fax: (614) 292-7695
E-mail: Hancock.2@osu.edu

◆ THE OHIO STATE UNIVERSITY, School of Teaching and Learning

Degree Offered: PhD with a concentration in TESOL.

Length of Program: 4 quarters. Students may be full-time or part-time and must begin their study at the beginning of the autumn quarter. The application deadline is January 1.

Program Requirements: 90 quarter hours beyond the master's degree. Competence in a language other than English is highly recommended. A comprehensive examination and a thesis are required. Practice teaching is not required.

Courses Offered: (*required) *Courses in second language acquisition, methods, materials, and testing; seminars; *thesis; *two minor areas of concentration in such related areas as linguistics, English language or literature, and teacher education; *courses in language, literacy, and culture.

Full-Time Staff: See program description for MA with a concentration in TESOL.

Requirements for Admission: See program description for MA with a concentration in TESOL.

Tuition, Fees, and Aid: For in-state students, $1,738 per quarter; for out-of-state students, $4,500 per quarter. Fees are $191 per quarter. Very limited teaching, research, and administrative assistantships are available on a competitive basis. Students may apply for additional competitive awards once they have been admitted.

General: The university, the second largest in the United States, is a state university with 19 different colleges. The TESOL program has been in existence for many years and is considered one of the top second language programs in the nation. The university's doctoral candidates have a high placement rate, and many return to their home countries for responsible, university-level positions.

A limited number of slots are available for visiting scholars (faculty) from international institutions.

Twelve students completed the program in 1996–1997.

The university has an intensive English language program for nonnative speakers of English.

Summer Session: Yes

Further Information: Professor Charles R. Hancock
Foreign/Second Language Program
School of Teaching and Learning
Arps Hall, Room 327
The Ohio State University
1945 High Street
Columbus, OH 43210-1172

Telephone: (614) 292-8047
Fax: (614) 292-7695
E-mail: Hancock.2@osu.edu

◆ OHIO UNIVERSITY, Department of Linguistics

Degree Offered: MA with a concentration in applied linguistics and TESOL.

Length of Program: 6 quarters. Students may be full-time or part-time and must begin their study at the beginning of the fall quarter. The application deadline is April 15.

Program Requirements: 75 quarter hours. Competence in a language other than English is required; English meets the requirement for nonnative speakers of English. Practice teaching plus either a thesis or an extensive research project are required. A comprehensive examination is not required.

Courses Offered: (*required) *Introduction to Linguistics; *Introduction to Graduate Studies; *Phonology I; *Syntax I; *Pedagogical Grammar; *Theories of Language Learning; *TESOL Methodology; *TESOL Materials; *Language Teaching Practicum; *Semantics; *Sociolinguistics; *Research in Linguistics; *Proseminar or Thesis; Theories of Bilingualism; Computers in Language Teaching; Testing in TESOL; Methods in K–12 TESL; Reading in TESOL; Topics in Applied Linguistics; Linguistics and Semiotics; Phonology II; Syntax II; Sociolinguistics II; electives in psychology, English, education, computer science, anthropology, philosophy, and foreign languages.

Full-Time Staff: Zinny S. Bond, James Coady, David Cross, Beverly Flanigan, Joung Hee Krzic, Richard McGinn (chair), Nasiombe Mutonyi, Hiroyo Oshita, Marmo Soemarmo, Yasuko Takata, Liang Tao.

Requirements for Admission: The university's requirements for admission are a baccalaureate degree with a minimum GPA of 3.0, transcripts, three letters of recommendation, and a minimum TOEFL score of 600 for nonnative speakers of English. For native speakers of English, knowledge of one language other than English (equivalent to 2 years of undergraduate course work) is required. A GRE score is recommended but not required.

Tuition, Fees, and Aid: For in-state students, $1,708 per 9–18 quarter hours; for out-of-state students, $3,281 per 9–18 quarter hours. Fees are $335 per quarter. Teaching assistantships in ESL, introductory linguistics courses, and non-Western languages (Chinese, Indonesian/Malaysian, Japanese, Swahili) are available. Graduate assistantships and tuition scholarships are also available.

General: The faculty work closely with the students and mentor them in developing research skills, and there are many opportunities to teach linguistics, languages, and ESL to both children and adults. Students have ample opportunity to gain valuable skills in the use of computers for language learning. The program leads to an Ohio credential in TESOL.

Regular employment opportunities are available in Japan and China.

Twenty students completed the program in 1996–1997.

The university has an intensive English language program for nonnative speakers of English.

Summer Session: Yes

Further Information: Graduate Chair
Department of Linguistics
Gordy Hall
Ohio University
Athens, OH 45701-2979

Telephone: (740) 593-4564
Fax: (703) 593-2967
E-mail: lingdept@ohiou.edu

◆ OKLAHOMA CITY UNIVERSITY, Department of Education

Degrees Offered: MEd (MA) with a concentration in TESOL.

Length of Program: 3–4 semesters. Students may be full-time or part-time and may begin their study at the beginning of any semester. Application deadlines are fall semester, July 30; spring semester, November 30; summer I, April 30; summer II, May 30.

Program Requirements: 36 semester hours. Competence in a language other than English is not required. Practice teaching and a comprehensive examination are required. A thesis is not required.

Courses Offered: (*required) *The English Language: Structure/Usage; *Studies in Linguistics; *Theory and Methods of TESOL; *ESL/EFL Assessment; *Practicum; *Methods of Research; *two of the following: American English Phonology, Sociolinguistics: Intercultural Issues in TESOL, American Culture Through American Literature, Foundations of Reading; *two of the following: Multicultural Concepts, Historical Thought of Education, Psychological Foundations of Education, Sociological Foundations of Education; two electives.

Full-Time Staff: Brooks Bar, Dilin Liu, Billie McElroy, Sherry Sexton (chair).

Requirements for Admission: The university's requirement for admission is a bachelor's degree with a minimum GPA of 3.0. Nonnative speakers of English must have a TOEFL score of 500. The program requires an academic writing sample.

Tuition, Fees, and Aid: $300 per credit hour. A few graduate assistantships and student loans are available.

General: The elective courses are extremely flexible. Students can take almost any graduate course that they think will further their future career, including but not limited to business and foreign language studies. The program will most likely become an MA program in fall 1998.

Study abroad programs with scholarships are available in South Korea, Japan, Taiwan, China, and East European and Latin American countries.

The university has an intensive English language program for nonnative speakers of English.

Summer Session: Yes

Further Information: Director
Department of TESOL
Walker Center 271
Oklahoma City University
2501 North Blackwelder
Oklahoma City, OK 73106

Telephone: (405) 521-5476
Fax: (405) 521-5447
E-mail: dliu@lec.okcu.edu

◆ OKLAHOMA STATE UNIVERSITY, Department of English

Degree Offered: MA in English with a TESL option.

Length of Program: 4 semesters. Students may be full-time or part-time and may begin their study at the beginning of the fall or spring semester. Application deadlines are fall semester, April 1 (February 15 for early admission); spring semester, October 1.

Program Requirements: 30 (thesis option)–34 (nonthesis option) credit hours. Competence in a language other than English is required; English meets the requirement for nonnative speakers of English. Practice teaching and a comprehensive examination are required. A thesis is optional.

Courses Offered: (*required) *TESL Theory and Methods; *Internship in TESL; *TESL Testing; *Social and Psychological Aspects of Language; *Studies in English Grammar; *Descriptive Linguistics; Seminar in Linguistics; Studies in TESL; Topics in Linguistics; Topics in Second Language Acquisition; Language in America; History of English; Teaching Technical and Business Writing; Theories of Communication; Qualitative Research Methods; Comparative Cultures; Psychology of Language; Computer Applications in Education; offerings in education, psychology, sociology, and anthropology.

Full-Time Staff: Carol Lynn Moder (Director), Susan Garzon, Gene B. Halleck, Ravi Sheorey.

Requirements for Admission: The university's requirements for admission are an undergraduate degree from an accredited institution, an acceptable academic record, and the recommendation of the English Department. The program requires a minimum overall undergraduate GPA of 3.0, two letters of recommendation, a 250-word statement of purpose, and a 7- to 15-page writing sample or a GRE score. Nonnative speakers of English must have a minimum TOEFL score of 550.

Tuition, Fees, and Aid: For in-state students, $95.91 per credit hour; for out-of-state students, $174.50 per credit hour. Fees are $14–$16 per credit hour. Teaching assistantships and a small number of fellowships and tuition waivers are available.

General: The program provides a broad range of courses from which students may individualize their programs of study to meet their particular career plans. Areas of faculty and student specialization include testing, simulation and gaming, curriculum design, discourse analysis, and ethnolinguistics. The department offers courses both on the main campus in Stillwater and at a branch campus in Tulsa. The program can include courses for an Oklahoma ESL endorsement.

Although no formal agreement with other institutions is in effect, the department encourages and assists students in finding teaching opportunities abroad. Students have taught in the People's Republic of China, Mexico, and Japan during their course work. The university also participates in a university consortium in Indonesia.

Ten students completed the program in 1996–1997.

The university has an intensive English language program for nonnative speakers of English.

Summer Session: Yes

Further Information: Graduate Coordinator
Department of English
205 Morrill Hall
Oklahoma State University
Stillwater, OK 70478

Telephone: (405) 744-9469
Fax: (405) 744-6326
E-mail: carol.moder@okway.okstate.edu
http://www.writing.okstate.edu/english

◆ OKLAHOMA STATE UNIVERSITY, Department of English

Degree Offered: PhD in English with a specialization in TESL/linguistics.

Length of Program: 8 semesters. Students may be full-time or part-time and may begin their study at the beginning of the fall or spring semester. Application deadlines are fall semester, April 1 (February 15 for early admission); spring semester, October 1.

Program Requirements: 60 credit hours beyond the MA. A reading knowledge of two languages or mastery of one language is required; English meets the requirement for nonnative speakers of English. A comprehensive examination and a thesis are required. Practice teaching is not required.

Courses Offered: (*required) *Introduction to TESL Research; TESL Theory and Methods; Internship in TESL; TESL Testing; Social and Psychological Aspects of Language; Studies in English Grammar; Descriptive Linguistics; Seminar in Linguistics; Studies in TESL; Topics in Linguistics; Topics in Second Language Acquisition; Language in America; History of English; Teaching Technical and Business Writing; Theories of Communication; Qualitative Research Methods; Comparative Cultures; Psychology of Language; Computer Applications in Education; offerings in education, psychology, sociology, and anthropology.

Full-Time Staff: See MA program description.

Requirements for Admission: The university's requirements for admission are a master's degree from an accredited institution, an acceptable academic record, and the recommendation of the English Department and the dean of the Graduate College. Nonnative speakers must have a minimum of 550 on the TOEFL. The program requires a minimum overall graduate GPA of 3.5, three letters of recommendation, a 250-word statement of purpose, and a 10- to 20-page writing sample or a GRE score. Nonnative speakers must have a TOEFL score near 600 and must submit a TWE score.

Tuition, Fees, and Aid: See MA program description.

General: The program provides a broad range of courses from which students may individualize their programs of study to meet their particular career plans. At the doctoral level students are encouraged to supplement second language acquisition and pedagogy courses with course work in psycholinguistics or sociolinguistics. There are many opportunities for students to be involved in research and curriculum design projects during their course of study. Areas of faculty and student specialization include testing, simulation and gaming, curriculum design, learning strategies, discourse analysis, Native American languages, and ethnolinguistics. The program can include courses for an Oklahoma ESL endorsement.

Although no formal agreement with other institutions is in effect, the department encourages and assists students in finding teaching opportunities abroad. Students have taught in the People's Republic of China, Mexico, and Japan during their course work. The university also participates in a university consortium in Indonesia.

Four students completed the program in 1996–1997.

The university has an intensive English language program for nonnative speakers of English.

Summer Session: Yes

Further Information: Graduate Coordinator, Department of English
205 Morrill Hall
Oklahoma State University
Stillwater, OK 74078

Telephone: (405) 744-9469
Fax: (405) 744-6326
E-mail: carol.moder@okway.okstate.edu
http://www.writing.okstate.edu/english

◆ OLD DOMINION UNIVERSITY, Department of English

Degree Offered: MA in applied linguistics.

Length of Program: 3 years. Students may be full-time or part-time and may begin their study at the beginning of any semester. Application deadlines are fall semester, July 1; spring semester, November 1; summer semester, April 1.

Program Requirements: 33 semester hours. Competence in a language other than English is required for native speakers of English. Practice teaching and an oral comprehensive examination are required. A thesis is not required.

Courses Offered: (*required) *Language and Communication Across Cultures; *General Linguistics; *Phonetics and Phonology; *Syntax; *Practicum; History of the English Language; American English; Descriptive Linguistics; Advanced History of the English Language; Semantics and Lexicography; Sociolinguistics; First and Second Language Acquisition.

Full-Time Staff: Janet M. Bing, John P. Broderick, Carole P. Hines, Charles E. Ruhl, Natalie Schilling-Estes.

Requirements for Admission: The university's requirement for admission is a BA from an accredited institution with a B average in the major field. The program requires 12 hours of undergraduate courses in language or literature (9 on the upper level). Nonnative speakers of English must submit a minimum TOEFL score of 570 (550 for provisional acceptance), a sample of scholarly writing, and three recommendations, one evaluating the applicant's proficiency in English.

Tuition, Fees, and Aid: For in-state students, $171 per credit hour; for out-of-state students, $453 per credit hour. Fees are $38. Teaching assistantships, writing assistantships, administrative assistantships, and fellowships are available.

General: The program cooperates closely with the English Language Center. There is a strong emphasis on computer skills. Graduates have an excellent employment record.

Students have the opportunity to do practice teaching in Brazil, and the university has exchange programs in Japan and Brazil.

Twenty-four students completed the program in 1996–1997.

The university has an intensive English language program for nonnative speakers of English.

Summer Session: Yes

Further Information: Dr. Janet M. Bing
Department of English
Old Dominion University
Norfolk, VA 23529-0078

Telephone: (757) 683-4030
Fax: (757) 683-3241
E-mail: jbing@odu.edu

◆ OREGON, UNIVERSITY OF, Department of Linguistics

Degree Offered: MA in linguistics with applied linguistics option.

Length of Program: 6 quarters. Students may be full-time or part-time and may begin their study at the beginning of any quarter. The application deadline for the fall quarter is August 15.

Program Requirements: 48 credits. Competence in a language other than English is required for native speakers of English. A comprehensive examination is required unless the student is invited by the faculty to write a thesis. Practice teaching is not required.

Courses Offered: Second Language Acquisition; Second Language Teaching Methods; Second Language Practice; Advanced Second Language Acquisition; Advanced Second Language Teaching Methods; Second Language Teaching Practicum; English Grammar; Applied ESL Phonetics and Phonology; Content-Based Second Language Teaching K–12; Phonetics, Phonology, Syntax, and Semantics I and II; Phonological Theory; Syntactic Theory; Semantic Theory; Empirical Methods in Linguistics; Languages of the World; Discourse Analysis; Psycholinguistics; Cognitive Lab; Cognitive Linguistics; Sociolinguistics; Language Planning and Policy; Historical and Comparative Linguistics; Seminars in Applied Linguistics; Seminars in General Linguistics.

Full-Time Staff: Kathie Carpenter, Scott DeLancey, Thomas Givon, Eric Pederson, Derry Malsch, Doris Payne (chair), Patricia Rounds, Jacquelyn Schacter, Russell S. Tomlin.

Requirements for Admission: The university's requirements for admission are graduation from an accredited 4-year college or university and acceptance by the major department. The program requires a statement of purpose, a GRE score, a TOEFL score for nonnative speakers of English, transcripts, and three letters of recommendation.

Tuition, Fees, and Aid: For in-state students, $1,496 per quarter; for out-of-state students, $3,354 per quarter. Teaching assistantships are available in linguistics and in the American English Institute. Research assistantships are available through faculty grant support.

General: The program assumes that a solid preparation in linguistics, applied as well as theoretical, is an indispensable requirement for any further specialization at the graduate level. Whereas the faculty and courses deal with a wide variety of linguistic topics and issues, three facets of linguistics are strongly emphasized: (a) a functional approach to the study of language structure and use; (b) an empirical, experimental, and cross-linguistic approach to the methodology of linguistic research; and (c) an interdisciplinary emphasis on the place of human language in its wider natural context. A joint program with the College of Education leads to a state endorsement in ESOL.

Five students completed the program in 1996–1997.

The university has an intensive English language program for nonnative speakers of English.

Summer Session: Yes

Further Information: Dr. Patricia L. Rounds
Department of Linguistics
233 Straub Hall
University of Oregon
Eugene, OR 97403

Telephone: (541) 346-3907
Fax: (541) 346-3917
E-mail: plrounds@oregon.uoregon.edu

◆ OREGON, UNIVERSITY OF, Department of Linguistics

Degree Offered: PhD in linguistics with applied linguistics option.

Length of Program: Variable. Students may be full-time or part-time and may begin their study at the beginning of any quarter. The application deadline for the fall quarter is August 15.

Program Requirements: 32 credits. Courses applied to the MA degree cannot count toward the PhD course requirements. Competence in two languages other than English is required; one may be the MA qualifying language. A doctoral examination, a dissertation, and an oral examination are required.

Courses Offered: (*required) *two seminars, one in syntax, semantics, or pragmatics; *a course in statistics; *a cognitive science laboratory course; *Empirical Methods in Linguistics. See MA program description for other courses.

Full-Time Staff: See MA program description.

Requirements for Admission: See MA program description.

Tuition, Fees, and Aid: See MA program description.

General: See MA program description.

Summer Session: Yes

Further Information: Dr. Patricia L. Rounds
Department of Linguistics
233 Straub Hall
University of Oregon
Eugene, OR 97403

Telephone: (541) 346-3907
Fax: (541) 346-3917
E-mail: plrounds@oregon.uoregon.edu

◆ OUR LADY OF THE LAKE UNIVERSITY OF SAN ANTONIO, Department of Education

Degrees Offered: BA with ESL endorsement; BA with bilingual certification.

Length of Program: 8 semesters. Students may be full-time or part-time and may begin their study at the beginning of any semester. Application deadlines are fall semester, August 9; spring semester, December 22; summer semester, May 23.

Program Requirements: Competence in a language other than English is not required. Practice teaching and a comprehensive examination are required. A thesis is not required.

Courses Offered: (*required) For the ESL endorsement: *Language Acquisition Processes; *Linguistic Applications; *General Linguistic Theory; *ESL Methodology. For bilingual certification: *ESL Methodology; *Language Arts/Reading: Bilingual; *Mexican-American Cultural History; *Linguistic Applications; *Advanced Spanish Grammar, *Reading Composition II; *Spanish Dialects of the Southwest.

Full-Time Staff: Hugh B. Fox III (director), David Sanor.

Tuition, Fees, and Aid: $261 per semester hour. Fees vary from course to course. Graduate assistantships, work study, and grants are available.

Summer Session: Yes

Further Information: Dr. Hugh B. Fox III
Department of Education
Moye 213
Our Lady of the Lake University of San Antonio
411 SW 24th Street
San Antonio, TX 78207-4689

Telephone: (512) 434-6711 extension 304

◆ OUR LADY OF THE LAKE UNIVERSITY OF SAN ANTONIO, Department of Education

Degrees Offered: MEd with a specialization in ESL; MEd with a specialization in bilingual education.

Length of Program: 4 semesters. Students may be full-time or part-time and may begin their study at the beginning of any semester. Application deadlines are fall semester, August 9; spring semester, December 22; summer semester, May 23.

Program Requirements: Competence in a language other than English is not required. A comprehensive examination is required. Neither practice teaching nor a thesis is required.

Courses Offered: (*required) *General Linguistic Theory; *ESL Methodology. For the bilingual education specialization: *Instructional Techniques for Content Areas: Bilingual; *Reading and Language Arts: Bilingual. For the specialization in ESL: *Language Acquisition Processes; *Linguistic Applications.

Full-Time Staff: See BA program description.

Tuition, Fees, and Aid: See BA program description.

Summer Session: Yes

Further Information: Dr. Hugh B. Fox III
Department of Education
Moye 213
Our Lady of the Lake University of San Antonio
411 SW 24th Street
San Antonio, TX 78207-4689

Telephone: (512) 434-6711 extension 304

◆ PACIFIC, UNIVERSITY OF THE, Benerd School of Education, Department of Curriculum and Instruction

Degree Offered: BA in liberal studies with a concentration in second language pedagogy.

Length of Program: 8 semesters. Students may be full-time or part-time and may begin their study at the beginning of any semester.

Program Requirements: 124 semester units. Competence in a language other than English is not required. Practice teaching is required. Neither a thesis nor a comprehensive examination is required.

Courses Offered: (*required) *Introduction to Language; *Syntax and Semantics; *Language Acquisition; *ESL: Theory and Practice; *Introduction to Bilingual Education.

Full-Time Staff: David P. Baral, Marilyn Draheim (chair).

General: The program includes the California CLAD emphasis as part of an elementary teaching credential.

Further Information: Marilyn Draheim, Chair
Department of Curriculum and Instruction
Benerd School of Education
University of the Pacific
3601 Pacific Avenue
Stockton, CA 95211

Telephone: (209) 946-2685
Fax: (209) 946-3110

◆ PENNSYLVANIA, UNIVERSITY OF, Language in Education Division

Degree Offered: MSEd in TESOL.

Length of Program: 4 semesters. Students may be full-time or part-time and may begin their study at the beginning of any semester. Rolling admissions are in effect for the fall semester. Application deadlines are spring semester, December 1; summer session, April 15.

Program Requirements: 12 credit hours. Competence in a language other than English is not required. Practice teaching and a comprehensive examination are required. A thesis is not required.

Courses Offered: (*required) *Fieldwork in Language in Education: TESOL Observation *or* *Fieldwork in Language in Education: TESOL Practice; *Educational Linguistics; *Sociolinguistics in Education; *Approaches to Teaching English and Other Modern Languages; Classroom Discourse and Interaction; Cross-Cultural Awareness; Cross-Cultural Variation in Language Use; Ethnographic Methods; Group Processes; Higher Education Systems; Issues and Approaches in Intercultural Education; Language and Gender; Language Diversity and Education; Language in the Professions; Language Planning and Education; Managing People; Multicultural Issues in Education; Second Language Acquisition.

Full-Time Staff: Morton Botel, Rebecca Freeman, Vivian Gadsen, Nancy Hornberger, Susan Lytle, Cheri Micheau, Teresa Pica (chair), Lawrence Sipe, Charles Dwyer, Frederick Erickson, Kathleen Hall.

Requirements for Admission: The university's requirements for admission are three letters of recommendation, a statement of purpose, and a GRE score. The program requires a TOEFL score for international students.

Tuition, Fees, and Aid: $8,256 per semester. Fees are $710. Teaching assistantships, research assistantships, merit-based fellowships, student employment, and loans are available.

General: The program focuses on both the practical and the theoretical aspects of the field. The program is classroom oriented, with a strong focus on intercultural communication and on the interaction of social behavior and language use. Together these form a dynamic backdrop to the more traditional aspects of teacher preparation. Students learn to teach English as a second, foreign, or international language and to design and administer English language programs. Faculty regularly engage in research and teaching abroad.

Thirty-five students completed the program in 1996–1997.

The university has an intensive English language program for nonnative speakers of English.

Summer Session: Yes

Further Information: Keith Watanabe
Language in Education Division
Graduate School of Education, Suite A-10
University of Pennsylvania
3700 Walnut Street
Philadelphia, PA 19104

Telephone: (215) 898-4800
Fax: (215) 573-2109
E-mail: keithw@nwfs.gse.upenn.edu

◆ THE PENNSYLVANIA STATE UNIVERSITY, Department of Speech Communication

Degree Offered: MA (TESL).

Length of Program: 4 semesters. Students may be full-time or part-time and must begin their study at the beginning of the fall semester. The application deadline is February 15.

Program Requirements: 36 credits. Competence in a language other than English is required; English meets the requirement for nonnative speakers of English. Practice teaching, a master's paper, and a comprehensive examination are required.

Courses Offered: (*required) *Theory: Second Language Acquisition; *TESL; *Introduction to Applied Linguistics; *Linguistic Structures for ESL; *American English Phonetics; *Cross-Cultural Communication *or* Communication in Second Language Classrooms; *Internship/Supervised College Teaching; *6 credits from courses offered by the College of Education and approved by the student's committee; Analysis of Discourse; Seminar in Second Language Acquisition; Research Problems in ESL; Second/Foreign Language Materials Development; Second/Foreign Language Assessment; Advanced Language Assessment; Theories of Communicative Competence.

Full-Time Staff: Sandra J. Savignon (director), Grant H. Henning, Karen E. Johnson.

Requirements for Admission: The university's requirements for admission are a bachelor's degree, a GRE score, three letters of reference, and a statement of goals and professional objectives. Nonnative speakers of English must have a minimum TOEFL score of 600. The program requires a BA in a related or appropriate major.

Tuition, Fees, and Aid: For in-state students, $3,151 per semester; for out-of-state students, $6,490 per semester. Teaching assistantships and graduate school fellowships are available.

General: The program stresses both theoretical and practical issues related to the learning and teaching of ESL/EFL. Course work emphasizes second language acquisition theory and research, applied linguistics, teaching methodology, and cross-cultural communication. The program also offers oral language proficiency testing and training of international teaching assistants for the Program in ESL. The MA program provides a foundation for those intending to continue study at the doctoral level in applied linguistics, speech communication, and second/foreign language education. Students completing the program can apply for entrance into the doctoral program in speech communication with an emphasis in TESL.

The university has an intensive English language program for nonnative speakers of English.

Summer Session: No

Further Information: Sandra J. Savignon, Director
Program in English as a Second Language
305 Sparks Building
The Pennsylvania State University
University Park, PA 16802

Telephone: (814) 865-7365
Fax: (814) 863-7986
E-mail: tesl@psu.edu
http://www.la.psu.edu/speech/esl/intro.htm

◆ PITTSBURGH, UNIVERSITY OF, Department of Linguistics

Degree Offered: MA in linguistics with a TESOL certificate.

Length of Programs: 6 semesters. Students may be full-time or part-time and may begin their study at the beginning of any semester, but fall semester is preferred. The application deadline for the fall semester is February 1.

Program Requirements: 30 credits. Competence in a language other than English is required for native speakers of English. Practice teaching and a thesis are required. A comprehensive examination is not required.

Courses Offered: (*required) *Syntactic Theory; *Phonetics and Phonemics; *Phonology; *Linguistic Structure of English; *Theory and Methods of Second Language Teaching; *Techniques and Procedures of TESOL; *Second Language Acquisition; Psycholinguistics; Sociolinguistics; Materials Development for TESOL; Current Issues in TESOL; Morphology; Historical Linguistics; Field Methods; American Indian Languages; Introduction to Computational Linguistics; Anthropological Linguistics.

Full-Time Staff: Robert DeKeyser, Daniel Everett (chair), Peter Gordon, Alan Juffs, Terrence S. Kaufman, Margaret MacEachern, Lionel Menasche, Christina Bratt Paulston, Charles Perfetti, Richmond H. Thomason, Sarah Grey Thomason, Paul Toth.

Requirements for Admission: The university's requirement for admission is a baccalaureate degree. Nonnative speakers of English must have a minimum TOEFL score of 550. The program requires 2 years of college-level foreign language study or residence abroad, a GRE score, a minimum GPA of 3.0, and, for nonnative speakers of English, a minimum TOEFL score of 600.

Tuition, Fees, and Aid: For in-state students, $3,855 per semester; for out-of-state students, $7,937 per semester. Fees are $212 per semester. Teaching assistantships in the English Language Institute and in the Department of Linguistics, as well as a limited number of research assistantships, are available.

General: The program combines a solid grounding in theories and analytic techniques of linguistics with specific training in TESOL. The department prides itself on its good faculty-student ratio and access to state-of-the-art computer facilities.

Ten students completed the program in 1996–1997.

The university has an intensive English language program for nonnative speakers of English.

Summer Session: Yes

Further Information: Admissions Officer
Department of Linguistics
University of Pittsburgh
2816 Cathedral of Learning
Pittsburgh, PA 15260

Telephone: (412) 624-5900
Fax: (412) 624-6130

◆ PITTSBURGH, UNIVERSITY OF, Department of Linguistics

Degree Offered: PhD in applied linguistics with a TESOL certificate.

Length of Program: Students may be full-time or part-time and may begin their study at the beginning of any semester, but fall semester is preferred. The application deadline for the fall term is February 1.

Program Requirements: 72 credits. Competence in two foreign languages is required. Practice teaching, a dissertation, and a comprehensive examination are required.

Courses Offered: See MA program description.

Full-Time Staff: See MA program description.

Requirements for Admission: See MA program description.

Tuition, Fees, and Aid: See MA program description.

General: See MA program description.

Summer Session: Yes

Further Information: Admissions Officer
Department of Linguistics
University of Pittsburgh
2816 Cathedral of Learning
Pittsburgh, PA 15260

Telephone: (412) 624-5900
Fax: (412) 624-6130

◆ PORTLAND STATE UNIVERSITY, Department of Applied Linguistics

Degrees Offered: TESL certificate; BA in linguistics.

Length of Program: 1 year. Students may be full-time or part-time and may begin their study at the beginning of the fall, winter, or spring quarter (fall or winter quarter only for international students). Application deadlines are fall quarter, February 1; winter quarter, September 1 (international students, July 1); spring quarter, November 1.

Program Requirements: 40 quarter credits. Competence in a language other than English is required; English meets the requirement for nonnative speakers of English. Practice teaching is required. A thesis is not required. A comprehensive examination is required only if the student has no proof of study of 2 years of a foreign language.

Courses Offered: (*required) *Introduction to Linguistics; *TESOL Methods; Syntax; Phonology; Linguistic Semantics; Linguistic Pragmatics; Discourse Analysis; Historical and Comparative Linguistics; How Do People Learn a Second Language?; Taking Stock: Assessment and Evaluation in Programs With Language Minority Students; Sociolinguistics; Psycholinguistics; Applied Linguistics; Language Acquisition; Language Testing; Introduction to Computational Linguistics; Natural Language Processing; Speech Recognition and Synthesis; Linguistics and Cognitive Science; Grammar for TESOL; Culture Learning in the Language Classroom; ESL in the Workplace; Curriculum Design and Materials Development in TESOL; TESOL Methods; World Englishes; History of the English Language; Structure of the English Language; Linguistics and Literature; Administration of ESL Programs.

Full-Time Staff: John Armbrust, Becky K. Boesch, Kimberley A. Brown, Ruth Chapin, Tucker Childs, Jeanette S. DeCarrico, Thomas G. Dieterich, M. Jane Dresser, Michael J. Harvey, Lena Koessler, Shirley A. Morrell, Marjorie Terdal, Judith Wild, Margaret Young.

Requirements for Admission: The university's requirements for admission are a postbaccalaureate application and, for nonnative speakers of English, a TOEFL score of 550.

Tuition, Fees, and Aid: For in-state students, $1,900 per term (full-time); for out-of-state students, $3,265 credits per term (full-time). A few graduate teaching assistantships are available.

General: The program emphasizes practice teaching and other practical experience, both in the ESL program and at other institutions in the community. The certificate program leads to an Oregon credential in TESOL.

The university has a faculty exchange program at the University of Freiburg, Germany, and student exchange opportunities are available in Germany and France.

Thirty students completed the program in 1996–1997.

The university has an intensive English language program for nonnative speakers of English.

Summer Session: Yes

Further Information: Chair
Department of Applied Linguistics
Neuberger Hall 467
Portland State University
724 SW Harrison
Portland, OR 97207

Telephone: (503) 725-4088
Fax: (503) 725-4139
E-mail: tittelk@nhl.nh.pdx.edu; westbys@pdx.edu

◆ PORTLAND STATE UNIVERSITY, Department of Applied Linguistics

Degree Offered: MA: TESOL.

Length of Program: 2 or more years. Students may be full-time or part-time and may begin their study at the beginning of the fall, winter, or spring quarter (fall or winter quarter only for international students). Application deadlines are fall quarter, February 1; winter quarter, September 1 (international students, July 1); spring quarter, November 1.

Program Requirements: 46 quarter credits. Competence in a language other than English is required; English meets the requirement for nonnative speakers of English. Practice teaching and a thesis are required. A comprehensive examination is required only if the student has no proof of study of 2 years of a foreign language.

Courses Offered: (*required) *4 credits from Syntax, Phonology, Linguistic Semantics, Linguistic Pragmatics, Discourse Analysis, Historical and Comparative Linguistics, Linguistics and Cognitive Science, History of the English Language; *4 credits from Second Language Acquisition, Selected Topics, Sociolinguistics, Psycholinguistics, Survey of Applied Linguistics, First Language Acquisition, Grammar for TESOL, World Englishes; *4 credits from Language Proficiency Testing, Administration of ESL/EFL Programs, ESL in the Workplace, Curriculum Design and Materials Development in TESOL, Linguistics and Literature; *8 credits in literature and cultural studies; *8 credits in TESOL Methods and Supervised Practice; *10 credits in research.

Full-Time Staff: See TESL certificate program description.

Requirements for Admission: The requirements for admission are a baccalaureate degree from an accredited institution with a minimum cumulative GPA of 3.0, two letters of reference, a personal statement, transcripts, 2 years of foreign language study, and, for nonnative speakers of English, a TOEFL score of 600.

Tuition, Fees, and Aid: See TESL certificate program description.

General: See TESL certificate program description.
Eighty students completed the program in 1995–1997.

Summer Session: Yes

Further Information: Chair
Department of Applied Linguistics
Neuberger Hall 467
Portland State University
724 SW Harrison
Portland, OR 97207

Telephone: (503) 725-4088
Fax: (503) 725-4139
E-mail: tittelk@nhl.nh.pdx.edu; westbys@pdx.edu

◆ PUERTO RICO, UNIVERSITY OF, Department of Graduate Studies, School of Education

Degree Offered: MEd in TESL.

Length of Program: 4 semesters. Students may be full-time or part-time and must begin their study at the beginning of the fall semester. The application deadline is February 1.

Program Requirements: 40 credits. Competence in a language other than English is required. Practice teaching is not required. A thesis and a comprehensive examination are required.

Courses Offered: (*required) Professional component: *Advanced Seminar: The Principles of Learning and Teaching ESL; *Advanced Methods for the Teaching of Oral English to Speakers of Other Languages; *Seminar: Curriculum, Instruction, and Evaluation of English Programs; *The Methodology of the Teaching of Literature to Students of ESL; *Methods and Techniques of Teaching Grammar and Composition in Modern English; *Theory and Practice in Bilingual Education; *three of the following: Critical Writing, Language and Educational Culture, Studies in Bilingualism, Problems in the Analysis of Contemporary English, Literature and Language of the English-Speaking Caribbean; directed electives: Research Methods in Education, Statistics for Education; free electives; *Thesis.

Full-Time Staff: María A. Irizarry (chair), John Vázquez, Eloína Vidal.

Requirements for Admission: The university's requirements for admission are a baccalaureate degree, command of Spanish and English, and a score on the Prueba de Aptitud para Estudios Graduados (Graduate Studies Aptitude Test) or GRE.

Tuition, Fees, and Aid: For in-state students, $75 per credit; for out-of-state students, $1,750 per semester. Teaching assistantships, scholarships, and loans are available.

General: The program emphasizes teaching performance to meet the needs and demands of the local setting.

Three students completed the program in 1996–1997.

The university has an intensive English language program for nonnative speakers of English.

Summer Session: Yes

Further Information: Coordinator, TESL Program
Department of Graduate Studies, School of Education
University of Puerto Rico
San Juan, PR 00976

Telephone: (787) 764-0000 extensions 2324, 4396
Fax: (787) 764-0000 extension 2283
E-mail: mirizarr@upracd.upr.clu.edu

◆ PUERTO RICO, UNIVERSITY OF, Department of Graduate Studies, School of Education

Degree Offered: EdD in curriculum and teaching in the area of TESL.

Length of Program: 14 semesters. Students may be full-time or part-time and must begin their studies at the beginning of the fall semester. The application deadline is February 1.

Program Requirements: 60 credits. Competence in Spanish is required. An internship, a dissertation, and a comprehensive examination are required.

Courses Offered: (*required) *Linguistics; *Models of Teaching, Supervision, and Evaluation in Programs of ESL; *Language Acquisition and the Application of Theories of Learning and Intellectual Development of TESL; Advanced Techniques in the Teaching of Reading in a Bilingual Setting; The Teaching of ESL to Exceptional Students; Language and Culture; Problems in the Analysis of Contemporary English; Seminar in Semantics; Seminar in English Phonology; Implications of Modern Linguistic Theory for TESL.

Full-Time Staff: See program description for MEd in TESL.

Requirements for Admission: The university's requirements for admission are a master's degree or its equivalent in TESL, a GPA of 3.0, and fluency in Spanish and English. The program requires an interview with the Admissions Committee and two letters of recommendation.

Tuition, Fees, and Aid: See program description for MEd in TESL.

General: Two students completed the program in 1996–1997.

The university has an intensive English language program for nonnative speakers of English.

Summer Session: Yes

Further Information: Coordinator, TESL Program
Department of Graduate Studies, School of Education
University of Puerto Rico
San Juan, PR 00976

Telephone: (787) 764-0000 extensions 2324, 4396
Fax: (787) 764-0000 extension 2283
E-mail: mirizarr@upracd.upr.clu.edu

◆ PUGET SOUND, UNIVERSITY OF, Continuing Education

Degree Offered: Washington State endorsement in ESL.

Length of Program: Students attend part-time and in the summer and may begin their study at the beginning of any quarter. There are no application deadlines.

Program Requirements: 24 quarter hours. Competence in a language other than English is not required. Practice teaching, a thesis, and a comprehensive examination are optional.

Courses Offered: (*required) *Language Acquisition and Learning Theories and Practice; *Whole Language and the ESL Classroom; *Learning Variables and the ESL Child; *Reading and the ESL Child; *The Writing Process and the ESL Child; *Oral Language Development in the ESL Child; *Content Area Instruction for ESL Students; *Testing and Evaluation of ESL Students.

Requirements for Admission: None. All courses are offered through continuing education.

Tuition, Fees, and Aid: $70 per quarter hour. No financial aid is available.

General: The program is designed for individuals who want to acquire experience in teaching ESL and for teachers who have students with limited English skills in their classrooms. The courses meet the guidelines of the Washington State Superintendent of Public Instruction for an ESL endorsement.

Fifteen students completed the program in 1996–1997.

Summer Session: Yes

Further Information: Kathy Brooke
School of Education
Howarth 301
University of Puget Sound
1500 North Warner
Tacoma, WA 98416

Telephone: (253) 756-3382
Fax: (253) 756-8312
E-mail: kmbrooke@ups.edu

◆ QUEENS COLLEGE OF THE CITY UNIVERSITY OF NEW YORK, Department of Linguistics and Communication Disorders

Degree Offered: BA in linguistics.

Length of Program: 4 semesters. Students may be full-time or part-time and must begin their study at the beginning of the fall semester. There are no application deadlines.

Program Requirements: 39 credits. Competence in a language other than English is optional. Practice teaching and a minor in secondary education are required. Neither a thesis nor a comprehensive examination is required.

Courses Offered: (*required) *Introduction to Language; *Introduction to Linguistic Analysis; *Phonetics; *The Structure of English Words; *Syntax I and II; *Sociolinguistics; *Bilingualism; *Phonology; *Introduction to Applied Linguistics; *Semantics and Pragmatics; *Methods and Materials of TESOL in Content Areas; *Issues in Linguistic Research.

Full-Time Staff: Charles E. Cairns, Robert Fiengo, Elaine C. Klein, Gita Martohardjono, Herbert Seliger, Alan Stevens, Robert Vago.

Requirements for Admission: The college's requirement for admission is a strong academic record in high school (a B+ average). Admission is based on GPA, academic program, and test scores. SAT scores are recommended (minimum 1050). The program requires a concentration form, generally at the end of the sophomore year.

Tuition, Fees, and Aid: For in-state students, $1,600 per semester; for out-of-state students, $3,400 per semester.

General: The program leads to a New York State credential in TESOL.
Nineteen students completed the program in 1996–1997.
The college has an intensive English language program for nonnative speakers of English.

Summer Session: Yes

Further Information: Professor Robert Vago
Department of Linguistics and Communication Disorders
Kissena Hall 347
Queens College of the City University of New York
Flushing, NY 11367

Telephone: (718) 997-2870
Fax: (718) 997-2873
E-mail: vago@qcvax.acc.qc.edu

◆ QUEENS COLLEGE OF THE CITY UNIVERSITY OF NEW YORK, Department of Linguistics and Communication Disorders

Degree Offered: MA in applied linguistics.

Length of Program: 3 semesters. Students may be full-time or part-time and may begin their study at the beginning of any semester. Application deadlines are fall semester, March 1; spring semester, December 1.

Program Requirements: 33 credits. Competence in a language other than English is not required. Practice teaching is required. Neither a thesis nor a comprehensive examination is required.

Courses Offered: (*required) *Introduction to Linguistics; *Structure of American English I and II; *Sociolinguistics; *Bilingualism; *Testing and Measurement; *Introduction to Second Language Acquisition; *Methods and Materials Through the Basic Skills; *Practicum in Adult TESOL; *Seminar in Research; one elective.

Full-Time Staff: Elaine C. Klein, Gita Martohardjono, Michael Newman, Herbert Seliger, Robert Vago.

Requirements for Admission: The requirement for admission is a BA with a minimum GPA of 3.0.

Tuition, Fees, and Aid: For in-state students, $185 per credit; for out-of-state students, $320 per credit.

General: Nineteen students completed the program in 1996–1997.

The college has an intensive English language program for nonnative speakers of English.

Summer Session: Yes

Further Information: Professor Robert Vago
Department of Linguistics and Communication Disorders
Kissena Hall 347
Queens College of the City University of New York
Flushing, NY 11367

Telephone: (718) 997-2870
Fax: (718) 997-2873
E-mail: vago@qcvax.acc.qc.edu

◆ QUEENS COLLEGE OF THE CITY UNIVERSITY OF NEW YORK, Department of Linguistics and Communication Disorders

Degree Offered: MS in education: TESOL.

Length of Program: 3 semesters. Students may be full-time or part-time and may begin their study at the beginning of any semester. Application deadlines are fall semester, March 1; spring semester, December 1.

Program Requirements: 33 credits. Competence in a language other than English is not required. Practice teaching is optional. Neither a thesis nor a comprehensive examination is required.

Courses Offered: (*required) *Foundations in Education; *Introduction to Linguistics; *Structure of American English I and II; *Sociolinguistics; *Bilingualism; *Testing and Measurement; *Introduction to Second Language Acquisition; *Methods and Materials Through the Basic Skills; *Methods and Materials Through the Content Areas; *Seminar in Research.

Full-Time Staff: See MA program description.

Requirements for Admission: See MA program description.

Tuition, Fees, and Aid: See MA program description.

General: The program leads to a New York State credential in TESOL.

Nineteen students completed the program in 1996–1997.

The college has an intensive English language program for nonnative speakers of English.

Summer Session: Yes

Further Information: Professor Robert Vago
Department of Linguistics and Communication Disorders
Kissena Hall 347
Queens College of the City University of New York
Flushing, NY 11367

Telephone: (718) 997-2870
Fax: (718) 997-2873
E-mail: vago@qcvax.acc.qc.edu

◆ RADFORD UNIVERSITY, Department of Educational Studies

Degree Offered: MS in education with a major in curriculum and instruction and a TESL concentration.

Length of Program: 4 semesters. Students may be full-time or part-time and may begin their study at the beginning of any semester. Application deadlines are fall semester, February 1; spring semester, October 1; summer semester, April 1.

Program Requirements: 30–46 semester hours, depending on licensure option. Competence in a language other than English is required for native speakers of English; English meets the requirement for nonnative speakers of English. Blocking and student teaching are required for the licensure option. A comprehensive examination is required. A thesis is not required.

Courses Offered: (*required) *Educational Research; *Instructional Technology; *Foundations of Education; *International Education; *Linguistics; *Advanced Study in Reading; *ESL: Analysis and Application of Instructional Technology; *Second Language Assessment Principles; ESL: Applied Linguistics; Second Language Curriculum Design; a modern foreign language; Blocking; Student Teaching.

Full-Time Staff: Anita L. Corey, Patricia M. Harris, Harvey R. Jahn, Donna C. Kauffman, Alvin Proffit (chair), Sheila S. Reyna, Paul W. Witkowsky.

Requirements for Admission: The university's requirements for admission are a GRE, NTE, or Miller Analogies Test score and, for nonnative speakers of English, a TOEFL score of 550.

Tuition, Fees, and Aid: For in-state students, $1,652 per semester; for out-of-state students, $3,244 per semester. Graduate assistantships and tuition waivers are available.

General: The TESL concentration allows students to develop knowledge of second language acquisition theory based on sound educational practices. Core requirements provide the background necessary to work in either administrative or teaching positions. Emphasis is given to the interconnection of planning, delivery, and assessment. The program can lead to a Virginia credential in TESOL.

Three students completed the program in 1996–1997.

Summer Session: Yes

Further Information: Director
English Language Institute
Radford University
707 Norwood Street (RUS Box 6936)
Radford, VA 24142

Telephone: (540) 831-5403
Fax: (540) 831-6023
E-mail: dkauffma@runet.edu

◆ RHODE ISLAND COLLEGE, Educational Studies Department

Degree Offered: MATESL.

Length of Program: 4 semesters and 2 summer sessions. Students may be full-time or part-time and may begin their study at the beginning of any semester. Application deadlines are fall semester, April 1; spring semester, November 1.

Program Requirements: 51 credits. Two semesters of a language other than English are required for native speakers of English. A 45-clock-hour practicum and a comprehensive examination are required. A thesis is not required.

Courses Offered: (*required) *Current Issues in ESL; *Language Acquisition and Learning; *Applied Linguistics in ESL; *TESL; *Teaching Reading and Writing to ESL Students; *Curriculum Development and Language Assessment in ESL; *Applied Research and TESL; *Psychological Perspectives on Learning and Teaching; *Contexts of Schooling; *Comparative Philosophies of Education; *Instructional Approaches to Children With Special Needs in Regular Classes; *Dimensions of Secondary Education; *Language Arts in the Elementary School; *Student Teaching; *Student Teaching Seminar.

Full-Time Staff: J. Botelho, Gale Goodwin-Gomez, C. Panofsky (chair), Willis Poole, Ezra Stieglitz.

Requirements for Admission: The college's requirements for admission are official transcripts, an official GRE or Miller Analogies Test score, and three letters of recommendation. Students who have not graduated from an institution of higher education in which English is the medium of instruction must present a TOEFL score of 550 or higher (this score may substitute for the GRE or Miller Analogies Test score).

Tuition, Fees, and Aid: For in-state students, $154 per credit; for out-of-state students, $300 per credit. The application fee is $25.

General: The program leads to Rhode Island ESL certification, K–12.

Six students completed the program in 1996–1997.

The college has an intensive English language program for nonnative speakers of English.

Summer Session: Yes

Further Information: Dr. Willis Poole
Educational Studies Department
Henry Barnard School, Room 217
Rhode Island College
600 Mount Pleasant Avenue
Providence, RI 02908

Telephone: (401) 456-8573
Fax: (401) 456-8018
E-mail: wpoole@grog.ric.edu

◆ RHODE ISLAND COLLEGE,
Educational Studies Department

Degree Offered: MEd in TESL.

Length of Program: 3 semesters and 1 summer session. Students may be full-time or part-time and may begin their study at the beginning of any semester. Application deadlines are fall semester, April 1; spring semester, November 1.

Program Requirements: 36 credits. Two semesters of a language other than English are required for native speakers of English. A 45-clock-hour practicum and a comprehensive examination are required. A thesis is not required.

Courses Offered: (*required) *Current Issues in ESL; *Language Acquisition and Learning; *Applied Linguistics in ESL; *TESL; *Teaching Reading and Writing to ESL Students; *Curriculum Development and Language Assessment in ESL; *Applied Research and TESL; *History of the English Language *or* Modern English Grammar; *Cultural Foundations of Education; *Instructional Approaches to Children With Special Needs in Regular Classes; *Instructional Technology; *one of the following: Issues in Child Growth and Development, Social Psychology of Adolescence, Psychological Perspectives on Learning and Teaching.

Full-Time Staff: See program description for MATESL.

Requirements for Admission: See program description for MATESL.

Tuition, Fees, and Aid: For in-state students, $154 per credit; for out-of-state students, $300 per credit. The application fee is $25. A limited number of graduate assistantships are available that pay $4,000 per academic year and include remissions of tuition for the academic year and a summer session.

General: The program leads to an state ESL endorsement.
Eleven students completed the program in 1996–1997.
The college has an intensive English language program for nonnative speakers of English.

Summer Session: Yes

Further Information: Dr. Willis Poole
Educational Studies Department
Henry Barnard School, Room 217
Rhode Island College
600 Mount Pleasant Avenue
Providence, RI 02908

Telephone: (401) 456-8573
Fax: (401) 456-8018
E-mail: wpoole@grog.ric.edu

◆ ROCHESTER, UNIVERSITY OF, Warner Graduate School of Education

Degree Offered: MS in TESOL.

Length of Program: 4 semesters. Students may be full-time or part-time and may begin their study at the beginning of any semester. Application deadlines are summer or fall semester, July 1; spring semester, November 1; summer semester, February 1 or April 1.

Program Requirements: 39 semester hours. Competence in a language other than English is required. Practice teaching and a thesis are required. A comprehensive examination is not required.

Courses Offered: (*required) *Teaching, Curriculum, and Change; *Master's Research Methods; *Theories of Human Development; *Language Development; *Second Language Acquisition and Bilingualism; *English Language Study for Educators; *Theory and Practice in TESOL; *Implementing Innovation in TESOL; *Reflective Teaching in TESOL; *Student Teaching in TESOL.

Full-Time Staff: Patricia Irvine (coordinator).

Requirements for Admission: The program's requirement for admission is a bachelor's degree with a GPA of at least 2.75.

Tuition, Fees, and Aid: $672 per credit hour. No financial aid is available.

General: The program leads to a New York State credential in TESOL.
Eight students completed the program in 1996–1997.

Summer Session: Yes

Further Information: Coordinator of TESOL Program
Department of Teaching and Curriculum
Warner School of Education
University of Rochester
PO Box 270425
Rochester, NY 14627

Telephone: (716) 275-0967
Fax: (716) 473-7598
E-mail: pdir@uhura.cc.rochester.edu

◆ ST. CLOUD STATE UNIVERSITY, Department of English

Degree Offered: BS minor in ESL and ESL licensure.

Length of Program: 4 semesters. Students may be full-time or part-time and may begin their study at the beginning of any semester. Application deadlines are fall semester, December 25; spring semester, January 10.

Program Requirements: 24 credits. Two years of college study of a language other than English are required; English meets the requirement for nonnative speakers of English. Practice teaching is required. For Minnesota licensure, a teacher qualification examination and 34 credits of education courses are required. Neither a thesis nor a comprehensive examination is required.

Courses Offered: (*required) *TESL Theory and Methods; *TESL Methods: Reading and Writing; *Literacy for Second Language Learners; *English Grammars; Sociolinguistics, Language, and Gender; Pragmatics; ESL and Culture; Bilingual-Bicultural Education; Assessment, Evaluation, and Testing.

Full-Time Staff: David Heine, James H. Robinson (director), Suzanne Ross, Suellen Rundquist, Ramon Serrano, Marya Teutsch-Dwyer.

Requirements for Admission: The university's requirement for admission is graduation from high school in the upper half of the graduating class or an ACT score of 25 or higher (PSAT of 100 or higher, or SAT of 1000 or higher). For licensure, students must have a GPA of 2.5.

Tuition, Fees, and Aid: For in-state students, $90 per credit; for out-of-state students, $110 per credit. Work study and in-state tuition grants are available.

General: The program focuses on preservice teacher preparation for teaching ESL in K–12 classrooms. The minor may also be taken by international students or students who seek preparation for teaching in the Peace Corps or in other positions in non-English-speaking countries.

Ten students completed the program in 1996–1997.

The university has an intensive English language program for nonnative speakers of English.

Summer Session: Yes

Further Information: James H. Robinson
English Department
106 Riverview
St. Cloud State University
720 4th Avenue South
St. Cloud, MN 56301-4498

Telephone: (320) 255-4956
Fax: (320) 654-5524
E-mail: nobinson@stcloudstate.edu

◆ ST. CLOUD STATE UNIVERSITY, Department of English

Degree Offered: MA in English with a concentration in TESL.

Length of Program: 2 years. Students may be full-time or part-time and may begin their study at the beginning of any semester. Application deadlines are fall semester, April 1; spring semester, October 1.

Program Requirements: 36 credits. Competence in a language other than English is required; English meets the requirement for nonnative speakers of English. Practice teaching is required for K–12 licensure. A thesis is optional. A comprehensive exam is not required.

Courses Offered: (*required) *Theories of Second Language Acquisition; *TESL Methods; *TESL Methods: Reading and Writing; *Research in English, *English Grammars; *Sociolinguistics; Bilingual-Bicultural Education; ESL and Culture; Literacy for Second Language Learners; American English; Assessment, Evaluation, and Testing; Pragmatics; Language and Gender.

Full-Time Staff: See BS minor program description.

Requirements for Admission: The university's requirement for admission is a bachelor's degree with a 2.75 GPA or a 480 on the verbal section of the GRE. The program requires 1 year of study of a language other than English and completion of an introductory course in linguistics.

Tuition, Fees, and Aid: For in-state students, $150 per credit; for out-of-state students, $200 per credit. Teaching assistantships in college ESL, the Intensive English Center, the Writing Center, and freshman composition are available.

General: The program is designed for both the K–12 and adult teaching markets, and many students complete the K–12 licensure program simultaneously with the MA. The program balances theory and practice with an additional emphasis on cross-cultural communication skills for teachers.

The program has internship programs with the Minnesota State University at Akita, Japan; Seirei Junior College in Akita, Japan; Chung Nam Junior College in Taejon, Korea; and the International Classroom in San José, Costa Rica.

Seven students completed the program in 1996–1997.

The university has an intensive English language program for nonnative speakers of English.

Summer Session: Yes

Further Information: James H. Robinson, Director
English Department
106 Riverview
St. Cloud State University
720 4th Avenue South
St. Cloud, MN 56301-4498

Telephone: (320) 255-4956
Fax: (320) 654-5524
E-mail: nobinson@stcloudstate.edu

◆ SAINT MICHAEL'S COLLEGE, School for International Studies

Degree Offered: MA in teaching ESL/EFL.

Length of Program: 3 semesters. Students may be full-time or part-time and may begin their study at the beginning of any semester.

Program Requirements: 36 credits. Competence in a language other than English is not required. Practice teaching and a comprehensive examination are required. A thesis is not required.

Courses Offered: (*required) *Introduction to Language and Linguistics; *English Grammar; *(for all nonnative speakers of English) Communication Skills; *Theory and Method in Second Language Teaching; *English Phonology and the Teaching of Oral Skills in ESL/FL; *Teaching Reading and Writing in ESL/FL; *Second Language Acquisition; *Practicum I: Seminar/Observation; *Practicum II: Classroom Teaching; Problems and Theory in Grammar; Computer-Assisted Language Learning; Audiovisual Communication (noncomputer) in ESL/FL; Content-Based Instruction and English for Specific Purposes; Literature in ESL/FL; Grammar in the Classroom; Ideas That Work in TESL/FL; English Vocabulary and Semantics; Studies in American Culture; History of the English Language; Discourse/Error Analysis: Practical Implications for Second Language Teaching; Sociopragmatics; Bilingualism and Multicultural Education; Testing and Evaluation in TESL/FL; Language Learning and Assessment for Children; Independent Study in TESL/FL; Special Seminar in TESL/FL; Thesis Research Seminar.

Full-Time Staff: Mahmoud T. Arani, Christine Bauer-Ramazani, Sheena M. Bloodgett, Sarah E. Cummings, Carolyn B. Duffy, Daniel W. Evans, Robert P. Fox, Matthew Handelsman, Polly O. Howlett, M. Kathleen Mahnke, M. Elizabeth O'Dowd, Barbara S. Sargent, Bonnie Tangalos, Alice M. Thayer, Robert S. Williams.

Requirements for Admission: The program's requirement for admission is a BA or BS degree from a U.S. college or university with at least a B average, or the equivalent. Nonnative speakers of English must have a TOEFL score of 550 or higher.

Tuition, Fees, and Aid: $280 per credit. Student assistantships are available. Some financial aid is available to international students.

General: Courses are taught year round, including the summer. The program leads to ESL endorsement and licensure for teaching ESL in public schools. The college, which is nationally and internationally acclaimed, is located in an attractive and safe environment. Students have the opportunity to do their practice teaching in such countries as Japan, Thailand, Morocco, Greece, Korea, and Colombia. Most faculty have overseas experience and teach in the college's cooperative MATESL programs overseas.

Sixty-five students completed the program in 1996–1997.

The college has an intensive English language program for nonnative speakers of English.

Summer Session: Yes

Further Information: Dr. Mahmoud T. Arani
School of International Studies
Saint Michael's College
Winooski Park
Colchester, VT 05439

Telephone: (802) 654-2300
Fax: (802) 654-2595
E-mail: sis@smcvt.edu

◆ SAM HOUSTON STATE UNIVERSITY, Department of Language, Literacy, and Special Populations

Degree Offered: MEd with a concentration in bilingual education.

Length of Program: 6 semesters. Students may be full-time or part-time and may begin their study at the beginning of any semester. Application deadlines are fall semester, August 1; spring semester, December 1; summer I, May 15; summer II, June 15.

Program Requirements: 36 semester credit hours. Competence in Spanish is required for a Texas ESL endorsement. Practice teaching is required for certification. A comprehensive examination is required. A thesis is not required.

Courses Offered: (*required) *Teaching Language Arts and Reading in Spanish; *Bilingual Program Development in the Content Areas. For ESL minor: *Applied Linguistics for Classroom Teachers; *TESL: Oral Language Communications; *Social, Cultural, and Language Influences on Learning. Language Acquisition and Development for Bilingual and ESL Programs; Integrating Current Technologies in Teaching; Advanced Methods in Classroom Management and Discipline; Assessment of Learning; Human Growth and Development Across the Lifespan; Critical Analysis and Reflection for Teaching; The Curriculum in the Elementary School *or* The Secondary Curriculum.

Full-Time Staff: Hollis Lowery-Moore (chair), Michele R. Hewlett-Gomez (coordinator), Patricia Morales, Judith Olson.

Requirements for Admission: The university's requirements for admission are a baccalaureate degree with a GPA of at least 2.5 from a college or university of recognized standing, official transcripts, and a GRE General Test score of 800 or above.

Tuition, Fees, and Aid: For in-state students, $803 per 12 credit hours; for out-of-state students, $3,371 per 12 credit hours. Competitive departmental aid and college work-study programs are available.

General: The program correlates current theoretical principles and field-based practices with course lectures and assignments. It focuses on teacher training for educators interested in bilingual/ESL education programs. Students with state teaching credentials may partially fulfill requirements for a Texas endorsement in bilingual education or ESL.

International fieldwork can be arranged in Spanish-speaking countries.

Two students completed the program in 1996–1997.

The university has an intensive English language program for nonnative speakers of English.

Summer Session: Yes

Further Information: Dr. Michele R. Hewlett-Gomez
Department of Language, Literacy, and Special Education
Teacher Education Center, Room 242
Sam Houston State University
2100 Sam Houston Street, Avenue J
Huntsville, TX 77341-2119

Telephone: (409) 294-1138
Fax: (409) 294-1131
E-mail: edu_mrh@shsu.edu

◆ SAN DIEGO STATE UNIVERSITY, Department of Linguistics

Degrees Offered: Basic and advanced certificates in applied linguistics and ESL.

Length of Program: 2 semesters. Students may be full-time or part-time and may begin their study at the beginning of any semester.

Program Requirements: 12 credits per semester. Competence in a language other than English is not required. Practice teaching is required. A thesis and a comprehensive examination are optional.

Courses Offered: (*required) Basic certificate: *Linguistics and English *or* Fundamentals of Linguistics; *Psycholinguistics *or* Language Acquisition; *Sociolinguistics *or* American Dialectology; *Theory and Practice of TESL. Courses for the advanced certificate are under review.

Full-Time Staff: Zev Bar-Lev, Soonja Choi (chair), Thomas S. Donahue, Ann M. Johns, Jeffrey P. Kaplan, Deborah Poole, Gail L. Robinson, Betty T. R. Samraj, Robert Underhill, Charlotte Webb.

Tuition, Fees, and Aid: For in-state students, no tuition; for out-of-state students; $246 per unit. Fees are in-state students, $618 per semester for 0–6 units, $951 per semester for 6.1 units or more.

General: The program provides a strong foundation in theory and description. Courses can apply to an undergraduate or graduate linguistics major.

Seventy-one students completed the program in 1996–1997.

Summer Session: Yes

Further Information: Jeffrey P. Kaplan, Adviser
Certificate Program in Applied Linguistics and ESL
Department of Linguistics and Oriental Languages
BA 327
San Diego State University
5500 Campanile Drive
San Diego, CA 92182-7727

Telephone: (619) 594-5879
Fax: (619) 594-4877
E-mail: jkaplan@mail.sdsu.edu

◆ SAN FRANCISCO, UNIVERSITY OF, International and Multicultural Education Program

Degree Offered: MA in TESL (with optional emphasis in educational technology).

Length of Program: 2 semesters and a summer. Students may be full-time or part-time and may begin their study at the beginning of the fall or spring semester. Application deadlines are fall semester, July 1; spring semester, November 1.

Program Requirements: 30 semester hours (33 semester hours with emphasis in educational technology). Competence in a language other than English is not required. A thesis is required. Neither practice teaching nor a comprehensive examination is required.

Courses Offered: (*required) *Applied Linguistics; *Structure of American English; *TESL; *Preparation and Evaluation of ESL Materials; *a culture course; *MA Field Project; *four additional courses.

Full-Time Staff: Alma Flor Ada, Denis Collins, Anita de Franz, Rosita G. Galang, Aida A. Joshi, Dorothy Messerschmitt, Emile Wilson.

Requirements for Admission: The university's requirements for admission are a bachelor's degree or its equivalent from an accredited institution with an undergraduate GPA of 2.7, two letters of recommendation, a statement of purpose, and a résumé. Nonnative speakers of English must submit a TOEFL score of 570 or higher.

Tuition, Fees, and Aid: $627 per unit. Loans are available.

General: In consultation with their adviser, students may take four courses in educational technology to obtain an emphasis in that area.
 Twenty students completed the program in 1996–1997.
 The university has an intensive English language program for nonnative speakers of English.

Summer Session: Yes

Further Information: Dorothy S. Messerschmitt
International and Multicultural Education
School of Education
University of San Francisco
2130 Fulton
San Francisco, CA 94117

Telephone: (415) 422-6878
Fax: (415) 422-2677

◆ SAN FRANCISCO STATE UNIVERSITY,
Department of English

Degree Offered: MA in English with a concentration in TESOL.

Length of Program: 4 semesters. Students may be full-time or part-time and may begin their study at the beginning of any semester. Application deadlines are fall semester, April 1; spring semester, November 15. International students applying from abroad are accepted only for the fall semester; the application deadline is March 1.

Program Requirements: 30 semester units. Some experience with a non-Indo-European Language is required; English meets the requirement for nonnative speakers of English. Practice teaching and a comprehensive examination are required. A thesis is optional.

Courses Offered: (*required) *TESOL: Pedagogical Grammar; *Introduction to Graduate Study: TESOL; *Practicum in TESOL (for students with less than 2 years' teaching experience); *Seminar in TESOL: Listening and Speaking Skills; *Seminar in TESOL: Reading and Writing Skills; *Student Teaching in TESOL; *Integrative Seminar; *one course each from Advanced Seminar (Psycholinguistics, Sociolinguistics, Assessment, Literature and Culture, Teaching English Overseas, Adult ESL Literacy, ESL in the Workplace, ESL Curriculum and Materials), linguistics, related courses (education, psychology, social science), and humanities.

Full-Time Staff: Bradford Arthur, H. Douglas Brown, Troi Carleton, Jagdish Jain, James Kohn, Sandra McKay, Patricia Porter, Thomas Scovel, May Shih, Barry Taylor, Rachelle Waksler, Gail Weinstein, Elizabeth Whalley (coordinator).

Requirements for Admission: The university's requirement for admission is a BA or BS with a minimum GPA of 2.5 in the last 60 semester units attempted. The program requires a 3.0 GPA in the last 60 semester units attempted. Students without the necessary language and literature backgrounds will need to complete prerequisite courses. Nonnative speakers of English must have a TOEFL score of 570 or higher.

Tuition, Fees, and Aid: For in-state students, $459 per semester for 0–6 units; $792 per semester for 6 or more units. For out-of-state students, $246 per unit in addition. Fees are $199.

General: The program emphasizes the preparation of professional teachers for the classroom, especially adult education and college-level programs in the United States and abroad. The focus is on teaching, the preparation of teaching materials, and a firm knowledge of literature in the field. Although the program does not train researchers, it fosters critical and scholarly attitudes.

Fifty-six students completed the program in 1996–1997.

The university has an intensive English language program for nonnative speakers of English.

Summer Session: Yes

Further Information: Coordinator, MATESOL Program
Department of English
San Francisco State University
1600 Holloway Avenue
San Francisco, CA 94132

Telephone: (415) 338-2266
E-mail: matesol@sfsu.edu

◆ SAN JOSÉ STATE UNIVERSITY, Department of Linguistics and Language Development

Degrees Offered: TESOL certificate: graduate and undergraduate.

Length of Program: 2 semesters. Students may be full-time or part-time and may begin their study at the beginning of any semester. Application deadlines are fall semester, September 1 (March 1 for international students); spring semester, February 1 (September 1 for international students).

Program Requirements: 18 units. Competence in a language other than English is not required. Neither practice teaching, nor a thesis, nor a comprehensive examination is required.

Courses Offered: (*required) *Introduction to Linguistics; *Patterns of English. Graduate certificate: *Second Language Acquisition; *Intercultural Communication and Second Language Acquisition; *Methods and Materials for TESOL; *Curriculum and Assessment in TESOL. Undergraduate certificate: *Introduction to Second Language Learning and Teaching; *Introduction to Second Language Development; *Sociolinguistics; one elective.

Full-Time Staff: Martha Bean, Thom Huebner, B. Kumaravadivelu, Peter Lowenberg, Denise Murray (chair), Patricia Nichols, Manjari Ohala, Roula Svorou, Swathi Vanniarajan.

Requirements for Admission: For undergraduate study, a high school diploma is required. For graduate study, a baccalaureate degree from a regionally accredited institution with a minimum GPA of 2.5 in the last 60 semester units is required. The program requires a minimum TOEFL score of 570 (or evidence of 3 years of schooling in English).

Tuition, Fees, and Aid: For in-state students, $669.50 per semester for 1–6 units, $1,002.50 per semester for more than 6 units; for out-of-state students, $246 per unit plus fees of $459 per semester. Three scholarships of up to $400 each are available on a competitive basis after the completion of 9 units.

General: This program places a strong emphasis on research findings in socio- and psycholinguistics as they apply to second language acquisition and to the teaching ESL/EFL at all levels.

Nineteen students completed the program in 1996–1997.

The university has an intensive English language program for nonnative speakers of English.

Summer Session: Yes

Further Information: TESOL Coordinator
Department of Linguistics and Language Development
San José State University
One Washington Square
San José, CA 95192-0093

Telephone: (408) 924-4413
Fax: (408) 924-4703
E-mail: linguist@email.sjsu.edu

◆ SAN JOSÉ STATE UNIVERSITY, Department of Linguistics and Language Development

Degree Offered: MA in TESOL (with optional emphasis in English for specific purposes).

Length of Program: 3 semesters. Students may be full-time or part-time and may begin their study at the beginning of any semester. Application deadlines are fall semester, September 1 (March 1 for international students); spring semester, February 1 (September 1 for international students).

Program Requirements: 30 units. Competence in a language other than English equivalent to 1 year of college study is required for native speakers of English. Practice teaching is required. Either a comprehensive examination or a thesis is required.

Courses Offered: (*required) *English Structures for Teaching I; *English Structures for Teaching II; *Second Language Acquisition; *Intercultural Communication and Second Language Acquisition; *Methods and Materials for TESOL; *Curriculum and Assessment in TESOL; *Practicum in TESOL; Topics in Linguistics and TESOL; Classroom Techniques for TESOL Professionals; Foundations in English for Specific Purposes (ESP); ESP Course Design; Special Topics in ESP; Developmental Reading/ Writing: Principles and Practice; Analyzing Classroom Language; Cross-Cultural Literacy; English in the Global Context; electives in linguistics (phonetics, phonology, syntax, semantics, psycholinguistics, and sociolinguistics).

Full-Time Staff: See TESOL certificate program description.

Requirements for Admission: See TESOL certificate program description.

Tuition, Fees, and Aid: See TESOL certificate program description.

General: See TESOL certificate program description.
　　Twenty-four students completed the program in 1996–1997.
　　The university has an intensive English language program for nonnative speakers of English.

Summer Session: Yes

Further Information: TESOL Coordinator
　　　　　　　　　　　Department of Linguistics and Language Development
　　　　　　　　　　　San José State University
　　　　　　　　　　　One Washington Square
　　　　　　　　　　　San José, CA 95192-0093

　　　　　　　　　　　Telephone: (408) 924-4413
　　　　　　　　　　　Fax: (408) 924-4703
　　　　　　　　　　　E-mail: linguist@email.sjsu.edu

◆ SANTA FE, COLLEGE OF, Department of Education

Degree Offered: MA with a focus on at-risk youth and a concentration in TESL.

Length of Program: Students may be full-time or part-time and may begin their study at the beginning of any semester. There are no application deadlines.

Program Requirements: 24 credits. Six credits of a language other than English are required. Practice teaching is required. Neither a thesis nor a comprehensive examination is required.

Courses Offered: (*required) *Bilingual/Multicultural Education; *Second Language Acquisition; *Introduction to Linguistics; *Bilingual or TESL Practicum;

*Literacy for Second Language Learners; *English Phonology and Grammar; *6 hours in an appropriate language.

Full-Time Staff: Barbara Rerden (chair), Wallace Pond, Sandra Rodriguez.

Requirements for Admission: The requirement for admission is a bachelor's degree from an accredited institution.

Tuition, Fees, and Aid: $237 per credit. Stafford loans are available.

General: The program is set in Santa Fe, the 400-year-old capital of New Mexico. Students may pursue a traditional program or a portfolio-based alternative program. The program leads to a New Mexico credential in TESOL.

Twenty students completed the program in 1996–1997.

Summer Session: Yes

Further Information: Professor Sandra Rodriguez
Department of Education
College of Santa Fe
1600 St. Michael's Drive
Santa Fe, NM 87505

Telephone: (505) 473-6130
Fax: (505) 473-6510
E-mail: Rodriguez@csf.edu

◆ SCHOOL FOR INTERNATIONAL TRAINING, Department of Language Teacher Education

Degrees Offered: MAT in ESOL, ESOL and Spanish, or ESOL and French.

Length of Program: 2 semesters (academic-year program), or 2 successive summers for qualified working teachers (summer program). Students must be full-time and must begin their study at the beginning of the fall or summer semester. There are no application deadlines, but recommended dates are academic-year program, July 1; summer program, May 1.

Program Requirements: 32–33 credits. Competence in a language other than English is not required. Practice teaching is required between the two semesters for the academic-year program and in the year between the two summers for the summer program. A portfolio is required for the academic-year program. An independent professional project is required for the summer program. A comprehensive examination is not required.

Courses Offered: (*required) *Approaches to Teaching Second Languages; *Teaching the English Language *or* English Structures; *Teaching the Four Skills; *English Applied Linguistics; Language Acquisition and Learning; *English Applied Linguistics; *Intercultural Communication for Language Teachers *or* Culture and the Language Teacher; *Language Acquisition and Learning *or* Second Language Acquisition; *(academic-year program only) Integrative Seminar *and* Diversity in Community; *(nonnative speakers only) Advanced English; *Foreign Language Study; *(teacher certification, academic-year program only) Human Development, Bilingual-Multicultural Education, Literacy in the ESL Classroom, Perspectives in Public Education, Contrastive Linguistics and Culture (bilingual-multicultural education endorsement); *(Spanish or French concentration) Advanced Spanish *or* Advanced French, Spanish Structures *or* French Structures, Spanish Applied Linguistics *or* French Applied Linguistics, Teaching Hispanic Culture *or* Teaching Francophone Culture, Teaching Practices *or* Windham Partnership Seminar (academic-year program only).

Full-Time Staff: Marti Anderson, Francis Bailey, Ray Clark, William Conley, Alvino Fantini, Beatriz Fantini, Donald Freeman, Kathleen Graves, Ani Hawkinson, Michael Jerald, Diane Larsen-Freeman, Paul Levasseur, Kathy Maston, Bonnie Mennell, Jack Millett, Patrick Moran, Carol Rodgers, Alex Silverman, Lise Sparrow, Claire Stanley, Elizabeth Tannenbaum, Elka Todeva, Leslie Turpin.

Requirements for Admission: The school's requirements for admission are a BA or the equivalent, demonstrated academic ability, and relevant professional and intercultural ability. Nonnative speakers of English must have a TOEFL score of 550. The program requires language teaching experience, good communication skills, the ability to critically analyze previous experience, and the ability to work well with others. Teaching experience and a current position teaching the language of concentration are required for the summer program.

Tuition, Fees, and Aid: $17,500 for the program. Fees are $1,033 for the academic-year program and $756 for the summer program. Grants, small scholarships, federal loans, and college work study are available.

General: Two distinctive formats are offered for completion of the degree: (a) the Academic Year MAT Program (September–June) and (b) the Summer MAT Program—two successive summers of study on campus with independent, supervised work and internship during the interim year (for currently employed language teachers only). Spanish, French, and ESOL concentrations are available in either format. The distinctive features of the MAT Program are an emphasis on effective classroom skills and on developing a personal approach to language teaching through an experiential and reflective process. The school features a dynamic international atmosphere (30–40% of the student body is composed of international students), and close contact with faculty is common. Working language teachers can integrate their studies with their job through the summer format. With additional course work and a second teaching internship, the academic-year format leads to a Vermont endorsement in TESOL; a bilingual-bicultural education endorsement is also available.

The variety of supervised internships is also unusual, with sites all over New England and Mexico, where teaching is combined with a family home stay, and in other oversea locations including Morocco, South Africa, and El Salvador.

Ninety-six students completed the program in 1996–1997.

The school has an intensive English program for nonnative speakers of English.

Summer Session: Yes

Further Information: Fiona Cook
MAT Admissions Office
School for International Training
Kiling Road, PO Box 676
Brattleboro, VT 05302

Telephone: (802) 257-7751; (800) 336-1616
Fax: (802) 258-3500
E-mail: admissions@sit.edu

◆ SCHOOL OF TEACHING ENGLISH AS A SECOND LANGUAGE, SEATTLE UNIVERSITY, School of Education

Degree Offered: Initial certificate in teaching English as a second or foreign language.

Length of Program: 1 quarter. Students may be full-time or part-time and may begin their study at the beginning of any quarter. There are no application deadlines.

Program Requirements: 12 quarter hours. Competence in a language other than English is not required. Extensive microteaching is required. Neither a thesis nor a comprehensive examination is required.

Courses Offered: (*required) *TESL: Theory and Application; Methods of Language Acquisition; Teaching Grammar to ESL Students; Materials Selection and Development in ESL; Developing ESL Literacy; Cultural Variables in TESL; Teaching Content to Students of Limited English Proficiency; Linguistics for the ESL Teacher; Testing and Evaluating ESL Students; Student-Centered Learning in ESL; Self-Analysis and Improvement in TESL; Classroom Speech for the Bilingual Instructor; Teaching English Pronunciation; Bilingual Education: Theory and Application; Curriculum and Program Design in ESL.

Full-Time Staff: Nancy A. Butler Tulare (chair), Bernice Ege-Zavala, Barbara Peterson, Josephine Hirschman, Christine Jenkins, Chuck Cox, Elizabeth Hanson.

Requirements for Admission: The program's requirement for admission is completion of a bachelor's degree. Matriculation in Seattle University is required for students who wish to use certificate credits toward a master's degree.

Tuition, Fees, and Aid: $180 per credit. Seattle University master's students may apply their financial aid to tuition.

General: Students can apply credits earned to certificates, master's degrees at Seattle University, and the Washington State ESL endorsement. Instructors consistently model the student-centered classroom they profess.

Two hundred sixteen students completed the programs in 1996–1997.

The university has a nonintensive English language program.

Summer Session: Yes

Further Information: Information Director
School of Teaching ESL
Seattle University School of Education
2601 NW 56th Street
Seattle, WA 98107

Telephone: (206) 781-8607
Fax: (206) 781-8922
E-mail: hasegawa@seattleu.edu
http://www.seattle.edu/soe/stesl

◆ SCHOOL OF TEACHING ENGLISH AS A SECOND LANGUAGE, SEATTLE UNIVERSITY, School of Education

Degree Offered: Advanced certificate in teaching English as a second or foreign language.

Length of Program: 2 quarters. Students may be full-time or part-time and may begin their study at the beginning of any quarter. There are no application deadlines.

Program Requirements: 24 quarter hours. Competence in a language other than English is not required. Practice teaching is required. Neither a thesis nor a comprehensive examination is required.

Courses Offered: (*required) *TESL: Theory and Application; *Self-Analysis and Improvement in TESL; Methods of Language Acquisition; Teaching Grammar to ESL Students; Materials Selection and Development in ESL; Developing ESL Literacy; Cultural Variables in TESL; Teaching Content to Students of Limited English Proficiency; Linguistics for the ESL Teacher; Testing and Evaluating ESL Students;

Student-Centered Learning in ESL; Classroom Speech for the Bilingual Instructor; Teaching English Pronunciation; Bilingual Education: Theory and Application; Curriculum and Program Design in ESL.

Full-Time Staff: See program description for initial certificate.

Requirements for Admission: See program description for initial certificate.

Tuition, Fees, and Aid: See program description for initial certificate.

General: See program description for initial certificate.
Twenty students completed the program in 1996–1997.

Summer Session: Yes

Further Information: Information Director
School of Teaching ESL
Seattle University School of Education
2601 NW 56th Street
Seattle, WA 98107

Telephone: (206) 781-8607
Fax: (206) 781-8922
E-mail: hasegawa@seattleu.edu
http://www.seattle.edu/soe/stesl

◆ SEATTLE PACIFIC UNIVERSITY, College of Arts and Sciences, Division of Humanities

Degree Offered: MA in TESOL.

Length of Program: Students may be full-time or part-time and may begin their study at the beginning of any quarter. Application deadlines are fall quarter, August 1; winter quarter, December 1; spring quarter, March 1; summer quarter, May 1.

Program Requirements: 54 quarter credits. One year of college-level study of a language other than English, or the equivalent, is required for native speakers of English. Practice teaching is required. Neither a comprehensive examination nor a thesis is required.

Courses Offered: (*required) *Phonology; *Morphology; *Syntax; *Second Language Acquisition; *Multicultures; *Values and Ethics in Education *or* Comparative Religion; *Methodology of Foreign Language Teaching; *Teaching ESL Grammar; *Teaching Listening and Speaking; *Teaching Reading; *Teaching Writing; Testing and Curriculum Development; *Language Learning Practicum; *Teaching Practicum Phase I; *Teaching Practicum Phase II; *three of the following: Learning With Technology, The School: A Multicultural Approach, Cultural Communication, Sociolinguistics, Comparative Syntax, Pragmatics and Semantics.

Full-Time Staff: Kathryn Bartholomew (director), Robert Drovdahl, Patricia Hammill, Elletta Kennison, William Nagy, Katya Nemtchinova, Debra Sequerra, Peter Smith, Michael Ziemann.

Requirements for Admission: The university's requirements for admission are a bachelor's degree from an accredited college or university with a GPA at least 3.0 in the last 45 quarter credits, two letters of recommendation, official transcripts from the institution granting the bachelor's degree and any attended since, and a GRE score of at least 950 or a Miller Analogies Test score of at least 5 (or, for nonnative speakers of English, a TOEFL score of at least 600). The program requires a personal statement, proficiency in a foreign language equivalent to at least 1 year's study at the college level, and one or more basic courses in linguistic theory (courses may be taken concurrently with the first year of course work).

Tuition, Fees, and Aid: $255 per quarter credit. A limited number of graduate assistantships are available.

General: The program offers a balance of practice and theory, with emphasis on preparation for effectiveness in teaching and on cultural sensitivity. A language learning practicum for native speakers gives them direct experience of the joys and frustrations ESL/EFL students face.

Ten students completed the programs in 1996–1997.

The university has an intensive English language program for nonnative speakers of English.

Summer Session: Yes

Further Information: Graduate Coordinator
MA-TESOL
Tiffany 120
Seattle Pacific University
3307 Third Avenue West
Seattle, WA 98119-1997

Telephone: (206) 281-2670
Fax: (206) 281-2771
E-mail: tesol@spu.edu

◆ SEATTLE PACIFIC UNIVERSITY, College of Arts and Sciences, Division of Humanities

Degree Offered: MA in TESOL with Washington State K–12 certification.

Length of Program: Students may be full-time or part-time and may begin their study at the beginning of any quarter. Application deadlines are fall quarter, August 1; winter quarter, December 1; spring quarter, March 1; summer quarter, May 1.

Program Requirements: 77 quarter credits. One year of college-level study of a language other than English, or the equivalent, is required for native speakers of English. Practice teaching is required. Neither a comprehensive examination nor a thesis is required.

Courses Offered: (*required) *Phonology; *Morphology; *Syntax; *Second Language Acquisition; *Values and Ethics in Education; *Foundations: Issues and Ideas in American Education; *Classroom Management; *Methodology of Foreign Language Teaching; *Teaching ESL Grammar; *Teaching Listening and Speaking; *Teaching Reading; *Teaching Writing; *Testing and Curriculum Development; *Language Learning Practicum; *Teaching Practicum Phase I; *Teaching Practicum Phase II; *K–12 Internship; *two of the following: Cultural Communication, Sociolinguistics, Teaching Reading and Language Arts, Learning With Technology, Teaching With Technology.

Full-Time Staff: See MA in TESOL program description.

Requirements for Admission: See MA in TESOL program description.

Tuition, Fees, and Aid: See MA in TESOL program description.

General: See MA in TESOL program description.

The university has an intensive English language program for nonnative speakers of English.

Summer Session: Yes

Further Information: Graduate Coordinator
MA-TESOL
Tiffany 120
Seattle Pacific University
3307 Third Avenue West
Seattle, WA 98119-1997

Telephone: (206) 281-2670
Fax: (206) 281-2771
E-mail: tesol@spu.edu

◆ SEATTLE UNIVERSITY, School of Education, Leadership and Service Division

Degrees Offered: MA and MEd in adult education and training.

Length of Program: 5 quarters. Students may be full-time or part-time and may begin their study at the beginning of any quarter. Application deadlines are fall quarter, August 20; winter quarter, November 20; spring quarter, February 20; summer quarter, May 20. Deadlines are earlier for international applicants.

Program Requirements: MA: 45 quarter credits; MS: 48 quarter credits. Competence in a language other than English is not required. A comprehensive examination is required. Practice teaching or another internship experience is required. A thesis is required for the MA.

Courses Offered: (*required) MA: *Adult Psychology and Learning; *Instructional Methods for Adults; *Internship in Adult Education Setting; *Introduction to Research and Graduate Study; *Evaluation of Educational Programs; *Philosophy of Education; *Planning Programs for Adult Learners; *12 credits from the following: English for Academic Purposes, Language Acquisition, Language in Society, Linguistics for Language Teachers, Methods of Language Acquisition, TESL: Theory and Application, Teaching Grammar to ESL Students, Bilingual Education: Theory and Application, Classroom Speech for the Bilingual Instructor, Cultural Variables in TESL, Curriculum and Program Design in ESL, Developing ESL Literacy; American Community College; Continuing Education for the Professional. MEd: *Foundations of Adult Education; *Multicultural Perspectives; *12 credits from the following: Linguistics for the ESL Teacher, Materials Selection and Development in TESL, Methods of Language Acquisition, Self-Analysis and Improvement in TESL, Student-Centered Learning in ESL, Teaching Content to Students of Limited English Proficiency, Teaching English Pronunciation, Teaching Methods in Basic Skills for Adults, TESL: Theory and Application, Testing and Evaluating ESL Students; Introduction to Administration in Adult Settings; Introduction to Mild Handicaps; Issues in Basic Skills for Adults; Leadership in Education I; Leadership in Education II; Philosophy and Methods of Skill Training; Reading in the Content Fields; Women as Transformational Leaders.

Full-Time Staff: Brita Butler-Wall, Carol C. Weaver, Delight C. Willing (coordinator).

Requirements for Admission: The university's requirements for admission are a bachelor's degree from a regionally accredited institution with a GPA of 2.75 or above on the last 90 graded quarter credits (60 semester credits), official transcripts, and two recommendations from recent supervisors or others who can assess the applicant's ability. Applicants with a GPA of below 2.75 and those with nonlettered grades must take the GRE or the Miller Analogies Test. Nonnative speakers of English must submit a TOEFL score.

Tuition, Fees, and Aid: $329 per quarter credit.

General: The programs allow students to specialize in adult basic education, adult developmental education, human resource training, or TESOL. All specializations focus on the adult educator as teacher/practitioner.

Thirty-five students completed the programs in 1996–1997.

The university has an intensive English program for nonnative speakers of English.

Summer Session: Yes

Further Information: Delight Willing, Program Coordinator
TESOL Program
Loyola Hall, Room 409
Seattle University
900 Broadway
Seattle, WA 98122-4340

Telephone: (206) 296-6168
Fax: (206) 296-5632
E-mail: dwilling@seattleu.edu

◆ SEATTLE UNIVERSITY, School of Education, Leadership and Service Division

Degrees Offered: MA and MEd in TESOL.

Length of Program: 5 quarters. Students may be full-time or part-time and may begin their study at the beginning of any quarter. Application deadlines are fall quarter, August 20; winter quarter, November 20; spring quarter, February 20; summer quarter, May 20. Deadlines are earlier for international applicants.

Program Requirements: MA: 45 quarter credits; MS: 48 quarter credits. Competence in a language other than English is not required. A comprehensive examination and a competency examination, plus practice teaching or another internship experience, are required. A thesis is required for the MA.

Courses Offered: (*required) MA: *Adult Psychology and Learning; *Instructional Methods for Adults; *Internship in Adult Education Setting; *Introduction to Research and Graduate Study; *Evaluation of Educational Programs; *Philosophy of Education; *Planning Programs for Adult Learners; English for Academic Purposes, Language Acquisition; Language in Society; Linguistics for Language Teachers; Methods of Language Acquisition; TESL: Theory and Application; Teaching Grammar to ESL Students; American Community College; Bilingual Education: Theory and Application; Classroom Speech for the Bilingual Instructor; Continuing Education for the Professional; Cultural Variables in TESL; Curriculum and Program Design in ESL; Developing ESL Literacy; Foundations of Adult Education; Introduction to Administration in Adult Settings; Introduction to Mild Handicaps; Issues in Basic Skills for Adults; Leadership in Education I; Leadership in Education II; Linguistics for the ESL Teacher; Materials Selection and Development in TESL; Methods of Language Acquisition; Multicultural Perspectives; Philosophy and Methods of Skill Training; Reading in the Content Fields; Self-Analysis and Improvement in TESL; Student-Centered Learning in ESL; Teaching Content to Students of Limited English Proficiency; Teaching English Pronunciation; Teaching Methods in Basic Skills for Adults; TESL: Theory and Application; Testing and Evaluating ESL Students; Women as Transformational Leaders.

Full-Time Staff: See program description for MA or MEd in adult education and training.

Requirements for Admission: See program description for MA or MEd in adult education and training.

Tuition, Fees, and Aid: See program description for MA or MEd in adult education and training.

General: The program is designed for the ESL/EFL practitioner and focuses on teaching the adult learner. Education is offered in all facets of ESL/EFL classroom teaching and beyond, including program administration and curriculum development.

Thirty-five students completed the programs in 1996–1997.

The university has an intensive English program for nonnative speakers of English.

Summer Session: Yes

Further Information: Brita Butler-Wall, Program Coordinator
TESOL Program
Loyola Hall, Room 409
Seattle University
900 Broadway
Seattle, WA 98122-4340

Telephone: (206) 296-2682
Fax: (206) 296-5632
E-mail: bbwall@seattleu.edu

◆ SETON HALL UNIVERSITY, College of Education and Human Services, Department of Secondary Education

Degree Offered: MA in ESL.

Length of Program: 4 semesters. Students may be full-time or part-time and may begin their study at the beginning of any semester. There are no application deadlines.

Program Requirements: 42 credits. Competence in a language other than English is not required. Practice teaching is required only for those pursuing initial New Jersey State certification. A thesis or a comprehensive examination is required.

Courses Offered: (*required) *Teaching English as a Second Language I and II; *General Linguistics; *Applied Linguistics; *Phonology and Structure; *Sociolinguistics or Psycholinguistics; *Language, Culture, and Civilization; *Human and Intercultural Relations; *Social Psychology of the Bilingual Child; *Field Experience in Bilingual Education; *Graduate Research Methods; *Research Seminar; *Psychological Issues and Implications.

Full-Time Staff: Juan Cobarrubias (chair), William E. McCartan, Dr. Skeele, Dr. Devlin-Schere.

Requirements for Admission: The university's requirements for admission are a Miller Analogies Test or GRE score, three letters of recommendation, and a résumé. The program requires a New Jersey teaching credential.

Tuition, Fees, and Aid: $472 per credit. Graduate assistantships and Stafford loans are available.

General: The university is located in a highly intercultural region with over 15,000 limited-English-speaking students in the immediate vicinity. Graduates of the program over the last 20 years have had nearly a 100% rate of job placement. The program leads to a New Jersey credential in TESOL.

Twenty-four students completed the program in 1996–1997.

The university has an intensive English language program for nonnative speakers of English.

Summer Session: Yes

Further Information: Dr. W. E. McCartan
Department of Secondary Education
Koslawski Hall, Room 441
Seton Hall University
400 South Orange Avenue
South Orange, NJ 07079

Telephone: (973) 275-2727
Fax: (973) 761-7642
E-mail: mccartwi@shu.edu

◆ SHENANDOAH UNIVERSITY, TESOL Department

Degree Offered: Undergraduate endorsement in TESOL.

Length of Program: Students may be full-time or part-time and may begin their study at the beginning of any trimester. Application deadlines are fall trimester, September 1; winter trimester, January 1; spring trimester, April 1; summer institute, July 1.

Program Requirements: 21 credits. Competence in a language other than English is required. Practice teaching is required. Neither a thesis nor a comprehensive examination is required.

Courses Offered: (*required) *Intercultural Education; *English Linguistics; *Second Language Acquisition; *Organization and Curriculum Development; *Second Language Teaching Methods I (Listening and Reading); *Second Language Teaching Methods II (Speaking and Writing); *Practicum.

Full-Time Staff: Ashley Hastings, Harold Smith.

Requirements for Admission: The requirement for admission to the program is prior grades averaging C (2.0) or better. Nonnative speakers of English must have a minimum TOEFL score of 500.

Tuition, Fees, and Aid: $7,200 per semester. Scholarships, on-campus employment, and student loans are available.

General: This program is designed to prepare baccalaureate graduates for a wider variety of jobs in the United States and other countries. The endorsement must be accompanied by a major in another field, such as biology, communications, education, math, music, psychology, or sociology.

The program has agreements for exchange of faculty and students with institutions in several countries.

The university has an intensive English language program for nonnative speakers of English.

Summer Session: Yes

Further Information: Chair
TESOL Department
Shenandoah University
1460 University Drive
Winchester, VA 22601

Telephone: (540) 678-4461
Fax: (540) 678-4474
E-mail: hsmith@su.edu

◆ SHENANDOAH UNIVERSITY, TESOL Department

Degree Offered: Professional certificate in TESOL.

Length of Program: Two summer institutes or year-round. Students may be full-time or part-time and may begin their study at the beginning of any trimester. Application deadlines are fall trimester, September 1; winter trimester, January 1; spring trimester, April 1; summer institute, July 1.

Program Requirements: 18 credits. Competence in a language other than English is not required. A practicum is optional. A thesis and a comprehensive examination are not required.

Courses Offered: (*required) *Intercultural Education; *English Linguistics; *Second Language Acquisition; *Organization and Curriculum Development; *Second Language Teaching Methods I (Listening and Reading); *Second Language Teaching Methods II (Speaking and Writing).

Full-Time Staff: See program description for undergraduate endorsement in TESOL.

Requirements for Admission: The requirement for admission to the program is a baccalaureate degree from an accredited university with prior grades averaging B (3.0) or better. Nonnative speakers of English must have a minimum TOEFL score of 500.

Tuition, Fees, and Aid: $450 per credit. Professional educator scholarships and student loans are available.

General: This graduate-level, nondegree program may stand alone or be a stepping-stone toward further graduate studies. All certificate courses completed with a grade of B or better may be applied toward the university's MSEd (TESOL). The certificate program may be completed in year-round study or in two summer institutes that meet during July and Early August. The program leads to a Virginia credential in TESOL.

The program has agreements for exchange of faculty and students with institutions in several countries.

Six students completed the program in 1996–1997.

The university has an intensive English language program for nonnative speakers of English.

Summer Session: Yes

Further Information: Chair
TESOL Department
Shenandoah University
1460 University Drive
Winchester, VA 22601

Telephone: (540) 678-4461
Fax: (540) 678-4474
E-mail: hsmith@su.edu

◆ SHENANDOAH UNIVERSITY, TESOL Department

Degree Offered: MSEd (TESOL).

Length of Program: Year-round or three summers. Students may be full-time or part-time and may begin their study at the beginning of any trimester. Application deadlines are fall trimester, September 1; winter trimester, January 1; spring trimester, April 1; summer institute, July 1.

Program Requirements: 33 credits. Competence in a language other than English is required for native speakers of English. A practicum plus a thesis or an internship is required. A comprehensive examination is not required.

Courses Offered: (*required) *English Linguistics; *Second Language Acquisition; *intercultural Education; *Organization and Curriculum Development; *Second Language Teaching Methods I (Listening and Reading); *Second Language Teaching Methods II (Speaking and Writing); *Practicum in TESOL; *Major Issues in TESOL; *Focal Skills Approach to Second and Foreign Language Teaching; *Internship or Thesis; *one of the following: a research/statistical methods course (if not taken before the program), one elective, more time on the internship or thesis.

Full-Time Staff: See program description for undergraduate endorsement in TESOL.

Requirements for Admission: The requirement for admission is a baccalaureate degree from an accredited university with prior grades averaging B (3.0) or better. Nonnative speakers of English must have a minimum TOEFL score of 550; provisional admission is available with a score of 500.

Tuition, Fees, and Aid: $4,950 per trimester. Teaching assistantships, professional educator scholarships, and student loans are available.

General: The program focuses on practical integration of language acquisition theory, communicative teaching methods, and effective curriculum and program development. The program may be completed in year-round study or in three or four summer institutes that meet during July and early August. All students get practical experience in school settings, university intensive programs, and community organizations. This program is the only professional preparation program offering a course on the focal skills approach, which is used at the university and several other universities' intensive English programs. The program leads to a Virginia credential in TESOL.

The program has agreements for exchange of faculty and students with institutions in several countries.

Twelve students completed the program in 1996–1997.

The university has an intensive English language program for nonnative speakers of English.

Summer Session: Yes

Further Information: Chair
TESOL Department
Shenandoah University
1460 University Drive
Winchester, VA 22601

Telephone: (540) 678-4461
Fax: (540) 678-4474
E-mail: hsmith@su.edu

◆ SHENANDOAH UNIVERSITY, TESOL Department

Degree Offered: EFL certificate.

Length of Program: Year-round or three summers. Students must be full-time and may begin their study at the beginning of the fall or winter trimester or the summer institute. Application deadlines are fall trimester, September 1; winter trimester, January 1; summer institute, July 1.

Program Requirements: 9 credits. Competence in a language other than English is not required. Neither a practicum, nor a thesis, nor a comprehensive examination is required.

Courses Offered: (*required) *Intercultural Education; *Focal Skills Approach to Second and Foreign Language Teaching; Second Language Teaching Methods; English Linguistics; Second Language Acquisition; Issues in TESOL; Organization and Curriculum Development.

Full-Time Staff: See program description for undergraduate endorsement in TESOL.

Requirements for Admission: The requirement for admission to the program is a baccalaureate degree from an accredited university with prior grades averaging B (3.0) or better. Nonnative speakers of English must have a minimum TOEFL score of 500.

Tuition, Fees, and Aid: $450 per credit. No financial aid is available.

General: This graduate-level, nondegree program is designed for persons wanting basic credentials for teaching English language in non-English-speaking countries. It may also be accepted toward further graduate studies at this university and others. Classes meet during three periods each year: July–early August in the intensive 5-week summer institute, September–early December in the fall trimester, and January–early April in the winter trimester.

The program began in 1998.

The university has an intensive English language program for nonnative speakers of English.

Summer Session: Yes

Further Information: Chair
TESOL Department
Shenandoah University
1460 University Drive
Winchester, VA 22601

Telephone: (540) 678-4461
Fax: (540) 678-4474
E-mail: hsmith@su.edu

◆ SIMMONS COLLEGE, Department of Education and Human Services

Degree Offered: MAT (ESL).

Length of Program: 2 semesters plus a summer session. Students may be full-time or part-time and may begin their study at the beginning of any semester. Application deadlines are fall semester, August 1; spring semester, December 1; summer semester, May 1.

Program Requirements: 40 credits. Competence in a language other than English is required for native speakers of English. Practice teaching is required. A classroom-based research project is required. Neither a comprehensive examination nor a thesis is required.

Courses Offered: (*required) *Introduction to Linguistics and English Grammar; *Teaching Strategies in the Inclusive Classroom; *Pluralism and Language Use; *TESL Methodology and Curriculum Development; *Second Language Acquisition; *Student Teaching Practicum; *Research and Evaluation in Schools; *Advanced Seminar in TESL Methods and Curriculum; *Clinical Teaching Experience.

Full-Time Staff: Paul Abraham (director), Janet Chumley.

Requirements for Admission: The university's requirements for admission are a bachelor's degree from an accredited college or university, official transcripts, a résumé, two recommendations, a 500-word statement of purpose, a GRE or Miller

Analogies Test score, and an interview. Nonnative speakers of English must submit a minimum TOEFL score of 550 and officially translated and evaluated transcripts if the originals are not written in English. Teachers seeking standard certification must submit copies of relevant teaching certificates.

Tuition, Fees, and Aid: $562 per credit. Scholarships are available.

General: The site of the program allows for intensive faculty-student interaction, and the program provides a strong foundation in theory coupled with intensive practice (2 semesters). The program leads to a Massachusetts credential in TESOL.

Fifteen students completed the program in 1996–1997.

Summer Session: Yes

Further Information: Stephanie Cichon, Staff Assistant
MATESL Program
Department of Education and Human Services
W303
Simmons College
300 The Fenway
Boston, MA 02115

Telephone: (617) 521-2579
Fax: (617) 521-3174
E-mail: scichon1@umsvax.simmons.edu

◆ SOKA UNIVERSITY OF AMERICA, Graduate School

Degree Offered: MA in second and foreign language education with a concentration in TESOL.

Length of Program: 3–4 semesters. Students must be full-time and must begin their study at the beginning of the fall semester. The application deadline is March 31.

Program Requirements: 33 semester credits (plus a 2-credit prerequisite if necessary). Competence in a language other than English is required; English meets the requirement for nonnative speakers of English. Practice teaching and a thesis are required. A comprehensive examination is not required.

Courses Offered: (*required) The Study of Language (prerequisite); Introduction to Language and Linguistics; *Basic TESOL Methodology; *Phonetics and Phonology; *Sociolinguistics and Education; *Modern English Grammar; *Survey of TESOL Materials; *Language Learning Theory; *Testing Language Skills; *MA Thesis/Project; *Practicum in ESL; Discourse Analysis; Topics in TESOL Methods and Materials: (1) K–12, (2) Postsecondary, (3) Innovative Methods, (4) Focus on Japanese Learners of English, (5) Content-Based Language Instruction, (6) Computer-Assisted Language Learning.

Full-Time Staff: Tomoko Takahashi (chair).

Requirements for Admission: The university's requirements for admission are a baccalaureate with a minimum GPA of 2.75 or a B– average, two letters of reference, and a personal statement detailing the applicant's background, plans for graduate study and a professional career, and other relevant information. Nonnative speakers of English must have a TOEFL score of 600 or higher. Competence in a foreign language is preferred.

Tuition, Fees, and Aid: $200 per credit. The registration fee is $80; the application fee is $50. Soka University of America Merit Scholarships, campus employment, student loans, and tuition deferral are available.

General: The program stresses linguistics, teaching and learning processes, and cross-cultural awareness. The university has small classes that cultivate close and supportive relationships among students and individual attention from faculty.

The university offers internship programs at its affiliated institution in Japan. Graduating students may apply for 3-year contract positions in teaching English at Soka University and Soka High School in Tokyo and at Kansai Soka High School in Osaka.

Eight students completed the program in 1996–1997.

Summer Session: No

Further Information: Director
Graduate Admissions Office
Soka University of America
26800 West Mulholland Highway
Calabasas, CA 91302

Telephone: (818) 880-3717
Fax: (818) 880-9326
E-mail: grad_admissions@soka.edu

◆ SONOMA STATE UNIVERSITY, Departments of Anthropology and Linguistics

Degree Offered: Certificate in TESL.

Length of Program: 2 semesters. Students may be full-time or part-time and may begin their study at the beginning of any semester. Students who enter in the spring will need 3 semesters to finish unless prerequisites have been met. Application deadlines are fall semester, November of the previous year (April 1 for international students); spring semester, August of the previous year (October 1 for international students).

Program Requirements: 24 credits. Competence in a language other than English is recommended. Practice teaching is required. Neither a thesis nor a comprehensive examination is required.

Courses Offered: (*required) *Introduction to Linguistic Studies (prerequisite); *Phonological Analysis; *Phonology and Pronunciation; *Linguistics and Second Language Teaching; *English Grammar and ESL; *Language and Content; *Internship in Applied Linguistics; *Grammatical Analysis; *Vocabulary Teaching and Learning; *Language in a Sociopolitical Context; *Multicultural Communication; *TESL; *Evaluation and Testing.

Full-Time Staff: Cherry Campbell, Shirley Silver (coordinator).

Requirements for Admission: The university's requirements for graduate admission are a baccalaureate degree from a regionally accredited institution with a minimum GPA of 2.5 in the last 60 semester units attempted. Nonnative speakers of English must have a TOEFL score of 550 or higher. Undergraduate applicants must have a high school diploma that includes 56 units completed with a minimum GPA of 2.0 and must present an SAT or ACT score. Nonnative speakers of English must have a TOEFL score of 500.

Tuition, Fees, and Aid: For in-state students, $1,065 per semester; for out-of-state students, $4,005 per semester. No financial aid is available.

General: The certificate is awarded only in conjunction with or after the receipt of a baccalaureate degree.

Twelve students completed the program in 1996–1997.

The university has an intensive English language program for nonnative speakers of English.

Summer Session: Yes

Further Information: Coordinator, TESL Certificate Program
Department of Anthropology-Linguistics
Stevenson Hall 2054
Sonoma State University
1801 East Cotati Avenue
Rohnert Park, CA 94928

Telephone: (707) 664-2419
Fax: (707) 664-3920
E-mail: silver@sonoma.edu

◆ SOUTH CAROLINA, THE UNIVERSITY OF, Linguistics Program

Degree Offered: Certificate in TEFL.

Length of Program: 2 semesters and a summer. Students may be full-time or part-time and must begin their study at the beginning of the summer or fall semester. Application deadlines are summer semester, April 1; fall semester, July 1.

Program Requirements: 18 semester hours. Competence in a language other than English is not required. A summer practicum is required. Neither a thesis nor a comprehensive examination is required.

Courses Offered: (*required) *Survey of Linguistics; *Introduction to Phonology *or* Introduction to Syntax; *Second Language Acquisition; *TEFL; *Practicum in TEFL; Phonological Theory; Syntactic Theory; Historical Linguistics; History and Methodology of Linguistics; Language Theory and Phonetics; Introduction to German Linguistics; Introduction to Spanish Linguistics; French Phonology; Language Change; Language and Gender; Philosophy of Language; Psychology of Language; Introduction to Language Development; Applied English Syntax; Semantics; Formal Semantics; History of the English Language; History of the French Language; History of the German Language; History of the Spanish Language; Introduction to Sociolinguistics; Analysis of Conversation; Varieties of American English; Studies in the Philosophy of Language; Discourse Analysis; Stylistics; Poetics; Theory and Methodology in Second Language Acquisition; Topics in Linguistics; Seminar in Syntax; Seminar in Language Variation; Seminar in Language Acquisition; Seminar in ESL.

Full-Time Staff: Simon Belasco, Anne Bezuidenhout, Donald Cooper, Dorothy Disterheft, Stanley Dubinsky, Kurt Goblirsch, Barbara Hancin-Blatt, Michael Montgomery, Christine Moritz, Carol Myers-Scotton (director), Bruce Pearson, Rene Schmauder.

Requirements for Admission: The university's requirements for admission are two letters of recommendation, transcripts, and a GRE composite score of 800 for native speakers of English and 700 for nonnative speakers of English. Nonnative speakers must also have a TOEFL score of 560 or higher. The program requires a personal statement outlining educational background and career goals.

Tuition, Fees, and Aid: For in-state students, $1,862 per semester; for out-of-state students, $3,817 per semester. No financial aid is available.

General: Three students completed the program in 1996–1997.

The university has an intensive English language program for nonnative speakers of English.

Summer Session: Yes

Further Information: Carol Myers-Scotton
Linguistics Program
Welsh Humanities Building
The University of South Carolina
Columbia, SC 29208

Telephone: (803) 777-2063
Fax: (803) 777-9064
E-mail: linguistics@sc.edu

◆ SOUTH CAROLINA, THE UNIVERSITY OF, Linguistics Program

Degree Offered: MA in linguistics.

Length of Program: 4 semesters. Students may be full-time or part-time and must begin their study at the beginning of the summer or fall semester. Application deadlines are summer semester, April 1; fall semester, July 1.

Program Requirements: 30 semester hours. Competence in a language other than English is required; English meets the requirement for nonnative speakers of English. A thesis and a comprehensive examination are required. Practice teaching is not required.

Courses Offered: (*required) *Survey of Linguistics; *Introduction to Phonology; *Introduction to Syntax; *Thesis Preparation; Phonological Theory; Syntactic Theory; Historical Linguistics; History and Methodology of Linguistics; Second Language Acquisition; TEFL; Practicum in TEFL; Language Theory and Phonetics; Introduction to German Linguistics; Introduction to Spanish Linguistics; French Phonology; Language Change; Language and Gender; Philosophy of Language; Psychology of Language; Introduction to Language Development; Applied English Syntax; Semantics; Formal Semantics; History of the English Language; History of the French Language; History of the German Language; History of the Spanish Language; Introduction to Sociolinguistics; Analysis of Conversation; Varieties of American English; Studies in the Philosophy of Language; Discourse Analysis; Stylistics; Poetics; Theory and Methodology in Second Language Acquisition; Topics in Linguistics; Seminar in Syntax; Seminar in Language Variation; Seminar in Language Acquisition; Seminar in ESL.

Full-Time Staff: See program description for certificate in TEFL.

Requirements for Admission: The university's requirements for admission are two letters of recommendation, transcripts, and a GRE composite score of 1000 for native speakers of English and 700 for nonnative speakers of English. Nonnative speakers must also have a TOEFL score of 560 or higher. The program requires a personal statement outlining educational background and career goals.

Tuition, Fees, and Aid: See program description for certificate in TEFL. Teaching assistantships for students with 18 graduate credit hours and a limited number of research assistantships are available.

General: The program requires all students to have a foundation in formal areas of linguistics (specifically phonology and syntax) but encourages specialization in areas such as second language acquisition, ESL, sociolinguistics, or others useful in the job market. The program's recognition of the values of both types of courses is its greatest strength.

Twelve students completed the program in 1996–1997.

The university has an intensive English language program for nonnative speakers of English.

Summer Session: Yes

Further Information: Carol Myers-Scotton
Linguistics Program
Welsh Humanities Building
The University of South Carolina
Columbia, SC 29208

Telephone: (803) 777-2063
Fax: (803) 777-9064
E-mail: linguistics@sc.edu

◆ SOUTH CAROLINA, THE UNIVERSITY OF, Linguistics Program

Degree Offered: PhD in linguistics.

Length of Program: Approximately 4 years. Students may be full-time or part-time and must begin their study at the beginning of the summer or fall semester. Application deadlines are summer semester, April 1; fall semester, July 1.

Program Requirements: Competence in three languages other than English is required for native speakers of English; English meets the requirement for one of the languages for nonnative speakers of English. Written and oral comprehensive examinations, a thesis, and a dissertation are required. Practice teaching is not required.

Courses Offered: (*required) *Survey of Linguistics; *Introduction to Phonology; *Introduction to Syntax; *Phonological Theory; *Syntactic Theory; *Historical Linguistics; *History and Methodology of Linguistics; *Dissertation Preparation; Second Language Acquisition; TEFL; Practicum in TEFL; Language Theory and Phonetics; Introduction to German Linguistics; Introduction to Spanish Linguistics; French Phonology; Language Change; Language and Gender; Philosophy of Language; Psychology of Language; Introduction to Language Development; Applied English Syntax; Semantics; Formal Semantics; History of the English Language; History of the French Language; History of the German Language; History of the Spanish Language; Introduction to Sociolinguistics; Analysis of Conversation; Varieties of American English; Studies in the Philosophy of Language; Discourse Analysis; Stylistics; Poetics; Theory and Methodology in Second Language Acquisition; Topics in Linguistics; Seminar in Syntax; Seminar in Language Variation; Seminar in Language Acquisition; Seminar in ESL.

Full-Time Staff: See program description for certificate in TEFL.

Requirements for Admission: The university's requirements for admission are two letters of recommendation, transcripts, and a GRE composite score of 1200 for native speakers of English and 800 for nonnative speakers of English. Nonnative speakers must also have a TOEFL score of 590 or higher. The program requires a personal statement outlining educational background and career goals.

Tuition, Fees, and Aid: See program description for certificate in TEFL.

General: See program description for MA in linguistics.
Eight students completed the program in 1996–1997.
The university has an intensive English language program for nonnative speakers of English.

Summer Session: Yes

Further Information: Carol Myers-Scotton
Linguistics Program
Welsh Humanities Building
The University of South Carolina
Columbia, SC 29208

Telephone: (803) 777-2063
Fax: (803) 777-9064
E-mail: linguistics@sc.edu

◆ SOUTH FLORIDA, UNIVERSITY OF, Division of Modern Languages and Linguistics

Degree Offered: MA in applied linguistics.

Length of Program: 4 semesters. Students may be full-time or part-time and must begin their study at the beginning of the fall or spring semester. Application deadlines are fall semester, March 31; spring semester, August 31.

Program Requirements: 39 semester hours. Competence in a language other than English is required for native speakers of English. Practice teaching and a comprehensive examination are required. A thesis is not required.

Courses Offered: (*required) *Introduction to Graduate Study in Linguistics; *Applied Linguistics; *The Grammatical Structure of English; *Methods of TESL; *TESL Curriculum; *Cross-Cultural Issues in ESL; *Second Language Acquisition; *Language Testing; *Contrastive Analysis; *Internship; Sociolinguistics; History of English; Computer-Assisted Language Learning; Linguistic Anthropology; Psychology of Language.

Full-Time Staff: Jacob C. Caflisch, Carol J. Cargill, Roger W. Cole (chair), Jeffra C. Flaitz.

Requirements for Admission: The university's requirements for admission are a BA from an accredited institution and a minimum combined GRE score of 1000. For nonnative speakers of English, the program requires a minimum TOEFL score of 600 and a TSE score of 55.

Tuition, Fees, and Aid: For in-state students, $1,098 per semester; for out-of-state students, $3,528 per semester. Teaching assistantships are available, usually after the first semester of a student's program.

General: The program, which leads to a Florida credential in TESOL, features a mentorship program and two full semesters of supervised teaching practice in the associated English Language Institute.

The university operates programs in Madrid, Spain, and Caracas, Venezuela, and offers exchange programs in France.

Eighteen students completed the program in 1996–1997.

Summer Session: Yes

Further Information: Director of Graduate Studies in Linguistics
Division of Languages and Linguistics
CPR 419
University of South Florida
Tampa, FL 33620

Telephone: (813) 974-2548
Fax: (813) 974-1718
E-mail: rogrcole@quijote.lang.usf.edu

◆ SOUTHEAST MISSOURI STATE UNIVERSITY, Department of English

Degree Offered: BA in English, language option.

Length of Program: 8 semesters. Students may be full-time or part-time and may begin their study at the beginning of any semester. Application deadlines are fall semester, July 15; spring semester, December 1; summer semester, May 15.

Program Requirements: 24 credits. Competence in a language other than English is required; English meets the requirement for nonnative speakers of English. Practice teaching is highly recommended. Neither a thesis nor a comprehensive examination is required. Honors students may write an extended paper.

Courses Offered: (*required) *Introduction to Creative Writing; *Advanced Composition; *Principles of Language; *Masterpieces of English Literature I; *Masterpieces of English Literature II; *Masterpieces of American Literature I; *Masterpieces of American Literature II; *Grammars of English; *Theories of ESOL Learning and Teaching; *Practicum for Teaching ESOL; *History of the English Language; *Methods and Techniques for Teaching ESOL; *Materials Development and Assessment.

Full-Time Staff: Carol Scates (chair), Nancy Blattner, Linda Burns, Robert Burns, Julie Chen, Jennie Cooper, Roy Dawson, Jacob Gaskins, Robert Hamblin, Dale Haskell, Pamela Hearn, Harvey Hecht, Michael Hogan, Dean Monahan, Katherine Parrish, Adelaide Parsons, Henry Sessoms, Susan Swartwout, Robert Zeller.

Requirements for Admission: The university's requirements for admission are an application, a processing fee, and official transcripts. Nonnative English-speaking students need a TOEFL score of 550 or higher. Non-U.S. students must submit evidence of financial resources, official copies of transcripts, and translations.

Tuition, Fees, and Aid: For in-state students, $93.30 per hour; for out-of-state students, $173.30 per hour. The general fee is $6.70. Aid is very limited. Some scholarships and work study are available.

General: The program emphasizes the practical application of theory to practice. Students develop a portfolio that includes a personal statement of the theory of learning and philosophy of teaching, a description of personal method, a curricular plan for a specific setting, materials developed and assessment tools selected for the curriculum, peer coaching reviews, and videotapes of coaching. The program, which leads to a state add-on endorsement, includes a nationally recognized University Studies Program.

Study abroad opportunities exist in Great Britain, Mexico, the Netherlands, and other places.

Five students completed the program in 1996–1997.

The university has an intensive English language program for nonnative speakers of English.

Summer Session: Yes

Further Information: Dr. Adelaide Heyde Parsons
English Department
Pacific Hall, Room 401
One University Plaza, MS 2250
Southeast Missouri State University
Cape Girardeau, MO 63701

Telephone: (573) 651-2551
Fax: (573) 651-5188
E-mail: ahparsons@semovm.semo.edu

◆ SOUTHEAST MISSOURI STATE UNIVERSITY, Department of English

Degree Offered: MA TESOL.

Length of Program: 3 semesters. Students may be full-time or part-time and may begin their study at the beginning of any semester. Application deadlines are fall semester, April 1; spring semester, September 1; summer semester, February 1.

Program Requirements: 36 hours. Competence in a language other than English is not required. Practice teaching is required. Either a comprehensive examination or a thesis is required.

Courses Offered: (*required) *Principles of Language; *Approaches to Grammar; *Theories of ESOL Learning and Teaching; *Methods and Techniques of TESOL; *Materials Development and Assessment in TESOL; *Special Problems in TESOL; *Practicum in TESOL *or* Seminars in Teaching ESOL at the University Level; *Sociolinguistics *or* Teaching in a Multicultural Society *or* Multicultural Literature in the Classroom.

Full-Time Staff: Nancy Blattner, Julie Chen, Adelaide Heyde Parsons (director), Katherine Parrish, Carol Scates (chair).

Requirements for Admission: The university's requirements for admission are an official transcript showing graduation from an accredited college or university, complete individual transcripts from all colleges attended, an evaluation fee of $20, and approval of the dean of graduate studies and the department chairperson. Nonnative English-speaking students need a TOEFL score of 550 or higher.

Tuition, Fees, and Aid: For in-state students, $99.30 per hour; for out-of-state students, $184.30 per hour. Research and teaching assistantships and a few scholarships are available.

General: The program emphasizes the practical application of theory to practice. Students develop a portfolio that includes a personal statement of the theory of learning and philosophy of teaching, a description of personal method, a curricular plan for a specific setting, materials developed and assessment tools selected for the curriculum, peer coaching reviews, and videotapes of teaching. The program leads to a Missouri credential in TESOL if the student is already certified. Courses are offered at other sites in Missouri.

Twenty-five students completed the program in 1996–1997.

The university has an intensive English language program for nonnative speakers of English.

Summer Session: Yes

Further Information: Dr. Adelaide Heyde Parsons
English Department
Pacific Hall, Room 401
One University Plaza, MS 2250
Southeast Missouri State University
Cape Girardeau, MO 63701

Telephone: (573) 651-2551
Fax: (573) 651-5188
E-mail: ahparsons@semovm.semo.edu

◆ SOUTHERN ILLINOIS UNIVERSITY AT CARBONDALE, Department of Linguistics

Degree Offered: MA in TESOL.

Length of Program: 3–4 semesters. Students may be full-time or part-time and must begin their study at the beginning of the fall semester. The application deadline is May 1.

Program Requirements: 32–38 semester hours. Competence in a language other than English is required for native speakers of English. Practice teaching and either a comprehensive examination or a thesis are required.

Courses Offered: (*required) *General Linguistics; *Phonetics; *TESOL Theory and Methods; *Pedagogical Grammar; *Second Language Acquisition; *Oral Practicum; *Written Practicum; electives in testing, English for specific purposes, computer-assisted language learning, and materials.

Full-Time Staff: Paul J. Angelis (chair), Colleen Brice, Joan Friedenberg, Janet Fuller, Glenn Gilbert, Usha Lakshmanan, Ruth Johnson, Geoffrey Nathan.

Requirements for Admission: The university's requirements for admission are an undergraduate degree with a GPA of 3.0 and letters of recommendation. The program requires a TOEFL score of 570 for nonnative speakers of English.

Tuition, Fees, and Aid: For in-state students, $98.80 per credit hour; for out-of-state students, $296.40 per credit hour. Fees are $443.72 per semester (9 credit hours). Teaching assistantships, fellowships, and a very limited number of research assistantships are available.

General: The program has a link with the intensive English program and good computer facilities.

Thirty-five students completed the program in 1996–1997.

The university has an intensive English language program for nonnative speakers of English.

Summer Session: Yes

Further Information: Chair
Department of Linguistics
Faner 3234
Southern Illinois University at Carbondale
Carbondale, IL 62901

Telephone: (618) 536-3385
Fax: (618) 453-6527
E-mail: ling@siu.edu

◆ SOUTHERN MAINE, UNIVERSITY OF, Department of Professional Education

Degree Offered: MSEd in literacy education with a concentration in ESL.

Length of Program: 3 semesters. Students may be full-time or part-time and may begin their study at the beginning of any semester. Application deadlines are spring semester, September 15; fall or summer semester, February 1.

Program Requirements: 33 credits. Competence in a language other than English is optional. Practice teaching and a comprehensive examination are required. A thesis is not required.

Courses Offered: (*required) *Methods of Teaching Second Languages; *Aspects of the English Language; *Seminar in L2 Literacy; *The Writing Process; *Improving Teaching in the Content Areas Through Literacy; *Reading Development and Instruction; *Teacher Research in Literacy; *Practicum in Literacy Education; The Multicultural Classroom; ESL Testing and Assessment; ESL Curriculum Design.

Full-Time Staff: Michael P. O'Donnell, Margo Wood.

Requirements for Admission: The university's requirements for admission are undergraduate college transcripts, three references, and a Miller Analogies Test or GRE score.

Tuition, Fees, and Aid: For in-state students, $173 per credit hour; for out-of-state students, $477 per credit hour. Fees are $12 per credit hour. A limited number of scholarships and graduate assistantships are available.

General: The program emphasizes a holistic, developmental approach to literacy development, with a special focus on language minority social and cultural concerns.

Six students completed the program in 1996–1997.

The university has an intensive English language program for nonnative speakers of English.

Summer Session: Yes

Further Information: Donald L. Bouchard
Professional Education: Literacy Education/ESL
Concentration
218 Bailey Hall
University of Southern Maine
Gorham, ME 04038

Telephone: (207) 780-5400
Fax: (207) 780-5315

◆ SOUTHERN MISSISSIPPI, THE UNIVERSITY OF, Department of Foreign Languages

Degree Offered: MA in the teaching of languages (TESOL emphasis).

Length of Program: 3 semesters. Students may be full-time or part-time and may begin their study at the beginning of any semester. Application deadlines are summer, May 15; fall, August 7; spring, December 18.

Program Requirements: 33 semester hours. Competence in a language other than English is required for native speakers of English; English meets the requirement for nonnative speakers. A practicum, a comprehensive examination, and a final reflective paper are required.

Courses Offered: (*required) *Methods of Teaching Second and Foreign Languages; *Applied Linguistics in Second and Foreign Languages; *Second Language Acquisition Theory and Practice; *Sociocultural and Sociolinguistic Perspectives in Language; *Practicum in Second and Foreign Language; *TESOL Seminar; *Pedagogical Grammar for TESOL; Teaching Reading in ESL/EFL; Curriculum Development in ESL/EFL; Testing and Assessment in ESL/EFL; Program Administration in ESL/EFL; Teaching Composition in ESL/EFL; Foundations in Multicultural Education; Multicultural Education: Curriculum and Pedagogy; Topics in Anthropological Linguistics; Language, Gender, and Culture; Language Planning, Culture, and Politics; History of the English Language; Language and Speech Development; Multicultural Issues in Communication Disorders.

Full-Time Staff: Karen Austin, J. Burnett, A. Cheng, J.-L. Dassier, Giovanni Fontecchio, William Powell, R. Sánchez-Alonzo (chair), Sam Slick, S. Hauer, A. Jaffe, S. Cloud, C. Reeves-Kazelskis.

Requirements for Admission: The university's requirements for admission are a baccalaureate degree approved by a recognized accrediting agency; official transcripts showing a GPA of at least 2.75 for the last 2 years of undergraduate study; and a GRE, Miller Analogies Test, NTE, or Praxis Series score. Nonnative speakers of English must present a TOEFL score of 560 or above, with no section score lower than 54.

Tuition, Fees, and Aid: For in-state students, $1,259 per 12-hour load; for out-of-state students, $2,669 per 12-hour load. Summer tuition for all students is $871 per 12-hour load. Assistantships in ESL or foreign languages, which include a tuition waiver, are available to qualified individuals. Perkins loans and work study are also available.

General: The degree can be completed in a single calendar year with full-time enrollment, or over the course of two or more summers. Distance-learning courses, a practicum in which teachers use their own classrooms for analysis, and the ability to transfer up to 6 hours of acceptable credit give students flexibility in their programs of study. The program can lead to a Mississippi credential in TESOL.

Core courses can be taken during summers in Morelia, Mexico.

The university has an intensive English language program for nonnative speakers of English.

Summer Session: Yes

Further Information: MATL Director
Department of Foreign Languages
George Hurst Building, Room 110
The University of Southern Mississippi
Hattiesburg, MS 39406

Telephone: (601) 266-4964
Fax: (601) 266-4853
E-mail: MATL@ocean.st.usm.edu

◆ SYRACUSE UNIVERSITY, Department of Languages, Literatures, and Linguistics

Degree Offered: MA in linguistics with a concentration in ESL.

Length of Program: 3 semesters. Students may be full-time or part-time and may begin their study at the beginning of any semester. There are no application deadlines.

Program Requirements: 30 semester hours. Competence in a language other than English is optional for native speakers of English. A comprehensive examination is required. Practice teaching and a thesis are optional.

Courses Offered: (*required) *Introduction to Linguistic Analysis; *Phonological Analysis; *Syntactic Analysis; *Topics in Sociolinguistics; *Introduction to Teaching ESL; *Methodology of Teaching ESL; electives.

Full-Time Staff: Tej Bhatia, Gerald Greenberg, Jaklin Kornfilt, William Ritchie, Susana Sainz.

Requirements for Admission: The university's requirements for graduate admission are a GRE score and, for nonnative speakers of English, a TOEFL score.

Tuition, Fees, and Aid: $555 per credit. Teaching assistantships and tuition scholarships are available.

General: This interdisciplinary program in linguistics provides students with the opportunity to interact with multiple disciplines and interests.

Nine students completed the program in 1996–1997.

The university has an intensive English language program for nonnative speakers of English.

Summer Session: No

Further Information: Gerald R. Greenberg
Department of Languages, Literatures, and Linguistics
340 HB Crouse
Syracuse University
Syracuse, NY 13244-2175

Telephone: (315) 443-2175
Fax: (315) 443-5376

◆ TEACHERS COLLEGE, COLUMBIA UNIVERSITY, Department of Arts and Humanities

Degree Offered: MA in TESOL.

Length of Program: Students may be full-time or part-time and must begin their study at the beginning of the fall semester. The application deadline is February 1.

Program Requirements: 34–40 points. Competence in a foreign language is not required. Practice teaching and a comprehensive examination are required. A thesis is not required.

Courses Offered: (*required) *Classroom Practices; *Specialized Practica (2–3 semesters); *Problems in Contemporary Grammar; *Phonetics and Phonology; *Second Language Acquisition; *Second Language Assessment; *one or two of the following: Sociolinguistics and Education, Semantic Systems and the Lexicon, Interlanguage Analysis, Trends in Second Language Acquisition; *(for state certification) TESOL Methods for Pre-K-6, Specialized Methods: Content 7–12, Special Education, a multicultural course, a bilingual course; *three electives from outside the department.

Full-Time Staff: Leslie M. Beebe (director), Pamela Martins, James E. Purpura.

Requirements for Admission: The college's requirements for admission are two or three references, a personal statement, and college transcripts. International students must have a TOEFL score of 600 or higher.

Tuition, Fees, and Aid: $610 per point. Fees are $250 per semester. A select number of scholarships and assistantships are available.

General: The program offers students two options: a pre-K–12 option, which leads to New York State certification, and a general option, for student teachers interested in teaching abroad or focusing on adults. Course requirements include a balance of methods, linguistics, learning theory, and elective classes.

One hundred students completed the program in 1996–1997.

Summer Session: Yes

Further Information: Patricia Juza
TESOL Program
316 Main Hall, Box 66
Teachers College, Columbia University
525 West 120th Street
New York, NY 10027

Telephone: (212) 678-3936
Fax: (212) 678-3428
E-mail: pg81@columbia.edu

◆ TEACHERS COLLEGE, COLUMBIA UNIVERSITY, Department of Arts and Humanities

Degree Offered: EdM in TESOL.

Length of Program: Students may be full-time or part-time and may begin their study at the beginning of the any semester. Application deadlines are fall semester, February 1; spring semester, November 1; summer semester, April 1.

Program Requirements: 60 points. Competence in a foreign language is not required. Practice teaching, and a thesis or an EdM project, are required.

Courses Offered: (*required) *Teacher Education Programs *or* Language Teacher Education Programs; *Semantic Systems and the Lexicon; *Sociolinguistics and Education; *Critical Review of Readings in ESOL and Applied Linguistics; *Seminar in Second Language Acquisition; *Second Language Assessment; *a course in statistics, measurement, and research design; *three electives from outside the department.

Full-Time Staff: See program description for MA in TESOL.

Requirements for Admission: The college's requirements for admission are two or three references, a personal statement, and college transcripts. The program requires an MA in TESOL/applied linguistics (or the equivalent) and a writing sample.

Tuition, Fees, and Aid: See program description for MA in TESOL.

General: The program is designed to complement former professional training at the MA level and sometimes serves as an initial preparation for entering the doctoral program.

The TESOL Program in Tokyo, Japan, is targeted for teachers who plan on teaching in Japan.

Twenty-five students completed the program in 1996–1997.

Summer Session: Yes

Further Information: Patricia Juza
TESOL Program
316 Main Hall, Box 66
Teachers College, Columbia University
525 West 120th Street
New York, NY 10027

Telephone: (212) 678-3936
Fax: (212) 678-3428
E-mail: pg81@columbia.edu

◆ TEACHERS COLLEGE, COLUMBIA UNIVERSITY, Department of Arts and Humanities

Degree Offered: EdD in TESOL.

Length of Program: Students may be full-time or part-time and may begin their study at the beginning of any semester. Application deadlines are fall semester, February 1; spring semester, November 1; summer semester, April 1.

Program Requirements: 90 points. Competence in a foreign language is not required. Practice teaching and a dissertation are required. A comprehensive examination is not required.

Courses Offered: (*required) *Research Paper; *Doctoral Seminar; *Dissertation Seminar; *Teacher Education Programs *or* Language Teacher Education Programs; *Phonetics and Phonology; *Discourse Analysis; *Semantic Systems and the Lexicon; *Problems in Contemporary English Grammar; *Seminar in Second Language Acquisition; *Sociolinguistics and Education; *Second Language Assessment; *15 points in statistics, measurement, and research design.

Full-Time Staff: See MA in TESOL program description.

Requirements for Admission: The college's requirements for admission are two or three references, a personal statement, and college transcripts. The program requires an MA in TESOL/applied linguistic (or the equivalent), a video- or audiotape recording of teacher performance, and a writing sample.

Tuition, Fees, and Aid: See MA in TESOL program description.

General: The program emphasizes research, especially in the areas of second language acquisition and teaching. It serves students interested in research, university teaching, teacher education, or curriculum development. A minor in bilingual education is available, as are concentrations in teacher education, English language analysis, second language acquisition, sociolinguistics, and second language assessment.

The TESOL Program in Tokyo, Japan, is targeted for teachers who plan on teaching in Japan.

Fifteen students completed the program in 1996–1997.

Summer Session: Yes

Further Information: Patricia Juza
TESOL Program
316 Main Hall, Box 66
Teachers College, Columbia University
525 West 120th Street
New York, NY 10027

Telephone: (212) 678-3936
Fax: (212) 678-3428
E-mail: pg81@columbia.edu

◆ TEMPLE UNIVERSITY, Department of Curriculum, Instruction, and Technology in Education

Degree Offered: MEd (TESOL).

Length of Program: 3 semesters. Students may be full-time or part-time and may begin their study at the beginning of any semester. Applications are considered monthly.

Program Requirements: 30 credits. Competence in a language other than English is not required. A comprehensive examination is required. Neither practice teaching nor a thesis is required.

Courses Offered: (*required) *TESOL Methods I; *TESOL Methods II; *Sound System of American English; *Applied Linguistics; *Teaching New Grammars; five electives.

Full-Time Staff: Kenneth Schaefer, Noël Houck, Ellen Sylvester-Skilton.

Requirements for Admission: The university's requirement for admission is an undergraduate degree with a GPA of at least 2.8. The program requires a GRE or Miller Analogies Test score for native speakers of English and a TOEFL score of 575 for nonnative speakers of English.

Tuition, Fees, and Aid: For in-state students, $308 per credit hour; for out-of-state students, $429 per credit hour. Some graduate assistantships are available to second-year students.

General: The program emphasizes the relationship between theory and practice and aims to provide a wide coverage of issues. Students can elect to complete all or part of the program at Temple University Japan.

Thirty students completed the program in 1996–1997.

The Philadelphia campus has an intensive English language program for nonnative speakers of English.

Summer Session: Yes

Further Information: Chair
Department of Curriculum, Instruction and Technology in Education
Ritter Hall (351)
Temple University
Philadelphia, PA 19027

Telephone: (215) 204-6387
Fax: (215) 204-1414

◆ TEMPLE UNIVERSITY, Department of Curriculum, Instruction, and Technology in Education

Degree Offered: EdD (TESOL).

Length of Program: Students may be full-time or part-time and may begin their study at the beginning of any semester. Application deadlines are fall semester, October 15; spring semester, March 15.

Program Requirements: Competence in a language other than English is not required. A comprehensive examination and a thesis are required. Practice teaching is not required.

Courses Offered: (*required) *All required MEd (TESOL) courses; *The Context of Education; *Psychology of the Learner; *Curriculum, Teaching, and Technology; *Research Design in Education; *Applied Statistics in Education; various TESOL electives.

Full-Time Staff: See MEd (TESOL) program description.

Requirements for Admission: The university's requirement for admission is an undergraduate degree with a GPA of at least 2.8 and a master's degree. The program requires a GRE or Miller Analogies Test score for native speakers of English and a TOEFL score of 575 for nonnative speakers of English.

Tuition, Fees, and Aid: See MEd (TESOL) program description.

General: The program aims to develop students' capacity to carry out research in a variety of research sites. It emphasizes pedagogically relevant research. Students can elect to complete all or part of the program at Temple University Japan.

Ten students completed the program in 1996–1997.

The Philadelphia campus has an intensive English language program for nonnative speakers of English.

Summer Session: Yes

Further Information: Chair
Department of Curriculum, Instruction and
Technology in Education
Ritter Hall (351)
Temple University
Philadelphia, PA 19027

Telephone: (215) 204-6387
Fax: (215) 204-1414

◆ TEXAS, UNIVERSITY OF, AT ARLINGTON, Program in Linguistics

Degree Offered: Certificate in TESOL.

Length of Program: Students may be full-time or part-time and may begin their study at the beginning of any semester. Application deadlines are fall semester, June 20; spring semester, October 17; summer semester, March 27.

Program Requirements: 19 semester hours. Competence in a language other than English is not required. Neither practice teaching, nor a thesis, nor a comprehensive examination is required.

Courses Offered: (*required) *Linguistic Analysis; *Sociolinguistics; *Language Acquisition; *Teaching English as a Second or Foreign Language; *Methods and Materials for Teaching English as a Second or Foreign Language; *Contrastive Analysis and Error Analysis in the Teaching of English as a Second or Foreign Language *or* Pedagogical Grammar; *Certificate in ESL Practicum.

Full-Time Staff: Donald A. Burquest, Jerold A. Edmondson (director), Irwin Feigenbaum, Susan C. Herring, John C. Paolillo, David J. Silva.

Requirements for Admission: The university's requirement for admission is submission of transcripts of previous college work showing evidence of an undergraduate degree. The program requires demonstration through previous academic performance of the potential for successful completion of the certificate.

Tuition, Fees, and Aid: For in-state students, $1,115.25 for 9 semester hours; for out-of-state students, $3,131.25 for 9 semester hours. No financial aid is available.

General: The program emphasizes the application of principle to practice. Knowledge about language structure, use, and acquisition is used in the decisions made by the classroom teacher.

Four students completed the program in 1996–1997.

The university has an intensive English language program for nonnative speakers of English.

Summer Session: Yes

Further Information: Graduate Advisor
Program in Linguistics
Room 403 Hammond Hall
The University of Texas at Arlington
701 South College
Arlington, TX 76019-0559

Telephone: (817) 273-3133
Fax: (817) 272-2731
E-mail: office@ling.uta.edu

◆ TEXAS, UNIVERSITY OF, AT ARLINGTON, Department of Foreign Languages and Linguistics

Degree Offered: MA in linguistics with a concentration/certificate in TESOL.

Length of Program: 3 semesters. Students may be full-time or part-time and may begin their study at the beginning of any semester. Application deadlines are fall semester, June 20; spring semester, October 17; summer semester, March 27.

Program Requirements: Competence in a language other than English is not required. A comprehensive examination is required. Neither practice teaching nor a thesis is required.

Courses Offered: (*required) *Sociolinguistics; *Language Acquisition; *Teaching English as a Second or Foreign Language; *Methods and Materials in Teaching English as a Second or Foreign Language; *Contrastive Analysis and Error Analysis *or* Pedagogical Grammar; *Certificate in ESL Practicum; *Phonological Theory I; *Phonological Theory II; *Grammatical Theory I; *Grammatical Theory II; *Survey of Linguistic Theories; *Structure of a Non-Western Language; electives in linguistics, English, anthropology, education, management, computer science, and foreign languages.

Full-Time Staff: See program description for certificate in TESOL.

Requirements for Admission: The university's requirements for admission are a bachelor's degree from an accredited college or university with a satisfactory GPA, satisfactory standing at the last institution attended, an acceptable and current score on the GRE, demonstration through previous academic performance of the potential for graduate work in the chosen field, and three letters of recommendation. The program requires combined GRE verbal and quantitative scores of at least 1000.

Tuition, Fees, and Aid: For in-state students, $1,461 per 12 semester hours; for out-of-state students, $4,149 per 12 semester hours. Teaching assistantships, research assistantships, and scholarships are available.

General: The program emphasizes the connection between linguistics and TESOL. The students gain knowledge about language structure, acquisition, and use by working with many languages of the world. With this foundation, the students can make decisions as teachers of ESL.

Six students completed the program in 1996–1997.

The university has an intensive English language program for nonnative speakers of English.

Summer Session: Yes

Further Information: Graduate Advisor
Program in Linguistics
Room 403 Hammond Hall
The University of Texas at Arlington
701 South College
Arlington, TX 76019-0559

Telephone: (817) 273-3133
Fax: (817) 272-2731
E-mail: office@ling.uta.edu

◆ TEXAS, UNIVERSITY OF, AT AUSTIN,
Department of Foreign Language Education

Degree Offered: MA in foreign language education with a specialization in teaching English as a second/foreign language.

Length of Program: 3 semesters. Students must be full-time and may begin their study at the beginning of any semester. Application deadlines are fall semester, February 1; spring semester, October 1; summer semester, February 1.

Program Requirements: 36 credits. Competence in a language other than English is not required. Practice teaching and either a thesis or a report is are required. A comprehensive examination is optional.

Courses Offered: (*required) *ESL Methods; *6 graduate hours from Research and Writing Methods in Foreign Language Education, Evaluation of Foreign Language Education, The Second Language Learner, and Second Language Acquisition; *Studies in English Grammar; *Studies in English Phonology; *6 hours of electives in English; *3 hours of electives in education; *1 year of teaching experience, 2 semesters of teaching assistant experience, *or* Internship.

Full-Time Staff: Judith W. Lindfors, Elaine K. Horwitz, Zena Moore, Kathleen Sowash, Diane L. Schallert.

Requirements for Admission: The university's requirements for admission are a baccalaureate degree with a GPA of 3.25 and a GRE score of 1100 (475 on the verbal section). The program requires an essay and three letters of recommendation.

Tuition, Fees, and Aid: For in-state students, $108 per semester hour; for out-of-state students, $321 per semester hour. Teaching assistantships and a limited number of fellowships are available.

General: The program strongly emphasizes the development of both teaching and research skills and has strengths in both ESL and EFL.

Twenty-six students completed the program in 1996–1997.

The university has an intensive English language program for nonnative speakers of English.

Summer Session: Yes

Further Information: Dr. Elaine K. Horwitz
Department of Foreign Language Education
FLE, SZB 528
University of Texas at Austin
Austin, TX 78712

Telephone: (512) 471-4078
Fax: (512) 471-4607
horwitz@mail.utexas.edu

◆ TEXAS, UNIVERSITY OF, AT AUSTIN,
Foreign Language Education

Degree Offered: PhD in foreign language education with a concentration in applied linguistics or teaching English as a second/foreign language.

Length of Programs: Students may be full-time or part-time and may begin their study at the beginning of any semester. Application deadlines are fall semester, February 1; spring semester, October 1; summer semester, February 1.

Program Requirements: 73–85 credits. Competence in a language other than English is not required for native speakers of English and is recommended for nonnative speakers of English. A dissertation and a comprehensive examination are required.

Courses Offered: (*required) *Syntax 1, *General Phonology; *an additional graduate linguistics course; *four language/literature courses; *Research and Writing Methods in Foreign Language; *Foreign Language Education Forum; *an introductory course in quantitative research methodology; *an introductory course in qualitative research methodology; *an advanced course in quantitative or qualitative research methodology; *Psychology of Human Learning *or* Psychology of Learning; *Second Language Acquisition; *a learning course; *Methods of Teaching English as a Foreign Language; *Evaluation of Language Teaching Education; 9 additional hours.

Full-Time Staff: See MA program description.

Requirements for Admission: See MA program description.

Tuition, Fees, and Aid: See MA program description.

General: See MA program description.
  Twenty-one students completed the program in 1996–1997.
  The university has an intensive English language program for nonnative speakers of English.

Summer Session: Yes

Further Information: Dr. Elaine K. Horwitz
  Department of Foreign Language Education
  FLE, SZB 528
  University of Texas at Austin
  Austin, TX 78712

  Telephone: (512) 471-4078
  Fax: (512) 471-4607
  horwitz@mail.utexas.edu

◆ TEXAS, UNIVERSITY OF, AT EL PASO,
Department of Languages and Linguistics

Degree Offered: MA in linguistics with options in applied or Hispanic linguistics.

Length of Program: 4 semesters. Students may be full-time or part-time and may begin their study at the beginning of any semester. Application deadlines are fall semester, April 1; spring semester, November 1.

Program Requirements: 36 semester hours. Competence in a language other than English is not required. A thesis is optional. Neither practice teaching nor a comprehensive examination is required.

Courses Offered: (*required) *Principles of Linguistic Analysis; *Generative Syntax *or* Functional Syntax; *Phonology; Second Language Teaching—English; Pedagogical Issues in English Structure; English Historical Linguistics; Computer-Assisted Language Learning; Teaching Second Language Composition; Second Language Acquisition; Linguistic Variation; Language Testing; Language Universals and Typology; Spanish Phonetics and Phonology; Spanish Morphology; Spanish Syntax; Spanish Historical Linguistics; Bilingualism; Problems in Language Instruction; Seminar in Linguistic Research; Thesis.

Full-Time Staff: Jon Amastae (graduate director), Nancy Antrim, Edward L. Blansitt, Grant Goodall, Joan Manley, Richard Teschner.

Requirements for Admission: The university's requirement for admission is a bachelor's degree with a satisfactory GPA. Nonnative speakers of English must have a TOEFL score of at least 550. The program requires a GRE score, a statement of purpose, three letters of recommendations, and a BA in linguistics or a related field.

Tuition, Fees, and Aid: For in-state students, $650 per semester (9 credits); for out-of-state students, $2,576 per semester. Teaching assistantships are available.

General: The program features the opportunity to study in a bilingual, bicultural, binational environment and to focus on applied linguistics with respect to either Spanish or English. The binational El Paso–Juárez area offers many opportunities for field practice and research.

Seven students completed the program in 1996–1997.

The university has an English language program for nonnative speakers of English.

Summer Session: Yes

Further Information: Graduate Advisor—Linguistics
Department of Languages and Linguistics
University of Texas at El Paso
El Paso, TX 79968

Telephone: (915) 747-5767
Fax: (915) 747-5292
E-mail: gradling@utep.edu

◆ TEXAS, THE UNIVERSITY OF, PAN AMERICAN, Department of English

Degree Offered: BA with a concentration in ESL and/or linguistics.

Length of Program: 4 semesters above the sophomore level. Students may be full-time or part-time and may begin their study at the beginning of any semester. Application deadlines are fall semester, July 17; spring semester, November 13; summer semesters I and II, April 17.

Program Requirements: 12 credits. Competence in a language other than English is required; English meets the requirement for nonnative speakers of English. Practice teaching is not required unless a degree in education is pursued. Neither a thesis nor a comprehensive examination is required.

Courses Offered: (*required) *Introduction to Descriptive Linguistics. *24 advanced hours (beyond sophomore level) from Language and Culture; English Grammar; Modern English Syntax; History of the English Language; Contrastive Grammar; Fundamentals of Language Development; Introduction to ESL; ESL Theory and Practice; Composition Techniques; Language Acquisition; Grammar, Dialect, and Language Performance Theories; and Grammar, Dialect, and Language Performance Problems.

Full-Time Staff: Pamela L. Anderson-Mejias, Beatrice Mendez Egle, Edward Heckler, Pamela McCurdy, Paul Mitchell, Wei Zhu.

Requirements for Admission: The university's requirements for admission are graduation from an accredited high school or a GED diploma, transcripts, and ACT scores. The program requires completion of freshman and sophomore English (two composition and two literature courses).

Tuition, Fees, and Aid: For in-state students, $615 per 12 credit hours; for out-of-state students, $2,331 per 12 credit hours. The student service fee is $10 per semester credit hour. Financial aid programs are extensive and include scholarships, grants, federal loans, work study, and tuition waivers.

General: This program is one of the few that emphasize ESL in a region where bilingual education is the norm. The majority of the population speaks a language other than English, and the university is located 15–20 minutes from the U.S.-Mexican border. Students may enroll in the graduate practicum course for ESL teachers and the ESL testing course for teachers by arrangement.

The university has an intensive English language program for nonnative speakers of English.

Summer Session: Yes

Further Information: Dr. Lee Hamilton, Chair
Department of English
The University of Texas—Pan American
Edinburg, TX 78539

Telephone: (210) 381-3421

◆ TEXAS, THE UNIVERSITY OF, PAN AMERICAN, Department of English

Degree Offered: MA in ESL.

Length of Program: 1½–2 years. Students may be full-time or part-time and may begin their study at the beginning of any semester. First application deadlines are summer sessions and fall semester, the first work day in February; spring semester, the first work day in September. The second application deadline is 30 days before the beginning of the semester.

Program Requirements: 36 semester hours. Competence in a language other than English is not required. Practice teaching and two 3-hour written exams are required. A thesis is optional.

Courses Offered: (*required) Thesis and nonthesis options: *Modern English Syntax; *Studies in Language and Culture; *Introduction to ESL; *Problems in ESL; *Introduction to Descriptive Linguistics for Teachers; *Practicum in ESL; *ESL Testing; English Phonological Systems; Problems in Grammar, Dialects, and Language Performance. Thesis option only: *Problems in Linguistics; *Thesis (two courses).

Full-Time Staff: Edward Heckler, Pamela L. Anderson-Mejias, Pamela McCurdy, Wei Zhu.

Requirements for Admission: The university's requirements for admission are a bachelor's degree from an accredited institution with a minimum GPA of 3.0 and a minimum GRE composite score of 1000. International students must submit a financial deposit, an English translation of educational records, and a minimum TOEFL score of 550. The program requires official transcripts, a letter explaining career goals and reasons for seeking graduate studies, and catalogs for evaluation of transcripts, if necessary.

Tuition, Fees, and Aid: For in-state students, $72 per semester credit hour; for out-of-state students, $266 per semester credit hour. A limited number of teaching assistantships are awarded on a competitive basis.

General: This program features small classes, an informal mentoring system, a great deal of interaction with faculty, evening courses for teachers, and a location in a multicultural-multilingual location that is a 15-minute drive from the U.S.-Mexican border. Collaborative programs under development may offer opportunities for international practice teaching and exchange.

Four students completed the program in 1996–1997.

The university has an intensive English language program for nonnative speakers of English.

Summer Session: Yes

Further Information: Lee Hamilton
Department of English
CAS 230
The University of Texas--Pan American
1201 West University Drive
Edinburg, TX 78539

Telephone: (956) 381-3422
E-mail: lHamilton@Panam.edu

◆ TEXAS, THE UNIVERSITY OF, AT SAN ANTONIO, Division of Bicultural-Bilingual Studies

Degree Offered: MA with a concentration in ESL.

Length of Program: 3–4 semesters. Students may be full-time or part-time and may begin their study at the beginning of any semester. Application deadlines are fall semester, July 1; spring semester, December 1; summer semester, May 1.

Program Requirements: 36 semester hours. Competence in a language other than English is not required. A comprehensive examination is required. A thesis is optional. Practice teaching is not required.

Courses Offered: (*required) *Linguistics—ESL; Foundations of Second Language Acquisition; Language Analysis for Second Language Specialists; Second Language Acquisition Research; Second Language Reading; Second Language Instruction in School Contexts; Family and Adult Literacy; Program and Syllabus Design; Second Language Writing; Assessment in Bilingual and Second Language Studies; Research Methods in Bilingual and Second Language Studies; Ethnographic Research Methods; Multicultural Groups in the United States; Cultural Adaptation in Bilingual Societies; Psychological Considerations in a Bicultural Environment; Latino Biculturalism in the United States.

Full-Time Staff: Robert J. Bayley, Ellen Riojas Clark, Carolyn L. Kessler, Robert D. Milk (director), Tom Ricento, Howard Smith, Armando Trujillo.

Requirements for Admission: The university's requirement for admission is a baccalaureate degree with a GPA of 3.0 in the last 60 hours of undergraduate work. The program requires a GRE score.

Tuition, Fees, and Aid: For in-state students, $1,191 per semester; for out-of-state students, $3,117 per semester. Graduate research assistantships are available.

General: The Division of Bicultural-Bilingual Studies is unique in providing a faculty fully devoted to the study of linguistic and cultural issues in pluralistic settings. The interdisciplinary nature of the program, offered in the context of San Antonio, provides an uncommon opportunity for exploring ESL issues.

The program leads to a state endorsement in ESL.
Thirty-two students completed the program in 1996–1997.

Summer Session: Yes

Further Information: Dr. Robert Milk, Director
Division of Bicultural-Bilingual Studies
MS 3.01.18
University of Texas at San Antonio
6900 North Loop 1604 West
San Antonio, TX 78249-0653

Telephone: (210) 458-4426
Fax: (210) 458-5962
E-mail: bcbldiv@lonestar.utsa.edu

◆ TEXAS TECH UNIVERSITY, Department of Classical and Modern Languages and Literatures

Degree Offered: MA in applied linguistics.

Length of Program: 4 semesters. Students may be full-time or part-time and may begin their study at the beginning of any semester. Application deadlines are fall semester, June 1; spring semester, October 8. International students outside the United States should apply a year in advance.

Program Requirements: 36 semester hours without thesis, or 30 semester hours plus 6 hours of thesis. Competence in a language other than English is required for native speakers of English; English meets the requirement for nonnative speakers of English. Practice teaching is not required. Either a comprehensive examination or a thesis is required.

Courses Offered: (*required) *Pedagogical Grammar of English; *Methods of Teaching English as a Second/Foreign Language *or* Methods of Teaching ESL to Pre-K–12 Students; *Second/Foreign Language Acquisition *or* First and Second Language Acquisition; *Linguistic Analysis; *Principles of Language; *Studies in Linguistics; *Seminar in Applied Linguistics; *Ethnolinguistics *or* Intercultural Communication; Thesis; Practicum; Applied Linguistics and the Teaching of Reading; Seminar in Cognition; Psychology of Reading; Teaching the Multicultural-Multilingual Student; Instructional and Management Issues in Bilingual Education and ESL; Teaching Strategies for ESL and Content-Area Teachers of Limited English Proficient Students.

Full-Time Staff: Sharon Myers, Rosslyn Smith (graduate advisor), Amie Beckett, Richard Gomez, James Goss, Nancy Hickerson, May Jane Hurst, Roman Taraban.

Requirements for Admission: The university's requirements for admission are official transcripts showing the award of a bachelor's degree substantially equivalent to one from Texas Tech University, an official GRE score that is no more than 5 years old, and transcripts from all higher education institutions attended. Nonnative speakers of English must submit TOEFL scores.

Tuition, Fees, and Aid: For in-state students, $32 per credit hour plus $21 per credit graduate program tuition; for out-of-state students, $246 per credit hour plus $21 per credit graduate program tuition. Fees are $91.50 per semester plus $36 per credit hour. The student services fee for full-time students is $79.20–$105.50 per semester. Teaching assistantships, chancellor's fellowships, on-campus employment, Texas Public Education grants, federal loans, and occasional departmental scholarships are available.

General: The program emphasizes working with adolescents and adults, although there are also courses for students wishing to work with children. Students have access to and training in modern equipment for computer-assisted language learning and speech analysis software. The library also has a direct link to Satellite Communications for Learning Associated (SCOLA), allowing downloading of international programming for language teaching and learning. The department houses the academic ESL program and the Texas Tech International Teaching Assistant Program, both of which provide opportunities for training and experience for students who plan to work with postsecondary international students.

Two students completed the program in 1996–1997.

The university has an intensive English language program for nonnative speakers of English.

Summer Session: Yes

Further Information: Graduate Adviser, Applied Linguistics
Department of Classical and Modern Languages and Literatures
Foreign Language Building, Room 207
Texas Tech University
Box 42071
Lubbock, TX 79409

Telephone: (806) 742-3145
Fax: (806) 742-3306
E-mail: rosslyn.smith@ttu.edu

◆ TEXAS WOMAN'S UNIVERSITY, Department of Reading and Bilingual Education

Degree Offered: MEd with a concentration in ESL.

Length of Program: 2 years. Students may be full-time or part-time and may begin their study at the beginning of any semester. Application deadlines are fall semester, July; spring semester, November; summer semester, March.

Program Requirements: 39 semester hours. Competence in a language other than English is required. Practice teaching, a thesis, and a comprehensive examination are required.

Courses Offered: ESL Methods; Psycholinguistics; Multicultural Education; Comparative Linguistics; Teaching Reading to Linguistically Different Learners.

Full-Time Staff: Rudy Rodriguez (chair), Luis Rosado, Martina Randeri, P. Dam.

Requirements for Admission: The university's requirements for admission are a GRE score of at least 700 and a GPA of at least 2.75 for the last 60 hours of undergraduate work.

Tuition, Fees, and Aid: For in-state students, $73 per semester hour; for out-of-state students, $287 per semester hour. Teaching assistantships are available contingent on the availability of funds.

General: The program, which leads to a Texas credential in TESOL, emphasizes the preparation of preservice and in-service teachers for elementary and secondary ESL programs.

Plans are under way to include international fieldwork.

Thirty students completed the program in 1996–1997.

Summer Session: Yes

Further Information: Rudy Rodriguez
Department of Reading and Bilingual Education
MLL 510F
Texas Woman's University
PO Box 425769
Denton, TX 76204-5769

Telephone: (940) 898-2227
Fax: (940) 898-2224
E-mail: d_rodriguez@twu.edu

◆ UNIVERSITY OF TOLEDO, Department of English and Department of Curriculum and Instruction

Degree Offered: MAEd in ESL.

Length of Program: 3–4 semesters. Students may be full-time or part-time and may begin their study at the beginning of any semester. Applications for admission are considered continuously; applicants requesting financial aid should apply 6 months in advance.

Program Requirements: 34–36 semester hours. Competence in a language other than English is required for native speakers of English. Practice teaching and a thesis or project are required. A comprehensive examination is not required.

Courses Offered: (*required) *Group Processes in Education; *Educational Testing and Grading; *Adolescent Development; *Foundations of Curriculum and Instruction; *Issues in Second Language Instruction; *Fundamentals of Linguistic Analysis; *History of the English Language; *Applied Linguistics Research and Theory I Laboratory; *Applied Linguistics Research and Theory II; *Seminar in English Instruction: ESL.

Full-Time Staff: Samir Abu-Absi, Douglas W. Coleman (director), Dwayne DeMedio, Melinda Reichelt, Dorothy Siegel.

Requirements for Admission: The university's requirement for admission is a bachelor's degree with a minimum undergraduate GPA of 2.7, acceptance by the Department of English and the Department of Curriculum and Instruction, three letters of recommendation, a TOEFL score for nonnative speakers of English, and a GRE score for international students.

Tuition, Fees, and Aid: For in-state students, $2,400 per semester; for out-of-state students, $5,200 per semester. Fees are $390 per semester. Teaching assistantships and fee-waiver scholarships are available.

General: This program is intended primarily for those who will teach ESL at the elementary and secondary levels. It leads to an Ohio credential in TESOL.
The university has an exchange agreement with the University of Lodz, Poland. Seven students completed the program in 1996–1997.
The university has an intensive English language program for nonnative speakers of English.

Summer Session: Yes

Further Information: Douglas W. Coleman
Department of English
University of Toledo
Toledo, OH 43606-3390

Telephone: (419) 530-2318
Fax: (419) 530-4440
E-mail: Douglas.Coleman@utoledo.edu
http://uhenglab.uhe.utoledo.edu

◆ UNIVERSITY OF TOLEDO, Department of English

Degree Offered: MA in English with a concentration in ESL.

Length of Program: 3–4 semesters. Students may be full-time or part-time and may begin their study at the beginning of any semester. Applications for admission are considered continuously; applicants requesting financial aid should apply 6 months in advance.

Program Requirements: 33–35 semester hours. Competence in a language other than English is required for native speakers of English. Practice teaching and a thesis are required. A comprehensive examination is not required.

Courses Offered: (*required) *Fundamentals of Linguistic Analysis; *History of the English Language; *Applied Linguistics Research and Theory I; *Applied Linguistics Research and Theory I Laboratory; *Applied Linguistics Research and Theory II; *Seminar in English Instruction: ESL; *Issues in Second Language Instruction; *English Structure and Language Teaching; *one course prescribed by the adviser; *6 semester hours approved by the adviser and drawn from English, linguistics, curriculum and instruction, and instructional technology.

Full-Time Staff: See program description for MAEd in ESL.

Requirements for Admission: The university's requirement for admission is a bachelor's degree with a minimum undergraduate GPA of 2.7, acceptance by the Department of English, three letters of recommendation, and a GRE score for international students. The program requires a writing sample.

Tuition, Fees, and Aid: See program description for MAEd in ESL.

General: This program, which began in fall 1997, is intended for those who wish to teach ESL at the college level in the United States or to go abroad to teach ESL.
   The university has an exchange agreement with the University of Lodz, Poland.
   The university has an intensive English language program for nonnative speakers of English.

Summer Session: Yes

Further Information: Douglas W. Coleman
Department of English
University of Toledo
Toledo, OH 43606-3390

Telephone: (419) 530-2318
Fax: (419) 530-4440
E-mail: Douglas.Coleman@utoledo.edu
Http://uhenglab.uhe.utoledo.edu

◆ UNITED STATES INTERNATIONAL UNIVERSITY, Department of Global Liberal Studies

Degree Offered: BA in TESOL.

Length of Program: 4 years. Students may be full-time or part-time and may begin their study at the beginning of any quarter. Application deadlines are 30 days before the quarter in which the applicant desires admission.

Program Requirements: 186 quarter units. Competence in a language other than English is required; English meets the requirement for native speakers of English. Neither practice teaching, nor a thesis, nor a comprehensive examination is required.

Courses Offered: (*required) *General education (86 units); *Second Language Teaching Theory and Methods; *Teaching Listening, Speaking, Reading, and Writing; *Second Language Assessment, Evaluation, and Placement; *Advanced English Composition; *English Language History; *English Grammar; *Introduction to Linguistics; *Teaching Pronunciation; *Curriculum Design and Materials Development; *Technology in the Second Language Classroom; *TESOL Seminar and Observation; *Literature and Culture; *Comparative Philosophy; *Community Service; *Integrated Seminar; *project or internship; electives.

Full-Time Staff: Judy Law, Linda Swanson.

Requirements for Admission: The university's requirements for admission are a minimum GPA of 2.5, SAT or ACT scores for U.S. students, a personal essay, and written recommendations. The program requires a minimum TOEFL score of 550 for nonnative speakers of English.

Tuition, Fees, and Aid: $3,600 per quarter for 12–16 units. Fees are $100 for full-time students. Various forms of financial aid are available.

General: The TESOL major prepares students to teach in both international and domestic settings or to continue their education at the graduate level. The university's undergraduate population is 40% international, providing the opportunity to develop a global perspective
The university has an intensive English language program for nonnative speakers of English.

Summer Session: No

Further Information: Dr. Linda J. Swanson, Chair
Department of Global Liberal Studies
LIS 200C
United States International University
10455 Pomerado Road
San Diego, CA 92025

Telephone: (619) 635-4713
Fax: (619) 635-4730
E-mail: lswanson@usiu.edu

◆ UNITED STATES INTERNATIONAL UNIVERSITY, Department of Education

Degree Offered: MEd with a concentration in TESOL.

Length of Program: 4–6 quarters. Students may be full-time or part-time and may begin their study at the beginning of any quarter. Application deadlines are fall quarter, August 1; winter quarter, December 1; spring quarter, March 1; summer quarter, May 1.

Program Requirements: 45 quarter hours. Competence in a language other than English is not required. Practice teaching is recommended. A thesis is required. A comprehensive examination is not required.

Courses Offered: (*required) *Theory and Method of Second Language Teaching; *Principles of Linguistics; *Techniques of Teaching Reading and Writing to Second Language Learners; *Techniques of Teaching Listening and Speaking to Second

Language Learners; *TESOL Practicum/Project; *Psycholinguistics *or* English Grammar for ESL and EFL Teachers; *Academic Instruction Designed for Culturally and Linguistically Diverse Students *or* Methods of Assessment; Interdisciplinary Readings; Using Technology to Facilitate Learning; Development of Cross-Cultural Competencies; New Models of Instruction and Learning.

Full-Time Staff: Mary Ellen Butler-Pascoe (chair), Linda Swanson, Linda Manney, Afia Dil, Janet Castanos, Suzanne Borman, Joel Levine.

Requirements for Admission: The university's requirements for admission are three academic references, a minimum GPA of 2.5, and a goal statement. The program requires a minimum TOEFL score of 550 and TWE score of 5 for nonnative speakers of English.

Tuition, Fees, and Aid: $245 per quarter unit. Fees are full-time, $100; part-time, $93. Work study is available.

General: The program focuses on preparing TESOL practitioners for leadership roles in a variety of institutions and second language learning settings in the United States and abroad. The program leads to a California credential in TESOL.

Students can utilize campuses in Kenya and Mexico for practica.

Forty-five students completed the program in 1996–1997.

The university has an intensive English language program for nonnative speakers of English.

Summer Session: Yes

Further Information: Dr. Mary Ellen Butler-Pascoe
Department of Education
M-13
United States International University
10455 Pomerado Road
San Diego, CA 92131

Telephone: (619) 635-4791
Fax: (619) 635-4714
E-mail: mbutler@USIU.edu

◆ UNITED STATES INTERNATIONAL UNIVERSITY, Department of Education

Degree Offered: EdD with a concentration in TESOL.

Length of Program: 12 quarters. Students may be full-time or part-time and may begin their study at the beginning of any quarter. Application deadlines are fall quarter, August 1; winter quarter, December 1; spring quarter, March 1; summer quarter, May 1.

Program Requirements: 92 quarter hours. Competence in a language other than English is not required. A dissertation and a comprehensive examination are required. Practice teaching is not required.

Courses Offered: (*required) *Issues in TESOL Theory and Methodology; *Research in Second Language Acquisition and Applied Linguistics; *Foundations for Planning Programs for Second Language Learners; *Design, Development, and Evaluation of Programs for Second Language Learners; *Sociopolitical Issues of Second Language Teaching; *Sociolinguistics; *Identity and Development: A Multicultural Focus; courses in educational leadership, instructional design, and learning and research.

Full-Time Staff: Mary Ellen Butler-Pascoe (chair), Linda Swanson, Linda Manney, Afia Dil, Janet Castanos, Suzanne Borman,

Requirements for Admission: The university's requirements for admission are a master's degree in a related field, a Miller Analogies Test or GRE score, three professional references, a goal statement, a writing test, and an interview. The program requires a minimum TOEFL score of 575 and TWE score of 5 for nonnative speakers of English.

Tuition, Fees, and Aid: $350 per quarter unit. Fees are full-time, $100; part-time, $93. Work study is available.

General: This concentration is designed to meet the global demand for specialists in TESOL and to prepare graduates for leadership roles in schools and universities in the United States and abroad. Students build upon a sound understanding of TESOL methodology and second language acquisition theory to develop expertise in ESL/EFL instruction and program development.

Students can utilize campuses in Kenya and Mexico for research.

The university has an intensive English language program for nonnative speakers of English.

Summer Session: Yes

Further Information: Dr. Mary Ellen Butler-Pascoe
Department of Education
M-13
United States International University
10455 Pomerado Road
San Diego, CA 92131

Telephone: (619) 635-4791
Fax: (619) 635-4714
E-mail: mbutler@USIU.edu

◆ UNIVERSITY OF UTAH, Linguistics Program

Degree Offered: ESL minor.

Length of Program: Students may be full-time or part-time and may begin their study at the beginning of any semester. Application deadlines are fall semester, June 1; spring semester, November 15; summer semester, April 15.

Program Requirements: 25 semester hours. Competence in a language other than English is not required. Practice teaching is required. Neither a thesis nor a comprehensive examination is required.

Courses Offered: (*required) *Pedagogical Structure of English; *Second Language Methodology: K–12; *Content-Based Language Teaching; *Practicum and Materials Development; *Bilingual/Bicultural Education; *Introduction to the Study of Language *or* Linguistics and Education *or* Graduate Survey of Linguistics; *Introduction to Multicultural Education *or* Issues and Research in Multicultural Education; *Minority Language Issues in Education *or* Bilingualism.

Full-Time Staff: Marianna DiPaolo (chair), David Dodd, Mushira Eid, Randall Gess, Thomas Huckin, David Iannucci, Mauricio J. Mixco, Adrian Palmer, Ed Rubin, Steven Sternfeld, Shelley Taylor, Johanna Watzinger-Tharp.

Requirements for Admission: The university's requirements for admission are a high school or GED diploma, and a GPA and SAT or ACT score that have an index number of at least 85 (e.g., 2.5 GPA plus 20 ACT). The program requires junior or higher standing, a minimum GPA of 3.0, and approval of the adviser. The program must be coupled with a secondary or elementary teaching certificate. Nonnative speakers of English must have a TOEFL score of 600 or higher.

Tuition, Fees, and Aid: For in-state students, $1,150 per semester; for out-of-state students, $3,118. Financial aid is available through the university.

General: The program features an excellent student-teacher ratio, faculty members with international expertise and field experience, and a variety of opportunities for supervised teaching. The program leads to a Utah credential in TESOL.

One student completed the program in 1996–1997.

The university has an intensive English language program for nonnative speakers of English.

Summer Session: Yes

Further Information: Coordinator
Linguistics Program
2300 LNCO
255 South Central Campus Drive, Room 2328
University of Utah
Salt Lake City, UT 84112

Telephone: (801) 581-8047
Fax: (801) 581-6255
E-mail: sbruhn@lrc.hum.utah.edu

◆ UNIVERSITY OF UTAH, Linguistics Program

Degree Offered: TESOL certificate.

Length of Program: 6 quarters. Students must be part-time and may begin their study at the beginning of the any semester. Application deadlines are fall semester, June 1; spring semester, November 15; summer semester, April 15.

Program Requirements: 19 semester hours. Competence in a language other than English is not required. Neither practice teaching, nor a thesis, nor a comprehensive examination is required.

Courses Offered: (*required) *Pedagogical Structure of English; *Second Language Methodology: Adult; *Practicum and Materials Development; *Second Language Testing; *Introduction to the Study of Language *or* Graduate Survey of Linguistics; one elective.

Full-Time Staff: See program description for ESL minor.

Requirements for Admission: See program description for ESL minor.

Tuition, Fees, and Aid: See program description for ESL minor.

General: The program features an excellent student-teacher ratio, faculty members with international expertise and field experience, and a variety of opportunities for supervised teaching.

Nine students completed the program in 1996–1997.

The university has an intensive English language program for nonnative speakers of English.

Summer Session: Yes

Further Information: Coordinator
Linguistics Program
2300 LNCO
255 South Central Campus Drive, Room 2328
University of Utah
Salt Lake City, UT 84112

Telephone: (801) 581-8047
Fax: (801) 581-6255
E-mail: sbruhn@lrc.hum.utah.edu

◆ UNIVERSITY OF UTAH, Linguistics Program

Degree Offered: MA in bilingual education.

Length of Program: 3 semesters. Students may be full-time or part-time and must begin their study at the beginning of the fall semester. The application deadline is June 1.

Program Requirements: 35 semester hours. One year of study of a language other than English is required. Practice teaching and a comprehensive examination are required. A paper is required.

Courses Offered: (*required) *Graduate Survey of Linguistics; *Pedagogical Structure of English; *Quantitative Analysis of Language; *Content-Based Language Teaching; *Practicum and Materials Development; *Second Language Testing; *Second Language Program Development and Administration; *Second Language Methodology: K–12; *Bilingual/Bicultural Education; *Multicultural Education *or* Issues and Research in Multicultural Education; *Bilingualism *or* Minority Language Issues in Education.

Full-Time Staff: Marianna DiPaolo (chair), David Dodd, Mushira Eid, Randall Gess, Thomas Huckin, David Iannucci, Mauricio J. Mixco, Adrian Palmer, Ed Rubin, Steven Sternfeld, Shelley Taylor, Johanna Watzinger-Tharp.

Requirements for Admission: The requirements for admission are a baccalaureate degree from an accredited college or university and a cumulative GPA of 3.0 or better. Nonnative speakers of English must have a TOEFL score of 600 or higher.

Tuition, Fees, and Aid: For in-state students, $1,150 per semester; for out-of-state students, $3,118. Teaching assistantships, a tuition scholarship, and other financial aid through the university are available.

General: The program features an excellent student-teacher ratio, faculty members with international expertise and field experience, and a variety of opportunities for supervised teaching. The program leads to a Utah credential in TESOL.
Nine students completed the program in 1996–1997.
The university has an intensive English language program for nonnative speakers of English.

Summer Session: No

Further Information: Coordinator
Linguistics Program
2300 LNCO
255 South Central Campus Drive, Room 2328
University of Utah
Salt Lake City, UT 84112

Telephone: (801) 581-8047
Fax: (801) 581-6255
E-mail: sbruhn@lrc.hum.utah.edu

◆ UNIVERSITY OF UTAH, Linguistics Program

Degree Offered: MA in second language acquisition.

Length of Program: 3 semesters. Students may be full-time or part-time and must begin their study at the beginning of the fall semester. The application deadline is June 1.

Program Requirements: 35 semester hours. One year of study of a language other than English is required. Practice teaching and a comprehensive examination are required. A paper is required.

Courses Offered: (*required) *Graduate Survey of Linguistics; *Pedagogical Structure of English; *Quantitative Analysis of Language; *Content-Based Language Teaching; *Practicum and Materials Development; *Second Language Testing; *Second Language Program Development and Administration; *Second Language Methodology: Adult; three electives.

Full-Time Staff: See program description for MA in bilingual education.

Requirements for Admission: See program description for MA in bilingual education.

Tuition, Fees, and Aid: See program description for MA in bilingual education.

General: The program features an excellent student-teacher ratio, faculty members with international expertise and field experience, and a variety of opportunities for supervised teaching.

Nine students completed the program in 1996–1997.

The university has an intensive English language program for nonnative speakers of English.

Summer Session: No

Further Information: Coordinator
Linguistics Program
2300 LNCO
255 South Central Campus Drive, Room 2328
University of Utah
Salt Lake City, UT 84112

Telephone: (801) 581-8047
Fax: (801) 581-6255
E-mail: sbruhn@lrc.hum.utah.edu

◆ UNIVERSITY OF WASHINGTON, Department of English

Degree Offered: MAT in ESL.

Length of Program: 6 quarters. Students may be full-time or part-time and must begin their study at the beginning of the summer or fall quarter. The application deadline is January 15. The second and last review of applications is April 1.

Program Requirements: 45–54 quarter hours. Competence in a language other than English is required for native speakers of English. Practice teaching is required. Neither a thesis nor a comprehensive examination is required.

Courses Offered: (*required) *Colloquium: Introduction to TESL; *Methods and Materials in TESL; *Research in TESL; *Testing in ESL; *Phonology I; *Syntax I; *Practicum in TESL; *three of the following: The Composition Process, Language and Social Policy, Language Variation and Language Policy in North America, Language Policy for Refugees, Introduction to Discourse Analysis, Comparative Grammars, Current Rhetorical Theory, Approaches to Teaching Composition,

Pedagogy and Grammar in Teaching ESL, Language Policy and Cultural Identity, Language Development, Phonology II; Syntax II; *an approved elective in anthropology, education, linguistics, psychology, speech and hearing sciences, independent study, *or* research.

Full-Time Staff: Heidi Riggenbach, Sandra Silberstein, James W. Tollefson.

Requirements for Admission: The university's requirements for admission are a bachelor's degree and a GRE General Test score. In addition, the program requires three letters of recommendation that preferably speak to academic ability and teaching experience, a statement of purpose, and an introductory linguistics course that may be taken on admission.

Tuition, Fees, and Aid: For in-state students, $1,681 per quarter; for out-of-state students, $4,158 per quarter. Teaching assistantships are available.

General: Thirteen students completed the program in 1996–1997.

The university has an intensive English language program for nonnative speakers of English.

Summer Session: Yes

Further Information: MATESL Advisor
Department of English
Box 354330
University of Washington
Seattle, WA 98195

Telephone: (206) 543-2017
Fax: (206) 685-2673
E-mail: marynell@u.washington.edu

◆ WASHINGTON STATE UNIVERSITY, Department of Teaching and Learning

Degrees Offered: EdM and MA in literacy education with a concentration in ESL/bilingual education.

Length of Program: 4 semesters. Students may be full-time or part-time and may begin their study at the beginning of any semester. There are no application deadlines.

Program Requirements: Competence in a language other than English is optional. Practice teaching and a thesis are required. A comprehensive examination is required.

Courses Offered: (*required) *Communicating in a Multilingual Society; *ESL Across the Content Areas; *Practicum in ESL/Bilingual Education; *two courses each in foundations, research methods, and content/methods.

Full-Time Staff: Gisela Ernst-Slavit (coordinator), Elsa Major, Monica Moore.

Requirements for Admission: The university's requirements for admission are a minimum GPA of 3.0, a GRE score, and letters of recommendation. Nonnative speakers of English must have a TOEFL score of 550.

Tuition, Fees, and Aid: For in-state students, $2,566 per semester; for out-of-state students, $6,433 per semester. Teaching and research assistantships are available.

General: The program's main focus is K–12 education. It leads to a Washington State credential in TESOL.

Twenty-six students completed the program in 1996–1997.

The university has an intensive English language program for nonnative speakers of English.

Summer Session: No

Further Information: Dr. Gisela Ernst-Slavit, Coordinator
Bilingual/ESL Education Program
Department of Teaching and Learning
Cleveland Hall 321
Washington State University
Pullman, WA 99164-2132

Telephone: (509) 335-0925
Fax: (509) 335-5046
E-mail: gernst@wsu.edu

◆ WEST CHESTER UNIVERSITY, English Department

Degree Offered: Certificate of preparation in ESL teaching.

Length of Program: 2 semesters. Students may be full-time or part-time and may begin their study at the beginning of any semester. Application deadlines are fall semester, July 1; spring semester, November 1; summer semester, April 1.

Program Requirements: 15 semester hours. Experience with a language other than English is required. Practice teaching is required. Neither a thesis nor a comprehensive examination is required.

Courses Offered: (*required) *Structure of English; *Techniques of Second Language Teaching; *ESL Practicum; Sociolinguistics *or* Sociolinguistic Issues in Second Language Education; *one of the following: Teaching Reading and Writing to ESL Students, Content-Based Second Language Instruction, Assessment of Second Language Students, Teaching Second Languages to Elementary and Secondary Students, Curriculum and Materials in TESL, Field Experiences in ESL, Practicum II.

Full-Time Staff: Cheryl L. Micheau, Dennis L. Godfrey, Garrett G. Molholt.

Requirements for Admission: The university's requirement for admission is a baccalaureate degree with a GPA of at least 2.5 overall and of at least 2.75 in the major discipline. The program requires a GPA of 3.0 in the undergraduate major; two recommendations; a résumé; 24 semester hours in the areas of English, linguistics, foreign language, and philosophy; 6 semester hours in the areas of anthropology, sociology, and psychology; Introduction to Linguistics, and foreign language learning experience. Nonnative speakers must have a TOEFL score of 580.

Tuition, Fees, and Aid: For in-state students, $187 per semester hour; for out-of-state students, $336 per semester hour. Fees are $31 per semester hour. Graduate assistantships in TESL and assistantships in the Tutoring Center are available.

General: The program is new.

The university has an intensive English language program for nonnative speakers of English.

Summer Session: Yes

Further Information: Cheri Micheau, Director
MA TESL Program/TESL Certificate Program
English Department
Main Hall 550
West Chester University
West Chester, PA 19383

Telephone: (610) 436-2898
Fax: (610) 436-3150
E-mail: cmicheau@wcupa.edu

◆ WEST CHESTER UNIVERSITY, English Department

Degree Offered: MA in TESL.

Length of Program: 4–5 semesters. Students may be full-time or part-time and may begin their study at the beginning of any semester. Application deadlines are fall semester, July 1; spring semester, November 1; summer semester, April 1.

Program Requirements: 36–39 semester hours. Experience in a language other than English is required; English meets the requirement for nonnative speakers of English. Practice teaching and a comprehensive examination are required. A thesis is not required.

Courses Offered: (*required) *Techniques of Second Language Teaching; *Curriculum and Materials for TESL; *Structure of Modern English; *Practicum in ESL; *Methods and Materials of Research in Second Language Education; *Sociolinguistics *or* Sociolinguistic Issues in Second Language Education; *Teaching Reading and Writing to Second Language Students; *Second Language Acquisition; Content-Based Second Language Instruction; Assessment of Second Language Students; Teaching ESL to Elementary/Secondary Students; Dialects of American English; History of English; Phonology and Morphology; Field Experiences in ESL; Practicum II; Culture in the Second Language Classroom.

Full-Time Staff: See program description for certificate of preparation in ESL teaching.

Requirements for Admission: See program description for certificate of preparation in ESL teaching.

Tuition, Fees, and Aid: See program description for certificate of preparation in ESL teaching.

General: The curriculum reflects a balance between theory and practice and provides a solid theoretical foundation in linguistics, second language acquisition, and second language pedagogy. Theory is applied to practical tasks such as curriculum and materials design, assessment of language needs and progress, and critical classroom observation and self-evaluation.

Four students completed the program in 1996–1997.

The university has an intensive English language program for nonnative speakers of English.

Summer Session: Yes

Further Information: Cheri Micheau, Director
MA TESL Program/TESL Certificate Program
English Department
Main Hall 550
West Chester University
West Chester, PA 19383

Telephone: (610) 436-2898
Fax: (610) 436-3150
E-mail: cmicheau@wcupa.edu

◆ WEST VIRGINIA UNIVERSITY, Department of Foreign Languages

Degrees Offered: MA in foreign languages (TESOL); BA in foreign languages (linguistics/TESL).

Length of Program: 4 semesters. Students may be full-time or part-time and may begin their study at the beginning of any semester. Application deadlines are open; deadlines for full consideration are fall semester, February 15; spring semester, October 15.

Program Requirements: 36 semester hours. Competence in a language other than English is required; English meets the requirement for nonnative speakers of English. A comprehensive examination is required. A thesis is optional. Practice teaching is not required.

Courses Offered: (*required) *ESL Methods; *ESL Theory; *ESL Linguistics; *Phonology; *American Culture; *Introduction to Research; *four courses in American English language, culture, and/or literature; Applied Linguistics; Discourse Analysis; ESL Materials and Syllabus Design; ESL Phonetics; History of Linguistics; Language Testing; Sociolinguistics; Second Language Writing; Transformational Grammar; Advanced Phonology; possible related courses in other departments.

Full-Time Staff: Frank W. Medley, Jr. (chair), Maria Amores, Susan M. Braidi, Ahmed Fakhri, Michael Reider, Jurgen Schlunk, Johan Seynnaeve, Sharon Wilkinson.

Requirements for Admission: The university's requirement for admission is submission of the application form and official transcripts. Nonnative speakers of English must submit official certification and translations of degrees and academic records. The program requires an application form, an official GRE score, and a statement of purpose in English. Nonnative speakers of English must have a minimum TOEFL score of 550.

Tuition, Fees, and Aid: For in-state students, $941 per semester; for out-of-state students, $3,499 per semester. Graduate teaching assistantships, tuition waivers, and meritorious scholarships are available.

General: The program features a focus on language, linguistics, culture, and literature in conjunction with different aspects of teaching English. The Foreign Language Department administers the university's intensive English program. Students may choose a curriculum that combines TESOL with another language. Students from different backgrounds have the flexibility to tailor the program to their needs.

The program has linkage agreements for teaching positions with the University of Valladolid, Spain, and the Colegio de Estudios Superiores de Administración and the Instituto Colombiano de Administración, Colombia.

Fourteen students completed the program in 1996–1997.

The university has an intensive English language program for nonnative speakers of English.

Summer Session: No

Further Information: Chair
Department of Foreign Languages
Chitwood Hall, Room 205
West Virginia University
PO Box 6298
Morgantown, WV 26506-6298

Telephone: (304) 293-5121
Fax: (304) 293-7655
E-mail: fmedley@wvu.edu

◆ WESTERN KENTUCKY UNIVERSITY, Department of English

Degree Offered: MA in English with a concentration in TESL.

Length of Program: 4 semesters. Students may be full-time or part-time and may begin their study at the beginning of any semester. Application deadlines are fall semester, May 15; spring semester, September 15; summer semester, February 15.

Program Requirements: 33 semester hours. Competence in a language other than English is not required. Practice teaching and a comprehensive examination are required. A thesis is not required.

Courses Offered: (*required) *Introduction to TESL; *TESL Methods and Materials; *Descriptive Linguistics; *Psycholinguistics and Sociolinguistics; *TESL Field Experience (Practicum); electives in literature.

Full-Time Staff: Lesa Dill, Ronald D. Eckard, Mary Ellen Pitts (chair), Ellen Johnson.

Requirements for Admission: The university's requirements for admission are a diploma from an accredited college or university with a minimum GPA of 2.75 and a minimum GRE score of 1200. The program requires a minimum of four courses in English and a minimum GPA of 3.0 in English. Nonnative speakers of English must have a TOEFL score of 550 or higher.

Tuition, Fees, and Aid: For in-state students, $1,135 per semester; for out-of-state students, $3,115 per semester. A limited number of teaching assistantships are available.

General: The program provides prospective ESL/EFL teachers with a background in linguistics, TESL methodology, and literature. The practicum provides valuable teaching experience in a variety of programs: university ESL, public elementary and high schools, and refugee and adult education programs. The program leads to a Kentucky endorsement in ESL.

Opportunities exist for fieldwork in Europe, Asia, and South America.

Six students completed the program in 1996–1997.

Summer Session: Yes

Further Information: Dr. Ronald D. Eckard, TESL Director
Department of English
Cherry Hall 111
1 Big Red Way
Western Kentucky University
Bowling Green, KY 42101

Telephone: (502) 745-6320
Fax: (502) 745-2533
E-mail: ronald.eckard@wku.edu

◆ WHEATON COLLEGE, Graduate School, Department of Intercultural Studies

Degree Offered: Graduate certificate in TESL.

Length of Program: 2 semesters. Students may be full-time or part-time and may begin their study at the beginning of any semester. Application deadlines are fall semester, May 1; spring semester, October 15.

Program Requirements: 24 semester hours. Competence in a language other than English is strongly recommended for native speakers of English; English meets the recommendation for nonnative speakers. Practice teaching is required. Neither a thesis nor a comprehensive examination is required.

Courses Offered: (*required) *Theoretical Foundations of TESL/TEFL Methodology; *Descriptive English Grammar; *Phonology for ESL/EFL Teachers; *Cross-Cultural Communication; *Cross-Cultural Teaching and Learning; *Teaching Reading and Composition to ESL/EFL Learners; *Principles of ESL/EFL Testing; *Practicum in TESL; *Introduction to Qualitative Research; *Curriculum Development and Materials Design for TESL/TEFL; Teaching ESL to Children, K–12.

Full-Time Staff: Lonna Dickerson, Gary Larson, Scott Moreau, Cheri Pierson, Alan Seaman (coordinator).

Requirements for Admission: The college's requirement for admission is a bachelor's degree from a regionally accredited college or university with a minimum GPA of 2.75. International students must have the equivalent. Nonnative speakers of English must have a TOEFL score of 600 or higher.

Tuition, Fees, and Aid: $350 per credit hour. Grants, scholarships, graduate assistantships, and loans are available.

General: The college is a nondenominational, broadly evangelical Christian institution. The program prepares both ESL and EFL teachers for cross-cultural work by emphasizing professional knowledge, cultural sensitivity, and creative teaching. Located in a suburb of Chicago, the college is connected with a number of ESL programs that provide opportunities for observation and practicum teaching experience. During the summer students can earn graduate credit in TEFL and second language acquisition through courses in the Institute for Cross-Cultural Training. The program leads to an Illinois credential in TESOL.

Students may elect to complete their teaching practicum overseas. The program has relationships with universities in Russia, China, Romania, and Korea.

Twenty-seven students completed the program in 1996–1997.

Summer Session: Yes

Further Information: Dr. Alan Seaman
Department of Intercultural Studies
Wheaton College Graduate School
Wheaton, IL 60187-5593

Telephone: (630) 752-7044
Fax: (630) 752-5935
E-mail: Alan.Seaman@wheaton.edu

◆ WHEATON COLLEGE, Graduate School, Department of Intercultural Studies

Degree Offered: MA in intercultural studies with a specialization in TESL.

Length of Program: 3 semesters. Students may be full-time or part-time and may begin their study at the beginning of any semester. Application deadlines are fall semester, May 1; spring semester, October 15.

Program Requirements: 40 semester hours. Competence in a language other than English is strongly recommended for native speakers of English; English meets the recommendation for nonnative speakers. Practice teaching and a comprehensive examination are required. A thesis is optional.

Courses Offered: (*required) *Theoretical Foundations of TESL/TEFL Methodology; *Descriptive English Grammar for ESL/EFL Teachers; *Cross-Cultural Communication; *Cross-Cultural Teaching and Learning; *Teaching Reading and Composition to ESL/EFL Learners; *Phonology for ESL/EFL Teachers; *Principles of ESL/EFL Testing; *Practicum in TESL; *Cross-Cultural Research; *Contextualization; Second Language Acquisition; 8 hours of electives.

Full-Time Staff: Evvy Campbell (chair), Lonna Dickerson, Gary Larson, Scott Moreau, Cheri Pierson, Alan Seaman (coordinator).

Requirements for Admission: See program description for graduate certificate in TESL.

Tuition, Fees, and Aid: See program description for graduate certificate in TESL.

General: The program provides a broad range of specialized training in TESL, with the opportunity to concentrate on Asian studies, Latin American studies, East European studies, community development, or more advanced course work in TESL. Located in a suburb of Chicago, the college is connected with a number of ESL programs that provide opportunities for observation and practicum teaching experience. During the summer students can earn graduate credit in TEFL and second language acquisition through courses in the Institute for Cross-Cultural Training. The program leads to an Illinois credential in TESOL.

Students may elect to complete their teaching practicum overseas. The program has relationships with universities in Russia, China, Romania, and Korea.

Twenty-one students completed the program in 1996–1997.

Summer Session: Yes

Further Information: Dr. Alan Seaman
Department of Intercultural Studies
Wheaton College Graduate School
Wheaton, IL 60187-5593

Telephone: (630) 752-7044
Fax: (630) 752-5935
E-mail: Alan.Seaman@wheaton.edu

◆ WICE/RUTGERS UNIVERSITY, Department of Continuing Education

Degree Offered: TEFL certificate.

Length of Program: 8 months (extensive, October–May); 1 month (intensive, September or June). Applications are accepted until courses fill.

Program Requirements: Competence in a language other than English is not required. Practice teaching is required. A project is required for the extensive course. Neither a thesis nor a comprehensive examination is required.

Courses Offered: Theories of Second Language Acquisition; Methods and Approaches; Presentation and Practice; Skills-Based Approaches; Integrating Skills; Lesson Planning; Group Management; Error Treatment; Pronunciation; Course Design; Language Awareness.

Full-Time Staff: Jacqueline Garçon, Rhoda McGraw, Hester Harris Poumellec.

Requirements for Admission: The requirements for admission are a native or nativelike ability in English, a good level of education, and a (telephone) interview. Competence in a foreign language is preferred.

Tuition, Fees, and Aid: Extensive course, 9,300 French francs; intensive course, 8,300 French francs. Fees must be paid in French francs. No financial aid is available.

General: The program is designed for people with little or no teaching experience. WICE organizes practice teaching on the premises that is concurrent with the academic component. The extensive course features morning, afternoon, or evening classes. Class size is limited to 12.

Fifty-six students completed the program in 1996–1997.

Summer Session: Yes

Further Information: WICE/Rutgers University TEFL Certificate Program
20 boulevard du Montparnasse
75015 Paris
France

Telephone: (33-1) 45-66-75-50
Fax: (33-1) 45-65-96-53
E-mail: wice@club-internet.fr
http://www.wice.org./teflcert.htm

◆ WICHITA STATE UNIVERSITY, Department of Curriculum and Instruction

Degrees Offered: BA in elementary education with TESL state teaching endorsement; add-on secondary endorsement.

Length of Program: 8–9 semesters. Students must be full-time for the last 4 semesters and may begin their study at the beginning of any semester. There are no application deadlines.

Program Requirements: 124 credit hours (including 28 hours for the ESL endorsement). Competence in a language other than English is not required. A practicum and a portfolio are required. Neither a comprehensive examination nor a thesis is required.

Courses Offered: (*required) *Applied Linguistics for ESL/Bilingual Education Teachers, Introduction to Linguistics, *or* The Nature of Language; *Multicultural Education, Sociomulticultural Education, *or* Language and Culture; *Second Language Acquisition; *TESL (Methods); *Second Language Assessment; Practicum in TESOL.

Full-Time Staff: Peggy J. Anderson (director), Tonya Huber, Dennis Kean (chair), Frank Kline.

Requirements for Admission: The university's requirement for admission is a high school diploma. Nonnative speakers of English must have a TOEFL score of 570 or higher and a TSE/SPEAK score of 240.

Tuition, Fees, and Aid: For in-state students, $81.50 per credit hour; for out-of-state students, $286.85 per credit hour.

General: The program emphasizes second language learning issues for teaching in elementary and secondary school settings. There are opportunities for off-campus field experiences and practica in public schools for 4 semesters. The university is located in a middle-sized urban environment with many speakers of other languages as well as Native American groups.

An Intensive English Language Center for nonnative speakers of English is located on the campus.

Summer Session: Yes

Further Information: Peggy J. Anderson, Director, TESOL Program
Department of Curriculum and Instruction
Corbin Education Center, Room 107
Wichita State University
1845 North Fairmount
Wichita, KS 67260-0028

Telephone: (316) 689-3322
Fax: (316) 978-3302
E-mail: panderso@wsuhub.uc.twsu.edu

◆ WICHITA STATE UNIVERSITY, Department of Curriculum and Instruction

Degrees Offered: Undergraduate certificate in TESOL; graduate certificate in TESOL with MA in liberal studies.

Length of Program: 1 year (certificate). Students may be full-time or part-time and may begin their study at the beginning of any semester. There are no application deadlines.

Program Requirements: 18 credit hours. Competence in a language other than English is not required. A practicum is required. A portfolio is required for the MA. Neither a comprehensive examination nor a thesis is required.

Courses Offered: See BA program description.

Full-Time Staff: See BA program description.

Requirements for Admission: The university's requirement for admission is a high school diploma for the undergraduate certificate. For the MA, the Graduate School requires a GPA of 3.0 in the most recent 60 hours, a GRE score of 917 or higher on two of the three General Test sections or a Miller Analogies Test score of 40 or above, proof of certification, 1 semester of satisfactory full-time teaching or equivalent professional experience, and a 500-word statement. For graduate admission, the program requires a BA degree from a regionally accredited institution and a minimum GPA of 2.75 in the last 60 hours of course work.

Tuition, Fees, and Aid: For in-state students, $81.50 per credit hour for undergraduates; $286.85 for graduate students. For out-of-state students, $286.85 per credit hour for undergraduates; $331.85 for graduate students. Some graduate teaching assistantships and research assistantships may be available in the Department of Curriculum and Instruction or the Intensive English Language Center.

General: The program focuses on both theoretical and practical issues related to the learning and teaching of ESL/EFL. Practical field experiences in ESL settings provide a direct opportunity to relate theory to practice. The certificate program may be taken as part of the MA in liberal studies.

The university has an intensive English language program for nonnative speakers of English.

Summer Session: Yes

Further Information: Peggy J. Anderson, Director, TESOL Program
Department of Curriculum and Instruction
Corbin Education Center, Room 107
Wichita State University
1845 North Fairmount
Wichita, KS 67260-0028

Telephone: (316) 689-3322
Fax: (316) 978-3302
E-mail: panderso@wsuhub.uc.twsu.edu

◆ WICHITA STATE UNIVERSITY, Department of Curriculum and Instruction

Degree Offered: State of Kansas endorsement in bilingual education/multicultural education.

Length of Program: 1 year. Students may be full-time or part-time and may begin their study at the beginning of any semester. There are no application deadlines.

Program Requirements: 18 credit hours. Competence in a language other than English is required; English meets the requirement for nonnative speakers of English. A practicum is required. Neither a comprehensive examination nor a thesis is required.

Courses Offered: (*required) *Applied Linguistics for ESL/Bilingual Education Teachers; *Mexico: Its People and Culture (or a similar course appropriate to the student's second language); *Second Language Acquisition; *TESL Methods; *Second Language Assessment; *Practicum: Bilingual Education.

Full-Time Staff: See BA program description.

Requirements for Admission: The requirements for admission are admission to the graduate school and a GPA of 2.75 in the last 60 hours of course work.

Tuition, Fees, and Aid: For in-state students, $286.85 per credit hour; for out-of-state students, $331.85 per credit hour. Graduate teaching assistantships are available.

General: The program emphasizes second language learning and bilingual education issues for teaching in elementary and secondary settings. There are opportunities for off-campus practica. The university is located in a middle-sized urban environment with many speakers of other languages as well as Native American groups.

The university has an intensive English language program for nonnative speakers of English.

Summer Session: Yes

Further Information: Peggy J. Anderson, Director, TESOL Program
Department of Curriculum and Instruction
Corbin Education Center, Room 107
Wichita State University
1845 North Fairmount
Wichita, KS 67260-0028

Telephone: (316) 689-3322
Fax: (316) 978-3302
E-mail: panderso@wsuhub.uc.twsu.edu

◆ WICHITA STATE UNIVERSITY, Department of Curriculum and Instruction

Degree Offered: MA in curriculum and instruction with a specialization in TESOL.

Length of Program: 2 years. Students may be full-time or part-time and may begin their study at the beginning of any semester. There are no application deadlines.

Program Requirements: 33 credit hours plus a 3-credit prerequisite course. Competence in a language other than English is not required. A practicum plus a portfolio or thesis is required. A comprehensive examination is not required.

Courses Offered: (*required) *Reflective Inquiry Into Teaching, Learning, and Schools; *Instructional Models and Practices; *Curriculum Models and Practices; *Seminars in Curriculum and Instruction; *Introduction to Educational Research; *Seminar on Research Problems; *Thesis *or* Portfolio; *12 hours selected from Applied Linguistics for ESL/Bilingual Education Teachers, Multicultural Education *or* Language and Culture, Second Language Acquisition, TESL, Second Language Assessment, Practicum in TESOL, and other courses available by arrangement with the student's committee.

Full-Time Staff: Alan Aagard, Robert Alley, Peggy J. Anderson, Geri Coffman, Bryna Fillian (graduate coordinator), Tonya Huber, Michael James, Dennis Kean (chair), Dennis Potthoff, Marlene Schommer, Johnnie Thompson, Candace Wells, John Wilson.

Requirements for Admission: The university's requirements for admission are a baccalaureate degree from a regionally accredited institution with a minimum GPA of 2.75 in the last 60 hours (including any postgraduate work) and no more than 9 hours of background deficiencies in the desired major field of study. Nonnative speakers of English must have a TOEFL score of 550 or higher. The Graduate School requires a GPA of 3.0 in the most recent 60 hours, a GRE score of 917 or higher on two of the three General Test sections or a Miller Analogies Test score of 40 or above, proof of certification, 1 semester of satisfactory full-time teaching or equivalent professional experience, and a 500-word statement.

Tuition, Fees, and Aid: For in-state students, $286.85 per credit hour; for out-of-state students, $331.85 per credit hour. Some graduate teaching assistantships and research assistantships may be available in the Department of Curriculum and Instruction or the Intensive English Language Center.

General: Individuals without a teaching certificate may gain TESL certification with an MA in liberal studies. Faculty and students have the opportunity to work with a Title VII Newcomers' Center in an urban school district.

Students may have opportunities for international fieldwork through Sister Cities (Cancún, Mexico), the Modern Language Department (Pueblo, Mexico) or the Anthropology Department (Great Plains Native American Reservations). Fulbright competitions and independent studies abroad may also be possible. Beginning in summer 1998, the program will be offered at Intercollege in Larnaca, Cyprus.

Thirty-five students completed the program in 1996–1997.

The university has an intensive English language program for nonnative speakers of English.

Summer Session: Yes

Further Information: Peggy J. Anderson, Director, TESOL Program
Department of Curriculum and Instruction
Corbin Education Center, Room 107
Wichita State University
1845 North Fairmount
Wichita, KS 67260-0028

Telephone: (316) 689-3322
Fax: (316) 978-3302
E-mail: panderso@wsuhub.uc.twsu.edu

◆ WILLIAM PATERSON UNIVERSITY, Department of Languages and Cultures

Degree Offered: MEd with a concentration in bilingual education/ESL.

Length of Program: Variable. Students may be full-time or part-time and may begin their study at the beginning of the fall or spring semester. Application deadlines are fall semester, April 1; spring semester, September 15.

Program Requirements: 33 credits. Competence in a language other than English is not required. Practice teaching, a thesis, and a comprehensive examination are required.

Courses Offered: (*required) *General Linguistics; *History and Cultural Roots of Bilingualism in the United States; *Language and Culture; *Social and Psychological Processes of the Multicultural Experience; *Applied Linguistics; *Structure of American English; *Research in Education I; *Research in Education II; Content Area Instruction in ESL; Methods, Materials, and Assessment in TESOL; Contrastive Linguistics; Content Areas in Bilingual Education; Bilingualism as an Individual and Social Phenomenon; Sociolinguistics.

Full-Time Staff: Angela Aguirre, Octavio de la Suarée, Joan Lesikin, Esther Martinez, Kara Rabbitt, William Rosa (chair), Orlando Saa, Bruce Williams, Keumsil Kim Yoon (director).

Requirements for Admission: The university's requirements for admission are a bachelor's degree from an accredited college or university with a cumulative GPA of 2.75 or better and a minimum score of 450 on the GRE verbal section or a score of 35 on the Miller Analogies Test. (The minimum score is being reconsidered.) In addition, the program requires a copy of the student's standard or provisional teaching certificate, two letters of professional recommendation, and a TOEFL score of 550 or higher for nonnative speakers of English.

Tuition, Fees, and Aid: For in-state students, $187 per credit; for out-of-state students, $266 per credit. Graduate assistantships are available.

General: The program provides courses leading to a New Jersey State endorsement certification in bilingual/bicultural education and ESL. Most of the courses for either certification can be transferred to the master's degree program.

Ten students completed the program in 1996–1997.

Summer Session: Yes

Further Information: Dr. Keumsil Kim Yoon, Director,
Bilingual/ESL Graduate Program
Department of Languages and Cultures
Atrium 245
William Paterson University
300 Pompton Road
Wayne, NJ 07470

Telephone: (973) 720-3041
Fax: (973) 720-3084
E-mail: yoonk@nebula.wilpaterson.edu

◆ WISCONSIN, UNIVERSITY OF, GREEN BAY, College of Education, Department of Communication and the Arts

Degree Offered: Education minor in ESL.

Length of Program: 4 semesters. Students may be full-time or part-time and may begin their study at the beginning of any semester. There are no application deadlines.

Program Requirements: 27 credits. Competence in a language other than English is required; English meets the requirement for nonnative speakers of English. Practice teaching is required. Neither a thesis nor a comprehensive examination is required.

Courses Offered: (*required) *ESL Methods; *Introduction to Language; *Language and Human Conflict; *Applied Linguistics; *Error Analysis; *Language and Literacy Development; *2 semesters of a language.

Requirements for Admission: At the graduate level, students must be certified teachers and must have been admitted to the education program.

General: The program, which leads to a Wisconsin credential in TESOL, has established a partnership with an inner-city school and is testing all incoming students.

Summer Session: No

Further Information: Barbara Law
College of Education
Wood Hall 432
University of Wisconsin, Green Bay
2420 Nicolet
Green Bay, WI 54303

Telephone: (414) 465-2835

◆ WISCONSIN, UNIVERSITY OF, MADISON, Department of English

Degree Offered: Certificate in TESOL.

Length of Program: 2–3 semesters. Students may be full-time or part-time and may begin their study at the beginning of any semester. Application deadlines are open.

Program Requirements: 21 credits. Competence in a language other than English is required for native speakers of English; English meets the requirement for nonnative speakers of English. Practice teaching is required. Neither a comprehensive examination nor a thesis is required.

Courses Offered: (*required) *Structure of English; *English Phonology; *two of the following: English Dialects, Studies of Interlanguage, ESL: Principles of Language Learning; *ESL: Theory and Practice; *ESL: Techniques and Materials; *ESL Academic Skills Workshop.

Full-Time Staff: Marian Bean, Cecilia Ford, Peter Schreiber, Charles T. Scott (director), Richard Young, Jane Zuengler.

Requirements for Admission: The university's requirement for admission is graduate or undergraduate standing. Special student status is available for post-BA/BS applicants. Nonnative speakers of English must submit appropriate TOEFL or MELAB scores.

Tuition, Fees, and Aid: For in-state students, $2,346 (graduate) or $1,217 (undergraduate or special) per semester; for out-of-state students, $7,198 (graduate) or $4,119 (undergraduate or special) per semester. No financial aid is available.

General: Students who do the certificate in conjunction with the MA program are eligible for consideration as salaried teaching assistants in the Program in ESL.

The university has an intensive English language program for nonnative speakers of English.

Summer Session: Yes

Further Information: Director
Programs in English Linguistics
Department of English
5134 Helen C. White Hall
University of Wisconsin—Madison
600 North Park Street
Madison, WI 53706

Telephone: (608) 263-3780
Fax: (608) 263-9305
E-mail: ctscott@facstaff.wisc.edu

◆ WISCONSIN, UNIVERSITY OF, MADISON, Department of English

Degree Offered: MA in English (applied English linguistics).

Length of Program: 2–4 semesters. Students may be full-time or part-time and must begin their study at the beginning of the fall semester. The application deadline is March 1 (January 15 for teaching assistantships).

Program Requirements: 27 credits plus 6 credits of prerequisites. Competence in a language other than English is required for native speakers of English; English meets the requirement for nonnative speakers. A comprehensive examination is required. Practice teaching is optional. A thesis is not required.

Courses Offered: (*required) *Structure of English; *English Phonology; *English Dialects; *Advanced English Syntax; *Advanced English Phonology; *Seminar in Applied English Linguistics; Studies in Interlanguage; ESL: Principles of Language Learning; ESL: Theory and Practice; ESL: Techniques and Materials; Discours Analysis; Research in ESL.

Full-Time Staff: Marian Bean, Deborah Brandt, Cecilia Ford, Martin Nystrand, Charles T. Scott (director), Richard Young, Jane Zuengler.

Requirements for Admission: The university's requirement for admission is the recommendation of the English Department, which is based on the undergraduate record, GRE score, letters of recommendation, a statement of purpose, and TOEFL scores (for nonnative speakers of English). Preference is given to applicants with strong undergraduate preparation in English, linguistics, or a foreign language. Completion of at least 4 semesters of a foreign language and a minimum grade of B in introductory courses in English syntax and English phonology are also required.

Tuition, Fees, and Aid: For in-state students, $2,346 per semester; for out-of-state students, $7,198 per semester. Teaching assistantships in the ESL Program, a very limited number of highly competitive, entry-level fellowships, and some support for dissertation research are available.

General: The program allows students to prepare for academic careers as teacher/ researchers in departments of English or applied linguistics. Students may concentrate their research interests in descriptive, historical, or applied areas. The current focus of much faculty research is in second language acquisition and discourse analysis. Students may have close links with the department's active and energetic Program in ESL. The university offers a wide variety of languages, including many of the less commonly taught languages of the world. A distributed minor in second language acquisition is available.

The university has an intensive English language program for nonnative speakers of English.

Summer Session: Yes

Further Information: Director
Programs in English Linguistics
Department of English
5134 Helen C. White Hall
University of Wisconsin—Madison
600 North Park Street
Madison, WI 53706

Telephone: (608) 263-3780
Fax: (608) 263-9305
E-mail: ctscott@facstaff.wisc.edu

◆ WISCONSIN, UNIVERSITY OF, MADISON, Department of English

Degree Offered: PhD in English (English language and linguistics).

Length of Program: 4–5 years. Students must take a full graduate course load (9–12 credits per semester; 6–9 credits for teaching assistants) until English course requirements have been met.

Program Requirements: At least seven graduate courses or seminars beyond the master's after background courses. Maintenance of a 3.5 GPA in English and a 3.25 GPA overall is required. Advanced competence in one foreign language and adequate competence in another are required; one language must be French, German, or Latin. Preliminary examinations are required in four of six areas, at least one of which is a core area (phonology and syntax; applied areas are discourse analysis, language variation, second language acquisition, and stylistics). A research seminar is required each fall semester until prelims have been passed. A dissertation is required.

Courses Offered: (*required) *background courses (if not completed at MA level): History of the English Language, English Dialects, Advanced English Phonology, Advanced English Syntax; *Structure of English; *minor of four courses (12 credits) in another department or in several departments. For courses, see program description for MA in English (applied English linguistics).

Full-Time Staff: Marian Bean, Donald Becker, Deborah Brandt, Robin Chapman, Thomas Cravens, Cecilia Ford, James Gee, Morton Gernsbacher, Raymond Harris, Robert Howell, Ya-fei Li, Marlys Macken, Kim Nilsson, Martin Nystrand, Ellen Rafferty, Charles Reed, Benjamin Rifkin, Joseph Salmons, Charles T. Scott (director), Andrew Sihler, Dennis Stampe, J. Randolf Valentine, Manindra Verma, Richard Young, Jane Zuengler.

Requirements for Admission: The university's requirement for admission is an MA degree from an Anglophone university in applied English linguistics or a related field.

Tuition, Fees, and Aid: For in-state students, $2,346 per semester; for out-of-state students, $7,198 per semester. Occasionally, limited-term teaching assistantships in the ESL Program are available for the first semester.

General: Students who have completed all the requirements for the MA except the final comprehensive examination normally have the opportunity to hold a salaried teaching assistantship in the English Language Institute offered each summer in the 8-week session. This experience under the mentorship of experienced ESL teachers provides an important counterbalance to the academic character of the program, which concentrates more on theoretical matters than on pedagogical ones. The program features a strong research orientation in second language acquisition studies and in discourse analysis.

Thirty-one students completed the program in 1996–1997.

The university has an intensive English language program for nonnative speakers of English.

Summer Session: Yes

Further Information: Director
Programs in English Linguistics
Department of English
5134 Helen C. White Hall
University of Wisconsin—Madison
600 North Park Street
Madison, WI 53706

Telephone: (608) 263-3780
Fax: (608) 263-9305
E-mail: ctscott@facstaff.wisc.edu

◆ WISCONSIN, UNIVERSITY OF, MILWAUKEE, Department of English

Degree Offered: MA in English with a concentration in English language and linguistics.

Length of Program: 3–5 years. Students may be full-time or part-time and may begin their study at the beginning of any semester. Application deadlines are fall semester, March 1; spring semester, October 1.

Program Requirements: 24–27 semester hours. Competence in a language other than English is not required. Practice teaching or a thesis is required. A comprehensive examination is not required.

Courses Offered: (*required) *Fundamentals of Linguistic Analysis; *Syntax; Practicum in University-Level ESL; Contrastive Analysis; ESL Composition; Historical/Comparative Linguistics; Language Typology and Language Universals; General Phonetics and Phonetics Practicum; Introduction to Linguistics; Introduction to English Linguistics; Phonology; Language and Society; Sociolinguistics; Language

Variation in English; Advanced Syntax; Advanced Phonology; History of the English Language; Semantics; Seminar in Linguistics; Discourse Analysis; Seminar in English Language; Survey of Modern English Grammar; Research Methods in Linguistics and ESL; Theory of Second Language Acquisition; Linguistics in Education; Linguistics and Grammar in ESL Education; Functional Syntax; Semantics and Pragmatics; Postsecondary Composition; Issues in Composition Studies; Research and Methodology in Rhetoric and Composition; Advanced English Grammar.

Full-Time Staff: Mary Louise Buley-Meissner, Pamela Downing (coordinator), Fred Eckman, Alice Gillam, Patricia Goldstein, Diane Highland, Gregory Iverson, Jean Mileham, Edith Moravesik, Michael Noonan, Rita Rutkowski-Weber, Peter Sands, Jessica Wirth.

Requirements for Admission: The university's requirements for admission are a bachelor's degree from an approved institution and a GPA of 2.5 or higher. Nonnative speakers of English must have a minimum TOEFL score of 550. The program requires three letters of recommendation, a statement of purpose, a GRE score, and transcripts.

Tuition, Fees, and Aid: For in-state students, $2,882 per semester; for out-of-state students, $7,718 per semester. Teaching assistantships, project assistantships, and fellowships are available.

General: Students may opt for either a master's thesis or a 3-credit teaching practicum. Subspecializations in linguistics, second language acquisition, and composition in a second language setting (CSLS) are available. The CSLS option is a unique course of study offered in conjunction with the Composition and Rhetoric Program. It provides instruction in the theory of second language acquisition and the theory and practice of teaching composition.

The program is in the process of developing international sites for the practicum. Three students completed the program in 1996–1997.

The university has an intensive English language program for nonnative speakers of English.

Summer Session: Yes

Further Information: Pamela Downing
Department of English
University of Wisconsin—Milwaukee
PO Box 413
Milwaukee, WI 53201

Telephone: (414) 229-4511
Fax: (414) 229-2643
E-mail: downing@uwm.edu

◆ WISCONSIN, UNIVERSITY OF, MILWAUKEE, Department of English

Degree Offered: PhD in English with a concentration in English language and linguistics.

Length of Program: 3–5 years. Students may be full-time or part-time and may begin their study at the beginning of any semester. Application deadlines are fall semester, March 1; spring semester, October 1.

Program Requirements: 27 semester hours. Competence in a language other than English is required; English meets the requirement for nonnative speakers of

English. A thesis, a preliminary written examination, and an oral dissertation defense are required. Practice teaching is not required.

Courses Offered: See MA program description.

Full-Time Staff: See MA program description.

Requirements for Admission: The university's requirement for admission is a bachelor's degree from an approved institution with a GPA of 2.5 or higher. Nonnative speakers of English must have a minimum TOEFL score of 550. The program requires an MA in linguistics or TESOL, three letters of recommendation, a statement of purpose, a GRE score, and transcripts.

Tuition, Fees, and Aid: See MA program description.

General: Two students completed the program in 1996–1997.

The university has an intensive English language program for nonnative speakers of English.

Summer Session: Yes

Further Information: Pamela Downing
Department of English
University of Wisconsin—Milwaukee
PO Box 413
Milwaukee, WI 53201

Telephone: (414) 229-4511
Fax: (414) 229-2643
E-mail: downing@uwm.edu

◆ WRIGHT STATE UNIVERSITY, Department of English Language and Literatures

Degree Offered: K–12 validation in TESOL.

Length of Program: 3 quarters. Students may be full-time or part-time and may begin their study at the beginning of any quarter. Application deadlines are 1 month before the quarter begins.

Program Requirements: 31–32 quarter hours. Competence in a language other than English is required for native speakers of English; English meets the requirement for nonnative speakers of English. Practice teaching, the NTE, and a portfolio are required. A thesis is not required.

Courses Offered: (*required) *Introduction to Linguistics (prerequisite); *Theory of ESL; *TESOL Methods and Materials; *Grammatical Structures of English; *ESL in the K–12 Classroom; *Sociolinguistics; Practicum in Education: ESL.

Full-Time Staff: Norman Cary, Chris Hall, Henry S. Limouze (chair), Marguerite MacDonald (director).

Requirements for Admission: The university's requirement for admission is an accredited high school or GED diploma. The program requires one course in the teaching of reading. Nonnative speakers of English must score 600 or higher on the TOEFL, 5 or higher on the TWE, and 55 or higher on the TSE.

Tuition, Fees, and Aid: For in-state students, $115 per quarter hour ($1,236 for 11–18 quarter hours); for out-of-state students, $230 per quarter hour ($2,472 for 11–18 quarter hours). Teaching assistantships are available for students who take the TESOL validation as part of the MA in TESOL, composition and rhetoric, or literature.

General: The program features a strong concentration in the teaching of writing.

Qualifying students may teach English for a 6-month period at Okayama University in Japan. Numerous international opportunities are available through the university's Center for International Education.

Two students completed the program in 1996–1997.

Summer Session: Yes

Further Information: Director, Programs in TESOL
Department of English Language and Literatures
438 Millet Hall
Wright State University
Dayton, OH 45435

Telephone: (937) 775-3136
Fax: (937) 775-2707
E-mail: mmacdonald@desire.wright.edu

◆ WRIGHT STATE UNIVERSITY, Department of English Language and Literatures

Degree Offered: Certificate in TESOL.

Length of Program: 3 quarters. Students may be full-time or part-time and may begin their study at the beginning of any quarter. Application deadlines are 1 month before the quarter begins.

Program Requirements: 22 quarter hours. Competence in a language other than English is highly recommended. Practice teaching and a portfolio are required. Neither a thesis nor a comprehensive examination is required.

Courses Offered: (*required) *Introduction to Linguistics (prerequisite); *Theory of ESL; *TESOL Methods and Materials; *Grammatical Structures of English; *Sociolinguistics; *Practicum; *Studies in World Literature *or* History of the English Language *or* ESL in the K–12 Classroom.

Full-Time Staff: Norman Cary, Robert Correale, Chris Hall, Henry S. Limouze (chair), Marguerite MacDonald (director).

Requirements for Admission: The university's requirement for admission is an accredited high school or GED diploma. The program requires a grade of B or better in Introduction to Linguistics. Nonnative speakers of English must score 600 or higher on the TOEFL, 5 or higher on the TWE, and 55 or higher on the TSE.

Tuition, Fees, and Aid: For in-state students, $115 per quarter hour ($1,236 for 11–18 quarter hours); for out-of-state students, $230 per quarter hour ($2,472 for 11–18 quarter hours). Teaching assistantships are available for students who take the TESOL certificate as part of the MA in TESOL, composition and rhetoric, or literature.

General: The program features a strong concentration in the teaching of writing.

Five native English-speaking students completed the program in 1996–1997.

Summer Session: Yes

Further Information: Director, Programs in TESOL
Department of English Language and Literatures
438 Millet Hall
Wright State University
Dayton, OH 45435

Telephone: (937) 775-3136
Fax: (937) 775-2707
E-mail: mmacdonald@desire.wright.edu

◆ WRIGHT STATE UNIVERSITY, Department of English Language and Literatures

Degree Offered: MA in TESOL.

Length of Program: 5–7 quarters. Students may be full-time or part-time and may begin their study at the beginning of any quarter. Application deadlines are 1 month before the quarter begins.

Program Requirements: 52 quarter hours (56 with prerequisite). Competence in a language other than English is highly recommended. Practice teaching and a portfolio are required. Neither a comprehensive examination nor a thesis is required.

Courses Offered: (*required) *Introduction to Linguistics (prerequisite); *Methods and Materials of Research in Writing and Language; *Rhetoric; *Issues in ESL Reading and Writing; *seminar in writing or language; *Theory of ESL; *TESOL Methods and Materials; *Grammatical Structures of English; *Sociolinguistics; *Practicum; *one of the following: ESL in the K–12 Classroom, History of the English Language, Studies in World Literature, Issues in Speaking and Listening, independent study in TESOL-related topic.

Full-Time Staff: Richard Bullock, Norman Cary, Robert Correale, Chris Hall, Henry S. Limouze (chair), Marguerite MacDonald (director), Nancy Mack.

Requirements for Admission: The university's requirement for admission is a baccalaureate degree from an accredited college or university with an overall GPA of 3.0 or an overall GPA of 2.57 but 3.0 or better for the last 93 quarter hours or 60 semester hours. The program requires Introduction to Linguistics or the equivalent; 20 hours of appropriate upper-division courses in literature, writing, language, or linguistics (or the equivalent) with a GPA of 3.5; and a paper (five pages or longer) using secondary sources written on a topic in English or a related field. Nonnative speakers of English must score 600 or higher on the TOEFL, 5 or higher on the TWE, and 55 or higher on the TSE.

Tuition, Fees, and Aid: For in-state students, $148 per quarter hour ($1,563 for 11–18 hours), for out-of-state students, $263 per quarter hour ($3,228 for 11–18 hours). Teaching assistantships are available.

General: The program features a strong concentration in the teaching of writing and leads to an Ohio credential in TESOL.
   Four students completed the program in 1996–1997.

Summer Session: Yes

Further Information: Director, Programs in TESOL
   Department of English Language and Literatures
   438 Millet Hall
   Wright State University
   Dayton, OH 45435

   Telephone: (937) 775-3136
   Fax: (937) 775-2707
   E-mail: mmacdonald@desire.wright.edu

◆ YOUNGSTOWN STATE UNIVERSITY, Department of English

Degree Offered: BA in English with a concentration in TESOL.

Length of Program: 4 years. Students may be full-time or part-time and may begin their study at the beginning of any quarter. Application deadlines are fall quarter, August 15; winter quarter, November 15; spring quarter, February 15; summer quarter, May 15.

Program Requirements: 48 quarter hours for the major plus 12 for the program. Competence in a language other than English is not required. Neither practice teaching, nor a comprehensive examination, nor a thesis is required.

Courses Offered: (*required for TESOL concentration) *Principles of Linguistic Study; *Language and Culture; *Development of the English Language; *TESOL Methods; *English Grammar; *Language Acquisition; *Sociolinguistics; TESOL Practicum.

Full-Time Staff: Salvatore Attardo, Rebecca Barnhouse, Steven Brown (coordinator), Thomas McCracken, Gail Okawa.

Requirements for Admission: Admission to the program is open to all full- and part-time students.

Tuition, Fees, and Aid: For in-state students, $942 per quarter; for out-of-state students, $2,200 per quarter. Scholarships and loans are available.

General: Students concentrating in TESOL take all the required classes for English majors and achieve a well-rounded background in English studies as well as a strong background in TESOL.

The university's Center for International Studies acts as a clearinghouse for overseas exchange.

Three students completed the program in 1996–1997.

The university has an intensive English language program for nonnative speakers of English.

Summer Session: No

Further Information: Dr. Steven Brown
English Department
Youngstown State University
1 University Plaza
Youngstown, OH 44555

Telephone: (330) 742-1654
Fax: (330) 742-2304
E-mail: srbrown@cc.ysu.edu

◆ YOUNGSTOWN STATE UNIVERSITY, Department of English

Degree Offered: MA in English with a concentration in TESOL.

Length of Program: 2 years. Students may be full-time or part-time and may begin their study at the beginning of any quarter. Application deadlines are fall quarter, August 15; winter quarter, November 15; spring quarter, February 15; summer quarter, May 15.

Program Requirements: 48 quarter hours. Competence in a language other than English is not required. A portfolio is required. Neither practice teaching, nor a comprehensive examination, nor a thesis is required.

Courses Offered: (*required for TESOL concentration) *TESOL Methods; *Language Acquisition; *Sociolinguistics; *Advanced Linguistics; *English Grammar; *TESOL Practicum.

Full-Time Staff: See program description for BA with a concentration in TESOL.

Requirements for Admission: Admission to the graduate school is granted by the dean upon recommendation of the department in which the applicant wishes to do major work.

Tuition, Fees, and Aid: For in-state students, $86 per quarter credit; for out-of-state students, $182 per quarter credit. Assistantships are available.

General: MA students concentrating in TESOL have an opportunity to take a variety of English courses. The TESOL program has a special interest in composition studies and works closely with colleagues in first language composition studies.

The university's Center for International Studies acts as a clearinghouse for overseas exchange.

Four students completed the program in 1996–1997.

The university has an intensive English language program for nonnative speakers of English.

Summer Session: No

Further Information: Dr. Steven Brown
English Department
Youngstown State University
1 University Plaza
Youngstown, OH 44555

Telephone: (330) 742-1654
Fax: (330) 742-2304
E-mail: srbrown@cc.ysu.edu

State Certification Requirements for Teaching English to Speakers of Other Languages

The information in this section was obtained from 51 state departments of education. Forty-six of the 50 states and the District of Columbia issue a credential in the field of TESOL.

Each state establishes its own teaching credentials, leading to differences in terminology and requirements. Some states license or certify individuals in TESOL as a primary teaching field; in other states, TESOL is an endorsement or validation added onto a teaching license or certification in another field, such as elementary or secondary education. Some states issue both types of credential.

The name in the first column is the person to whom a prospective teacher or interested person should write for further information. Specific requirements indicated on the questionnaires are given in the third column.

State and Contact	Credential in TESOL	Requirements and comments
Alabama Teacher Education and Certification Office State Department of Education PO Box 302101 Montgomery, AL 36130-2101 Telephone: (334) 242-9977 Fax: (334) 242-0498 E-mail: tcert@ sdenet.alsde.edu	Certification	The requirements are (a) eligibility for baccalaureate certification in a teaching field, (b) completion of an approved master's-level ESL program that includes one third course work in ESL, (c) a passing score on a norm-referenced test, and (d) completion of a 300-clock-hour internship.
Alaska Teacher Education and Certification Alaska Department of Education 801 West 10th Street, Suite 200 Juneau, AK 99801-1894 Telephone: (907) 465-2831 E-mail: certify@ educ.state.ak.us	Certification	The requirement is completion of an approved teacher education program at a regionally accredited institution whose teacher education standards meet or exceed national standards.
Arkansas Dr. André Guerrero Equity Assistance Center Arkansas Department of Education 4 State Capitol Mall, #405-B Little Rock, AR 72201	Add-on endorsement	The requirements are courses in methods of teaching second languages, second language acquisition, teaching people of other cultures, and second language assessment; and a minimum score of 642 on the NTE Core Battery, Professional Knowledge test.

State and Contact	Credential in TESOL	Requirements and comments
Arizona Certification Unit Arizona Department of Education PO Box 6490 Phoenix, AZ 85007 Telephone: (602) 542-4367	Endorsement	The ESL endorsement is an attachment to a teaching certificate. The requirements are (a) a valid Arizona elementary, secondary, or special education certificate and (b) a valid ESL certificate from another state; *or* (a) a valid Arizona elementary, secondary, or special education certificate, (b) completion of an approved program in ESL, or 21 hours of course work in selected areas and (c) a second language learning experience.
California Phillip A. Fitch, Executive Director Commission on Teacher Credentialing Information Services 1812 Ninth Street Sacramento, CA 95814-7000	Certificate	Individuals who successfully complete an approved CLAD emphasis preparation program at a college or university receive a multiple- or single-subject teaching credential with a CLAD emphasis. Teachers must (a) possess an appropriate California teaching credential or permit; (b) have experience learning a second language; and (c) pass Tests 1, 2, and 3 of the CLAD/ Bilingual CLAD Exams or complete 12 upper-division semester units of college course work in specified areas.
Colorado Educator Licensing Office of Professional Services Colorado Department of Education 201 East Colfax Avenue Denver, CO 80203 Telephone: (803) 866-6628	Licensure or endorsement	ESL may be issued as a primary license endorsement or added as a subsequent endorsement to an existing Colorado license or certificate. The requirements are completion of (a) a broad liberal arts preparation; (b) the state-approved program of professional education; (c) a prerequisite endorsement in early childhood, middle childhood education, early adolescence, or young adult education; and (d) an approved program in bilingual education or ESL.

State and Contact	Credential in TESOL	Requirements and comments
Connecticut Abigail Hughes, Chief Bureau of Certification and Teacher Preparation Connecticut Department of Education PO Box 2219 Hartford, CT 06145-2219 Telephone: (860) 566-5201	Certification and cross-endorsement	TESOL certification is issued for Grades pre-K–12 and adult education. The requirements include (a) a bachelor's degree from an approved institution with a minimum of 39 semester hours' credit in general education and either a major in TESOL or at least 39 semester hours of credit in TESOL, and (b) a minimum of 30 semester hours of credit in professional education in a planned program of study. To add TESOL as a cross-endorsement to a teaching certificate requires 30 semesters hours of credit in specific course work in TESOL.
Delaware Certification Office Delaware Department of Education Townsend Building PO Box 1402 Dover, DE 19903 Telephone: (302) 739-4688	Certification and endorsement	The requirements for standard ESOL K–12 certification are (a) a bachelor's degree from an accredited college; (b) completion of an approved teacher education program in ESOL or a minimum of 24 hours with specific distributions; and (c) a major in ESOL, or the completion of an approved teacher education program in ESOL, or completion of a program in English, a foreign language, or elementary education with specific course requirements, plus completion of the elementary level of a foreign language. In addition, an ESOL endorsement is required in Grades 9–12, in Grades 5–8 in departmentalized middle schools, and in adult education for those teaching primarily content area courses to classes primarily for students who are speakers of other languages.

State and Contact	Credential in TESOL	Requirements and comments
District of Columbia Yvonne D. Holt, Acting Director Teacher Education and Licensure Branch 215 G Street, NE Room 101A Washington, DC 20002 Telephone: (202) 724-4246 Fax: (202) 724-8784	Certification and endorsement	The requirements for certification in ESL (K–12) include (a) a bachelor's degree from an accredited institution, (b) completion of appropriate tests as mandated by the Board of Education, (c) 48 semester hours in a program of general or liberal education, (d) 18 semester hours in professional education requirements, (e) 30 semester hours of courses in ESL, and (f) competency in English and a language of specialty other than English. Endorsement in ESL (adult) requires (a) a valid teaching certificate in ESL and (b) 12 semester hours in adult education.
Florida Bureau of Teacher Certification Florida Department of Education 325 West Gainer Street Tallahassee, FL 32399-0400 Telephone: (850) 488-2317 E-mail: huggina@ mail.doe.state.fl.us	Certification and endorsement	Coverage in ESOL is a full certification area based on a degree major in ESOL allowing the individual to teach English or language arts to limited English proficient students. The requirement is a bachelor's degree or higher with a stated major in ESOL. The endorsement complements a full coverage, allowing the individual to teach a subject or subjects to limited English proficient students. Requirements are 15 semester hours of specific course work in ESOL.
Georgia Roan Garcia-Quintana, Director Title I Programs 1852 Twin Towers East Atlanta, GA 30334 Telephone: (404) 656-2436 E-mail: rgarcia@doek12.ga.us http://www.doe.k12.ga.us	Endorsement	An endorsement in ESOL may be added to all teaching certificates and to the service fields of school counselor and language pathologist. Fifteen quarter hours must be earned as follows: (a) 5 quarter hours in applied or contrastive linguistics or both, (b) 5 quarter hours in culture and society, and (c) 5 quarter hours in instructional methods and materials.

State and Contact	Credential in TESOL	Requirements and comments
Hawaii Clara Burrows Office of Personnel Services Department of Education PO Box 2360 Honolulu, HI 96804 Telephone: (808) 586-3476 Fax: (808) 586-3419 E-mail: clara_burrows/LILI/ HIDOE@notes.k12.hi.us	Certification	The requirements are (a) the completion of a state-approved teacher education program in TESOL and (b) NTE/Praxis Series tests PPST (W, R, M), PLT K–6 or K–12, and TESL 0360.

Idaho
Larry Norton
Certification
State Department of
  Education
PO Box 83720
Boise, ID 83720-0027
Telephone: (208) 332-6800
Fax: (208) 334-4664
E-mail:
  lnorton@sde.state.id.us
	Endorsement	ESL is an endorsement on an elementary or secondary certificate. The requirements are 20 credits to include a foreign language, ESL methods, and a course in cultural diversity.

Illinois
J. Reddy, Principal
  Consultant
Teacher Education and
  Certification
Illinois State Board of
  Education
100 North First Street
Springfield, IL 62777
Telephone: (217) 782-2805
Fax: (217) 524-1289
	Endorsement or certification	The requirements for an ESL endorsement include (a) an Illinois elementary, secondary, or early childhood teaching certificate; (b) 100 clock hours of ESL clinical experience; and (c) 18 semester hours of required courses. Teachers are certified in ESL only for the level of their teaching certificate. Teachers may apply for a K–12 certificate with 32 semester hours of ESL course work.

Indiana
Elizabeth Schurz, Director of
  Teacher Licensing
Indiana Professional
  Standards Board
Two Market Square Center
251 East Ohio Street
Indianapolis, IN 46204-2133
	Certification	ESL is not required on a license to teach ESL, but those who plan to teach ESL are strongly encouraged to complete the certification. Course work requirements for the ESL all-grade minor are (a) general linguistics and English linguistics, (b) psycholinguistics and sociolinguistics, (c) culture and society, (d) literature, (e) methods and materials, and (f) a practicum in an ESL setting.

State and Contact	Credential in TESOL	Requirements and comments

Iowa
Anne Kruse, Executive
  Director
Board of Educational
  Examiners
Grimes State Office Building
Des Moines, IA 50319-0147
Telephone: (515) 281-3611
	Endorsement	ESL teachers must meet the professional education core requirements common to all preparation programs. An ESL endorsement for Grades K–12 requires 24 semester hours of course work in ESL, including teaching ESL, applied linguistics, bilingual education, language in culture, the nature of language, and language acquisition.

Kansas
Susan Helbert, Certification
  Specialist
Certification Department
Kansas State Board of
  Education
120 SE 10th Avenue
Topeka, KS 66612-1182
Telephone: (913) 296-2289
	Endorsement	ESL is an added endorsement to a standard teaching certificate. It is available as a K–9, 7–12, or K–12 endorsement depending on the type of program completed. For full ESL certification, an applicant must hold or qualify for a standard Kansas teaching certificate, complete a state-approved ESL program, and submit an application and certification fee.

Kentucky Ronda Tamme Office of Teacher Education and Certification 1024 Capital Center Drive Frankfort, KY 40601 Telephone: (502) 573-1722	Endorsement	The requirements for ESL endorsement on K–12, 5–8, and 9–12 certificates include (a) 12 semester hours of additional course work in linguistics, applied linguistics, methods and materials, and understanding language; (b) 6 semester hours in a foreign language; and (c) proficiency in speaking English.

Louisiana
Rossana R. Boyd
Bilingual Education/ESOL
  Program
Division of Standards,
  Accountability, and
  Assistance
Louisiana Department of
  Education
PO Box 94064
Baton Rouge, LA 70804
Telephone: (504) 342-3454
Fax: (504) 342-0308
E-mail:
  rboyd@mail.doe.state.la.us
	Add-on certification	ESL is an add-on certification (12 semester hours) to a standard Louisiana teaching certificate. Teachers are required to take four courses: (a) Methods for Teaching ESL, (b) Introduction to Language and Culture, (c) The Structure of the English Language, and (d) Curriculum Design for the Multicultural Classroom.

State and Contact	Credential in TESOL	Requirements and comments
Maine Nancy Ibarguen Certification Office Maine Department of Education 23 State House Station Augusta, ME 04333-0023 Telephone: (207) 287-5944	Endorsement	The requirements include (a) a K–12, 7–12, or K–8 teaching certificate in another endorsement and (b) 3 credits each in ESL methods and materials, linguistics and language acquisition, culture studies, curriculum development, and assessment and testing.
Maryland Jill Bayce Division of Certification and Accreditation Maryland State Department of Education 200 West Baltimore Street Baltimore, MD 21201 Telephone: (410) 767-0344	Certification	The requirements include (a) a bachelor's degree from an accredited university; (b) course work in American English and linguistics (6 semester hours), foreign language (6 semester hours), cross-cultural studies (3 semester hours), and language learning (6 semester hours); and (c) course work in professional education, including foundations of education (6 semester hours), ESOL methodology (12 semester hours), student teaching (12 semester hours), and special education (3 semester hours).
Massachusetts Office of Certification Customer Service Center 350 Main Street PO Box 9120 Malden, MA 02148-9120 Telephone: (781) 388-3300 extension 665 Fax: (781) 388-3475	Certification	ESL certificates are issued for Grades pre-K–9, and 5–12. The requirements are (a) a demonstrated proficiency in reading, writing, and speaking American English at a level determined by the Board of Education; (b) 24 hours of course work in ESL; (c) the completion of a prepracticum consisting of 18 semester hours of course work and other experience related to effective teaching; and (d) the successful completion of a practicum made up of 150 clock hours of supervised teaching.

State and Contact	Credential in TESOL	Requirements and comments
Michigan Carolyn Logan, Director Office of Professional Preparation and Certification Michigan Department of Education 608 West Allegan, 3rd Floor Lansing, MI 48933 Telephone: (517) 373-3310	Endorsement	ESL is an endorsement added to either an elementary or a secondary certificate. The requirements are English language proficiency, experience learning a second language, and at least 20 hours in the following areas: linguistics, language acquisition, language and culture, pedagogy, and practicum.
Minnesota Judy McGilvrey, Licensing Specialist Personnel Licensing Capitol Square Building, No. 801 550 Cedar Street St. Paul, MN 55101 Telephone: (612) 296-2046 Fax: (612) 296-2403 E-mail: judy.mcgilvrey@ state.mn.us	Licensure	The requirements for a K–12 license include (a) a bachelor's degree, (b) 2 years of college-level or 4 years of high school–level study of a foreign language, and (c) completion of an approved ESL professional preparation program.
Mississippi Carolyn Alexander, Director Office of Education and Licensure Mississippi State Department of Education PO Box 771 Jackson, MS 39205 Telephone: (601) 359-3483	Endorsement	Holders of a standard teaching license may add ESL by completing 18 hours in the area or by completing a degree in the area.
Missouri John Miller, Director Teacher Certification Missouri Department of Elementary and Secondary Education PO Box 480 Jefferson City, MO 65102 Telephone: (573) 751-0051	Endorsement-only certificate	The requirements are (a) a valid Missouri elementary or secondary teaching certificate and (b) at least 21 semester hours in specific ESOL course work, including methods and materials, second language acquisition, linguistics, and a practicum.

State and Contact	Credential in TESOL	Requirements and comments
Montana Marilyn Roberts, Certification Specialist Office of Public Instruction PO Box 202501 Helena, MT 59620-2501 Telephone: (406) 444-3150 Fax: (406) 444-2843 E-mail: cert@opi.mt.gov	Certification	The requirements include (a) completion of an approved TESL program at a state- or regionally accredited college or university; (b) competence in English language, linguistics, and language and culture; (c) training in K–12 methods; (d) professional education course work; and (e) experience learning a second language.
Nebraska Robert W. Crosier, Director Teacher Education and Certification Nebraska Department of Education PO Box 94987 Lincoln, NE 68509 Telephone: (402) 471-2496	Endorsement	An ESL endorsement requires another endorsement as a prerequisite. The requirements are 1 year of another language or the equivalent and 3 undergraduate semester hours each in (a) English language and linguistics, (b) cross-cultural communication, (c) methods in ESL, and (d) a practicum in ESL.

Nevada
Branch of Teacher
Licensure
Nevada Department of
Education
1850 East Sahara, Suite
207—State Mailroom
Las Vegas, NV 89158
	Endorsement	A limited endorsement to teach ESL, K–12, requires (a) a valid elementary or secondary license and (b) completion of 6 semester hours of credit in methods and materials for TESL, theories of second language acquisition, testing and evaluation for ESL, and curriculum development for ESL.
		    An endorsement requires (a) above and 12 semester hours in the areas in (b).
		    A professional endorsement requires a master's degree, (a) above, 18 semester hours in the areas in (b), and 3 years of teaching experience.

State and Contact	Credential in TESOL	Requirements and comments
New Hampshire Richard Monteith Alexander Blastos Credentialing New Hampshire Department of Education State Office Park South 101 Pleasant Street Concord, NH 03301 Telephone: (603) 271-3874, 3871	Certification	The state prefers that teachers complete a regular course of study in ESL teaching methods, linguistics, and theory of language acquisition. Teachers with other certification may apply for alternative certification in ESL by writing a thesis enumerating their experience and relevant courses and participating in relevant professional development workshops. Such credentials are reviewed by a board.
New Jersey Ida B. Graham Director of Licensing and Credentials State Department of Education PO Box 500 Trenton, NJ 08625-0500 Telephone: (609) 292-2070 Fax: (609) 292-3768	Certification	ESL certification requires completion of a New Jersey college approved program. Applicants who complete out-of-state programs may submit their transcripts for review.
New Mexico Professional Licensure Unit New Mexico State Department of Education Education Building, Room 101 Santa Fe, NM 87503 Telephone: (505) 827-6587 Fax: (505) 827-6696	Endorsement	The requirements are possession of a New Mexico teaching license and 24 semester hours of credit in TESOL course work.

State and Contact	Credential in TESOL	Requirements and comments
New York Charles C. Mackey, Jr. Office of Teaching State Education Department Education Building, Room 5 North Albany, NY 12234 Telephone: (518) 474-3901	Certification	The requirements for a provisional ESL teaching certificate are either (a) completion of an approved program in TESOL, pre-K–12, and (b) a satisfactory level of performance in oral and written English on the state Teacher Certification Examinations; or (a) a baccalaureate degree, (b) 6 semester hours of college-level credit each in English, mathematics, science, and social studies, (c) 36 semester hours of college-level credit each in one of the liberal arts and sciences, (d) 15 semester hours in professional education, (e) 15 semester hours in TESOL, (e) 1 year of college-level study or the equivalent of a language and culture other than English, (f) college-supervised student teaching, (g) a satisfactory level of performance in oral and written English on the state Teacher Certification Examinations, and (h) 1 year of teaching experience.

North Carolina
Frances S. Hoch, Chiek
Second Languages, ESL,
  Information and Computer
  Skills
Department of Public
  Instruction
Education Building
301 North Wilmington Street
Raleigh, NC 27601-2825
Telephone: (919) 733-1797
Fax: (919) 715-2229
	Licensure	The field-based program allows the K–12 ESL licensure to be added to a North Carolina certificate in some other area. The requirement is completion of an approved competency-based program and the ESL Praxis.

State and Contact	Credential in TESOL	Requirements and comments
North Dakota Education Standards and Practice Board 600 East Boulevard Avenue Bismarck, ND 58505-0540 Telephone: (701) 328-2264	Endorsement	The requirement for a K–12 bilingual education or ESL endorsement for any certified teacher is 16 semester or 24 quarter hours of college course work in (a) foundations (4 semester or 6 quarter hours in multicultural education and bilingual education); (b) linguistics (6 semester or 9 quarter hours in linguistics, psycholinguistics, and sociolinguistics); (c) methods (2 semester or 3 quarter hours); (d) assessment (2 semester or 3 quarter hours); and (e) field experience (2 semester or 3 quarter hours).
Ohio Dr. Nancy Eberhart, Director Professional Development and Licensing 65 South Front Street, Room 1009 Columbus, OH 43239 Telephone: (614) 466-2761	Validation	Validation in ESL is attached to a teaching license. It requires the completion of a program at a college or university approved to offer this subject area.
Oklahoma Cindy Marose Director, Professional Studies 2500 North Lincoln Boulevard, #212 Oklahoma City, OK 73105-4599 Telephone: (405) 521-3337 Fax: (405) 522-1520	Special endorsement (optional)	A special endorsement must be attached to a major certificate area. The employing district makes the assignment based on expertise as determined by the local school board. The requirements are 24 semester hours selected from (a) linguistics and second language acquisition (6 semester hours minimum); (b) cultural history of the U.S. (6 semester hours minimum); (c) TESL, assessment and interpretation of language proficiency, and instruction of limited English proficient students (9 semester hours minimum); and (d) electives from the above categories or related areas.

State and Contact	Credential in TESOL	Requirements and comments
Oregon Janet Madland, Coordinator of Teacher Preparation Teacher Standards and Practices Commission Public Services Building 255 Capitol Street NE, Suite 105 Salem, OR 97310-1332 Telephone: (503) 378-3586	Optional endorsement	ESL is an elective endorsement in combination with a subject-area or special education endorsement. The endorsement will be required as of January 15, 2001. The requirements are (a) a teaching license and (b) 18 quarter hours in an approved ESL teacher education program.
Pennsylvania Don Lunday, Director Bureau of Teacher Preparation and Certification Pennsylvania Department of Education 333 Market Street Harrisburg, PA 17126-0333 Telephone: (717) 787-6376 Fax: (717) 787-3356 E-mail: ioocertifica@ psupen.psu.edu	None	A person who holds any Level I or Level II certificate and who possesses certification appropriate to the achievement of the planned course objectives may teach ESL and bilingual classes. The department also recommends that (a) the ESL teacher demonstrate the acquisition of the knowledge and skill to teach English as a foreign language, (b) the bilingual education teacher demonstrate fluency in both English and the language of the target population, and (c) all teachers possess an awareness and knowledge of the culture(s) of the target population.

State and Contact	Credential in TESOL	Requirements and comments

Rhode Island
Office of Teacher
  Certification and
  Professional Development
Rhode Island Department of
  Education
Shepard Building
255 Westminster Street
Providence, RI 02903
Telephone: (401) 277-4600
	Certification and endorsement	A provisional certificate as an ESL specialist in all grades requires (a) a bachelor's degree, (b) completion of an approved program for the preparation of ESL teachers *or* at least 6 semester hours of student teaching in ESL at both the elementary and secondary levels and at least 24 semester hours of course work in certain content areas, and (c) for applicants not previously certified, completion of the Core Battery of the NTE.
		  There are additional requirements for a life professional certificate. ESL endorsements for holders of elementary, early childhood, secondary English, and foreign language teaching certificates and for subject content teachers have separate course work and other requirements.

South Carolina
James H. Turner, Education
  Associate
Teacher Certification
State Department of
  Education
1429 Senate
Columbia, SC 29201
Telephone: (803) 734-8560
	None	

South Dakota
Lynda Sederstrom, Director
  of Teacher Education and
  Certification
Office of Policy and
  Accountability
South Dakota Department of
  Education and Cultural
  Affairs
700 Governors Drive
Pierre, SD 57501-2291
Telephone: (605) 773-4774
Fax: (605) 773-6139
	None	If adopted, a proposed endorsement in English as a new language would take effect January 1, 2000. The proposal calls for the requirement of 18 semester hours in linguistics, curriculum and instruction for new language acquisition, language and culture, program assessment, reading for limited English proficient students, and methodology.

State and Contact	Credential in TESOL	Requirements and comments

Tennessee
Sharon Evans
Office of Teacher Licensing
710 James Robertson
  Parkway
Nashville, TN 37243-0377
Telephone: (615) 741-1644
Fax: (615) 532-1448
E-mail: sevans@
  mail.state.tn.us
	Endorsement (licensure)	ESL is currently an add-on endorsement; however, as of September 1, 1999, there will be both initial licensure and add-on endorsement. The requirements for an add-on ESL endorsement, K–12, are (a) 6 semester hours in linguistics and English linguistics, (b) 8 semester hours in ESL pedagogy, (c) 4 semester hours in related studies, and (d) 2 semester hours in supervised ESL field experience. Initial licensure will require completion of studies in TESL course work, field experiences, and professional practice.

Texas Mary L. Charley State Board for Educator Certification 1001 Trinity Street Austin, TX 78701-2603 Telephone: (512) 469-3000 Fax: (512) 469-3018	Certification	The requirements are (a) a bachelor's degree; (b) a valid Texas teacher's certificate based on completion of an approved teacher education program; (c) 12 semester hours in language acquisition and development (psycholinguistics), methods of TESL, and descriptive/ contrastive linguistics; (d) evidence of a successful student teaching experience in an approved ESL program or 1 year of successful classroom teaching experience on a permit in an approved ESL or bilingual education program; and (e) ExCET requirement: ESL (12).

Utah
Diana Cortez
Bilingual/ESL Endorsement
  Program
Utah State Board of
  Education
250 East 500 South Street
Salt Lake City, UT 84111
	Endorsement	An ESL endorsement requires a basic or standard teaching certificate, fulfillment of competency requirements in English and in the strategies used in teaching second language learners, and completion of an approved program in teacher education.

State and Contact	Credential in TESOL	Requirements and comments
Vermont Licensing Office Vermont Department of Education 120 State Street Montpelier, VT 05620 Telephone: (802) 828-2445 Fax: (802) 828-3146	Endorsement	Candidates must demonstrate competencies in (a) linguistics and language acquisition; (b) linguistic and cultural diversity; (c) assessment; (d) methodology and curriculum development; and (e) program planning, consultation, and coordination.
Virginia Patty Pitts, Certification Specialist Virginia Department of Education PO Box 2120 Richmond, VA 23216-2120	Endorsement	ESL is an add-on endorsement to basic certification. Requirements are of course work in (a) the teaching of developmental reading (3 hours), (b) English linguistics (3 hours), (c) cross-cultural education (3 hours), (d) modern foreign language (6 hours), (e) electives (6 hours), and (f) methods for teaching ESL (3 hours).
Washington Professional Education and Certification Superintendent of Public Instruction PO Box 47200 Olympia, WA 98504-47200 Telephone: (206) 753-6773	Endorsement	A K–12 endorsement in ESL requires 24 hours of course work in (a) the structure of language or language acquisition, (b) culture and learning for the ESL student, (c) instructional methods in reading for the ESL student, (d) instructional methods in language arts for the ESL student, and (e) instructional methods in ESL.
West Virginia Amelia Davis Certification Building 6, Room B-337 Capitol Complex Charleston, WV 25305 Telephone: (304) 558-2691	None	

State and Contact	Credential in TESOL	Requirements and comments
Wisconsin Sue Harris, Consultant Teacher Licensing Wisconsin Department of Public Instruction PO Box 7841 Madison, WI 53707 Telephone: (608) 266-1027	Licensure	To obtain a license, teachers must complete a state-approved program. Requirements are (a) a bachelor's degree; (b) 34 semester hours in an approved TESOL major, or 22 semester hours in an approved TESOL minor if licensed based on a major in another area; and (c) a recommendation for teaching from the preparing institution.
Wyoming Linda Stowers, Director Professional Teaching Standards Board Hathaway Building, 2nd Floor 2300 Capitol Avenue Cheyenne, WY 82001 Telephone: (307) 777-6261	Endorsement	A K–12 endorsement may be obtained on completion of an ESL teacher preparation program meeting the standards set by the state.

U.S. Institutions With Doctoral Programs

Ball State University
University of California, Los Angeles
University of Cincinnati
University of Delaware
Florida State University
Georgetown University
University of Georgia
University of Hawai'i at Manoa
University of Houston
Illinois State University
Indiana University of Pennsylvania
University of Kansas
University of Maryland, College Park
University of Massachusetts at Amherst
State University of New York at Buffalo

New York University
Northern Arizona University
The Ohio State University
Oklahoma State University
University of Oregon
University of Pittsburgh
University of Puerto Rico
The University of South Carolina
Teachers' College, Columbia University
Temple University
University of Texas at Austin
United States International University
University of Wisconsin, Madison
University of Wisconsin, Milwaukee

U.S. Institutions With Master's Programs

Adelphi University
University of Alabama
The University of Alabama in Huntsville
American University
American University in Cairo
Universidad de las Américas—Puebla
The University of Arizona
Arizona State University
Azusa Pacific University
Ball State University
Biola University
Boston University
Bowling Green State University
Brigham Young University
University of California, Davis
University of California, Los Angeles
California State University,
    Dominguez Hills
California State University, Fresno
California State University, Fullerton
California State University, Hayward
California State University, Los Angeles
California State University, Northridge
California State University, Sacramento
Cardinal Stritch University
Carson-Newman College
Central Connecticut State University
Central Michigan University
Central Missouri State University
Central Washington University
University of Cincinnati
University of Colorado at Boulder
University of Colorado at Denver
Colorado State University
Columbia International University
University of Delaware

East Carolina University
Eastern College
Eastern Kentucky University
Eastern Mennonite University
Eastern Michigan University
Fairfield University
Fairleigh Dickinson University
The University of Findlay
Florida International University
Florida State University
Fordham University
Fresno Pacific University
Georgetown University
University of Georgia
Georgia State University
Gonzaga University
Grand Canyon University
University of Hawai'i at Manoa
Hofstra University
University of Houston
University of Houston—Clear Lake
Hunter College of the City University
    of New York
University of Idaho
University of Illinois at Chicago
University of Illinois at Urbana-
    Champaign
Illinois State University
Indiana State University
Indiana University
Indiana University of Pennsylvania
Inter American University of Puerto
    Rico, San Germán Campus
The University of Iowa
Iowa State University
Jersey City State College

University of Kansas
Long Island University,
   Brooklyn Campus
Manhattanville College
Mankato State University
University of Maryland,
   Baltimore County
University of Maryland, College Park
Marymount University
University of Massachusetts at Amherst
University of Massachusetts at Boston
University of Memphis
Meredith College
Michigan State University
University of Minnesota
The University of Montana
Montclair State University
Monterey Institute of
   International Studies
Mount Vernon College
Murray State University
National-Louis University
Nazareth College of Rochester
University of Nevada, Reno
University of New Hampshire
University of New Mexico
New Mexico State University
College of New Rochelle
State University of New York at Albany
State University of New York at Buffalo
State University of New York at
   Stony Brook
New York University
University of North Carolina at Charlotte
University of North Texas
Northeastern Illinois University
Northern Arizona University
Northern Illinois University
University of Northern Iowa
Notre Dame College
Nova Southeastern University
The Ohio State University
Ohio University
Oklahoma City University
Oklahoma State University
Old Dominion University
University of Oregon
Our Lady of the Lake University of
   San Antonio
University of Pennsylvania
The Pennsylvania State University
University of Pittsburgh
Portland State University

University of Puerto Rico
Queens College of the City University
   of New York
Radford University
Rhode Island College
University of Rochester
St. Cloud State University
Saint Michael's College
Sam Houston State University
University of San Francisco
San Francisco State University
San José State University
College of Santa Fe
School for International Training
Seattle University
Seattle Pacific University
Seton Hall University
Shenandoah University
Simmons College
Soka University of America
The University of South Carolina
University of South Florida
Southeast Missouri State University
Southern Illinois University at
   Carbondale
University of Southern Maine
University of Southern Mississippi
Syracuse University
Teachers' College, Columbia University
Temple University
University of Texas at Arlington
University of Texas at Austin
University of Texas at El Paso
University of Texas—Pan American
University of Texas at San Antonio
Texas Tech University
Texas Woman's University
University of Toledo
United States International University
University of Utah
University of Washington
Washington State University
West Chester University
West Virginia University
Western Kentucky University
Wheaton College
Wichita State University
William Paterson University
University of Wisconsin, Madison
University of Wisconsin, Milwaukee
Wright State University
Youngstown State University

U.S. Institutions With Graduate Certificate Programs

The University of Alabama in Huntsville
American University
The American University of Paris
Brigham Young University
University of California,
  Berkeley Extension
University of California, Santa Barbara
California Polytechnic State University
California State University,
  Dominguez Hills
California State University, Fullerton
California State University, Los Angeles
Central Missouri State University
University of Cincinnati
Clark University
Columbia University in the
  City of New York
Fairfield University
University of Florida
Fresno Pacific University
George Mason University
Georgetown University
Hamline University

Hawaii Pacific University
Indiana University
The University of Montana
Montclair State University
Monterey Institute of International
  Studies
Mount Vernon College
Portland State University
San Diego State University
San José State University
School of Teaching English as a
  Second Language
Shenandoah University
Sonoma State University
The University of South Carolina
University of Texas at Arlington
University of Utah
West Chester University
Wheaton College
Wichita State University
University of Wisconsin, Madison
Wright State University

U.S. Institutions With Undergraduate Programs

American University
Beloit College
Biola University
Brigham Young University—Hawaii
University of California, Riverside
California State University, Northridge
Carroll College
Central Connecticut State University
Central Washington University
Eastern Kentucky University
Eastern Mennonite University
Eastern Washington University
University of Florida
Florida Atlantic University
Florida International University
Goshen College
University of Hawai'i at Manoa
Hawaii Pacific University
Hobe Sound Bible College
Illinois State University
Indiana State University
University of Kansas
Mankato State University
University of Memphis

The University of Montana
Montclair State University
University of New Mexico
Northwestern College
Ohio University
Our Lady of the Lake University of
  San Antonio
University of the Pacific
Portland State University
Queens College of the City University
  of New York
St. Cloud State University
San Diego State University
San José State University
Shenandoah University
Southeast Missouri State University
United States International University
University of Utah
West Virginia University
Wichita State University
University of Wisconsin, Green Bay
University of Wisconsin, Madison
Wright State University
Youngstown State University

U.S. Institutions With TEFL Certificate Programs

University of California,
  Berkeley Extension
University of California,
  Irvine Extension
Hamline University

Saint Michael's College
  School of Teaching English as a
  Second Language
Shenandoah University
WICE/Rutgers University

U.S. Institutions With Programs Leading to a State Credential in TESOL

Adelphi University
The University of Alabama in Huntsville
American University
Azusa Pacific University
Ball State University
Beloit College
Boston University
Brigham Young University
University of California,
  Berkeley Extension
University of California, Los Angeles
Cardinal Stritch University
Carroll College
Carson-Newman College
Central Connecticut State University
Central Missouri State University
Central Washington University
University of Cincinnati
Clark University
University of Delaware
East Carolina University
Eastern Kentucky University
Eastern Mennonite University
Eastern Washington University
Fairfield University
Fairleigh Dickinson University
The University of Findlay
Florida Atlantic University
Florida International University
Florida State University
Fordham University
Fresno Pacific University
Goshen College
Grand Canyon University
Hamline University
Hobe Sound Bible College
Hofstra University
University of Houston
University of Houston—Clear Lake
Hunter College of the City
  University of New York
Illinois State University
Indiana State University
Inter American University of
  Puerto Rico—San Germán Campus

Iowa State University
Jersey City State College
Lamar University
Long Island University,
  Brooklyn Campus
Manhattanville College
Mankato State University
University of Maryland,
  Baltimore County
University of Maryland, College Park
Marymount University
University of Massachusetts at Amherst
University of Massachusetts at Boston
Meredith College
University of Minnesota
The University of Montana
Montclair State University
National-Louis University
Nazareth College of Rochester
University of Nevada, Reno
University of New Hampshire
University of New Mexico
College of New Rochelle
State University of New York at Albany
State University of New York at Buffalo
New York University
University of North Carolina at
  Charlotte
University of North Texas
Northeastern Illinois University
Northwestern College
Notre Dame College
Nova Southeastern University
Oklahoma State University
University of Oregon
Our Lady of the Lake University of
  San Antonio
University of the Pacific
Portland State University
University of Puget Sound
Queens College of the City University
  of New York
Radford University
Rhode Island College
University of Rochester

St. Cloud State University
Saint Michael's College
Sam Houston State University
College of Santa Fe
School for International Training
School of Teaching English as a
  Second Language
Seattle Pacific University
Seton Hall University
Shenandoah University
Simmons College
University of South Florida
Southeast Missouri State University

University of Southern Mississippi
University of Texas at San Antonio
Texas Woman's University
University of Toledo
United States International University
University of Utah
Washington State University
Western Kentucky University
Wheaton College
Wichita State University
William Paterson University
University of Wisconsin, Green Bay
Wright State University

PART 2

CANADA

Introduction

The Canadian programs in TESOL listed in the *Directory* include universities, which grant bachelor's degrees, graduate degrees, certificates, or diplomas; and community colleges and other autonomous schools, which offer certificate programs that train prospective teachers for local, noncredit ESL programs or for teaching English overseas. All the institutions described offer a designated program in TESOL rather than simply several courses that form part of another program.

In Canada, a teacher's certificate, which usually accompanies a bachelor of education degree, qualifies a teacher to work in the public school system; a diploma or graduate degree qualifies a teacher to work in some aspect of adult education or overseas or offer additional, specialized qualifications for practicing teachers.

In Ontario, TESL training most commonly takes the form of in-service courses, known as ESL Part I (dealing with pedagogical, linguistic, and cultural aspects of TESL), Part II (an in-depth continuation of Part I), and Part III (preparation for administrative and leadership positions in TESL). To register for these courses, a person must be employed as an officially certified teacher at an Ontario school.

In Quebec (and at some universities in other parts of Canada), teacher-training programs are incorporated within the bachelor's degree as part of a *baccalaureat d'enseignement* (B.Ens., or teaching baccalaureate). Prospective teachers who have an English degree and want to enroll in the equivalent of a bachelor of education program in Quebec should look for postbaccalaureate diploma or certificate programs. Most TESOL preparation programs in Quebec focus on training teachers of homogeneous francophone classes, and some courses are taught in French.

The structure of the school system in Quebec differs from that in other provinces. Children in Quebec attend 6 years of primary school and 5 years of secondary school followed by a program at a *collège d'enseignement général et professionnel* (CEGEP), which serves either as a bridge between high school and university or as a practical program for students who go directly into the work force after completion. After CEGEP, some students attend undergraduate university programs, which often last only 3 years.

U.S. readers should note that in Canada the word *college* does not carry the same meaning as the word *university*. Only universities have the power to grant degrees (and entitle someone to qualify for a government teaching permit). The term *college* either (a) refers to a subsection of a large university; (b) indicates a community college that tends to specialize in short-term, vocational, technical, or professional programs; or (c) is used in a general way to lend a school an air of distinction—at private boarding schools and CEGEPs but also in virtually all areas of education and training.

◆ ALGONQUIN COLLEGE, Continuing Education, Applied Arts and Technology

Degree Offered: Certificate in teaching English as a second/foreign language.

Length of Program: 2 semesters. Students may be full-time or part-time and may begin their study at the beginning of the fall or winter semester. Application deadlines are fall semester (full-time or part-time), March 1; winter semester (part-time), December 1.

Program Requirements: 9 credits. Competence in a language other than English is not required. Neither practice teaching, nor a thesis, nor a comprehensive examination is required.

Courses Offered: (*required) *An Introduction to Language; *Methodology in TESL/TEFL; *Language Learning and Culture; *Practicum I; *Practicum II; *Practicum III; *Adult Literacy and Beginner ESL; *Teaching Reading and Writing; *Pedagogical Grammar.

Full-Time Staff: Sophie Beare, Bernice Klassen (coordinators).

Requirements for Admission: The program's requirement for admission is an undergraduate degree or 3-year college diploma in a related discipline (e.g., education, sociology, English, linguistics, education). Nonnative speakers of English must submit a writing sample.

Tuition, Fees, and Aid: For Canadian students, $559.75 per semester; for non-Canadian students, $2,626.25 per semester. The Ontario Student Aid Program is available for Ontario residents.

General: The program focuses on practical training. Cross-cultural training is offered, and three courses are offered through distance education. The program leads to an Ontario credential in TESOL.

Forty students completed the program in 1996–1997.

Summer Session: No

Further Information: Sophie Beare or Bernice Klassen
TESL/TEFL Program
Room B442
1385 Woodroffe Avenue
Algonquin College
Nepean, ON K2G 1V8

Telephone: (613) 727-4723 extension 5743 or 5762
Fax: (613) 727-7757
E-mail: beares@algonquinc.on.can *or*
klassenb@algonquinc.on.can

◆ BROCK UNIVERSITY, Department of Applied Language Studies

Degree Offered: BA (honours) with a specialization in TESL.

Length of Program: 4 years. Students may be full-time or part-time and must begin their study at the beginning of the fall semester. The application deadline is June 1.

Program Requirements: 20 full courses. Competence in a foreign language is required. Practice teaching, a comprehensive examination, and a thesis are optional.

Courses Offered: (*required) *Introduction to Linguistics; *Phonetics; *Phonology; *Morphology; *Syntax; *Semantics; *Theories of Language Learning and Teaching;

*Methods; *Testing; *Curriculum Design; additional methodology and other optional courses.

Full-Time Staff: G. H. Irons, C. Luo, H. M. McGarrell, D. Patrick, M. Sanchez, J. N. Sivell, R. Welland.

Requirements for Admission: The university's requirement for admission is 6 Ontario academic credits. International students must submit high school transcripts to the registrar for equivalence assessment. The program requires demonstrated fluency in English.

Tuition, Fees, and Aid: Canadian students, $685 per full course; non-Canadian students, $1,885 per full course. Seminar assistantships are available for qualified students in Years 3 and 4.

General: The program, which began in 1997, is flexible and features small classes held on a beautiful campus in a convenient location.

The university offers a number of exchange programs in Asia, Europe, Australia, and the United States. Additional programs are pending.

The university has an intensive English language program for nonnative speakers of English.

Summer Session: No

Further Information: Chair
Department of Applied Language Studies
Brock University
St. Catharines, ON L2S 3A1

Telephone: (905) 688-5550 extension 3374
Fax: (905) 688-1912
E-mail: lvolterm@spartan.ac.BrockU.ca

◆ BROCK UNIVERSITY, Department of Applied Language Studies

Degree Offered: MEd (TESL).

Length of Program: 12–15 months. Students must be full-time until they complete their course work and must begin their study at the beginning of the fall semester. The application deadline is April 15.

Program Requirements: 9–10 half courses. Competence in a foreign language is optional. Practice teaching and a comprehensive examination are optional. A thesis or a project is required.

Courses Offered: (*required) *Foundation Course in Education; *Pedagogical Grammar; *Critical Developments in Second Language Reading; *Theory and Practice in Second Language Writing; *Speech Processing in a Second Language; *Project or Thesis Proposal; *Introduction to Educational Research Methods; electives.

Full-Time Staff: G. H. Irons, C. Luo, H. M. McGarrell, J. N. Sivell.

Requirements for Admission: The university's requirements for admission are undergraduate transcripts; a background in linguistics, TESL, education, or a similar, related area; and ESL teaching experience.

Tuition, Fees, and Aid: Canadian students, $472 per half-credit; non-Canadian students, $1,700 per half-credit. Research and teaching assistantships and entrance scholarships are available for qualified candidates.

General: The program, which began in 1997, is flexible and features small classes held on a beautiful campus in a convenient location. Students' programs are individualized.

The university has an intensive English language program for nonnative speakers of English.

Summer Session: Yes

Further Information: Assistant Registrar
Graduate Studies
Brock University
St. Catharines, ON L2S 3A1

Telephone: (905) 688-5550 extension 4467
Fax: (905) 688-5488
E-mail: graduate@spartan.ac.BrockU.ca

◆ CARLETON UNIVERSITY, Department of Linguistics and Applied Language Studies

Degree Offered: Certificate in TESL.

Length of Program: 2 semesters. Students may be full-time or part-time and may begin their study at the beginning of any semester. The application deadline for the fall semester is June 1.

Program Requirements: 5 Carleton credits (1 credit equals approximately 6 hours at a U.S. university; most courses are 3-credit half-courses). Competence in a language other than English is not required. Practice teaching is required. Neither a thesis nor a comprehensive examination is required.

Courses Offered: (*required) *Introduction to Linguistics; *TESL Methodology; *TESL Practicum; *Second Language Acquisition; *Major Structures of English; Phonetics; Language Analysis; Writing: Theory and Practice; Sociolinguistics; Gender and Language; Bilingualism; Psycholinguistics; Adult Literacy; Discourse Analysis; Language Testing; ESL Literacy; Selected Topics in Applied Linguistics.

Full-Time Staff: Ellen Cray, Patricia Currie, Richard Darville, Aviva Freedman, Stan Jones, Ann Laubstein, Peter Medway, Ian Pringle (director), Hans-George Ruprecht, Jaromira Rakusan, Devon Woods, Lynne Young, Helmut Zobl.

Requirements for Admission: The requirements for admission are an honours BA degree in a related field with high honours standing.

Tuition, Fees, and Aid: For Canadian students, $3,527 per two terms; for non-Canadian students, $9,157 per two terms. Some scholarships and graduate assistantships are available.

General: The certificate program concentrates on teaching English to adults, particularly in the Canadian context. Inside Canada, it is recognized extensively as a qualification for teaching at the postsecondary level, in private language schools, colleges, and universities. Students may complete the BA honours in linguistics and applied language studies and the certificate simultaneously, as certificate courses count toward the honours BA.

Summer Session: Yes

Further Information: Professor Lynne Young, Assistant Director
School of Linguistics and Applied Language Studies
Room 249 Paterson Hall
Carleton University
1125 Colonel By Drive
Ottawa, ON K1S 5B6

Telephone: (613) 788-2802
Fax: (613) 520-2642
E-mail: linguistics@carleton.ca
http://www.carleton.ca/slals

◆ CARLETON UNIVERSITY, Department of Linguistics and Applied Language Studies

Degree Offered: MA in applied language studies.

Length of Program: 3 semesters. Students may be full-time or part-time and may begin their study at the beginning of any semester. The application deadline for fall semester is July 1 (March 1 for teaching assistantships).

Program Requirements: 5 Carleton credits (1 credit equals approximately 6 hours at a U.S. university; most courses are 3-credit half-courses). Competence in a language other than English is not required. A thesis or research essay is required. Neither practice teaching nor a comprehensive examination is required.

Courses Offered: (*required) *Directions in Applied Language Studies; *Inquiry Strategies in Applied Language Studies; Language Classroom Research; Curriculum Design in ESL; Language in the Classroom; Issues in English Language Training/ Teaching; Written Language: Representation and Cognition; Language Testing; Evaluation in Applied Language Programs; Language Acquisition; Aspects of Language Development; Writing Research and Theory: Overview of Recent and Current Approaches; Second Language Writing: Research and Theory; Adult Literacy Acquisition; Linguistic Aspects of Canadian Bilingualism; Academic and Workplace Genres; Research in Adult Literacy; Writing Research and Theory: Social and Cultural Dimensions; Tutorial in Applied Language Studies; Special Topics in Applied Language Studies.

Full-Time Staff: See certificate program description.

Tuition, Fees, and Aid: For permanent residents of Canada, $1,865 per term; for others, $3,337 per term. Some graduate assistantships and scholarships are available.

General: The program focuses on language acquisition, development, and use, especially the acquisition of literacy and second languages, in a variety of contexts. The program is geared largely toward practitioners in the field, and courses are individualized according to career goals. Student may choose a concentration in ESL, the acquisition and development of writing abilities, or adult literacy.

Beginning in September 1998, students residing in Japan can follow the program at sites in Tokyo and Osaka, Japan.

Summer Session: Yes

School of Linguistics and Applied Language Studies
Room 249 Paterson Hall
Carleton University
1125 Colonel By Drive
Ottawa, ON K1S 5B6

Telephone: (613) 788-2802
Fax: (613) 520-2642
E-mail: linguistics@carleton.ca
http://www.carleton.ca/slals

◆ COLUMBIA COLLEGE, Department of English

Degree Offered: Certificate in English language teaching to adults (CELTA).

Length of Program: Students must be full-time.

Program Requirements: Competence in a language other than English is required; English meets the requirement for nonnative speakers of English. Practice teaching and a comprehensive examination are required. A thesis is not required.

Full-Time Staff: Elizabeth Gowland, James R. Janz (chair), Marie Morgan.

Requirements for Admission: The program requires a relevant BA or the equivalent.

Tuition, Fees, and Aid: $2,500 for the program.

General: The program leads to a British Columbia credential in TESOL.
Twelve students completed the program in 1996–1997.
The college has an intensive English language program for nonnative speakers of English.

Summer Session: Yes

Further Information: James R. Janz
Room 682
Columbia College
555 Seymour Street
Vancouver, BC V6A 3J3

Telephone: (604) 683-8360
Fax: (604) 682-7191
E-mail: jrjanz@columbiacollege.bc.ca

◆ CONCORDIA UNIVERSITY, TESL Centre

Degree Offered: BEd TESL.

Length of Program: 8 terms. Students may be full-time or part-time and may begin their study at the beginning of the fall or winter term. Application deadlines are fall term, July 1; winter term, November 1.

Program Requirements: 120 credits. Competence in English and French is required. Five ESL internships are required. Neither a comprehensive examination nor a thesis is required.

Courses Offered: (*required) *English Composition (Stage I); *English Composition (Stage II); *Canadian English literature elective; *Canadian or other English literature elective; *6 credits from advanced ESL, intermediate/advanced French, and other languages at any level; *The Inclusive Classroom: Educating Exceptional

Children; *Psychology of Learning; *Education in Quebec; *6 credits in education, adult education, and psychology; *Phonology for Teachers; *Modern English Grammar; *Grammar for Teachers; *Language Acquisition; *History of the English Language; Multicultural and Multilevel Classes; *Introduction to Teaching and Classroom Observation; *Pedagogy: General; *Microteaching; *Computers in Language Learning; *Testing, Evaluation, and Course Design; *Pedagogy: Primary; *Pedagogy: Secondary; *Internship: Primary I; *Internship: Secondary I; *Internship: Primary II; *Internship: Secondary II; *Internship Seminar; 6 credits of electives in TESL or linguistics.

Full-Time Staff: Palmer Acheson (chair), Nancy L. Brown, Elizabeth Gatbonton, Marlise Horst, Patsy M. Lightbown, Ronald Mackay, Gwendolyn S. Newsham, Lori Morris, V. Alex Sharma, Joanna L. White.

Requirements for Admission: The university's requirements for admission are satisfactory completion of Grade 13 or its equivalent, original transcripts, two reference letters, a biodata form, and a curriculum vitae.

Tuition, Fees, and Aid: For Quebec residents, $55.61 per credit; for Canadian, non-Quebec residents, $95.61 per credit; for non-Canadian residents, $275.61 per credit. Fees are $20 per term and $8.83 per credit. Financial aid is limited and generally unavailable to non-Canadian residents.

General: During 1998, the TESL Centre celebrated its 25th anniversary as the first academic unit of its kind in Canada. The university is located in the heart of a predominantly Francophone province, but there are many different cultural and linguistic minorities in Montreal, which many people consider to be the liveliest city in Canada. Extensive information is available regarding employment in TESL within Quebec, the rest of Canada, and abroad. The Centre hosts visiting professors from the United States, the United Kingdom, Cuba, Venezuela, and other countries. The program leads to a Quebec credential in TESOL.

Thirty-eight students completed the program in 1996–1997.

The university has an intensive English language program for nonnative speakers of English.

Summer Session: Yes

Further Information: Coordinator of the TESL BEd Program
TESL Centre
Concordia University
1455 de Maisonneuve Boulevard West
Montreal, QC H3G 1M8

Telephone: (514) 848-2449
Fax: (514) 848-4295
E-mail: barclay@alcor.concordia.ca
http://artsci-ccwin.concordia.ca/tesl/tesl.html

◆ CONCORDIA UNIVERSITY, TESL Centre

Degree Offered: Certificate in TESL.

Length of Program: 2 terms. Students may be full-time or part-time and may begin their study at the beginning of the fall or winter term. Application deadlines are fall term, July 1; winter term, November 1.

Program Requirements: 30 credits. Competence in English is required; competence in French is optional but preferred. Practice teaching is required. Neither a thesis nor a comprehensive exam is required.

Courses Offered: (*required) *Phonology for Teachers; *Modern English Grammar; *Grammar for Teachers; *Language Acquisition; *Methodology I; *Methodology II; *Testing, Evaluation, and Course Design; *Practicum; *English Composition (Stage I); *English Composition (Stage II).

Full-Time Staff: See BEd (TESL) program description.

Requirements for Admission: The university's requirements for admission are satisfactory completion of an undergraduate degree from a recognized college or university and original transcripts from all institutions attended. The program requires applicants to be trained teachers (of any subject) or to be able to document at least 400 hours of second language teaching, to supply two reference letters and a curriculum vitae, and to take a test of written and spoken English.

Tuition, Fees, and Aid: See BEd (TESL) program description.

General: See BEd (TESL) program description.
   Sixty students completed the program in 1996–1997.
   The university has an intensive English language program for nonnative speakers of English.

Summer Session: Yes

Further Information: Coordinator of the TESL Certificate Program
TESL Centre
Concordia University
1455 de Maisonneuve Boulevard West
Montreal, Quebec H3G 1M8

Telephone: (514) 848-2449
Fax: (514) 848-4295
E-mail: barclay@alcor.concordia.ca
http://artsci-ccwin.concordia.ca/tesl/tesl.html

◆ CONCORDIA UNIVERSITY, TESL Centre

Degree Offered: MA in applied linguistics.

Length of Program: 1½ years. Students may be full-time or part-time and may begin their study at the beginning of any semester. Application deadlines are fall semester, June 1; winter semester, November 1; summer semester, May 1. The deadlines are flexible.

Program Requirements: 45 credits. Competence in a foreign language is required. Practice teaching and a comprehensive examination are required. A thesis is optional.

Courses Offered: (*required) *Grammars of English; *Research Methods; *Language Development; *Bilingualism; *Methodology; *Research Paper; Syllabus Design; Testing and Evaluation; Supervision of Student Teachers; Program Evaluation; Pragmatics; ESL Administration.

Full-Time Staff: Palmer Acheson (chair), Nancy Brown, Elizabeth Gatbonton, Marlise Horst, Patsy M. Lightbown, Ronald Mackay, Alex Sharma, Joanna White.

Requirements for Admission: The university's requirements for admission are a bachelor's degree, three letters of recommendation, and a statement of purpose. International students must have a TOEFL score of 600 or above. The program requires full-year courses in English grammar, language teaching methods, and linguistics and half-year courses in phonetics/phonology and language acquisition. Preference is given to students with teaching experience.

Tuition, Fees, and Aid: For Quebec students, $1,500 (Canadian) per year; for other Canadian students, $2,500 per year; for out-of-country students, $U.S.5,000 per year. ESL teaching positions, research assistantships, and competitive university fellowships are available.

General: This program mainly serves experienced teachers. It is an advanced professional development program, not a teacher-training course.

Ten students completed the program in 1996–1997.

Summer Session: Yes

Further Information: Graduate Program Coordinator
TESL Centre
Concordia University, EN
1455 de Maisonneuve Boulevard, West
Montreal, QC H3G 1M8

Telephone: (514) 848-2445
Fax: (514) 848-4295
E-mail: parkins@vax2.concordia.ca;
lightbn@vax2.concordia.ca

◆ MANITOBA, UNIVERSITY OF, Department of Curriculum: Humanities and Social Sciences

Degree Offered: MEd (TESL).

Length of Program: 2 semesters. Students may be full-time or part-time and must begin their study at the beginning of the fall semester. Application deadlines are March 1 (Canadian students) and November 16 (non-Canadian students).

Program Requirements: 21 credits with thesis; 33 credits with a comprehensive examination. Competence in a language other than English is optional. Practice teaching, a thesis, and a comprehensive examination are optional.

Courses Offered: (*required) *Applied Linguistics; *Fundamentals of ESL Instruction; *Grammar in ESL Learning and Instruction; *Seminar in ESL Theory and Practice; *Introduction to Educational Research; *Research Issues and Application in TESL; *Perspectives in Curriculum; *Curriculum Theory and Design; *Inquiry in Curriculum and Instruction; *Master's Thesis or Master's Comprehensive Examination; ESL Materials Development and Practicum; TESL Pronunciation; TESL Vocabulary; TESL Literacy; Computers in TESL; Second Language Acquisition; Cross-Cultural Education; Adult Education.

Full-Time Staff: Patrick G. Mathews, Roy Graham, Paul Madak, Sheldon Rosenstock.

Requirements for Admission: The program's requirements for admission are a 4-year BEd or other degree with a minimum B average in the last 60 credits, 2 years of successful teaching experience, and English proficiency. Nonnative speakers of English must have a TOEFL score of at least 550.

Tuition, Fees, and Aid: For Canadian students, $3,722 for the program; for non-Canadian students, $4,134 for the program. A very limited number of fellowships are available.

General: Areas of focus from which to choose are K–12 ESL (early, middle, senior years), adult ESL (settlement, literacy, English for specific purposes), and international English (TEFL).

Seven students completed the program in 1996–1997.

The university has an intensive English language program for nonnative speakers of English.

Summer Session: Yes

Further Information: Dr. Patrick G. Mathews
Department of Curriculum: Humanities and
   Social Sciences
287 Education Building
University of Manitoba
Winnipeg, MB R3T 2N2

Telephone: (204) 474-9042
Fax: (204) 474-7550
E-mail: pmathews@ms.umanitoba.ca

◆ McGILL UNIVERSITY, Faculty of Education, Department of Second Language Education

Degree Offered: BEd (TESL).

Length of Program: Students must be full-time and must begin their study at the beginning of the fall semester. Application deadlines are January 15 for students outside Canada, February 1 for students from Canadian high schools outside Quebec, March 1 for CEGEP students in Quebec, and May 1 for exchange students.

Program Requirements: 120 credits. Competence in English is required. Practice teaching is required. A thesis and a comprehensive examination are optional.

Courses Offered: Introduction to Linguistics; Linguistic Aspects of Bilingualism; Survey of English Literature; Literature for Young Adults; Foundations of Second Language Education; Sociolinguistics and Second Language Education; Second Language Learning in Classroom Settings; Policy Issues in Quebec Education; Educational Psychology; Philosophical Foundations of Education; TESL in Elementary Schools; TESL in Secondary Schools; Measurement and Evaluation in TESL; Language Study for ESL Teachers; Computer/Internet and Second Language Learning; Exceptional Students; Literacy Development; First-, Second-, Third-, and Fourth-Year Professional Seminars; First-, Second-, Third-, and Fourth-Year Field Experience.

Full-Time Staff: Janet Donin, Roy Lyster, Mary Maguire (chair), Nina Spada, Carolyn Turner, Lise Winer.

Requirements for Admission: The program's requirements for admission are a diploma of college studies in any program and a GPA of 2.8. The program requires a score on the English proficiency examination of 80%.

Tuition, Fees, and Aid: For Quebec students, $2,439.03 per year; for Canadian students from outside Quebec, $3,639.03 per year; for international students, $8,471.41 per year. Entrance fellowships are available.

General: The program prepares students well to teach ESL at both the primary and the secondary levels.
   Fifty students completed the program in 1996–1997.
   The university has an intensive English language program for nonnative speakers of English.

Summer Session: No

Further Information: Joyce Gaul
Department of Second Language Education
Education 431A8
McGill University
3700 McTavish Street
Montreal, QC H3A 1Y2

Telephone: (514) 398-6982
Fax: (514) 398-5595
E-mail: gaul@education.mcgill.ca

◆ McGILL UNIVERSITY, Department of Second Language Education

Degree Offered: Certificate in TESL.

Length of Program: 3 semesters. Students may be full-time or part-time and may begin their study at the beginning of the September, January, or July term. Application deadlines are fall term, June 1; winter term, October 1; spring-summer term, February 1.

Program Requirements: 30 credits. Competence in a language other than English is not required. Practice teaching is required. Neither a thesis nor a comprehensive examination is required.

Courses Offered: (*required) *TESL: Elementary School; *ESL Pedagogy; *Practicum in Second Language Teaching I; *Practicum in Second Language Teaching II; *Language Study for Teachers of ESL; *one academic course in language, linguistics, or literature; four elective courses.

Full-Time Staff: Mary Maguire (chair), Roy Lyster.

Requirements for Admission: The program's requirements for admission are a teaching permit and completion of the English Language Proficiency Exam.

Tuition, Fees, and Aid: For Quebec students, $195.33 per course ($1,953.30 for the program); for Canadian students from outside Quebec, $320.33 per course ($3,203.30 for the program).

General: Twenty students completed the program in 1996–1997.

The university has an intensive English language program for nonnative speakers of English.

Summer Session: Yes

Further Information: T. Habib, Student Affairs Assistant
Certificate Program
Department of Second Language Education
Education Building
McGill University
3700 McTavish Street
Montreal, QC H3A 1Y2

Telephone: (514) 398-6985
Fax: (514) 398-5595
E-mail: Habib@Education.McGill.ca

◆ ONTARIO INSTITUTE FOR STUDIES IN EDUCATION OF THE UNIVERSITY OF TORONTO, Department of Curriculum, Teaching, and Learning

Degrees Offered: MA and MEd in second language education.

Length of Program: MA, 4 semesters; MEd, 3 semesters. Students may be full-time or part-time and must begin their study at the beginning of the autumn semester. The application deadline is January 15, though later applications are considered.

Program Requirements: 8 half-courses. Competence in a language other than English is not required. For the MA, a thesis is required; for the MEd, a research project is required. Neither practice teaching nor a comprehensive examination is required.

Courses Offered: (*required) *(MEd) Foundations of Bilingual and Multicultural Education; *(MA) Research Colloquium in Second Language Education; Methodology and Organization of Second Language Teaching; Theory of Second Language Teaching; Language Awareness and its Role in Teacher Development; Current Issues in ESL; Descriptive and Educational Linguistics of English; Seminar in Language and Communication; Critical Pedagogy, Language, and Minority Students; Education for Linguistic and Cultural Minorities; Second Language Learning; Bilingual Education and Bilingualism; Communicative Competence; Second Language Assessment; Collaborative Learning in Second Language Classrooms; Seminar in Second Language Literacy Education; Minority Groups and Cultural Determinants of the Curriculum; Reading in a Second Language; Language Planning and Policy; Research Themes in Canadian French as a Second Language Education; Writing in a Second Language; Pedagogical Grammar of French; Languages in Aboriginal Education; The French Canadian From Educational and Sociolinguistic Viewpoints; Individual Reading and Research; Second Language Classroom Research; Research Seminar in Multilingual/Multicultural Education; Ethnographic Research in the Language Disciplines; Advanced Colloquium in Educational Linguistics of English; Aspects of Second Language Acquisition; Language, Culture, and Education; Diversity and the Ethics of School Administration; Language Policy Across the Curriculum.

Full-Time Staff: Patrick Allen, Barbara Burnaby, Stacy Churchill, David Corson, Alister Cumming (head), Jim Cummins, Antoinette Gagne, Esther Geva, Monica Heller, Normand Labrie, Sharon Lapkin, Birgit Harley, Merrill Swain, Miles Turnbull.

Requirements for Admission: The university's requirements for admission are a 3- or 4-year bachelor's degree with mid-B or better standing in the final year from a recognized university (equivalent to a University of Toronto degree). Students from outside of Canada whose mother tongue or first language is not English must have a TOEFL score of at least 580 (with a TWE score of 5), an IELTS score of at least 7, or a MELAB score of at least 85. The program requires at least 1 year of teaching or other relevant professional experience.

Tuition, Fees, and Aid: For Canadian students, $3,700 per year for the MA; $4,580 per year for the MEd; for non-Canadian students, $7,500 per year for the MA; $11,000 per year for the MEd. Scholarships, research assistantships, and bursaries from the university, province, federal government, and other agencies are available on a limited basis.

General: The graduate program is the largest and most extensive in Canada. It focuses on curriculum, instruction, learning, and policy for education in second, foreign, and minority languages, particularly in reference to English and French in Canada but also other languages and settings. Areas of study include language learning, methodology, and organization of classroom instruction, language education policies and planning, and student and program evaluation as well as issues related to bilingualism, multilingualism, cultural diversity, and literacy.

Faculty conduct research internationally, and there are linkages with centers and universities in other parts of the world.

Seven students completed the MA and 21 students completed the MEd in 1996–1997.

The university has an intensive English language program for nonnative speakers of English.

Summer Session: Yes

Further Information: Registrar's Office, Graduate Studies
Ontario Institute for Studies in Education
of the University of Toronto
252 Bloor Street West
Toronto, ON M5S 1V6

Telephone: 1-800-785-3345; 416-923-6641, ext. 2663, 2664
Fax: 416-323-9964, 416-926-4725
E-mail: gradstudy@oise.utoronto.ca
http://www.oise.utoronto.ca/

◆ ONTARIO INSTITUTE FOR STUDIES IN EDUCATION OF THE UNIVERSITY OF TORONTO, Department of Curriculum, Teaching, and Learning

Degrees Offered: PhD and EdD in second language education.

Length of Program: 4 years. PhD students must be full-time for 2 years; EdD students must be full-time for 1 year. All students must begin their study at the beginning of the autumn semester. The application deadline is January 15, though later applications are considered.

Program Requirements: 6–8 half-courses. Competence in a language other than English is not required. A thesis and a comprehensive examination are required. Practice teaching is not required.

Courses Offered: (*required) *Research Colloquium in Second Language Education; Foundations of Bilingual and Multicultural Education; Methodology and Organization of Second Language Teaching; Theory of Second Language Teaching; Language Awareness and Its Role in Teacher Development; Current Issues in ESL; Descriptive and Educational Linguistics of English; Seminar in Language and Communication; Critical Pedagogy, Language, and Minority Students; Education for Linguistic and Cultural Minorities; Second Language Learning; Bilingual Education and Bilingualism; Communicative Competence; Second Language Assessment; Collaborative Learning in Second Language Classrooms; Seminar in Second Language Literacy Education; Minority Groups and Cultural Determinants of the Curriculum; Reading in a Second Language; Language Planning and Policy; Research Themes in Canadian French as a Second Language Education; Writing in a Second Language; Pedagogical Grammar of French; Languages in Aboriginal Education; The French Canadian From Educational and Sociolinguistic Viewpoints; Individual Reading and Research; Second Language Classroom Research; Research Seminar in Multilingual/Multicultural Education; Ethnographic Research in the Language Disciplines; Advanced Colloquium in Educational Linguistics of English; Aspects of Second Language Acquisition; Language, Culture, and Education; Diversity and the Ethics of School Administration; Language Policy Across the Curriculum.

Full-Time Staff: See MA/MEd program description.

Requirements for Admission: The university's requirements for admission are a master's degree with a thesis and B+ or better standing in courses from a recognized university (equivalent to a University of Toronto degree) and, for students from outside Canada whose mother tongue or first language is not English, a TOEFL score of at least 580 (with a TWE score of 5), an IELTS score of at least 7, or a MELAB score of at least 85. The program requires at least 2 years of teaching or other relevant professional experience.

Tuition, Fees, and Aid: For Canadian students, $3,700 per year for the PhD; $4,326 per year for the EdD. For non-Canadian students, $7,500 per year for the PhD; $11,000 per year for the EdD. Scholarships, research assistantships, and bursaries from the university, province, federal government, and other agencies are available on a limited basis.

General: See MA/MEd program description.

Eight students completed the PhD program and seven students completed the EdD program in 1996–1997.

The university has an intensive English language program for nonnative speakers of English.

Summer Session: Yes

Further Information: Registrar's Office, Graduate Studies
Ontario Institute for Studies in Education
of the University of Toronto
252 Bloor Street West
Toronto, ON M5S 1V6

Telephone: 1-800-785-3345; 416-923-6641, ext. 2663, 2664
Fax: 416-323-9964, 416-926-4725
E-mail: gradstudy@oise.utoronto.ca
http://www.oise.utoronto.ca/

◆ OTTAWA, UNIVERSITY OF, Faculty of Education

Degree Offered: MEd in second language teaching (English or French).

Length of Program: 10 courses. Students may be full-time or part-time.

Program Requirements: Practice teaching is optional. Neither a thesis nor a comprehensive examination is required.

Courses Offered: (*required) *Introduction to Research; *Synthesis Seminar; *five of the following: Sociocultural Factors in Second Language Teaching and Learning, Bilingual Education, Major Trends in Second Language Teaching, Second Language Program Development, Integrated Approaches for Teaching Oral Communication and Literacy, Language Issues in the Education of Minority Groups, Educational Implications of Language Assessment Practices, Teaching the Receptive Skills, Special Topics; three electives in linguistics, educational counseling, teaching and learning, and organizational studies.

Full-Time Staff: Johanne Bourdages, Pierre Calvé, Cécile Champagne-Muzar, Diana Masny, Ruth Taaffe, Larry Vandergrift, Claudette Cornaire, Sima T. Paribakht, Marjorie Wesche.

Requirements for Admission: The program's requirements for admission are a bachelor's degree and a teaching certificate. Students without a teaching certificate must take education prerequisites.

Tuition, Fees, and Aid: Canadian students, $1,595 per session (summer session, $797.50); international students, $2,900 per session (summer session, $1,450). A limited number of scholarships are available.

General: The unique bilingual university and national capital surroundings are reflected in the program, its professors, and its students. Courses are generally offered in English and French in alternate years. Individual programs may be undertaken at the Faculty of Education. A structured program proposal in language education (encompassing the teaching of French and English as first or second languages in varied settings) is expected to be approved shortly.

Further Information: Richard Chénier
Graduate Admissions
Faculty of Education
Lamoureux Hall, Room 109
University of Ottawa
Ottawa, ON K1N 6N5

Telephone: (613) 562-5800 (extension 4022)

◆ UNIVERSITÉ DU QUÉBEC À TROIS-RIVIÈRES, Département des langues modernes et traduction

Degree Offered: BA (ESL), enseignement des langues secondes—anglais et espagnol.

Length of Program: 4 years. Students must be full-time and must begin their study at the beginning of the fall term. The application deadline is March 1.

Program Requirements: 120 credits. Proficiency in French and English is required. Practice teaching and a comprehensive examination is required. A thesis is not required.

Courses Offered: (*required) *Advanced Grammar; *History of Language Teaching; *Oral Presentations; *Le système scolaire au Québec; *Espagnol intermédiare; *Stage I: Sensibilization; *Advanced Writing; *TESL Program and Practice: Elementary School Level; *Applied Phonetics; *Psychologie de l'enfant et de l'adolescent; *Espagnol intermédiare II; History of the English Language; *TESL Program and Practice: Secondary School Level; Young People's Literature; *Interventions pédagogiques adaptées; *Espagnol avancé; *Survey of English Literature; *Canadian and American Cultures; *Second Language Acquisition; *Gestion de la classe; *Stage II: Observation; *Version et thème espagnols; *Laboratoire d'interventions pédagogiques; *Nouvelles technologies et l'enseignement des langues; Stage III: Intervention en anglais; *Civilisation espagnole; *Lexicology; *Second Language Testing; *Didactique de l'espagnole; *Panorama de la littérature espagnole; *The Short Story; *Civilisation hispano-américaine; *Panorama de la littérature hispano-américaine; *Stage IV: Intervention en espagnol; *Internat en anglais au primaire ou au secondaire; *one of the following: Great Writers of the 20th Century, Communication administrative écrite en anglais, Anglais avancé en situation professionnelle; *L'apprentissage: Théories et implications pédagogiques; elective.

Full-Time Staff: Judith Cowan, Ronald Sheen, Egan Valentine.

Requirements for Admission: The university's requirement for admission is a Quebec college diploma. The program requires an entrance exam.

Tuition, Fees, and Aid: For in-province students, $1,000 per term; for out-of-province students, $1,500 per term.

General: This new program combines English and Spanish. It leads to a Quebec credential in TESOL.

Summer Session: No

Further Information: Egan Valentine
Département des langues modernes et traduction
Modules des langues
CP 500
Université du Québec à Trois Rivières
Trois Rivières, QC G9A 5H7

Telephone: (819) 376-5170 extension 3485
Fax: (819) 376-5169

◆ QUEEN'S UNIVERSITY, Faculty of Education

Degree Offered: Additional qualifications courses in ESL.

Length of Program: 3 semesters. Students must be part-time. Application deadlines are summer semester, June 15; fall semester, August 15; winter semester, December 15.

Program Requirements: 125 hours per course. Competence in a language other than English is not required. Practice teaching is required. Neither a thesis nor a comprehensive examination is required.

Courses Offered: ESL Part 1, Part 1, and Part 3.

Requirements for Admission: The program's requirement for admission is an Ontario certificate of qualification as a teacher if Ontario ESL certification is to be recommended.

Tuition, Fees, and Aid: $750 per course.

General: The program leads to an Ontario credential in TESOL.
Summer courses are available in Beijing, People's Republic of China.
Sixty students completed the program in 1995–1996.
The university has an intensive English language program for nonnative speakers of English.

Summer Session: Yes

Further Information: Office of the Faculty Registrar
Faculty of Education
Queen's University
Kingston, ON K7L 3N6

Telephone: (613) 545-6205
Fax: (613) 545-6203
E-mail: regoff@educ.queensu.ca

◆ SASKATCHEWAN, UNIVERSITY OF, Extension Division

Degree Offered: Certificate in TESL (CERTESL).

Length of Program: Designed as a part-time program. Application deadlines are fall semester, August 15; winter semester, December 15; spring/summer semester, May 1.

Program Requirements: 6 courses (507) semester hours. Competence in a language other than English is not required. Practice teaching is required. Neither a thesis nor a comprehensive examination is required.

Courses Offered: (*required) *Overview of Teaching ESL; *TESL Theory and Skill Development *or* TESL/Teaching English as a Second Dialect for Indian and Metis

Students; *TESL Materials Selection and Development; *Applied English Grammar and Phonetics; *TESL Methods; *Supervised Practicum or Professional Project.

Full-Time Staff: Ruth Epstein, Shirley Fredeen, Grace Milashenko, Roy Wagner (chair), Rena DeCoursey.

Requirements for Admission: The university's requirement for regular admission is complete secondary-level standing. Candidates who are at least 21 years of age may qualify for special (mature) admission.

Tuition, Fees, and Aid: For Saskatchewan students, $313.70 per course plus materials fees; for others, $470.55 per course plus materials fees. No financial aid is available.

General: The CERTESL program is aimed at current or prospective ESL or EFL instructors. The certificate is completed through distance education on a part-time basis, with a practicum that may be taken either on or off campus. The program leads to a Saskatchewan credential in TESOL.

Thirty-nine students completed the program in 1996–1997.

The university has an intensive English language program for nonnative speakers of English.

Summer Session: Yes

Further Information: CERTESL Program, Extension Credit Studies
Room 326 Kirk Hall
117 Science Place
University of Saskatchewan
Saskatoon, SK S7N 5C8

Telephone: (306) 966-5563
Fax: (306) 966-5590
E-Mail: extcred@usask.ca

◆ SIMON FRASER UNIVERSITY, Linguistics Department

Degree Offered: Certificate in TESL linguistics.

Length of Program: 4–5 semesters. Students may be full-time or part-time and may begin their study at the beginning of any semester. Application deadlines are spring semester, September 30; summer semester, January 31; fall semester, April 30.

Program Requirements: 31 credits. Competence in a language other than English is strongly recommended. Practice teaching is required. Neither a thesis nor a comprehensive examination is required.

Courses Offered: (*required) *Practical Phonetics; *Introduction to Linguistics; *The Wonder of Words; *Introduction to English Grammatical Description; *Introduction to Language Acquisition; *Linguistics and Language Teaching: Theory; *Linguistics and Language Teaching; *TESL Theory; *TESL Practice; *Curriculum and Instruction in TESL; 6 credits in electives

Full-Time Staff: Murray J. Munro, Neville J. Lincoln (chair), Gloria Sampson, Kelleen Toohey.

Requirements for Admission: Monolingual students who have never studied another language are strongly advised to take at least 6 credit hours in a language other than English.

Tuition, Fees, and Aid: For in-province students, $77 per credit hour; for out-of-province students, $231 per credit hour. Scholarships, bursaries, and awards are available.

General: The program provides the specialized linguistic knowledge and practical classroom methodology necessary to teach in a variety of TESOL settings. It leads to a British Columbia credential in TESOL.

Fifty-eight students completed the program in 1996–1997.

Summer Session: Yes

Further Information: Rita Parmar, Departmental Assistant
Department of Linguistics
Classroom Complex
Simon Fraser University
Burnaby, BC V5A 1S6

Telephone: (604) 291-5739
Fax: (604) 291-5659
E-mail: rita_parmar@sfu.ca

◆ SIMON FRASER UNIVERSITY, Linguistics Department

Degree Offered: Postbaccalaureate diploma in TESL.

Length of Program: 4–5 semesters. Students may be full-time or part-time and may begin their study at the beginning of any semester. Application deadlines are spring semester, September 30; summer semester, January 31; fall semester, April 30.

Program Requirements: 31 credits minimum. Competence in a language other than English is required. Practice teaching is required. Neither a thesis nor a comprehensive examination is required.

Courses Offered: Phonology; Syntax; Morphology; Linguistics and Language Teaching; TESL Theory; Topics in Linguistics; Curriculum and Instruction; Testing in Schools; Literacy; Education and Culture; Recent Advances in TESL; Instructional Psychology; Classroom Management; Canadian Ethnic Minorities.

Full-Time Staff: See certificate program description.

Requirements for Admission: The program's requirement for admission is a baccalaureate degree in a related field or completion of the TESL certificate.

Tuition, Fees, and Aid: See certificate program description.

General: The program offers a unique opportunity for practicing ESL teachers and graduates of related disciplines to gain access to advanced courses in TESL through distance education.

Six students completed the program in 1996–1997.

Summer Session: Yes

Further Information: Rita Parmar, Departmental Assistant
Department of Linguistics
Classroom Complex
Simon Fraser University
Burnaby, BC V5A 1S6

Telephone: (604) 291-5739
Fax: (604) 291-5659
E-mail: rita_parmar@sfu.ca

◆ TORONTO, UNIVERSITY OF, WOODSWORTH COLLEGE, Professional and International Programs

Degree Offered: Certificate in TESL (CERTESL).

Length of Program: 1 year. Students may be full-time or part-time and must begin their study in May or September. Application deadlines are summer session, April 1; winter session, July 1.

Program Requirements: 6 credits. Competence in a language other than English is not required. Practice teaching is optional. Neither a thesis nor a comprehensive examination is required.

Courses Offered: (*required) *Introduction to General Linguistics; *Pedagogical Grammar; *Methodology of TESL; *Theoretical Issues in Second Language Teaching and Learning; Language in Anthropological Thought; Language Acquisition; Language and Society; Sociolinguistics; Psychology of Language; Canadian English; Structure of English; Phonetics; Morphological Patterns in Language; Syntactic Patterns in Language; TESL Practicum.

Requirements for Admission: The program's requirement for admission is an acceptable average in 6 specified Ontario academic credits or the equivalent. Most applicants hold an undergraduate degree.

Tuition, Fees, and Aid: For Canadian students, $639.20 per course; for non-Canadian students, $1,600 per course. Fees are $246.82 per session. Bursaries and scholarships are available.

General: The program provides specialized academic and professional preparation primarily for teaching English to adults. The program offers a strong academic approach to second language instruction in response to the research in linguistics and second language acquisition. This is coupled with the opportunity to gain practical skills. Students are taught the analytical skills necessary to evaluate classroom materials, assess the language and cultural needs of a class, and record the progress of individual students.

Sixty-one students completed the program in 1996–1997.

The university has an intensive English language program for nonnative speakers of English.

Summer Session: Yes

Further Information: Professional and International Programs
University of Toronto
119 St. George Street
Toronto, ON M5S 1A9

Telephone: (416) 978-8713
Fax: (416) 946-3516
E-mail: certificates@woodsworth.utoronto.ca

◆ VANCOUVER COMMUNITY COLLEGE, Continuing Education Division

Degree Offered: TESL certificate.

Length of Program: 2 quarters. Students may be full-time or part-time and may begin their study at the beginning of any quarter. Application deadlines are fall quarter, August 15; winter quarter, December 1; spring quarter, March 15.

Program Requirements: 325 hours. Competence in a foreign language is optional. Practice teaching is required. A thesis is optional. A comprehensive examination is not required.

Courses Offered: (*required) *Overview of Teaching ESL; *Teaching Grammar One: Theory and Practice; *Teaching Grammar Two: Theory and Practice; *Teaching Pronunciation; *Teaching Listening and Speaking; *Teaching Writing; *Teaching Reading; *Teaching English for Academic Purposes; *TESL Internship; 30 hours of TESL elective courses.

Full-Time Staff: Jennifer House (coordinator), Jayeson Van Bryce (coordinator), Emma Chang, Joann Chernen, Chris Clark, Joanna Daley, Katherine Elliott, Corry Flader, Jane Forward, Arlene Howard, Raymonde Jajabi, Patricia Kennedy, John Kostoff, Nina Kozakiewicz, Marion Lovelace, Lorena McCafferty, Mary Jane Nehring, Alison Norman, Michael Pidgeon, Michael Plumb, Nan Poliakoff, Eugene Sayson, Richard Sim, Judy Taylor.

Requirements for Admission: The program's requirements for admission are an undergraduate degree; satisfactory completion of An Overview of Teaching ESL or an equivalent; a standard of spoken English equivalent to that of a native speaker and a good command of grammar, usage, spelling, and punctuation in written English; and an interview with program staff. Nonnative speakers of English must have a TOEFL score of 550, an IELTS score in Band 7, or a Cambridge Proficiency in English score of B.

Tuition, Fees, and Aid: For Canadian students, $1,000 for the program; for non-Canadian students, $6,000 for the program.

General: The program, which leads to an British Columbia credential in TESOL, is a pragmatic training course featuring the theory and practice of teaching the English language. It is the largest in Canada and is internationally recognized as an outstanding training program.

The program is in the process of setting up international fieldwork opportunities in China and Mexico.

One hundred students completed the program in 1996–1997.

The college has an intensive English language program for nonnative speakers of English.

Summer Session: Yes

Further Information: Jennifer House, Program Coordinator
TESL Certificate Program
Continuing Education
Vancouver Community College
1155 East Broadway
Box 24785, Station F
Vancouver, BC V5N 5V2

Telephone: (604) 871-7056
Fax: (604) 871-7300
E-mail: jhouse@vcc.bc.ca

◆ VANCOUVER COMMUNITY COLLEGE, Continuing Education Division

Degree Offered: International TESL certificate.

Length of Program: 2 quarters. Students must be full-time and may begin their study at the beginning of the fall or winter quarter. Application deadlines are fall quarter, August 15; winter quarter, November 15.

Program Requirements: 325 hours. Competence in a foreign language is optional. Practice teaching and a comprehensive examination are required. A thesis is optional.

Courses Offered: See TESL certificate program description.

Full-Time Staff: See TESL certificate program description.

Requirements for Admission: See TESL certificate program description.

Tuition, Fees, and Aid: See TESL certificate program description.

General: See TESL certificate program description.
Twenty students completed the program in 1996–1997.
The college has an intensive English language program for nonnative speakers of English.

Summer Session: No

Further Information: Jennifer House, Program Coordinator
TESL Certificate Program
Continuing Education
Vancouver Community College
1155 East Broadway
Box 24785, Station F
Vancouver, BC V5N 5V2

Telephone: (604) 871-7056
Fax: (604) 871-7300
E-mail: jhouse@vcc.bc.ca

◆ VANCOUVER COMMUNITY COLLEGE, Continuing Education Division

Degree Offered: TESL in-service qualification certificate.

Length of Program: 2 quarters. Students may be full-time or part-time and may begin their study at the beginning of the fall or spring quarter. Application deadlines are fall quarter, August 15; spring quarter, February 1.

Program Requirements: 300 hours. Competence in a foreign language is optional. Practice teaching and a comprehensive examination are required. A thesis is not required.

Courses Offered: (*required) *Foundations for English Language Instruction; *Teaching Grammar; *Teaching Pronunciation; *Teaching Listening and Speaking Skills; *Teaching Reading and Writing; *Practicum.

Full-Time Staff: Joanna Daley, Jennifer House, Ellen Kurz, Marion Lovelace, Nan Poliakoff, Tanis Sawkins, Judy Taylor, Patricia Watson, Maureen Zetler.

Requirements for Admission: The program's requirements for admission are an undergraduate university degree; satisfactory completion of An Overview to Teaching ESL or an equivalent; a standard of spoken English equivalent to that of a native speaker and a good command of grammar, usage, spelling, and punctuation in written English; and a successful interview with program staff. Nonnative speakers of English must have a Cambridge Proficiency in English score of B, a TOEFL score of 550, or an IELTS band score of 7.

Tuition, Fees, and Aid: For Canadian students, $1,650 for the program; for non-Canadian students, $3,500 for the program.

General: The program leads to a British Columbia credential in TESOL.

About 30 students completed the program in 1996–1997.

The college has an intensive English language program for nonnative speakers of English.

Summer Session: No

Further Information: Jennifer House, Program Coordinator
TESL Certificate Program
Continuing Education
Vancouver Community College
1155 East Broadway
Box 24785, Station F
Vancouver, BC V5N 5V2

Telephone: (604) 871-7056
Fax: (604) 871-7300
E-mail: jhouse@vcc.bc.ca

◆ VANCOUVER COMMUNITY COLLEGE, Continuing Education Division

Degree Offered: Tutoring ESL certificate.

Length of Program: Students may be full-time or part-time and may begin their study at the beginning of any quarter. Application deadlines are fall quarter, August 15; winter quarter, December 1; spring quarter, March 15.

Program Requirements: 120 hours. Competence in a foreign language is optional. Practice teaching and a comprehensive examination are required. A thesis is optional.

Courses Offered: (*required) *An Overview of Teaching ESL; *ESL Tutoring; *Tutoring Grammar; *Tutoring Pronunciation; *Tutoring ESL Practicum; Tutoring for the TOEFL; Tutoring ESL for Business People; Tutoring ESL Students for the BC Provincial Exam; Tutoring for the Language Proficiency Index; Tutoring for Elementary-Level ESL Students; Tutoring for Secondary-Level ESL Students; Tutoring for Conversation Skills; Basic Accounting for ESL Tutors.

Full-Time Staff: Emma Chang, Joann Chernen, Chris Clark, Corry Flader, Jennifer House, Arlene Howard, Pat Kennedy, Maria McLellan, Alison Norman, Maureen Zetler.

Requirements for Admission: See certificate in TESL program description.

Tuition, Fees, and Aid: For Canadian students, $900 for the program; for non-Canadian students, $1,800 for the program.

General: About 15 students completed the program in 1996–1997.

The university has an intensive English language program for nonnative speakers of English.

Summer Session: Yes

Further Information: Jennifer House, Program Coordinator
TESL Certificate Program
Continuing Education
Vancouver Community College
1155 East Broadway
Box 24785, Station F
Vancouver, BC V5N 5V2

Telephone: (604) 871-7056
Fax: (604) 871-7300
E-mail: jhouse@vcc.bc.ca

◆ VANCOUVER COMMUNITY COLLEGE, Continuing Education Division

Degree Offered: Certificate in TESL (CERTESL).

Length of Program: Students must be part-time and may begin their study at the beginning of any quarter. Application deadlines are fall quarter, August 15; winter quarter, November 15; spring-summer quarter, March 15.

Program Requirements: 6 courses. Competence in a foreign language is not required. A comprehensive examination is required. Practice teaching is optional. A thesis is not required.

Courses Offered: (*required) *An Overview of Teaching ESL; *TESL Theory and Skill Development *or* TESL/TESD for Indian and Metis Students; *TESL Materials Selection and Development; *Applied English Grammar and Phonetics; *TESL Methods; *Supervised Practicum *or* Professional Project.

Full-Time Staff: Jayeson Van Bryce (coordinator).

Requirements for Admission: The college's requirement for admission is completion of Grade 12 or the equivalent. The program requires a standard of English equal to that of a native speaker.

Tuition, Fees, and Aid: For Canadian students, $2,217 for the program; for non-Canadian students, $3,325 for the program. Fees are Canadian students, $313 per course; non-Canadian students, $470 per course.

General: This distance education program is offered in conjunction with the University of Saskatchewan. The program leads to a British Columbia credential in TESOL.

The university has an intensive English language program for nonnative speakers of English.

Summer Session: Yes

Further Information: Jayeson Van Bryce, Coordinator
Continuing Education
King Edward Campus
Vancouver Community College
1155 East Broadway
Box 24785, Station F
Vancouver, BC V5N 5V2

Telephone: (604) 871-7070
Fax: (604) 871-7300
E-mail: jvanbryce@vcc.bc.ca

◆ VICTORIA, UNIVERSITY OF, Department of Linguistics

Degree Offered: Diploma in applied linguistics.

Length of Program: 1 year. Students may be full-time or part-time and may begin their study at the beginning of any semester. Application deadlines are fall semester, May; winter semester, September; summer session, November.

Program Requirements: 15 units. Study of a language other than English is required. Practice teaching is required. Neither a thesis nor a comprehensive examination is required.

Courses Offered: (*required) *Theories in Applied Linguistics; *Techniques in Applied Linguistics; *Practicum in Applied Linguistics; *Grammar of English; Developmental Psycholinguistics; Growth of Modern English; Sociolinguistics; Issues in Cross-Cultural Communication; Language and Gender; Acoustic Phonetics; Second Language Acquisition; structure, context, and usage of a variety of languages.

Full-Time Staff: J. Arthurs, J. Esling, B. Harris, M. Warbey.

Requirements for Admission: The university's requirement for admission is a BA or BS.

Tuition, Fees, and Aid: For in-province students, $2,548 per year; for out-of-province students, $3,700 per year. A few work-study placements are available.

General: The program includes an extensive supervised classroom practicum as well as opportunities to observe a variety of language classes and instructors. Practicum placements are adjusted to suit students' interests and plans. Emphasis is placed on creative, innovative language instruction techniques based on sound theoretical and pedagogical principles as well as on sharing of insights and a thorough understanding of the human capacity for language acquisition. The program fulfills the requirements for the Association of British Columbia Teachers of English as an Additional Language Level 1 instructor.

Forty-two students completed the program in 1996–1997.

The university has an intensive English language program for nonnative speakers of English.

Summer Session: Yes

Further Information: Advisor, Applied Linguistics Diploma Program
Department of Linguistics
Box 3045
University of Victoria
Victoria, BC V8W 3P4

Telephone: (250) 721-7424
Fax: (250) 721-7423

◆ VICTORIA, UNIVERSITY OF, Department of Linguistics

Degrees Offered: BA, MA, and PhD in applied linguistics.

Length of Program: Students may be full-time or part-time and may begin their study at the beginning of any semester. Application deadlines are fall semester, May; winter semester, September; summer session, November.

Program Requirements: 30 units for the MA. Competence in a language other than English is required. Practice teaching is required. Either a thesis, or a major paper plus a comprehensive examination, is required.

Courses Offered: Applied Linguistics; Theoretical Linguistics; Acoustic Phonetics; Sociolinguistics.

Full-Time Staff: J. Arthurs, J. Esling, B. Harris, M. Warbey.

Requirements for Admission: The university's requirement for admission is a BA or BS. The program requires a GRE score and either a BA in linguistics or a qualifying year in linguistics.

Tuition, Fees, and Aid: About $2,000 per year. Teaching assistantships, scholarships, and fellowships are available.

General: See program description for diploma in applied linguistics. Research opportunities are abundant.

Three students completed the MA program in 1996–1997.

The university has an intensive English language program for nonnative speakers of English.

Summer Session: No

Further Information: Graduate Advisor
Department of Linguistics
Box 3045
University of Victoria
Victoria, BC V8W 3P4

Telephone: (250) 721-7424
Fax: (250) 721-7423

◆ THE WATERLOO CENTRE FOR APPLIED LINGUISTICS, TESL Program

Degree Offered: Certificate in TESL (CERTESL).

Length of Program: 2 semester. Students must be full-time and must begin their study in September. The application deadline is September 1.

Program Requirements: 370 hours. Competence in a foreign language is preferred. Practice teaching is required. Neither a thesis nor a comprehensive examination is required.

Courses Offered: (*required) *Language; *Second Language Acquisition; *The Adult Learner A: Learning Styles; *Linguistics A and B; *TESL Methodology A: Historical Overview; *TESL Methodology B: Lesson Planning/Classroom Management; *TESL Methodology C: Curriculum and Materials; *Structure of English; *Linguistics A: Segmentals; Linguistics B: Suprasegmentals; *Teaching Grammar; *Teaching Pronunciation; *Teaching Reading; *Teaching Writing; *Teaching Listening; *Teaching Speaking; *Language Assessment; *Teaching Observation and Practicum.

Full-time Staff: Janet D. Stubbs (director).

Requirements for Admission: The requirements for admission are an undergraduate degree, a writing sample, and a diagnostic grammar test. Candidates may be required to provide evidence of English language proficiency.

Tuition, Fees, and Aid: $5,000.

General: Students receive a solid grounding in both theory and practice, have extensive observation opportunities at various levels of ESL proficiency, teach in a supervised practicum, and receive membership in TESL Ontario.

Thirty students completed the program in in 1996–1997.

Summer Session: No

Further Information: Janet D. Stubbs
TESL Program Director
The Waterloo Centre for Applied Linguistics Inc.
561 Sugarbush Drive
Waterloo, ON N2K 1Z7

Telephone: (519) 725-9070
Fax: (519) 725-3644
E-mail: jstubbs@mgl.ca

◆ WESTERN ONTARIO, THE UNIVERSITY OF,
Western Centre for Continuing Studies

Degree Offered: Certificate in second language teaching.

Length of Program: 2–3 years part-time. Students must begin their study in September. The application deadline is March 1.

Program Requirements: Three degree-credit and five certificate-credit courses. Competence in a language other than English is not required for native speakers of English; competence in English is required for nonnative speakers of English. Practice teaching is required. Neither a thesis nor a comprehensive examination is required.

Courses Offered: (*required) *Introduction to Linguistics; *Applied Linguistics; *Teaching a Second Language: An Introduction; *Intercultural Communication; *Practicum; *Seminar; electives from linguistics and education psychology; Teaching English Grammar, Teaching Pronunciation in the Second Language Classroom.

Requirements for Admission: The university's requirement for admission is completion of high school with Ontario academic credits. The program requires some college- or university-level courses and some related experience.

Tuition, Fees, and Aid: $4,400 for the program. Financial aid from the Ontario Student Assistance Program is available to Ontario residents.

General: The program is relevant to the teaching of any second language, and students may complete assignments and practice in their specific language of interest. Some courses may be credited toward an undergraduate degree.

The university has an intensive English language program for nonnative speakers of English.

Summer Session: Yes

Further Information: Diploma and Certificate Programs
The Western Centre for Continuing Studies
Stevenson-Lawson Building, Room 23
The University of Western Ontario
London, ON N6A 5B8

Telephone: (519) 661-3632

◆ WESTERN ONTARIO, THE UNIVERSITY OF,
Faculty of Education

Degree Offered: Professional training for teachers: ESL.

Length of Program: Three 125-hour sections. Students must be part-time and must take the program in summer or fall-winter. Application deadlines are June for summer entry and September for fall-winter entry.

Program Requirements: Competence in a language other than English is not required. Practice teaching is required. Neither a thesis nor a comprehensive examination is required.

Courses Offered: ESL, Part 1.

Requirements for Admission: The university's requirement for admission is an Ontario teacher's certificate.

Tuition, Fees, and Aid: $630 per course.

General: The program leads to an Ontario credential in TESOL.

Summer Session: Yes

Further Information: Ruth Heard
Continuing Teacher Education, Faculty of Education
Althouse College, Room 1044
The University of Western Ontario
London, ON N6G 1G7

Telephone: (519) 661-2092

◆ YORK UNIVERSITY, Department of Languages, Literature, and Linguistics

Degree Offered: MA in theoretical and applied linguistics.

Length of Program: 3 semesters. Students may be full-time or part-time and may begin their study at the beginning of any semester. The application deadline is March 1.

Program Requirements: Six 1-semester courses plus a research paper or four 1-semester courses plus a thesis. Competence in a foreign language is not required. Neither practice teaching nor a comprehensive examination is required.

Courses Offered: (*required) Both streams: *Languages in Contact; *Second Language Acquisition *or* Second Language Instruction; Interlanguage; Implications of Languages in Contact; Developmental Psycholinguistics; English as a World Language; Language, Culture, and Ideology; Sociolinguistics and the Individual; Discourse and Pragmatics. Theoretical stream: Phonological Theories; Grammatical Theories; Historical Reconstruction: Phonology; Historical Reconstruction: Morphology and Syntax; Explanation in Historical Linguistics; Language Contact and Language Structure; Sociolinguistics and Linguistic Systems: The Speech Community; Sociolinguistics and Linguistic Systems: Linguistic Mechanisms; Research Seminar in Theoretical Linguistics; special topic; independent study. Applied stream: English Language Education in Canada; Planning in EL2 Institutions and Projects; Second Language Acquisitions for Language Education; Race, Culture, and Schooling; The Teacher as Researcher; Text Analysis for Teachers; Research Seminar in Applied Linguistics.

Full-Time Staff: David Mendelsohn (director), Ellen Bialystok, Michael J. Cummings, Sheila Embleton, Gregory R. Guy, Ruth King, Raymond Mougeon, Jull S. Bell, David Cooke, Susan Ehrlich, Ian Martin, Neil Naiman, Razika Sanaoui, Ian Smith, Nick Elson.

Requirements for Admission: The requirements for admission for the theoretical stream are an honours BA in linguistics or the equivalent with a B+ or higher average in the last 2 years of study, sufficient background in historical linguistics or sociolinguistics, and one acceptable upper-year 1-semester course each in syntax and phonology. In the absence of these courses, students may be required to complete additional courses. For the applied stream, applicants must have an honours degree with a B+ or higher average in the last 2 years of study in an appropriate field. Nonnative speakers of English must have a TOEFL score of 600.

Tuition, Fees, and Aid: For Canadian students, $5,000 per year; for non-Canadian students, $10,800 per year. Teaching assistantships, graduate assistantships, and research assistantships are available.

General: The program begins in fall 1998. The theoretical stream focuses on historical linguistics, sociolinguistics, and language contact. The applied stream focuses on language education, specifically TESL/TEFL; applied linguistics; and language contact.

The university has an intensive English language program for nonnative speakers of English.

Summer Session: No

Further Information: Professor David Mendelsohn, Director
MA in Theoretical and Applied Linguistics
S567 Ross Building
York University
4700 Keale Street
North York, ON M3J 1P3

Telephone: (416) 650-8046
Fax: (416) 736-5483
E-mail: gradling@yorku.ca

Provincial Certification Requirements for Teaching English to Speakers of Other Languages

The information in this section was obtained from provincial ministries of education. Of the eight provinces responding, four issue certification or add-on qualification in ESL. Requirements for teaching certificates differ from province to province in Canada and are not easily transferred between provinces.

The name in the first column is the person to whom a prospective teacher or interested person should write for further information. Specific requirements returned by the provinces are in the third column.

Province and Contact	Credential in TESOL	Requirements and comments
Alberta No official contact	None	
British Columbia British Columbia College of Teachers 1385 West Eighth Avenue #405 Vancouver, BC V6H 3V9 Telephone: (604) 731-8170	Specialty	Programs for TESL are given at the graduate level as specialties after initial teacher certification. Requirements are (a) 120 credits of postsecondary course work beyond the equivalent of BC Grade 12, including 30 credits of education course work and an acceptable practicum; and (b) mandatory academics for elementary and for secondary.
Manitoba Al Tataryn Professional Certification and Student Records Box 700 Russell, MB R0J 1W0	None	
Newfoundland Robert Parsons, Registrar of Teacher Certification Department of Education PO Box 8900 St. Johns, Newfoundland A1B 4J6 Telephone: (709) 729-3020	Add-on	Teachers employed in TESL programs must hold a standard teaching certificate and must have completed a recognized university program in TESL of not less than 30 semester hours.
Nova Scotia No official contact	None	
Ontario T.A.S.I.S., Ministry of Education and Training 12th Floor, Mowat Block 900 Bay Street Toronto, ON M7P 1R2	Add-on	ESL is an additional qualification to basic certification. The requirements are additional courses in ESL at a recognized university.

Province and Contact	Credential in TESOL	Requirements and comments

Quebec
Madame Louise Giroux
Direction de la formation et
  de la tutularisation du
  personnel scolaire
150, boulevard René
  Lévesque, 15e étage
Québec City, QC G1R 5W8
Telephone: (418) 643-8610
Fax: (418) 643-2149
E-mail: DeniseGiroux@
  meq.gouv.qc.ca
	None	

Saskatchewan Teacher Services 1500 4th Avenue Regina, SK S4P 3V7 Telephone: (306) 787-6085 Fax: (306) 787-0035 E-mail: lgraham@ sasked.gov.sk.ca	Certification	TESOL is an acceptable major or minor in a secondary teacher education program. The requirements are 4 years of postsecondary education, including 1½ years of teacher education and an 8-week practicum.

Canadian Institutions With Doctoral Programs

Ontario Institute for Studies
in Education

University of Victoria

Canadian Institutions With Master's Programs

Brock University
Carleton University
Concordia University
University of Manitoba
Ontario Institute for Studies in Education

University of Ottawa
University of Victoria
York University

Canadian Institutions With Undergraduate Programs

Brock University
Concordia University
McGill University

Université du Québec à Trois Rivières
Simon Fraser University
University of Victoria

Canadian Institutions With Certificate or Diploma Programs

Algonquin College
Carleton University
Columbia College
Concordia University
McGill University
University of Saskatchewan
Simon Fraser University

University of Toronto,
   Woodsworth College
Vancouver Community College
University of Victoria
The Waterloo Centre for
   Applied Linguistics
The University of Western Ontario

Canadian Institutions With Programs Leading
to a Provincial Credential in TESOL

Algonquin College
Columbia College
Concordia University
University of Ottawa
Université du Québec à Trois Rivières
Queen's University

University of Saskatchewan
Simon Fraser University
Vancouver Community College
University of Victoria
The University of Western Ontario

Acronyms

ACT	American College Test
BA	bachelor of arts
BEd	bachelor of education
BS	bachelor of science
CEGEP	*collège d'enseignement général et professionnel*
CLAD	cross-cultural, language, and academic development
EdD	doctor of education
EdM	master of education
EFL	English as a foreign language
ESL	English as a second language
ESOL	English to speakers of other languages
GED	General Educational Development
GPA	grade point average (based on a 4.0 scale unless otherwise indicated)
GRE	Graduate Record Examination
IELTS	International English Language Testing Service
MA	master of arts
MAT	master of arts in teaching
MEd	master of education
MELAB	Michigan English Language Assessment Battery
MS	master of science
NTE	National Teachers Examination
PACE	Premium for Academic Excellence
PhD	doctor of philosophy
PSAT	Preliminary Scholastic Aptitude Test
SAT	Scholastic Aptitude Test
SPEAK	Speaking Proficiency English Assessment Kit
TEFL	teaching English as a foreign language
TESL	teaching English as a second language
TESOL	Teachers of English to Speakers of Other Languages
TESOL	teaching English to speakers of other languages
TOEFL	Test of English as a Foreign Language
TSE	Test of Spoken English
TWE	Test of Written English

Geographic Index

Canada

British Columbia

Burnaby, Simon Fraser University, 307
Vancouver, Columbia College, 296
Vancouver, Vancouver Community
    College, 309
Victoria, University of Victoria, 313

Manitoba

Winnipeg, University of Manitoba, 299

Ontario

Kingston, Queen's University, 306
London, The University of Western
    Ontario, 316
Nepean, Algonquin College, 292
North York, York University, 317
Ottawa, Carleton University, 294
Ottawa, University of Ottawa, 304
St. Catharines, Brock University, 292
Toronto, Ontario Institute for Studies in
    Education, 301
Toronto, University of Toronto,
    Woodsworth College, 309
Waterloo, The Waterloo Centre for
    Applied Linguistics, 315

Quebec

Montreal, Concordia University, 296
Montreal, McGill University, 300
Trois Rivières, Université du Québec, 305

Saskatchewan

Saskatoon, University of Saskatchewan,
    306

United States

New England

Connecticut

Fairfield, Fairfield University, 71
New Britain, Central Connecticut State
    University, 50

Maine

Gorham, University of Southern Maine,
    222

Massachusetts

Amherst, University of Massachusetts,
    132
Boston, Boston University, 23
Boston, University of Massachusetts, 134
Boston, Simmons College, 213
Worcester, Clark University, 57

New Hampshire

Durham, University of New Hampshire,
    150
Manchester, Notre Dame College, 169

Rhode Island

Providence, Rhode Island College, 191

Vermont

Brattleboro, School for International
    Training, 202
Colchester, Saint Michael's College, 195

Mid-Atlantic

District of Columbia

Washington, American University, 5
Washington, Georgetown University, 84
Washington, Mount Vernon College, 145

Delaware

Newark, University of Delaware, 63

Maryland

Baltimore, University of Maryland, 128
College Park, University of Maryland,
    131

New Jersey

Jersey City, Jersey City State College, 121
South Orange, Seton Hall University, 209
Teaneck, Fairleigh Dickinson University,
    72
Upper Montclair, Montclair State
    University, 142
Wayne, William Paterson University, 257

Utah

Provo, Brigham Young University, 26
Salt Lake City, University of Utah, 242

The Southwest

Arizona

Flagstaff, Northern Arizona University, 164
Phoenix, Grand Canyon University, 92
Tempe, Arizona State University, 12
Tucson, University of Arizona, 11

New Mexico

Albuquerque, University of New Mexico, 151
Las Cruces, New Mexico State University, 152
Santa Fe, College of Santa Fe, 201

West Coast and Pacific

California

Azusa, Azusa Pacific University, 13
Berkeley, University of California, 29
Calabasas, Soka University of America, 214
Carson, California State University, Dominguez Hills, 37
Davis, University of California, 30
Fresno, California State University, 38
Fresno, Fresno Pacific University, 82
Fullerton, California State University, 39
Hayward, California State University, 41
Irvine, University of California, 31
La Mirada, Biola University, 19
Los Angeles, University of California, 32
Los Angeles, California State University, 42
Monterey, Monterey Institute of International Studies, 144
Northridge, California State University, 44
Riverside, University of California, 34
Rohnert Park, Sonoma State University, 215
Sacramento, California State University, 46
San Francisco, University of San Francisco, 198
San Francisco, San Francisco State University, 199

San Diego, San Diego State University, 197
San Diego, United States International University, 239
San José, San José State University, 200
San Luis Obispo, California Polytechnic State University, 36
Santa Barbara, University of California, 35
Stockton, University of the Pacific, 180

Hawaii

Honolulu, University of Hawai'i at Manoa, 96
Honolulu, Hawaii Pacific University, 99
Laie, Brigham Young University, 27

Oregon

Eugene, University of Oregon, 177
Portland, Portland State University, 184

Washington

Cheney, Eastern Washington University, 70
Ellensburg, Central Washington University, 55
Pullman, Washington State University, 246
Seattle, School of Teaching English as a Second Language, 203
Seattle, Seattle Pacific University, 205
Seattle, Seattle University, 207
Seattle, University of Washington, 245
Spokane, Gonzaga University, 89
Tacoma, University of Puget Sound, 187

Puerto Rico

San Germán, Inter American University of Puerto Rico, 119
San Juan, University of Puerto Rico, 186

Other U.S. Accredited or Affiliated

Cairo, Egypt, American University in Cairo, 8
Paris, France, The American University of Paris, 9
Paris, France, WICE/Rutgers University, 252
Puebla, Mexico, Universidad de las Américas, 10

Index to Institutions

Master's Degree in TESL
Applied Linguistics & English as a Second Language
Georgia State University / Atlanta, USA

Come Join Our Multicultural, Urban Environment!

Graduate faculty *Areas of Specialization* include second language *Theory and Practice* in . . .

> Academic Literacy, English Grammar, Intercultural Communication, Listening Comprehension, Oral Communication, Reading-Writing Relationships, Materials Design, Modern Technologies, Psycholinguistics, Second Language Acquisition, Sociolinguistics, Teacher-Learning & Development, Testing/Assessment.

Graduate Faculty:

> Patricia Byrd, Patricia L. Carrell, Joan Carson, Patricia Dunkel, John Murphy, Gayle Nelson, & Sara Cushing Weigle.

Qualified candidates are provided opportunities to

> * teach in an intensive English program
> * assist in language classes taught by ESL professionals
> * gain teaching experience in a practicum course
> * work alongside faculty as graduate research assistants
> * tutor ESL students at various levels of proficiency
> * teach in ESL programs in Atlanta
> * participate in professional development activities
> * live in an invigorating, urban environment

> Contact: Dr. Gayle Nelson, *Director of Graduate Studies*
> (e-mail: gnelson@gsu.edu)
> Department of Applied Linguistics/ESL
> Georgia State University
> P.O. 4099
> Atlanta, GA   30302-4099
> Phone: (404) 651-2940, 3650   Fax: (404) 651-3652

Visit our web site at: http://www.gsu.edu/~wwwesl/alesl/

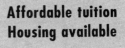

TESL at
Hawaii Pacific University

CHOICE OF TWO PROGRAMS
- Bachelor of Arts in Teaching English as a Second Language
- TESL Certificate (24 credit hours; open to BA or BS graduates)

BALANCED CURRICULUM
- Theory
- Pedagogy
- Practicum

FACULTY
- Dedicated, experienced faculty who have taught in Europe, Asia, Latin America, the Middle East, and the Pacific

PRACTICUM
- On-campus practice teaching in HPU's English Foundations Program
- One of the largest ESL programs in the U.S.
- Over 600 students per semester on 4 levels
- Students from over 50 countries

ACADEMIC CALENDAR
- Programs start in January, May, June and September

LOCATION
- Perfect location to combine serious study with year-round outdoor activities on Hawaii's mountains and beaches.

--- cut & mail ---

YES, I WOULD LIKE MORE INFORMATION ON HAWAII PACIFIC UNIVERSITY'S TESL PROGRAMS

Name_____

Address_____

_____

Country_____ M373

Send to: **Office of Admissions**
1164 Bishop Street
Honolulu, Hawaii 96813 USA
E-mail: admissions@hpu.edu
WWW: www.hpu.edu